the TRUTH about MONEY

3rd edition

the TRUTH about MONEY

3rd edition

RIC EDELMAN, CFS, RFC, CMFC, CRC, QFP

RODALE

For Jean
whose love, boundless support, endless patience, intuitive
understanding, deep personal sacrifice, endless patience, total dedication,
ceaseless work, endless patience, unwavering commitment, and
endless patience serve as my inspiration.

I am both grateful and humbled by her presence in my life, and
whatever success I attain is my tribute to her.

To My Dad
who taught me everything I know about business

and To My Mom
who let him

Here's the New Advice You'll Discover in This Edition

PLUS ALL NEW REVISED FIGURES AND STATS!

Here's More of the Unique, Award-Winning Advice in This Book

15,272 Reasons
You Need This Book

How to Use This Book

Table of Contents

Part IV - Equities

Part V - Packaged Products

Part VI - The Best Investment Strategies

Part VII - The Best Financial Strategies

Part VIII - The Best Strategies for Buying, Selling and Owning Homes

NON SEQUITUR   WILEY

HOW WE REALLY COMPREHEND FINANCIAL PLANNING...

Part IX - Taxes, Taxes, Taxes

Part X - Retirement Planning

Part XI - Insurance

Part XII — Estate Planning

Part XIII - How to Choose a Financial Advisor

Sources 617

About the Author 621

Index 625

BROOM HILDA   RUSSELL MYERS

© Tribune Media Services, Inc. All Rights Reserved. Reprinted with permission.

Acknowledgments

The Truth About Money began as a course I created in 1992 and which I then taught at Georgetown University for nine years. Many excellent ideas and crucial help for the original program came from my longtime colleague and valued friend, Ed Moore, CFP®, president of Edelman Financial Services Inc.

The book was first published in 1996. Its tremendous success (70 weeks on the best-seller lists — 22 at #1 — and named "Business Book of the Year" by *Small Press* magazine) led to a second edition in 1998. Considering that it was published before Internet Mania (let alone September 11, Enron, the War on Terrorism and three major new tax laws), it's safe to say that this third edition is way overdue.

Despite many requests from my publisher and others, I delayed producing a third edition largely because of the enormity of the work. With most books, the author merely writes a manuscript, then turns it over to the publisher who handles layout and design. But *The Truth About Money* isn't like most books. Not only are massive statistical research and analysis required, my staff and I create the entire layout and design, providing my publisher with camera-ready page proofs. As a result, I don't just write the book, we build it — and having done that twice already (and survived), it simply wasn't a task I was looking forward to repeating.

That's why I am so grateful to Suzi Fenton, senior graphic designer for Edelman Financial Services. Although the layout and design of this third edition is identical to the first two (and which were designed by EFS Communications Director Will Casserly), new book dimensions forced Suzi to manually reconstruct each page. Considering all the graphic elements — the text, page and line sidebars, charts and graphs, quotes, footnotes and cartoons — that's one Herculean effort, and she did a superb job under a tight deadline. Suzi was ably assisted by her colleague, EFS graphic designer Rodel Berber.

I'm also thankful for Jerry Mason, PhD, a highly respected veteran in the personal finance field. Jerry joined my staff as editor of my newsletter two years ago and he proved invaluable in helping me update many of the statistics and calculations peppered throughout the text. He also reviewed the manuscript and I've incorporated almost all of his comments.

Indeed, accuracy is the most important aspect in work of this type. It all needs to be said, and it all needs to be accurate, complete and intelligible. I am thus indebted to the following EFS staff who read the manuscript, found innumerable errors (all of which I hope I fixed!) and gave me many helpful comments: Senior Financial Planners Jim Baker, CPA, CFP®, Jack Bubon, CFP®, Cindee Berar, MBA, RFC, CRC, Diane Jensen, MS, CFP® and Betty O'Lear, MBA, CFP®; Financial Planner Brandon Corso, CMFC, BCE, AAMS, Associate Planners Mike Attiliis, CFS and Debbie Smith, MBA, CFP®; Planning Assistant Dawn Lanphier, Insurance Coordinator Carol Roberts, Administrative Assistant Evy Sheehan and Front Desk Manager Cheryl Schrettenbrunner. Kudos also to my agent, Gail Ross, and to the gang at HarperCollins.

To everyone involved in this effort, I thank you very much.

Foreword

Few subjects are as intimidating as money. Like the weather, almost everyone has an opinion about money, but how many know with any confidence or degree of certainty what to do about it?

Most individuals and families don't have a real financial plan, and those who do claim to have one really have based it on myth, hearsay, what their parents did, or advice given by friends, neighbors or co-workers. A lot of this advice is dangerous because it doesn't work and is not based on truth. Even the most intelligent among us who (we believe) always think and behave rationally and reasonably, display irrational and unreasonable behavior when it comes to money.

When my wife and I started making a little more money than we were paying out in bills (a mistake, I know — we should have started much earlier), we decided it was time to consult a financial advisor. We had an individual retirement account through a bank where our interest was falling and we had a little money in a savings and loan account where interest was under four percent.

Because we were fans of Ric Edelman's radio program on WMAL in Washington, D.C., we decided to call him first. We never made a second call.

Ric impressed us not only with his knowledge of money, but with his desire to work out a financial plan built upon our needs. There was no pressure. There was no attempt to sell us a particular line of stocks and bonds because he might receive a higher commission (and I'm getting nothing in return for writing this foreword except the satisfaction of sharing someone I believe in with others in need of similar help).

Actually, we weren't entirely sure what our needs were until Ric began asking questions about our circumstances, goals, and spending habits. Our visit with him was one of the most pleasurable professional experiences we have ever had. The man knows his subject and conveys a sincerity about helping his clients that is not always found in business today.

It is one thing to be knowledgeable. It is another to be able to communicate. Ric communicates with everyone, from expert to novice, without a sense of superiority, as you will discover in this book. Using humor as well as illustrations, Ric drives his points home in a way that is not intimidating (even for people like me who can't balance their checkbook and long ago gave up doing their own taxes). He makes learning about money fun and interesting and he does it without an ax to grind.

Were Ric Edelman secretary of the treasury, he would get us out of debt if his "clients" in Congress and the president would do what he says.

You could not read a better book about your money than *The Truth About Money* because Ric Edelman tells the truth — and that is one of the few things worth more than money.

So sure am I that not only are you going to like this book, but that you will benefit by following its advice, that were it my book I would offer you a money back guarantee if you don't like it. Yes, if you don't like this book, I guarantee you that you won't get your money back!

But you will like it, and while nothing is certain in life, I can safely predict that this book will make a significant contribution to your financial planning needs and when you are finished you will feel a lot more intelligent than before you started. That alone is worth the price of the book.

Cal Thomas
Syndicated Columnist

the
TRUTH
about
MONEY

3rd edition

The Rules of Money Have Changed. Again.
But the strategies haven't.

Never buy the first edition of a personal finance book. Instead, get the third edition. Like this one.

Okay, I'm kidding.

But only a little. That's because there really is some Truth (no pun intended) here. You see, thousands of personal finance books have been published, but few have ever been revised and released as a second or third edition. Why not? Because most of the advice offered these days fails the test of time. That makes them un-revisable: you can't "update" a book whose advice has proved to be completely wrong. Instead, it's easier to publish a brand new book, where you get to say brand-new things. So what if what you're saying today completely contradicts what you said before?

And that explains why I felt such trepidation when I began this third edition. The first two editions — published in 1996 and 1998 — were written during the greatest economic expansion in our nation's history. The strategies, the concepts, the advice — the Truth —were easy to follow, and the ideas made perfect sense.

But the 1990s are over. Is the Truth as I've explained it still valid? Have the strategies and concepts survived intact? Or did the "perfect storm" of the stock market's three-year decline, radical tax law changes, recession, inflation and terrorism render outdated and moot the advice I've been offering for the past 18 years?

I've seen this happen to dozens of pundits and authors. But as I updated all of *Truth*'s charts and statistics, applying up-to-date performance data and adjusting for new tax laws and a radically different economic, political and social environment, it soon became clear that, as far as the advice offered in this book is concerned, nothing has changed. All of the ideas, concepts and strategies first published in 1996 remain completely valid.

What is new is the book's timeliness. Now fully revised, these pages give you the latest information on the newest tax laws and proves, having gone through the 2000–2002 bear market, that you can indeed rely on its advice and strategies. This is very reassuring to the hundreds of thousands of Americans who have turned to this book for information on handling their investments, taxes, mortgages, insurance, estate planning, college, retirement, and all other aspects of personal finance.

As in its preceding editions, I again welcome you to learn for yourself how to take advantage of the realities and opportunities available to you, for both the protection and the prosperity of you and your family. Above all, I invite you to learn *The Truth About Money*.

Ric Edelman
November 2003

ric's money quiz

Here's your chance to discover how much (or how little!) you know about personal finance. Don't worry if you get stumped — the answers follow the quiz, along with the corresponding page numbers so you can quickly explore each topic. You'll discover how easily this book gives you the knowledge you need to achieve financial success!

1. **Of the following choices, which offers both extensive diversification and relatively low volatility?**

   ○ a. asset allocation funds
   ○ b. equity income funds
   ○ c. balanced funds
   ○ d. growth and income funds

2. **Gap insurance for a leased car:**

   ○ a. pays the difference between the car's residual value and the car's actual value
   ○ b. pays for any damage to the car during the lease
   ○ c. pays any missed payments during the lease
   ○ d. both b and c

3. **When contributing to a company retirement plan, _____ of your money should be invested in the stock mutual fund.**

   ○ a. 100%
   ○ b. 75%
   ○ c. 50%
   ○ d. 25%

4. **The relationship between interest rates and bond prices is as follows: As interest rates move up or down,**

   ○ a. bond prices stay the same
   ○ b. bond prices move in the same direction
   ○ c. bond prices move in the opposite direction
   ○ d. bond maturity dates change as well

5. **A planner gives his client a brochure describing the planner's fee schedule. Which of the following fee schedules is prohibited by NASD rules?**

   ○ a. a fee schedule that charges a flat fee of more than $500 per year
   ○ b. a fee schedule that charges both fees and commissions
   ○ c. a fee schedule where the planner shares in the profits earned in the client's account
   ○ d. a fee schedule where the planner charges commissions only

6. **FDIC:**

   O a. is funded by the U.S.
      government
   O b. guarantees that your money
      is safe
   O c. is a private insurance company
      for banks
   O d. will completely pay off all
      depositors if a bank goes broke

7. **Regarding withdrawals from your IRA account, there are penalties if you:**

   I.   withdraw money at too young
        an age
   II. don't begin making withdrawals
        by a certain age
   III. withdraw too little in a given year
   IV. withdraw too much in a given year

   O a. I only
   O b. I and II
   O c. I, II, and III
   O d. I, II, III and IV

8. **An "optimal" portfolio is one which:**

   O a. makes the most amount
      of money
   O b. takes the least amount of risk
   O c. minimizes expenses, including
      transaction costs, carrying costs
      and tax effects
   O d. balances return against risk

9. **When selling your primary residence, the first $500,000 of gain for married couples ($250,000 for singles) is excluded from the capital gains tax if you are what age?**

   O a. at least 70½
   O b. at least 59½
   O c. over 55
   O d. Age doesn't matter. It matters
      only that you have lived in
      your home for two of the
      last five years.

10. **What percentage of Americans 65 or older have an annual income below $15,000?**

   O a. 11%
   O b. 39%
   O c. 51%
   O d. 81%

11. **Which of the following is an example of Dollar Cost Averaging?**

   O a. placing 100% of your company
      retirement plan contributions
      into the stock fund each month
   O b. buying U.S. savings bonds via
      payroll deduction
   O c. placing equal amounts of
      money into four different
      kinds of mutual funds
   O d. buying 100 shares of a given
      stock every time the price
      changes by $10

12. According to a study by the Journal of the American Medical Association, nearly _____ of 2,000 critically-ill patients lost their life savings as a result of the illness.

  O a. 5%
  O b. 12%
  O c. 16%
  O d. 31%

13. When working with a planner, it is okay to:

  O a. write a check for the money you wish to invest payable to the planner
  O b. list your planner as joint owner or beneficiary on your accounts
  O c. give your planner discretionary authority
  O d. none of the above

14. Which of the following is not a reason to carry a big, long mortgage?

  O a. mortgages affect home values
  O b. if you don't borrow when you buy, you can't deduct interest later
  O c. a 30-year mortgage is better than a 15-year mortgage
  O d. you get a tax deduction for the interest you pay

15. The stock market is a:

  O a. leading economic indicator
  O b. lagging economic indicator
  O c. coincident economic indicator
  O d. none of the above

16. After paying for child-rearing and work-related costs, how much might a spouse take home in net after-tax income, assuming a gross salary of $30,000?

  O a. $20,000 per year
  O b. $1250 per month
  O c. $275 per week
  O d. $1.25 per hour

17. After a revocable living trust has been created for you, you need to:

  O a. rewrite your will
  O b. name new beneficiaries
  O c. retitle assets into the trust
  O d. name a trustee

18. Bypass trusts are best suited for:

  O a. widows trying to avoid probate
  O b. married couples with a net worth of more than $1,500,000
  O c. beneficiaries wishing to bypass their inheritance
  O d. everyone needs a bypass trust

19. Which of the following will not help you avoid losing principal due to interest rate risk?

- ○ a. buying gold
- ○ b. keeping bonds until they mature
- ○ c. buying government bonds only
- ○ d. do not buy bonds

20. An "accidental death benefit" rider:

- ○ a. provides additional money if your death is caused by an accident
- ○ b. increases your premiums
- ○ c. is a waste of money
- ○ d. all of the above

21. Variable annuities are popular because profits are:

- ○ a. tax-free
- ○ b. tax-exempt
- ○ c. tax-deferred
- ○ d. tax-deductible

22. What portion of Americans die without a will?

- ○ a. 0%
- ○ b. 20%
- ○ c. 40%
- ○ d. 80%

23. A bank CD is:

- ○ a. a stock
- ○ b. a bond
- ○ c. neither
- ○ d. both

24. A mortgage is a loan based on:

- ○ a. the current value of the house
- ○ b. the future value of the house
- ○ c. your income
- ○ d. your car payment

25. In the past 10 years, how many times has the performance of the U.S. Stock Market ranked among the top 5 worldwide?

- ○ a. once
- ○ b. four times
- ○ c. seven times
- ○ d. all 10 times

26. Assuming a 10% annual return, a 30-year-old would have to save how much each month to raise $100,000 by age 65?

- ○ a. $26
- ○ b. $95
- ○ c. $143
- ○ d. $217

Answers:
1-c (pg.174)	7-c (pg.480)	13-d (pg.609)	19-c (pg.100)	25-a (pg.128)
2-a (pg.321)	8-d (pg.242)	14-a (pg.408)	20-d (pg.548)	26-a (pg.17)
3-a (pg.490)	9-d (pg.424)	15-a (pg.122)	21-c (pg.198)	
4-c (pg.100)	10-b (pg.11)	16-d (pg.347)	22-a (pg.558)	
5-c (pg.610)	11-a (pg.269)	17-c (pg.583)	23-b (pg.54)	
6-c (pg.62)	12-d (pg.509)	18-b (pg.445)	24-c (pg.369)	

Part I
Introduction to
Financial Planning

There's a quiz at the end of this part!

To see how much you already know, skip to the end of this part and take the quiz now. Then, read the part and take the quiz again. You'll discover how much you've learned!

Part I — Introduction to Financial Planning

Overview - The 11 Reasons You Need to Plan

Thirty-five years ago, the financial planning profession did not even exist, yet today, hundreds of thousands of people claim to be financial planners (and some of them actually are!). What is financial planning, anyway, and is it really necessary?

After all, your parents didn't plan for their future — so why should you? The reason your parents didn't plan is the same reason you haven't packed for Europe: You're not going! Likewise, our parents and grandparents never planned for their future for the simple reason that they weren't going to have one. Why worry about developing cancer at age 88 if you are going to be dead of tuberculosis at 45? Since people weren't expecting to live past 65, there simply was no need for planning.

Today, of course, things are different. And among these differences is the need for financial planning. Here are 11 reasons why you need to plan.

Reason #1: To Protect Yourself and Your Family Against Financial Risks

Notice the word *financial*. As a financial planner, I cannot protect you from the risks you face in life — no planner can — but I can protect you from suffering the financial loss that may result when any of those risks become reality. What are those risks? The four major ones are injury, illness, death, and lawsuits, and you'll learn how to manage and reduce those risks in Part XI.

Lawsuits? You bet! For perspective, the odds that your house will burn down are 1 in 1,200 — yet according to *Forbes* magazine, the odds are just 1 in 200 that you will be sued at some point in your lifetime. (To learn how to protect yourself from the financial threat of a lawsuit, see Chapter 75.)

Reason #2: To Eliminate Personal Debt

For some people, a proper goal is to become worthless. If you owe lots of money to credit cards, auto loans, and student loans, becoming worthless would be a real improvement. You must move from *owing* money to *owning* money.

Indeed, total consumer debt in this country (excluding mortgages) exceeds $1.4 trillion, according to cardweb.com. Its research reveals that Americans hold an average of 8 credit cards each, with an average balance of $8,400 per card.

You've heard the joke about "running out of money before you run out of month," but it's not so funny to run out of money before the end of your *life*! You must make sure you don't outlive your income, and that means you've got to accumulate assets so you can support yourself for a lifetime. That's impossible to do if you have debts, so you must eliminate them. Chapter 51 will show you how.

Reason #3: Because You're Going to Live a Long, Long Time

At the time of the American Revolution, life expectancy at birth was 23 years. By 1900, Americans were expected to live only to age 47. Thus, throughout most of our nation's history, almost everyone worked; there was no such thing as retirement.

Today, though, life expectancy tables from such diverse groups as the IRS, life insurers, the National Institutes of Health and the Centers for Disease Control and Prevention all say roughly the same thing: A child born in 2004 has a life expectancy of 77 years (up from 47 in 1900); a 77-year-old today is expected to live to 88; an 88-year-

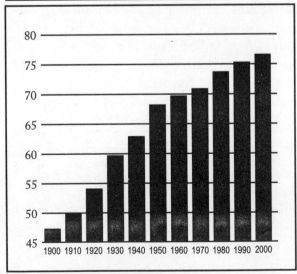

FIGURE 1-1

old to 94; and people who reach 100 are expected to live to 103. Soon, half of all deaths in the U.S. will occur after age 80. These life expectancies are a big part of why we need to plan.

How Old Will You Be in 2100?

The ridiculous part of all those life expectancy tables is that they all assume that life expectancies will remain at current levels. But that is not likely to be the case. Indeed, research suggests that people will continue to live longer and longer. In fact, even those as old as 45 today might be alive in the 22nd Century.

YOUR LIFE EXPECTANCY

People who are this age today	Are expected to live to this age
0	77
15	78
25	79
35	80
45	81
55	82
65	83
75	87
85	91

FIGURE 1-2

Why are these figures important? Well, to determine how much money you'll need in retirement, you need to project how long that retirement might be. Based on the actuarial data provided by various government agencies, most financial planners assume their clients will live to age 90, and conservative planners (my firm included) use age 95 (because the longer you live, the more money you'll need).

However, even "conservative" figures like age 95 could be too low. Based on the relatively new fields of gerontology, microbiology, and biotechnology, some believe that in the year 2050, people could be expected to live to age 140. No typo there: That's one hundred forty years of age.

This is not science-fiction. In 2050, your kids could still be having kids. For example, in 2050, I'll be 92. Will I make it? Well, that's still nine years younger than the age my Grandmom Fannie reached — and she was born in 1899. Let's face it: For many of us, 2050 is a done deal.

"If you can see yourself in possession of your goal, it's half yours."

—Tom Hopkins

If that's not startling enough, try this: It's now being suggested that lots of us who are here today could see the year 2100. The implications for society boggle the mind. Let's look closer at what such long life spans could mean.

You'll Have Multiple Marriages

First, you would be likely to have four or five spouses during your lifetime. Like all the other futurisms to follow, this one is not as far-fetched as it may first appear. After all, 75% of all married Americans eventually find themselves single again — either through divorce or death of their spouse — and most people who were married once eventually remarry. Thus, we're already a multiple-marriage society. It'll just become more so: More people will do it and more people will do it more often. (After all, can you imagine marrying someone at age 20 and living with that same person for the next 120 years!? Honey, I love you, but...)

You'll Have Multiple Careers

Second, you will have five or six careers. You'll go to school, get a degree, develop expertise in a given field, devote yourself to it for 20 or 30 years, then quit and start again, doing something entirely different. Think that's crazy? Millions of military retirees, police officers, firefighters, and schoolteachers already do this. They "retire" at 40 or 50 with 20 or 30 years of service and, with their monthly pension checks in the mail, they head off to new challenges. This strategy will become more common in the new millennium and the phrase "double-dipper" will give way to "quintuple-dipper" as people have five or six 20-year careers in their lifetime. The notion of "retirement" as we know it today will fade away. For more on this, read Rule 88 of *The New Rules of Money*.

You'll Extend Your Rites of Passage

As our lifetimes become extended, so too will our rites of passage. As recently as 1960, marrying in your late teens was common; the phrase "old maid" applied to women who failed to marry by age 20. You were expected to have children (plural) before you were 25, Jerry Rubin told us not to trust anyone over 30, middle age and mid-life crises hit at 45, and the "elderly" were 65.

As I bet yours does, my own life provides examples of this brave new world: My former college roommate is no closer to marriage now than

> *"I'd like to be rich enough so I could throw soap away after the letters are worn off."*
> —**Andy Rooney**

when we were in school; my oldest brother will be 72 when his youngest daughter graduates from medical school; one of my nieces has three daddies (one biological, one marital, and one legal); my 77-year-old father has renounced retirement (for the fourth time); and my grandmother defied the actuaries when she passed at 101.

If today's trends continue unabated, the year 2050 will find people marrying (for the first time) at age 50, having kids in their 60s (in France, they already are), facing middle age in their 80s, retiring in their 120s, and dying in their 140s.

These prognostications remind us that financial planning is a process, not a product. A financial plan must be periodically reviewed, with its assumptions challenged and altered based on changes in the economy and in your circumstances. One key circumstance is the fact that you may live much longer than you envision. If you plan to retire at 65 and are assuming a life expectancy of age 90, you're assuming a 25-year retirement. But what if you live to 140? Will you have enough income for a 75-year retirement?

Finally, who's going to pay for it all?

This question suggests that the most politically explosive social issue in America today — the right to life — will evolve into a new debate. In the 21st Century, with people living for so many years beyond their resources, with society forced to pay the tab, some will argue that those who cannot take care of themselves in old age, those who are living in pain or discomfort, those who do not have a family or support group on whom to rely, and those who cannot afford to pay for their care should have the right to choose death. To some, Dr. Kevorkian is evil, deserving of the 10-to-25-year prison sentence he received in 1999. To others he was a godsend, and to the remainder, he was a mere curiosity. Whatever you think of him, one thing is certain: Dr. Kevorkian is a prelude to the future. In the year 2050, his cause will be center stage as the nation deals with the next great social debate: euthanasia.

Welcome to the 22nd Century. I hope you'll be ready.

Reason #4: To Pay for the Costs of Raising Children

You're earning — and you'll continue to earn — a huge income. Take a 35-year-old making just $3,000 a month. Even without salary increases, that's more than $1 million in career earnings!

While that might sound like good news, it actually works against us. When making a lot of money, people often develop an attitude that says, "Gee, with this good income, life will take care of itself. It did for my parents. It did for my grandparents. It certainly will for me."

The issue, however, is not how much money you *earn*, but how much you *keep*. Look at the money your parents and grandparents earned over their careers. How much do they have left?

You easily could have little left from a lifetime of work, because you don't get to keep all the money you earn. You have expenses — lots of expenses. Can you name your biggest expense?

Children!

YOU ARE EARNING A HUGE AMOUNT OF MONEY

If you are age...	...and each month you earn...	...by age 65 you will earn a total of...
35	$3,000	$1,080,000
45	$5,000	$1,200,000
55	$7,500	$ 900,000

...Even If You Never Get a Raise!

FIGURE 1-3

According to the USDA, a baby born in 2001 will cost highest income families $337,690. As shown in Figure 1-4, lowest income families will still spend $169,920, while those inbetween will rack up expenses of $231,470. That's per child — and only for the first 17 years! To explore the financial issues of raising young children, see Chapter 54.

THE COST OF KIDS

Year	Age	INCOME GROUP		
		Lowest	Middle	Highest
2001	<1	$ 6,490	$ 9,030	$ 13,430
2002	1	6,710	9,340	13,890
2003	2	6,940	9,650	14,360
2004	3	7,330	10,240	15,170
2005	4	7,580	10,590	15,680
2006	5	7,840	10,940	16,220
2007	6	8,200	11,320	16,580
2008	7	8,480	11,700	17,150
2009	8	8,770	12,100	17,730
2010	9	9,090	12,420	18,120
2011	10	9,400	12,840	18,730
2012	11	9,720	13,280	19,370
2013	12	11,290	14,850	21,300
2014	13	11,680	15,350	22,020
2015	14	12,070	15,870	22,770
2016	15	12,350	16,740	24,220
2017	16	12,770	17,310	25,050
2018	17	13,210	17,900	25,900
Total		**$169,920**	**$231,470**	**$337,690**

FIGURE 1-4

Reason #5: To Pay for College

Guess what happens when the kids turn 18? They go to college!

It's estimated that, for a baby born in 2002, the cost of college in 2020 will be $100,000 for an in-state school and $265,000 for private and out-of-state schools. To learn the proper way to approach the cost of college, turn to Chapter 53.

THE COST OF A 4-YEAR COLLEGE DEGREE 2002-2006

Penn State*	$106,521
Maryland*	98,319
Berkeley*	122,161
Notre Dame	147,271
Harvard	157,267
Georgetown	158,116
Princeton	166,060
Yale	154,730

Assumes 6% annual increase in the cost of tuition, room and board — based on 2002-2003 prices.
*Out-of-State tuition

FIGURE 1-5

THE COST OF A WEDDING

Reception	$7,630
Rings	3,576
Honeymoon	3,296
Photography/ Videography	2,123
Miscellaneous	2,184
Apparel	1,274
Music	1,050
Flowers	782
Invitations	445
Total	**$22,360**

FIGURE 1-6

Reason #6: To Pay for a Daughter's Wedding

And if you made the foolish decision to have daughters instead of sons, get ready for another major expense: The wedding! According to Conde Nast Bridal Group, the average cost is $22,360; *Washingtonian* magazine puts it at $28,000.

Reason #7: To Buy a Car

The average price of a new car is $26,670, according to the National Automobile Dealers Association. Thus, that purchase is

"It's a question of priorities, Martha. Do you want lots of kids or <u>one</u> with a college education?"

From the Wall Street Journal - Permission, Cartoon Features Syndicate

one of your biggest — and most confusing — financial decisions. Should you pay cash, accept dealer financing, or use home equity? Is leasing right for you? To learn the answer, go to Chapter 52.

Reason #8: To Buy a Home

Americans devote the largest portion of their incomes to housing. Consequently, how you handle the purchase of your home will have far-reaching implications on virtually every facet of your financial life, including your ability to save, pay for college and plan for your retirement. For this reason, I devote four chapters (56-59) exclusively to this subject, and it's referenced in many other chapters as well, including those dealing with debt elimination (Chapter 51), paying for college (Chapter 53), and the costs of raising children (Chapter 54).

Reason #9: To Be Able to Retire When — and in the Style — You Want

Consider food. Assuming you and your spouse retire at 65 and live to your normal life expectancy of 85, you're going to eat 43,800 meals in retirement! (That's three meals a day, 365 days a year over 20 years for two people.) If each of those meals costs five dollars, you'll spend $219,000 on food. Where will that money come from?

Most people are ignorant of this message. Of today's retirees 65 and older, 39% have incomes below $15,000 a year, according to the Social Security Administration. I'm not saying these people never earned more than $15,000 a year while they were working. Rather, their income dropped below $15,000 when they retired.

Only 15% of retirees earn more than $50,000 a year. Yet the masses didn't plan to fail. They simply failed to plan, because under the old rules, planning wasn't necessary. It used to be that a worker and his family could be comfortable if he retired at 62 on a pension and Social Security. That doesn't happen anymore. Today, you don't retire as young as 62 — unless you've been downsized out of work. And you're going to live much longer than your parents and grandparents did, aren't you? Therefore, your money must last much longer. And that is the dilemma: If you fail to plan, you face the possibility of a retirement filled with poverty, welfare, and charity.

A Gallup survey showed that 75% of workers want to retire before age 60, yet only 25% think they will. That suggests people don't know how they are going to achieve their goals. One thing is sure, it's not going to happen by itself. It's going to require effort and attention. Part X will help.

WILL YOU RETIRE WHEN YOU WANT?

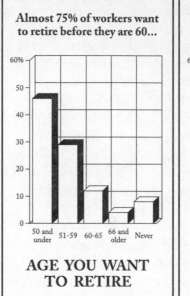

Almost 75% of workers want to retire before they are 60...

AGE YOU WANT TO RETIRE

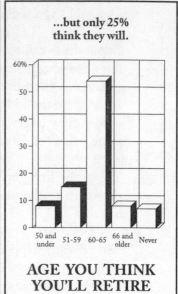

...but only 25% think they will.

AGE YOU THINK YOU'LL RETIRE

FIGURE 1-7

Reason #10: To Pay for the Costs of Long-Term Care

Prior generations did not have to deal with the costs of long-term care, but we must: Of those who reach age 65, according to the U.S. Department of Health & Human Services and Americans for Long-Term Care Security, 40%

> *"If you don't know where you're going, you'll probably end up somewhere else."*
> —David Campbell

will spend time in a nursing home and 5% will require long-term care at some point. The average annual cost of a nursing home now exceeds $61,000; neither your health insurance nor Medicare will pay for it. The result: A growing number of senior citizens today are supported by others because they don't have the money to care for themselves. For more, see Chapter 73.

Reason #11: To Pass Wealth to the Next Generation

This is more difficult than ever before, because living longer means it is increasingly likely that you will spend your money before you have the chance to bequeath it.

Economists call this *transference of wealth*. Historically, money was passed from father to son. It started with our immigrant ancestors, who built homes and had children. When the children married, they moved into the house with Mom and Dad. Then the kids had kids, making it three generations in one house. As the family grew larger, each generation built new rooms, increasing the size — and the value — of the family's wealth.

When the first generation died, the second generation inherited the house, later passing it to the next generation, with each growing more affluent than the previous one.

That doesn't happen today. We don't have three generations living in one house as often as we once did. Today, when our grandparents die, we're more likely to sell their house because we have our own home and we don't need theirs.

Furthermore, we find that our grandparents live so much longer than before — longer than they expected — that they often run out of assets and have nothing to leave to their children. Therefore, instead of passing wealth down to the children, the kids send money up to the parents. Thus, in many cases, the transfer of wealth is going backwards, and economists worry that most Americans are not prepared for this reality. Learn how to avoid that problem by reading Part XII.

It is for all these reasons — to protect against risk; to eliminate debt; you're going to live a long time; to handle such major expenses as children, college costs and weddings; to buy cars and homes; to afford a comfortable retirement; to protect against long-term care costs; and to pass wealth to your heirs — that **you need to create a financial plan**.

> *"Americans tend to plan for everything — except success."*
> — Ric Edelman

Chapter 1 - The Four Obstacles to Building Wealth

As you begin trying to accumulate wealth, you'll encounter four major obstacles. The first is the most deadly, but if you think it's the economy or taxes, you're wrong. Your biggest enemy, as I can attest from having worked with thousands of people just like you, is *yourself*. Without question, *procrastination* is the most common cause of financial failure.

To understand this, consider the story of Jack and Jill. You know Jack fell down the hill, but you didn't know that he suffered head injuries. As a result, Jack decided not to go to college. Instead, at age 18, he got a job, enabling him to contribute $3,000 to his IRA each year. After eight years, he stopped, having invested a total of $24,000.

Meanwhile, his sister Jill, inspired by Jack's accident, went to medical school. At age 26, she began her practice and started contributing $3,000 to her IRA. And she did so for 40 years, from age 26 to 65. She invested a total of $120,000 and she put her money into the same investment as her brother Jack. Thus, Jill started investing the same year Jack stopped, and she saved for 40 years compared to just eight years for her brother.

By age 65, whose IRA account do you think was worth more money?

Assuming Jack and Jill each earned a 10% return, Jill accumulated $1,324,778, but Jack collected $1,552,739 — $227,961 more than his sister!

CLOSE TO HOME   JOHN MCPHERSON

© 1994 John McPherson/Dist. by Universal Press Syndicate   3-29

© John McPherson. Reprinted with permission of Universal Press Syndicate. All rights reserved.

"I've been going over our finances. According to my calculations, our monthly retirement income will be either $2,124 or $42,798, depending on whether or not we win the Publishers Clearing House sweepstakes."

"Knowledge is power."
—Francis Bacon

While Jack had invested only $24,000 to Jill's $120,000, his money earned interest for eight years longer than his sister. It wasn't the money that made him successful — it was the *time value of money*. Jack didn't procrastinate, and by investing sooner than Jill, his account grew larger.

I have heard the complaint that procrastination does not belong at the top of my "Enemies of Money" list. There must be other, more serious causes for financial failure, right?

Wrong!

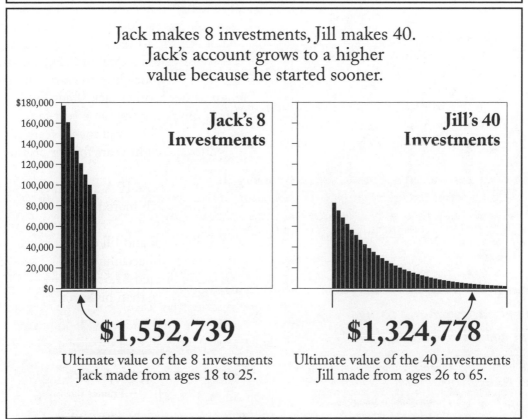

JACK AND JILL

Jack makes 8 investments, Jill makes 40.
Jack's account grows to a higher
value because he started sooner.

Jack's 8 Investments

Jill's 40 Investments

$1,552,739

Ultimate value of the 8 investments
Jack made from ages 18 to 25.

$1,324,778

Ultimate value of the 40 investments
Jill made from ages 26 to 65.

FIGURE 1-8

Obstacle #1: Procrastination

I cannot stress enough the need for you to get started right now. Procrastination says you'll do it tomorrow. It's easy to see why you put planning off until later: After all, who has time? You've got lots of deadlines and you don't need another one. You've got to get to work on time, get your kid to soccer practice and prepare for out-of-towners who will be visiting you this weekend. With today's deadlines, you don't have time to work on something whose effects will not be felt for 20 years. But that's okay because you're young and you'll still have plenty of time later! Right?

Wrong!

Maybe this is why so few of my firm's clients are under 30. It just seems that young people don't want to talk about something 40 years away: They're more concerned about this weekend's party!

In fact, I've heard all the excuses: If you're in your 20s, you figure you've got 40 years to deal with it, so you'll put it off until you are in your 30s...

...but by then, you've got a new house, new spouse, and new kids — and you're spending money like never before. Who can think about saving at a time like this? You'll deal with it later, after things settle down in your 40s...

...when indeed you're making more money than ever, but now you find that your older children are entering college. On top of that, your income growth isn't as rapid as it used to be. No problem, you say, because by the time you hit your 50s, you think your major expenses will be behind you...

> *"There are so many things that we wish we had done yesterday, so few that we feel like doing today."*
> —**Mignon McLaughlin**

...only to discover that your younger kids are entering college and the older ones are starting to get married (with you footing all these bills) and maybe the graduates need help buying a house, too. Your parents probably need some help as well, because they're getting up in years. And you can't remember the last time you got a promotion; after all, you've moved up so high in the company that the only way you'll get promoted is for somebody to retire or die.

You're also finding that the cost of living has never been higher, so planning for retirement will just have to wait a bit longer...

...and when you hit 65, you lament your anemic savings and wish you had started 40 years ago.

I see this all the time.

If there is only one thing in this entire book that you need to take on faith, it's this: There is never an ideal time for planning, and while you can always find a reason to put it off, don't. Do it now. Procrastination will cause you financial ruin more effectively, more completely, than the worst advice a crooked broker could ever give you.

The Cost of Procrastination

There is, in fact, a specific cost to procrastination. If you are 20 years old and you want to raise $100,000 by age 65, you need to invest only $1,372 today (ignoring taxes for the moment and assuming a 10% annual return).

But a 50-year-old would need to invest nearly $24,000 to obtain that same $100,000. This is the cost of procrastination. As you can see, it's not money that makes people financially successful, it's time.

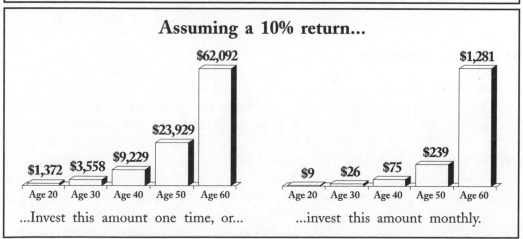

TO RAISE $100,000 BY AGE 65

Assuming a 10% return...

Invest this amount one time						invest this amount monthly				
$1,372	$3,558	$9,229	$23,929	$62,092		$9	$26	$75	$239	$1,281
Age 20	Age 30	Age 40	Age 50	Age 60		Age 20	Age 30	Age 40	Age 50	Age 60

...Invest this amount one time, or...   ...invest this amount monthly.

FIGURE 1-9

> While presenting this in a seminar, an elderly gentleman rose to object to my comments. "Excuse me," he said, "but I can't do that."
>
> "Why not?" I asked. "Don't you have a hundred bucks?"
>
> "I have the hundred dollars," he replied. "But I don't have the 30 years!"

The cost of procrastination can be shown just as easily for those who save monthly: Our 20-year-old would need to save less than $10 a month, but the 50-year-old would need to save $239 a month. You tell me: Who has an easier task?

Why $1,200 = $37,125

A lot of folks reading this will concede that starting young has its advantages. But I'm plenty young, you might be thinking, so I'll just start next year. After all, next year, I'll still be young enough, but I'll be making more money, and it'll be easier for me to start. After all, what difference can one year make?

A big difference.

If a 30-year-old saves $100 a month until age 65, earning 10% per year, the resulting account would be worth **$379,664**.

But if this person waited just one year, beginning her savings at 31 instead of 30, her account at age 65 would be worth only **$342,539**.

Thus, the cost of not saving $100 a month for just one year is **$37,125**. Can you really afford to blow thirty-seven grand?

Don't procrastinate. Start now.

Out the Door by Twenty-Four

Like so many other things in life, procrastination is a learned art. As with most basic attitudes, we learn about this one from our parents.

A listener, Bob, once called my radio show. Age 23, he asked, "Ric, what should I do with my money? I have $24,000 and no debt." I was impressed. Most of the 20-somethings I know are broke and have lots of credit cards. Bob said the bulk of his money was an inheritance and it was just sitting in his bank account.

I asked him about his monthly expenses, expecting Bob's reply to be in the range of $1,000 to $3,000; such an amount would be typical for folks in their 20s. To my surprise, he said, "Oh, I spend about two hundred dollars a month." Then the truth came out. Bob, 23 and a college graduate, lives at home.

> *"Human beings are the only creatures on earth that allow their children to come back home."*
>
> **—Bill Cosby**

Upon graduation, he became an official member of The Boomerang Generation. Mom and Dad shipped him off to college at age 18, paid the bill, and prepared to celebrate the fact that their child-rearing and child-supporting days were over.

But when Bob graduated, he didn't move on with his life. Instead, he moved back. Bob once again lives with his parents, at their expense, and his total monthly spending of $200 goes to whatever he wants — parties, hanging out with friends, movies, eating out with the guys, weight-lifting at the club, and other activities of the financially secure.

Bob is able to participate in these avocations, of course, because "someone else" does his laundry, cooks his meals, and pays for the home he lives in.

Occupationally speaking, Bob is in a rut. Upon graduation, he missed the career track: Unable to get the job of his choice, he chose not to work at all. I asked, "When are you going to move out?" He said, "I'm in no hurry."

I can see his point. Why should he move to a 700-square-foot, three-room apartment that costs $1,200 per month (plus utilities, Internet and telephone)? He'd

CALVIN AND HOBBES BILL WATTERSON

> *"Life is like riding a bicycle; you don't fall off unless you stop pedaling."*
> —Claude Pepper

have to buy furniture and a TV, drag his laundry to the Laundromat, shop for his own groceries, and cook his own meals.

Why should Bob do that, when he can live in a 3,000-square-foot, multi-level single family home on a quarter-acre lot in the suburbs, where somebody else takes care of his laundry, does the food shopping, and prepares dinner nightly?

Let's face it, Bob's got a great thing going here, and the operative initials are M-O-M.

Bob can come and go as he pleases, has no bills to pay, and if something goes wrong, the landlord takes care of it, spelled D-A-D.

This is an issue of "tough love." Without exception, all my clients who have kids love them dearly, and they'd do anything for them — but enough is enough. Parents must recognize that at 23, these "kids" are adults — and they need to act like it. Parents are not doing their children any favors by coddling and protecting them against the cold, cruel realities of life.

In Bob's case, Mom and Dad need to charge him rent, just like any other landlord. They need to collect an amount equal to (a) what Bob would pay elsewhere, or (b) what Mom and Dad would charge if Bob were a stranger.

If they were to charge $1,200 a month, two things would happen: Bob would get a job to pay for it, and he'd move out. Both are exactly what Bob needs to do if he's to develop and thrive in our society.

> *"If you can count your money, you don't have a billion dollars."*
> —J. Paul Getty

And to all you Moms and Dads who hate the thought of collecting rent from your own children, here's a neat trick: Collect the rent and invest it for your son or daughter without telling them. When they finally move out (we hope, one day, they will), you can give them the money as a moving-out gift, allowing them to use the money you've saved for them to help them get settled in a new home.

Don't get me wrong. I don't have a problem with kids living at home; it can be a smart financial move — for kids trying to save money. Rather, my problem is with kids who live at home as freeloaders — and there is a big difference between the two.

> *"Do not handicap your children by making their lives easy."*
> —Lazarus Long

Take the example of Mike, one of my clients. He is 26 and, like Bob, lives at his parents' home. He didn't go to college, but he's been working since he was 16. Mom and Dad have always covered his expenses because Mike has always had a job and he contributes to running the household (doing chores, cooking, cleaning, and shopping). He's diligent, conscientious, and — most important — Mike is good at saving money.

In fact, he is *really* good at saving money: Mike has $60,000, which he saved on his own — no gifts or inheritances. He's accumulated his money throughout the 10 years he's worked.

And that's why Mom and Dad have no problem with him living at home for free: They know that rather than forcing Mike to pay rent to them or some other landlord, he's paying himself. So when he does decide to move out, he can afford to buy a place, not just rent it. Besides, like most suburbanites, Mom and Dad can afford to have Mike live in the house and they love to have him around, so it's a great deal for everybody.

The Bobs of our nation won't be 20-something forever and if they don't learn to pay their way now, if they don't start preparing to do so, they never will. Are you prepared to support your kids for your entire life?

Give your kids a push. Don't let them procrastinate. It could be the best thing you ever do for them.

CALVIN AND HOBBES   BILL WATTERSON

Obstacle #2: Spending Habits

Again, the problem is you, not the economy or world politics!

To see what I mean, look at the Newmans, married, with a combined annual income of $60,000. They felt they didn't spend extravagantly, but they were nonetheless concerned that they couldn't seem to save any money. "We don't drive fancy cars or take big vacations and our kids don't have the latest Reeboks," they told me. "But we can't seem to get ahead."

Needless to say, the Newmans didn't know where their money was going, so my firm helped them figure it out. The Newmans commuted to work separately and here's what we found:

When they each got to the office, each would buy a newspaper for fifty cents, coffee ($1.25), and a doughnut ($1.00). In a mid-afternoon break, they'd buy a candy bar ($.75). Without knowing the other was also doing this, each was spending $3.50 a day, for a daily total of $7.00.

With 20 working days per month, they were spending $140 per month, or $1,680 a year.

And guess what happens to the money you earn before you receive it? It gets taxed. In other words, the Newmans had to earn $2,400 in order to net the $1,680 that they frittered away on candy and soda. Then they came to us saying, "We can't seem to save any money."

CATHY   CATHY GUISEWITE

Where Does My Money Go?

Have you ever withdrawn $50 from an automatic teller machine, yet find your wallet or purse empty just a few days later?

Have you ever asked yourself, "Where does all my money go?" Like the Newmans, you probably are piddling it away. You have no idea you're doing it, because if you did know, you would stop instantly, for there isn't a rational human being in the world who would tolerate such nonsense.

"A study of economics usually reveals that the best time to buy anything is last year."
—Marty Allen

But we all piddle money away because we don't pay attention. The Newmans were spending 3% of their annual income on... *nothing!* To avoid this problem, you've got to look at your spending habits, for that's where you'll find the key to your financial future. If your spending habits are causing you trouble, you can learn how to fix them in Chapter 51.

INFLATION

1978	9.0	1991	3.1
1979	13.3	1992	3.0
1980	12.4	1993	2.8
1981	8.9	1994	2.7
1982	3.9	1995	2.5
1983	3.8	1996	3.6
1984	4.0	1997	1.9
1985	3.8	1998	1.6
1986	1.1	1999	2.2
1987	4.4	2000	3.4
1988	4.4	2001	2.8
1989	4.7	2002	1.4
1990	6.1		

25-Year Average: 4.4%

FIGURE 1-10

Obstacle #3: Inflation

The most onerous of money's enemies, inflation is perhaps the best illustration of how **The Rules of Money Have Changed**.

Over the past 25 years, inflation averaged 4.4% per year, according to Ibbotson Associates. At that rate, a 50-year-old earning $50,000 a year, who plans to retire at 65 on that same income, will need a net worth

"Inflation is when the buck doesn't stop anywhere."
—Anonymous

$1,000 TODAY

In this many years...	$1,000 will be worth...	...and it will take this much money to buy what $1,000 buys today:
5	$806	$1,240
10	650	1,538
15	524	1,907
20	422	2,365
25	340	2,934
30	274	3,639
35	221	4,513
40	178	5,597

assuming 4.4% annual inflation

FIGURE 1-11

CONSUMER PRICES

	25 Years Ago	Today	25 Years from Now*
Automobile	$4,098	$26,670	$73,000
Postage Stamp	.06	.37	1.09
Gallon of Milk	1.23	2.89	8.48
Movie Ticket	1.50	7.50	16.60
Physician's Office Visit	6.75	114.00	335.00
Electric Shaver	15.00	115.50	338.00
Running Shoes	20.00	48.80	143.20
Gallon of Gasoline	.32	1.41	4.14

*based on 4.4% annual inflation

FIGURE 1-12

of $1.7 million — and his income in his first year of retirement needs to be $95,000.

Indeed, to look into the future, you need not 20/20 vision but an inflation-adjusted 50/50 vision!

In fact, 4.4% annual inflation means $1,000 will be worth less than two-thirds as much in 10 years. Put another way, you'll need $1,538 in 10 years to buy what $1,000 buys today. Are you old enough to remember when President Nixon announced a 90-day wage and price freeze? Inflation was rampant and nobody could stop it — not Congress, the Federal Reserve Board, the President's Council of Economic Advisors, the banks, or Wall Street.

Nixon and the nation panicked. Convinced that inflation was going to cause an economic calamity worse than the Great Depression, the President stopped inflation artificially. For 90 days, nobody was permitted to raise salaries or prices. And the strategy worked — until the 91st day, anyway. When President Nixon established his freeze in 1971, the inflation rate was just four percent. If that were the case 10 years later, Jimmy Carter would have been reelected! By the time Jimmy left office in 1980, inflation was 13% and banks were offering 15% CDs.

But you didn't buy those CDs, because you were convinced that next month, CD rates would be 16% and you didn't want to be stuck with "only" 15%! So you kept your money in daily accounts. You rode the interest wave up and right back down again!

Inflation — even very low inflation — once panicked our nation, but no longer. How can that be? The reason is the frog.

Yes, the frog.

"If you had your life to live over again, you'd need more money."
—**Anonymous**

The Boiling Frog Syndrome

If you throw a frog into a pot of boiling water, he'll jump out. But if you place a frog into a pot of lukewarm water and slowly turn up the heat, it will boil to death.

And so it is with inflation. We've grown accustomed to inflation over the past 25 years, but that doesn't mean we don't continue to be hurt by its effect. We are hurt even at "low" rates of inflation.

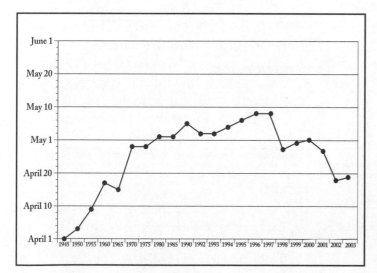

TAX FREEDOM DAY

FIGURE 1-13

Obstacle #4: Taxes

We all love to hate taxes.

According to the Tax Foundation, Tax Freedom Day is April 19, meaning that every dollar you earn for the first four months of the year goes to taxes. Put another way, you work nearly three hours of each workday just to pay taxes. No wonder we find it difficult to save money!

In addition to federal income taxes, you also must contend with state income taxes, as shown in Figure 1-14, plus personal property taxes, sales

25

taxes, user taxes, intangibles taxes, excise taxes, capital gains taxes, and estate taxes.

The amazing thing is that everybody thinks taxes are a natural part of life. Have we all forgotten why we revolted against England?

Our federal income tax wasn't even created until 1913 — and it took a constitutional amendment to do it. And when the tax was established, it was quite low: There was no tax on the first $20,000 of income and only a 1% tax on income between $20,000 and $50,000 — and $20,000 was a lot of income in 1913!

You can guess what the politicians said back then, too. "Don't worry," I'll bet they claimed, "tax rates will never rise!"

It's the Boiling Frog Syndrome all over again.

> *"Noah must have taken into the Ark two taxes, one male and one female. And did they multiply bountifully! Next to guinea pigs, taxes must have been the most prolific animals."*
> —**Will Rogers**

> *"Our Founding Fathers objected to taxation without representation. They should see it today with representation."*
> —**Anonymous**

STATE INCOME TAXES

State	Top Rate	State	Top Rate
Alabama	5.00%	Nebraska	6.80%
Alaska	None	Nevada	None
Arizona	5.04%	New Hampshire	Limited
Arkansas	6.50%	New Jersey	6.37%
California	9.30%	New Mexico	8.20%
Colorado	4.63%	New York	6.85%
Connecticut	4.50%	North Carolina	8.25%
Delaware	5.95%	North Dakota	5.54%
Florida	None	Ohio	7.50%
Georgia	6.00%	Oklahoma	7.00%
Hawaii	8.30%	Oregon	9.00%
Idaho	7.80%	Pennsylvania	2.80%
Illinois	3.00%	Rhode Island	25% of Federal
Indiana	3.40%	South Carolina	7.00%
Iowa	8.98%	South Dakota	None
Kansas	6.45%	Tennessee	Limited
Kentucky	6.00%	Texas	None
Louisiana	6.00%	Utah	7.00%
Maine	8.50%	Vermont	9.50%
Maryland	4.75%	Virginia	5.75%
Massachusetts	5.30%	Washington	None
Michigan	3.90%	Washington, D.C.	8.70%
Minnesota	7.85%	West Virginia	6.50%
Mississippi	5.00%	Wisconsin	6.75%
Missouri	6.00%	Wyoming	None
Montana	11.00%		

Average State Income Tax Rate: 5.6%

FIGURE 1-14

Chapter 2 - The Story of Taxes and Inflation

Together, taxes and inflation create a web of incredible treachery, serving as another example of how **The Rules of Money Have Changed**.

At the turn of the century, taxes and inflation were not a concern. Homes cost $5,000 (Sears used to sell them from their catalog) and if you wanted to borrow money to buy your house, the bank charged you from 4% to 6%. If you deposited money into the bank, the bank paid you 2%; its profit was the difference between what it charged and what it paid.

Why were our parents and grandparents willing to accept a 2% return on their savings? Because it was profitable for them to do so: With no inflation, the 2% they earned was a real 2% and, with no taxes to pay, they got to keep it all. Thus, our parents and grandparents were able to prosper from a 2% return on their money and banks were able to prosper by charging only 4% or 6% for their loans.

Banks were willing to offer 30-year mortgages at these low rates because it had always been profitable to do so. Indeed, from 1879 to 1965, mortgage rates in the U.S. (Figure 1-15) were very stable, consistently at 5.3%, give or take half a point.

But something happened in 1966. Rates began to rise and they've been fluctuating ever since.

Amazing! Interest rates that had remained constant since the end of the Civil War suddenly began to fluctuate, rocketing from 5.7% to 16.5% and crashing back down again.

> *"Man is not like other animals in the ways that are really significant: Animals have instincts, we have taxes."*
>
> —Eric Goffman

> *"In 1790, the nation which had fought a revolution against taxation without representation discovered that some of its citizens weren't much happier about taxation with representation."*
>
> —Lyndon Johnson

MORTGAGE RATES 1879-1965

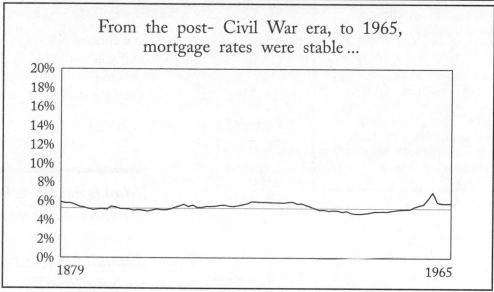

From the post- Civil War era, to 1965,
mortgage rates were stable ...

FIGURE 1-15

1966-2002

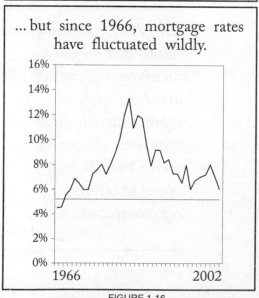

... but since 1966, mortgage rates
have fluctuated wildly.

FIGURE 1-16

*"The further backward
you can look, the further
forward you are likely
to see."*

—Winston Churchill

Too often, people get hung up explaining things rather than accepting them. For example, I can't explain the principles of internal combustion, but I can safely drive a car.

Handle money the same way: Recognize things for what they are, even if you can't explain them. As a judge once said, "I can't explain what pornography is, but I know it when I see it."

Why did this happen? Well, I'll tell you:

I don't know.

But I can tell you what happened to banks as a result: They got killed. In 1965, they gave borrowers 30-year, fixed-rate loans at 5.83%, but by 1980, they were paying 21% in CD rates. So, the banks found themselves earning 5.83% but paying out 21%. Yup, that's a good way to kill a bank, and that's why, in the 1980s, more banks failed than in any period since the Depression.

Bankers — some of the smartest economic minds in the nation — didn't see inflation coming, so it's no surprise that ordinary consumers didn't, either.

My point is that our parents and grandparents were able to succeed financially with a 2% bank account, yet if we do what they did — if we handle our money the way they handled theirs — we will fail where they succeeded.

Here's why: Assume CD rates are 2%. If you are in the 33% combined federal/state income tax bracket, you lose to taxes a third of everything you earn. Thus, if you earn 2%, you lose 0.667%, and keep only 1.34%.

But because of inflation, which at this writing is almost 2%, you're actually losing money.

This is why many people fail financially. They focus on how much they earn instead of how much they *keep*. What counts is your *after-tax, after-inflation rate of return*.

HOW TAXES AND INFLATION AFFECT YOUR INVESTMENT EARNINGS

If You Earn	6%
You Pay Taxes of (33% Combined Fed/State Brackets)	- 2%
What's Left is	4%
Minus Inflation (25-year average CPI)	- 4.4%
Net Earnings	-0.4%

To beat the effects of taxes and inflation, you *must* earn nearly 7% per year!

FIGURE 1-17

As I say on my radio and TV shows, you've got to earn more than the current combined rate of inflation and taxes in order for your money to grow in real terms. To determine the minimum rate of return that you need to earn to beat taxes and inflation, look at Figure 1-18.

The irony is that everybody is lamenting today's low interest rates, compared to those of the past thirty years, and my firm gets lots of calls from people complaining that interest rates have dropped. "I can no longer get 6% or 8% CDs," they say. "Banks are not paying good rates any more."

My colleagues and I find this quite funny, because banks never paid "good rates." It's just that you're noticing for the first time! You see, CD rates — like all interest rates — simply track inflation. When inflation rates are high, interest rates are high, and when inflation drops, interest rates drop. In 1980, for example, when interest rates were 15%, inflation was 13%.

WHAT YOU MUST EARN TO MAINTAIN YOUR MONEY'S PURCHASING POWER

Inflation Rate

Tax Rate	2%	3%	4%	5%	6%	7%	8%	9%	10%	11%	12%
0%	2.0	3.0	4.0	5.0	6.0	7.0	8.0	9.0	10.0	11.0	12.0
10%	2.2	3.3	4.4	5.6	6.7	7.8	8.9	10.0	11.1	12.2	13.3
15%	2.4	3.5	4.7	5.9	7.1	8.2	9.4	10.6	11.8	12.9	14.1
20%	2.5	3.8	5.0	6.3	7.5	8.8	10.0	11.3	12.5	13.8	15.0
25%	2.7	4.0	5.3	6.7	8.0	9.3	10.7	12.0	13.3	14.7	16.0
30%	2.9	4.3	5.7	7.1	8.6	10.0	11.4	12.9	14.3	15.7	17.1
35%	3.1	4.6	6.2	7.7	9.2	10.8	12.3	13.8	15.4	16.9	18.5
40%	3.3	5.0	6.7	8.3	10.0	11.7	13.3	15.0	16.7	18.3	20.0
45%	3.6	5.5	7.3	9.1	10.9	12.7	14.5	16.4	18.2	20.0	21.8

Example: If inflation is 4% and you pay 35% in taxes, your investments must earn 6.2% to break even.

FIGURE 1-18

Do the math: If you earned 15% on a CD, you netted 10% after taxes. But with 13% inflation, you were still losing in real terms. In other words, you were just as broke earning 15% in 1980 as you are earning 2% today. You simply never noticed. Now that you are thoroughly demoralized, let me assure you that there is a way out of this tax-and-inflation trap. And that leads us to the next chapter.

> *"Why does a small tax increase cost you two hundred dollars and a substantial tax cut save you thirty cents?"*
>
> —Peg Bracken

FRANK & ERNEST   BOB THAVES

Frank and Ernest is copyright by Thaves. Used here with permission. All rights reserved.

Chapter 3 - The Greatest Discovery of the 20th Century

Albert Einstein is often quoted as having said that the greatest discovery of the 20th century was compound interest. Of course, the story's not true, but it is a fun anecdote that makes a good point.

Here's why: If you were to invest $10,000 at 5% interest for 20 years, your profit from the investment would be $16,533 (ignoring taxes). But if you doubled the rate of interest to 10%, how much money would you earn?

Although it would seem that doubling the rate would double the return, this is not the case: Increasing the rate by 100% increases the *return* by nearly 350%. In other words, instead of earning $16,533 in interest, you would earn $57,275.

That's the power of compound interest: Money doesn't grow linearly — it grows exponentially! Take it a step further: If you earn 15% instead of 5%, your profit would be $153,665. Thus, three times the rate produces more than nine times the return. And at 20% — a four-fold increase in rate — your profit would be $373,376, or a return 23 times higher than that provided by 5%.

THE MAGIC OF COMPOUND INTEREST

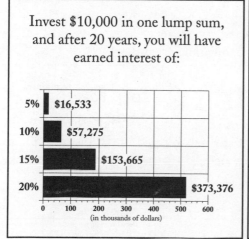

Invest $10,000 in one lump sum, and after 20 years, you will have earned interest of:

5%	$16,533
10%	$57,275
15%	$153,665
20%	$373,376

(in thousands of dollars)

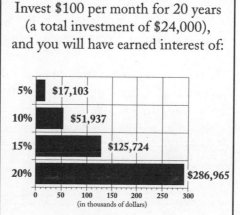

Invest $100 per month for 20 years (a total investment of $24,000), and you will have earned interest of:

5%	$17,103
10%	$51,937
15%	$125,724
20%	$286,965

(in thousands of dollars)

FIGURE 1-19

Investing monthly works just as well when investing a lump-sum: If you invest $100 a month over 20 years, you'll have invested a total of $24,000. At 5%, your money would earn $17,103 in interest, but doubling the rate to 10% would once again increase your profit by 350%, just as before.

At 15%, you would have earned $125,724; at 20%, you'd have arned $286,965.

For nine years, I taught a class on this subject at Georgetown University, and it was usually about this time that my students would raise a question: Where can you earn 20%?

> *"Make use of time, let not advantage slip."*
> —**William Shakespeare**

The Secret to Earning 20% with No Risk

Would you like me to tell you how to earn a guaranteed 20% per year with no risk? Well, I'll tell you:

I don't know how.

And if I *did* know how, why would I tell you?

Ask yourself that question the next time someone cold-calls you with the hottest deal around. After all, if they have such a great investment, why would they tell you about it? Look, I'm a nice guy, but let's face it: If I had a "sure thing," I'd be so busy investing my own money that I certainly wouldn't have the time to tell you about it. And assuming I did have time to make a few phone calls, why would I call you — a total stranger — instead of telling my family and friends?

Actually, Wall Street has pondered the question of "why tell me?" for some time, and identified two theories: The first says that the only *sure* way to make money from investments is to earn commissions by selling them, and brokers can do that only by convincing someone that he or she will get rich in the process. Thus, this theory says a broker tells a client to buy or sell because it's good for the broker, not necessarily good for the investor.

The second theory says that Wall Street sharks who are on TV, the radio, or in some magazine or newspaper telling you to buy a certain stock often already own it, and they want to unload it. But they can't sell until the price goes up, or up again, and what better way to get the price of a stock to go up than by telling a few million people to buy it? So, they tout the stock on CNBC or *Wall Street Week* or *Money* magazine, and the masses oblige.

> *"The rich are taking their advice from professional financial advisors. The poor are getting their advice from* **Money** *magazine."*
> —Robert Veres

The stock briefly goes up — long enough for the guy who pitched it to get out — and he goes *back* on these programs to say, "See? I was right!"

Wall Street is full of these self-fulfilled prophecies.

You think I'm kidding? Studies have shown that in the 48 hours after a stock is touted on a popular TV show or news column, the stock rises significantly as tens of thousands of people call their brokers with buy orders. The run-ups last just long enough for the sharks who fed the information to the media to cash out at big profits. After that, the stocks quickly return to their original levels, leaving investors with stocks they bought at very high prices.

Consider the example of Kidder Peabody broker A. Karl Kiplee. According to *Financial Planning on Wall Street*, Kiplee admitted that he planted inaccurate stories in the media about Epitope, Inc., a small biotech company. Allegedly, he gave CNBC and then-*Money* magazine reporter Dan Dorfman (perhaps the best-known financial journalist in the nation at the time), false information, causing Dorfman to report in March 1994 that Epitope's AIDS test stood only a 1% chance of receiving FDA approval. This allegedly caused the stock to drop in value, yet in December of that year, the test was indeed approved.

DILBERT   SCOTT ADAMS

Reprinted by permission of Newspaper Enterprise Associate, Inc.

Epitope, alleging false and misleading statements, settled a suit with Kiplee, and even considered a suit against Dorfman, merely because Dorfman quoted Kiplee. As Dorfman later told *Business Week*, one "just can't be sure that everyone [you] speak to is 100% ethical."

But that wasn't Dorfman's only brush with controversy. *Business Week* reported in late 1995 that Dorfman was under investigation by federal authorities regarding his relationship with a Wall Street publicist. According to *Business Week*, the allegations were that corporate clients paid fees to the publicist, a good friend of Dorfman's, in exchange for having Dorfman say positive things about the company. There is no indication that any money was exchanged between the publicist and Dorfman. However, Dorfman was fired by *Money* magazine; and he later left CNBC.

Think this story is dated? Then consider the more recent accounting scandals that have implicated dozens of companies and their auditors and the brokerage firms that promoted their stocks to hapless investors. For a complete discourse on this, read Chapter 6 of *Discover the Wealth Within You*.

Think about it. Stock prices are based on the laws of supply and demand. Supply (the number of shares of a stock that exist) is fixed; thus the price goes up and down based on demand. If lots of people want to buy, the price goes up, and if few want to buy, or if many want to sell, the price goes down.

Match these fundamentals with how one succeeds in the stock market. You make money by buying low and selling high. First, you buy a stock that has a low price. Then you go on television or radio, or get quoted in the newspaper, telling everyone that the price is really low and that you think the price of the stock is going to go up. Better yet, get someone like Dorfman to do it for you.

DILBERT   SCOTT ADAMS

Reprinted by permission of Newspaper Enterprise Associate, Inc.

By distributing your message to millions of people, several hundred thousand will oblige, and this new demand will cause the price to rise within a day or two. You know when the show is going to air, or when the story is going to be printed (since you planted it), so you buy a few days in advance, and after the news breaks, you quickly sell while the stock is high, making a bundle. The masses, of course, get ripped-off: They buy the stock after the news report, as the stock is on its way up (they BUY HIGH) and as soon as the media attention ends (which it does quickly) demand softens and the stock falls back to its original level, causing them to SELL LOW. Thus, the knowing-no-better consumers lose money while the promoters make money. This becomes a vicious trap for the unwary, because the promoters return to the media, saying, "The stock went up, so I was right. Therefore, you should listen to me next time and do what I tell you to do." Thus, they get invited back onto these shows, and they can be quoted again and again, and people continue to follow their "advice" and unwittingly help them make millions time after time. (This is one of the reasons why there is often a big difference between *investment returns and investor returns* — see Chapter 37.)

Several law school students at Georgetown University figured out how to engage in this "pump and dump" scheme on the Internet, and they bilked investors nationwide for hundreds of thousands of dollars before the SEC forced them to stop. But the university allowed them to graduate anyway, and today they all have law degrees. (And that explains why I stopped teaching there — I resigned in protest.)

So whenever you see a "hot tip" touted in a financial newsletter, magazine, or newspaper, or you hear some pundit claiming on radio or TV, or on some Internet site, that you need to buy or sell a certain stock, you've got to ask yourself, "What is the motivation of the person who's saying this?" After all, how relevant to your particular circumstances can the advice be when it is simultaneously being provided to millions of people?

DILBERT   SCOTT ADAMS

Reprinted by permission of Newspaper Enterprise Associate, Inc.

Even when motivation is not suspect, there's another potential problem: Lots can happen between the time an article is written and the time you read it. In its April 1995 issue, *Smart Money* magazine named Sports & Recreation as one of its "favorite midcap stocks," encouraging its readers to buy the company's shares. In the following issue, *Smart Money* apologized, saying, "Now we hate [the stock]." The magazine explained that "just as readers were starting to get their [April] issues in the mail," the stock dropped 42% in two days. Although the magazine's editors put a sell signal on the stock, readers saw the magazine's buy recommendation.

That must have been embarrassing for *Smart Money*'s editors. Imagine, then, how they felt when it happened again in the very next issue! Yup, whereas the May issue apologized for April, the June issue found itself apologizing for May, whose cover story, "Where to Invest Now," said to buy the stock of United Wisconsin Services. Yet as *Smart Money* reported in June, "Just after we sent our [May] cover story to the printers, [there was] some disturbing news... [W]ith the May issue already in some subscribers' hands, UWS dropped a bombshell... its shares sank as low as $19, less than half their 1995 high."

To *Smart Money*'s credit, they admitted their mistake. Still, you need to think again before you act on information contained in a personal finance magazine.

Keep that in mind the next time you hear some financial wizard say, "The market's going to have a 20% correction." He might really mean, "The stock market's too high right now for me to buy more, so I want you to sell your holdings, which will force the stock market down by 20% so I can get in at the lower prices."

This is why I never tout stocks, mutual funds, or other investments by name in this or any of my books, or in my newsletter, on my radio and TV shows, on my web site, or in my seminars. Be wary of those who do. Like all investment advisors, I have my favorites, but my role here is to provide you with a fundamental financial education, not to get you to buy or sell something. By focusing on education, you'll understand how the financial world works, making you able to make decisions that are best for you. And that, in turn, will allow you to take control of your financial future so you can ignore all the pundits.

How Did the Millionaires Get That Way?

Our inability to tell you how to get guaranteed 20% annual returns aside, I bet you can name the one asset that has produced more millionaires in our nation's history than any other. No, it's not the Internet — it's real estate (although technology may overtake the #1 position in the coming years). So, let's take a little quiz:

1. Which of the following is the most valuable real estate?

(a)   Maui

(b)   Hong Kong

(c)   Manhattan

(d)   Monaco

(e)   Tokyo

The answer is (c). Manhattan Island's real estate is the most expensive in the world.

2. From whom did we buy the island and how much did we pay?

These are easy questions. After all, you learned this in third grade! We bought Manhattan Island from Native Americans, for blankets and beads worth $24.

3. What was the year?

This is a bit tougher. The year was 1626.

The Rule of 72

Before I ask you the final question, let me teach you about the Rule of 72. Great fun at cocktail parties,[1] the Rule of 72 allows you to determine how long it will take for money to double at various interest rates.

It works like this: Say you want your money to double in 10 years. To determine how much interest you need to earn, just divide 10 into 72. Therefore, in order for your money to double in 10 years, you must earn 7.2% annually. If you earn 15% and want to know how long it will take to double your money, just divide 72 by 15. The answer: 4.8 years.

So, simply divide whatever number you have — either the interest rate or the time — into the number 72, and the answer will be the number you need. If you divide the interest rate into 72, you'll get the *time*. If you divide the time into 72, you'll get the *interest rate*. What fun![2]

Now, on to our quiz's final question:

---

[1] Maybe not.
[2] Maybe not.

4. If the Indians had invested their $24 at 7.2% interest, so their money would double every 10 years (as the Rule of 72 shows you), how much money would they have by 2004?

By 2004, the Indians would have $5.7 trillion — on a $24 investment! The power of compounding is astounding! The key is interest earning interest on top of interest.

Yet many people spend the interest they earn. Do you? All too often, people deposit into their checking accounts the interest and dividends they get from CDs, stocks, and bonds and away the money goes, never to be seen again. If the Indians had done that — if they had deposited their $24 into a bank and spent the $1.73 that they earned each year (at 7.2%) instead of letting it compound — they would have earned (and spent) $653.94 in interest over the entire 378 years and the original $24 today still would be just $24.

THE POWER OF COMPOUNDING

$24 Invested at 7.2% in 1626...

$24.00
48.00
96.00
192.00
384.00
768.00
1,536.00
3,072.00
6,144.00
12,288.00
24,576.00
49,152.00
98,304.00
196,608.00
393,216.00
786,432.00
1,572,864.00
3,145,728.00
6,291,456.00
12,582,912.00
25,165,824.00
50,331,648.00
100,663,296.00
201,326,592.00
402,653,184.00
805,306,368.00
1,610,612,736.00
3,221,225,472.00
6,442,450,944.00
12,884,901,888.00
25,769,803,776.00
51,539,607,552.00
103,079,215,104.00
206,158,430,208.00
412,316,860,416.00
824,633,720,832.00
1,649,267,441,664.00
3,298,534,883,328.00
$5,752,801,116,572.00

...grew to $5.7 Trillion, by 2004!

FIGURE 1-20

> *"Money doesn't buy happiness. The fellow with $50 million is no happier than the fellow with $40 million."*
>
> —Anonymous

How Big is a Trillion?

Most people's eyes glaze over at talk of really big numbers. Do you really appreciate the size of a trillion? Let's put it this way: If you were to count from one to a trillion, counting one number each second, it would take you more than 11 days to reach one million. To reach one billion, you'd have to count for 31.7 years, while one trillion would take you 31,688 years.

If you like to go shopping, consider this: If you were to spend $1,000 a day, here's how long it would take you to spend:

$1 million	—	3 years
$1 billion	—	3 thousand years
$1 trillion	—	3 million years

That's a lot of shopping!

The message is this: *Invest your money, leave it alone, and don't touch it!* Allowing the interest to earn interest is the difference between six hundred dollars and $5.7 trillion.

Do You Want to Work Hard or Work Smart?

If you could save twice what you're saving now, you'd be twice as well off, right?

Yes, it's true that you'd double your return if you doubled your savings, but few people can afford to increase their savings by such a large amount.

But you can succeed financially without doubling your savings. Or rather, without doubling the amount of money you save. Here's what I mean:

Say you save $150 per month at a 5% annual return. In 40 years, you'd have $228,903. If you doubled your savings to $300 per month, you'd double your return, to $457,806. But clearly, in order to double the amount you save, you'd have to work harder — and most of us work hard enough as it is.

So let's try working smarter instead. If you continue to save the same $150 per month, but now earn 10% instead of 5%, your account in 40 years will be worth $948,612 — or four times more than if you had earned 5%. Indeed working smart is twice as profitable as working hard.

"I am a great believer in luck, and I find the harder I work, the more I have of it."
—**Stephen Leacock**

And if you're really smart, you'll do both: By boosting your monthly savings to $300 and earning 10%, you'll have $1,897,224.

Chapter 4 - The Good News and the Bad News About Planning for Your Future

Recall my comments in Chapter 1 about needing 50/50 vision in order to succeed. I said that a 50-year-old earning $50,000 would need $1.7 million in order to retire comfortably. Did that number scare you?

All too often, the media use statistics like this one to intimidate consumers, and financial advisors often recite similar numbers to bully their clients into action. The most common use is in the area of college planning. Sadistic planners enjoy telling people that college will cost their infant children and grandchildren hundreds of thousands of dollars — effectively scaring the beejeebers out of their clients.[3]

Unfortunately, I have discovered that such numbers lead to a different reaction: Upon seeing such huge figures — numbers that certainly seem impossible to attain — clients respond by *doing nothing*. After all, clients typically say, "There's no way I can save that much money, so why bother doing anything?"

They have a point. Planners often discuss the future in black and white, rather than in shades of gray. They lead people to believe — or they allow people to conclude on their own — that if they fail to accumulate *every penny* they need, none of the pennies they collect will be of any help. Of course, that's nonsense, for while you might not be able to save a million dollars, having half a million ain't too shabby, either.

But even taking this failing on the part of planners into consideration, consumers still are getting it wrong — because they look only at the bad news, and not at the good news.

The bad news, in case you haven't already figured it out for yourself, is that *you will be unable to save all the money you need by the time you need it*. To see my point, just look at the numbers behind my 50/50: That 50-year-old earning $50,000 has 15 years until he retires. Even if he saves 100% of his gross income — with nothing siphoned off for taxes or current needs — he'll amass only $750,000, or roughly a third of his goal. Thus, it seems that he won't be able to retire comfortably, for it is clearly impossible for him to save enough money.

---

[3] Of course, I would never stoop to such a tactic in this book.

"If only God would give me some clear sign! Like making a deposit in my name in a Swiss bank account."

—Woody Allen

That's the bad news — and it's so bad, in fact, that many people never even try to plan. But that's only the bad news. While it is true that you will be unable to save enough money to meet all your financial goals, the good news is that you don't have to.

You need to go beyond my 50/50 story to our Indian story in Chapter 3: By making a one-time deposit of $24, the Indians were able to earn interest totaling $653.94 over a period of 378 years. But that $653.94, in turn, produced another $5.7 trillion in interest. Thus, you needn't worry about saving huge amounts of money. All you need to do is start the process: Invest the first dollar, and that dollar will do the rest. All it needs is an effective rate of return, and time.

So, when planning for your future, getting started now and saving whatever you can is half your answer. The other half is to boost the rate your savings earns — and you can learn how in Part VI.

"'A penny saved is a penny earned'? What are you, some kind of nut?"

© 2004; Reprinted courtesy of Bunny Hoest and Parade Magazine.

ric's money quiz

Here's a chance to see how well you learned the information contained in Part I – Introduction to Financial Planning. Don't worry if you get stumped — just re-read this part until it sinks in. Remember, your financial future depends on it.

The answers are at the end of the quiz. No peeking!

---

1. You need a financial plan to protect against which of the following risks?

   I.   illness
   II. injury
   III. death
   IV. lawsuits

   O a. I and II
   O b. I, II, and III
   O c. III
   O d. I, II, III, and IV

2. What percentage of Americans 65 or older have an annual income below $15,000?

   O a. 11%
   O b. 39%
   O c. 51%
   O d. 81%

3. What did Einstein supposedly call "The Greatest Discovery of the 20th Century"?

   O a. the atomic bomb
   O b. compound interest
   O c. the theory of relativity
   O d. modern portfolio theory

4. According to government statistics, middle income American households earning more than $56,000 can expect to spend how much money raising a child from age 0-17?

   O a. $93,624
   O b. $141,576
   O c. $231,470
   O d. $334,629

5. The cost of a four-year education at Harvard University is:

   O a. $93,981
   O b. $119,463
   O c. $157,267
   O d. $191,542

6. Assuming a 10% annual return, a 30-year-old would have to save how much each month to raise $100,000 by age 65?

   O a. $26
   O b. $95
   O c. $143
   O d. $217

7. Financial experts generally agree that the most common reason people fail financially is:

   O a. not making enough money
   O b. having to pay too much in taxes
   O c. procrastination
   O d. an inflationary economy

8. When President Nixon declared a 90-day Freeze on Wages and Prices in 1971, he was concerned that rampant inflation would destroy the economy. What was the inflation rate when Nixon enacted the freeze?

   O a. 4%
   O b. 8%
   O c. 13%
   O d. 18%

9. Imagine that, beginning on January 1st, the government withheld 100% of your income for taxes, until your total taxes for the year were paid. On what day would you finish paying your taxes for the year?

   O a. February 12
   O b. April 19
   O c. May 5
   O d. September 9

10. The federal income tax has existed since:

   O a. 1776
   O b. 1812
   O c. 1863
   O d. 1913

Answers: 1-d (pg.3)   3-b (pg.33)   5-c (pg.10)   7-b (pg.17)   9-c (pg.25)
          2-b (pg.11)   4-c (pg.9)   6-a (pg.18)   8-a (pg.24)   10-d (pg.26)

Part II
Understanding the Capital Markets

There's a quiz at the end of this part!

To see how much you already know, skip to the
end of this part and take the quiz now. Then, read
the part and take the quiz again. You'll discover
how much you've learned!

Part II — Understanding the Capital Markets

Overview - Of All the isms, Ours Is Capitalism

A society can take many forms. There's socialism, communism, fascism, and lots of other "isms", some of which I don't pretend to understand. In America, we operate under capitalism and, whether you like it or not, whether you agree with it or not, you must take advantage of its rules if you are to succeed in our society.

Under capitalism, government and business need capital (money) to achieve their goals. Obtaining capital is their first task, for it allows them to further their objectives — whether social, political, or financial.

Businesses and governments raise capital by printing and selling certificates, which they claim have value and are worth buying. Like innocent children, we believe them. This faith is vital, for without it, our economic system would collapse. (Now you know what they're measuring in the Consumer Confidence Survey: faith in our economy.)

All certificates, whether produced by business or government, are said to contain value because they (allegedly) will do one of two things:

- generate income   or   • grow in value.

That's it. The entire world of capitalism, our financial markets, and Wall Street can be reduced to these two premises. It's as simple as that.

To see how this concept works in the real world, let's go to the marketplace. It begins with the manufacturing process. Let's say a company manufactures a product. It then sells that product to a distributor, who distributes (sells) it to a retailer, who resells it to you, the consumer. Eventually, you do one of four things with that product:

- you consume it   • you donate it
- you throw it away   • you have a yard sale.

One of those four things happens to every product you buy.

Chapter 5 - The Manufacturing Process

You can see this process in almost any industry. In real estate, for example, a developer buys land, obtains zoning, builds roads and sewers, then sells parcels to builders.

The builders erect homes and then hire real estate agents to sell the homes to consumers (this is called the new home market). And the consumer later resells the house through the existing home market.

General Motors does the same thing: GM manufactures a car and sells it to a Buick dealer, which is a distributor; the dealer hires a salesperson to sell the car to a consumer, who later sells it to someone else through the used car market.

Corporate America does this, too, when it needs to raise cash. Say a big company needs $100 million to build a new factory. To raise the money (i.e., capital), the company manufactures (prints) certificates and proclaims they are worth $100 million. These certificates might be bond certificates, or they might be stock certificates (more on that later).

Next, the company sells the certificates to a securities broker/dealer.

By agreeing to buy the certificates from the company, the b/d now must sell them. To do so, it hires stockbrokers to peddle the certificates to investors (consumers). This process, called an Initial Public Offering, is handled in what's known as the *primary* (or first) *market*, as this is the first time these certificates are being offered to consumers.

The brokers continue to sell the certificates until they are sold out. If you buy one and later want to sell it, or if you did not buy one at first but later want to, you would do so in the secondary market, called a stock exchange. It's a place where people trade (or exchange) certificates with each other.

The New York Stock Exchange is the world's largest stock market. It's just like a grocery market, but instead of buying food, you buy certificates, and you can sell them as well. There are several secondary markets (exchanges) in the U.S.: the American Exchange, the Philadelphia Exchange, the Denver Exchange, and more. Most countries also have exchanges, although usually only one. (It's a testament to the U.S.'s size and power that it has so many exchanges. Other big ones are found in London, Frankfurt and Tokyo.) There even is a tertiary (or third) marketplace, where certificates trade electronically. There are other markets for trading commodities, such as oil, pork bellies, soybeans, and orange juice. The Mercantile Exchange and the Chicago Board Options Exchange are the biggest of these.

People often say stockbrokers and financial advisors are in the service business, but that's wrong. Wall Streeters sell products, each with its own unique features, benefits, costs, and risks — just like televisions and other products.

Stockbrokers sell securities while insurance agents sell policies. Traditionally, both are salespeople who work on commission. If you go to a Ford dealer, guess what kind of car he's going to sell you? It's the same with brokerage firms: Brokers sell whatever they have in inventory. Let's face it: If a car dealer has 27 station wagons on the lot, they're going to be pushing station wagons that day. Likewise, stockbro-

THE MANUFACTURING PROCESS

Manufacturer	Developer	General Motors	Corporation
Distributor	Builder	Buick	Broker/Dealer
Retailer	Realtor	Car Salesman	Stockbroker
Consumer	Home Buyer	Car Buyer	Investor
• Donation • Yard Sale • Trash	Realtor for Existing Home Sales	Used Car Market	Stock Exchange

FIGURE 2-1

51

kers have quotas and are under pressure from management to sell certain types and amounts of products each day, each week, and each month.

The Two Types of Certificates

There are two kinds of certificates: bonds, also known as income or debt, and stocks, also known as growth or equity.

If Acme Widgets Inc. issues a bond certificate, it must pay you interest and eventually return your money to you, but it does not give you control of, or ownership of, the company.

If Acme issues a stock certificate, it does not have to pay interest (called dividends in this case) or ever give your money back to you, but you become an owner, and thus you and the others who buy the stock now have control over the company.

If you were Acme and needed to raise money, which type of certificate would you issue?

TWO MAJOR TYPES OF CERTIFICATES

Bonds also known as Income or Debt	**vs.**	**Stocks** also known as Growth or Equity
Yes	**Must pay interest or dividends?**	No
Yes	**Must capital be repaid?**	No
No	**Must give up control?**	Yes

FIGURE 2-2

Like so many aspects in the world of money, the answer is: *It depends*. In this case, it depends on what Acme is trying to accomplish. That's why some companies issue stock while others issue bonds — and why lots of companies do both. Let's take a closer look at these two types of certificates.

If you are a bond holder, you are a *lender*. You are lending money to Acme. You do not care whether Acme makes or loses money. As long as Acme stays in business, you will receive a specific rate of interest and you will get your money back at a predefined date (called the *maturity date*). If Acme goes broke, you rank very high on the list of creditors in bankruptcy court. In fact, next to the IRS and Acme employees, bondholders typically are the highest-ranking creditors.

> *"The trouble with experience is that by the time you have it you are too old to take advantage of it."*
> —Jimmy Connors

By contrast, a stockholder is an *owner* of the company. You have no idea how much money you're going to earn and there is no specific date in which your money will be returned. If Acme does not make any money, neither do you, and if Acme goes broke, so do you. If Acme goes bankrupt, you rank last in bankruptcy court.

All investments are either equity (meaning ownership, like stocks) or debt (meaning loanership, like bonds), although sometimes they don't look like it. Wall Street pays lots of money to lots of people for creative packaging of these products. Today, you can find dozens of different types of investments, as Figure 2-3 shows. But in the final analysis, each fundamentally remains either debt or equity — just as a station wagon is still a car.

> **All the details about a particular bond are included on the bond's certificate (which is just a printed piece of paper). It states:**
>
> - **the value of the bond (known as the face value since it is printed directly on the certificate);**
> - **the interest rate;**
> - **how often the interest is paid;**
> - **who issued the bond; and**
> - **the maturity date.**

Remember that when choosing between stocks and bonds, "the greater the risk, the greater the reward." It is *impossible* to earn more money without taking a higher degree of risk, so if someone is offering you an investment that promises a better return than normal, you can be sure there also is a higher degree of risk than normal. As we learn more about investments in this book, we'll look more closely at these risks.

Is a CD: (a) a stock, (b) a bond, or (c) neither?

Think about it: You have a stated rate of interest; you have a stated maturity date; and your earnings are not dependent on the profits of the bank. CDs, therefore, are bonds.

FINANCING INSTRUMENTS

Bonds

Bankers Acceptance	Exchangeable Debt
Bridge Loan	Event-Risk Protected Debt
Bunny Bond	Flip-Flop Note
Certificate of Deposit	Increasing Rate Debt
Commercial Paper	Indexed Debt
Covered Option Security	Junk Bond
Convertible Debt	Floating-Rate Note
Convertible With Premium Put	Medium-Term Note
Debt With Deferred Rate Setting	Nondollar Debt
Debt With Equity Warrants	Option-Related Debt
Debt With a Forward Commitment	Pay-in-Kind Debenture
Dutch Auction Note	Poison Put
Dual-Currency Bond	Variable-Coupon Renewable Note
Eurocommercial Paper	Zero-Coupon Bond
European Currency Unit Bond	

Stocks

Adjustable-Rate Preferred
Convertible to Preferred
Increasing Rate Preferred
Money Market Preferred
Pay-in-Kind Preferred
Poison Preferred
Remarketed Preferred

Derivatives

Debt-for-Equity Swap
Securities With a Put Option
Options
Futures
Interest Rate Swaps
Currency Forward
Options on Futures

FIGURE 2-3

Chapter 6 - Building Cash Reserves

15,000 Reasons Why You Need Reserves

What if your car breaks down or the roof leaks? You might need cash fast. Therefore, you need cash reserves to provide you with ready cash in the event of an unforeseen crisis. The reason you need reserves, quite simply, is because every single day in America, tens of thousands of washing machines break down.

People lose jobs, kids need braces, daughters get married, cars need repairs, businesses go broke. Like the saying, "Life is what happens while you're making other plans," something expensive is sure to happen when you least expect it. For all of life's unexpected events — both good and bad — you need cash reserves to get you through them.

Two Factors Determine How Much You Should Keep in Reserves

The amount you should keep in reserves depends on two factors: your monthly expenses and the stability of your income.

First, focus on how much you spend each month. If you don't know the amount, refer to Chapter 51. Your reserves should be at least six months' worth of spending, and preferably 12. However, the actual multiple depends on the stability of your income: The more stable your income, the lower your multiple need be.

For example, if you and your spouse each have highly secure jobs, or if your income is based on government pension checks, a smaller cash cushion might be acceptable. But considering today's world — not to mention those with uncertain incomes — it's much more prudent to maintain in cash reserves a full 12 months' worth of spending. The point is that you should maintain in cash reserves enough to get you through rough times. But it's equally important that you maintain only enough, because the interest rate your reserves will earn is terribly low — lower, in fact, than what you'll earn on virtually any other investment.

And leave your reserves alone.

If you determine, say, that $50,000 is the right amount of reserves for you, do what it takes to amass that 50 grand and never touch it for anything but a crisis — just as you never touch your umbrella unless it starts raining.

If you know you're going to incur a large expense within the next two years, such as home improvements, the purchase of a car, wedding or college costs, or other big-ticket expense, stash those amounts away in addition to your reserves. The same is true for occasional expenses, such as Christmas shopping. If you know you're going to spend $1,000 over the holidays, boost your reserves by that amount during the year.

The goal is to maintain your reserves at their fully-funded level at all times. If a crisis forces you to spend some or all of your reserves, your first task is to build your reserves back up again.

Once you determine how much you need for reserves, you must keep your reserves safe (meaning you cannot incur investment losses) and *liquid* (meaning you can get the money at any time without penalty).

Six Places to Store Your Reserves

Six places qualify:

- your mattress
- savings accounts
- checking accounts
- money market funds
- U.S. Treasury Bills, and
- short-term bank CDs and commercial paper

Nothing else qualifies, including everything listed next. Although the following list consists of investments that are *cash equivalents* (meaning they are the same as cash), and although many people often use these investments to store their reserves, they are nonetheless unsuitable.

U.S. Treasury Notes. Unlike *T-Bills*, which mature in as little as 30 days, *Notes* mature in two to ten years. That's too long to have to wait to get your money back so you can fix your car.

U.S. Treasury Bonds. These mature in more than ten years. If the 2-year note is too long, 30-year bonds are waaaay too long. (The government is not currently issuing new 30-year bonds, but existing ones can be bought in the marketplace.)

U.S. EE Savings Bonds. These don't qualify as reserves until one year after you buy them, because you cannot cash them in for that long. That's too long to wait if you need cash in a hurry.

Bank CDs and Commercial Paper. Unless, of course, they mature within one year. Commercial paper is a CD-like investment that is offered by large corporations instead of banks.

Life Insurance Cash Value. Yes, this is a cash equivalent. (Why do you think they call it "*cash* value"?) But no, it is not suitable for use as reserves, because of potentially large surrender penalties, tax risks, and other restrictions.

Fixed Annuities. The insurance industry's version of bank CDs, typically offering a slightly higher rate. These investments offer a tax advantage discussed in Chapter 28. Annuities are not acceptable as reserves because of tax penalties and surrender charges.

SHOE   JEFF MacNELLY

TYPES OF CASH EQUIVALENTS

Type of Asset	Offered By	Source of Protection	Taxable?	Suitable as Cash Reserves?
Checking Account	Banks, S&Ls, Credit Unions	Federal Deposit Insurance	Federal and State	Yes
Savings Account	Banks, S&Ls, Credit Unions	Federal Deposit Insurance	Federal and State	Yes
Certificate of Deposit	Banks, S&Ls, Credit Unions	Federal Deposit Insurance	Federal and State	If maturity is less than 1 year
Money Market Fund	Investment Companies	Based on underlying security	Federal and State, unless Tax-exempt	Yes
Treasury Bill, Note, Bond	United States Government	Federal Guarantee	Federal Only	Bills Only
U.S. Savings Bond	United States Government	Federal Guarantee	Federal Only	see footnote*
Life Insurance Cash Value	Insurance Companies	Guaranteed by Insurance Company	Only if withdrawn via policy surrender	No
Fixed Annuity	Insurance Companies	Guaranteed by Insurance Company	Only upon withdrawal 10% penalty if under age 59½	No
Commercial Paper	Corporations	Guaranteed by Issuer	Federal and State	If maturity is less than 1 year

FIGURE 2-4

* Because EE bonds cannot be cashed in for one year after purchase, EE bonds you currently own (and which are more than one year old) are suitable as cash reserves. New ones you buy would not be suitable for one year.

The interest rates offered by all these choices are both very similar and very low. Furthermore, the rates change constantly, rising and falling with inflation. This becomes quite apparent in Figure 2-5, which compares the 30-day T-Bill with inflation rates. Notice that as inflation has risen or fallen, so have interest rates.

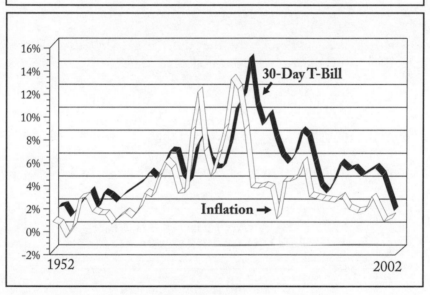

FIGURE 2-5

Although I've stated that you should place into cash equivalents only the amount needed for reserves, many Americans place 100% of their money into accounts like these. Why?

"I can't afford to gamble with my money," is the common answer. "I need to know my money is safe."

Sound familiar? The irony here is that CDs are among the most volatile of all investments — even considering the stock market's decline of the early 2000s. But consumers don't realize how volatile CDs are because they don't look at CDs the correct way.

If you had invested $10,000 in a 1-year CD in 1981, your rate would have been 15.5%, meaning you would have earned $1,550 in interest that year. And who was the most likely buyer of that CD? Conservative retirees who needed income and who wanted safety for their money.

But that rate only lasted one year. By 1986, the rate was only 7.02%. Thus, the income on that CD dropped by more than half, to just $702. By 2002, the CD was earning only $155. Not only did retirees watch their income plummet, the cost of living jumped during that time — meaning that retirees needed $3,041 in 2002 to buy what $1,550 bought in 1981. Yet their income from CDs in 2002 was just $155!

Many retirees are going broke and they don't know why. After all, they had invested safely; they hadn't done anything wrong... had they?

This horror story is replayed over and over for people who have all their money in CDs. This is a very volatile investment, one whose income stream is both unpredictable and, ironically, far more uncertain than the "risky" stock market.

Do you want your money to be safe? Well, you're going broke... safely!

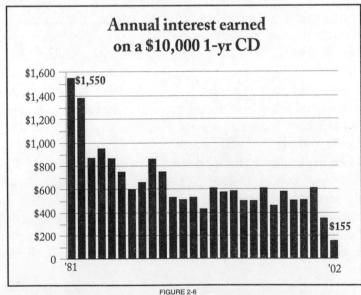

FIGURE 2-6

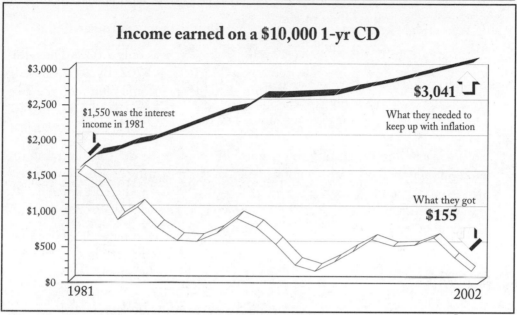

RETIREES AND THEIR CDs

Income earned on a $10,000 1-yr CD

$1,550 was the interest income in 1981

$3,041

What they needed to keep up with inflation

What they got
$155

1981   2002

FIGURE 2-7

The True Job of Banks

This is not intended to be an indictment against banks. You don't make any money in bank accounts (in real economic terms) simply because you're not supposed to. The bank is not tricking you; rather, making money for you is simply not the bank's job!

Actually, you should use a bank for only three reasons: to store your reserves, to get a loan, and to execute financial transactions. Think about it: What do you do with your paycheck? You put it in your checking account so you can write checks to pay your bills. The bank simply processes the transaction for you.

Thus, banks serve as short-term depositories of cash, as you move money from one place to another. For example, have you ever sold a house to buy another? Typically, you sell one house a few weeks or months before you settle on the other. In the meantime, what do you do with the cash you got from selling the first house?

You've got to put it somewhere; you certainly don't want to gamble with it, since you need it as a down payment on the new house. So what do you do? You put it in the bank, where you receive enough interest to keep pace with inflation.

The bank thus keeps your money current with inflation, and banks do this extremely well while maintaining a very high degree of safety.

Similarly, those who have brokerage accounts know that when they sell a stock, their broker automatically "sweeps" the proceeds of the sale into a money market fund, so the cash can earn interest until they buy other investments.

So if you've ever noticed that you seem to be working harder than ever and making more money than ever, yet you don't feel like you're getting ahead, now you know why: You've been keeping your money in banks, S&Ls, and credit unions, and your money — in real terms — hasn't been growing. Like pedestrians on a treadmill, money in a bank works hard but doesn't get anywhere.

The Myth of FDIC

It's ironic that those who choose banks are primarily concerned with safety, because banks are not the ultimate safe haven. In fact, for the savviest safety-conscious investors, banks are far too risky. Banks, after all, are nothing more than private businesses, and like any private business, a bank can go broke at any time, taking customers' money with it.

But what about FDIC? Doesn't that guarantee your money is safe?

Not at all! FDIC is widely misunderstood, so here's the truth about it:

The Great Depression saw more than 50% of the nation's banks go out of business, leaving their depositors penniless. This destroyed consumer confidence in banks. To restore that confidence, the federal government in 1933 created the Federal Deposit Insurance Corporation. Although chartered by Congress, FDIC is a private insurance company and receives no federal funding.

Rather, its money comes from banks, which pay insurance premiums to FDIC, much as you pay premiums to your auto insurer. Thus, when a bank fails, it files a claim with FDIC requesting that it pay off the bank's depositors, just as you would

If you think government-sponsored deposit insurance makes your money safe, talk to a depositor at Old Court Savings & Loan. When this Maryland S&L failed, thousands of depositors thought their money was safe. Unfortunately, Old Court, like many thrifts across the country, was a member of the state deposit fund, not the federal program. When several S&Ls went broke in the early '80s, the state fund ran out of money.

In 1986, the state treasurer offered a plan to return all the money to Old Court's depositors. The plan would have required Maryland to issue new bonds. When Wall Street threatened to lower Maryland's AAA bond rating — which would have increased the state's borrowing costs — the governor rejected the plan, deciding that the state's bond rating was more important than the money its citizens had lost.

ask your auto insurer to pay your repair bill when you have an accident. Thus, FDIC was designed to reassure consumers that their money would be safe even if their bank was to fail. Similar systems were created for S&Ls (The Federal Savings and Loan Insurance Corporation), credit unions (The National Credit Union Share Insurance Fund) and pension funds (The Pension Benefit Guaranty Corporation).

These agencies, all of which have demonstrated their ability to handle occasional failures, never were designed to cope with a system-wide collapse. And indeed, the 1980s proved too much for some of them. When the S&L crisis loomed in 1986, FSLIC found itself technically bankrupt, with only 12 cents on deposit for each $100 it was insuring. FDIC was little better, with only 23 cents on hand for each hundred dollars it was protecting. Even today, FDIC, although improved, still has only $1.25 per $100.

By the late 1980s, Congress was forced to create the Resolution Trust Corporation to manage what was left of FDIC and the defunct FSLIC. Today, cleanup of the mess left by failed S&Ls and banks continues, and the FDIC, although stronger now that the wave of failures has ebbed, still has little in reserves to handle further failures.

Insurance, after all, is only as good as the company providing it, and this is too uncertain for the most risk-averse of investors. That's why, for these investors, there is only one choice for their money: U.S. Government Securities. We'll learn more about them in the next chapter.

Chapter 7 - The Most Fundamental of All Investment Risks - And How to Avoid It

Many people place their life savings in banks because they think doing so keeps their money safe. But safe from what?

As we saw in Chapter 2, money that you keep in banks is not safe from inflation or taxes. So what is it that people are thinking of when they talk about bank accounts being "safe"?

The risk that banks help you avoid — even though you may not realize it — is *default risk*. Because of FDIC protection, people feel that they do not need to fear the bank going broke, taking their money with it. Like Will Rogers once said, "I am more interested in the return of my principal than the return on my principal!"

Although banks are perceived to be free of default risk, there's another — even better — way to avoid default risk: by investing in securities issued by the Federal Government of the United States, issuer of the world's safest investments.

Why are these investments so safe? Because the U.S. Government guarantees (not merely insures) them. This guarantee, printed on each bond the government issues, is a "full faith and credit obligation" of the Government of the United States of America "for the timely payment of principal and interest."

This guarantee is the investment standard of the world, because it is the only investment that absolutely frees you from default risk. This is deemed so because the United States has never defaulted on an interest or principal payment in the entire history of our nation. No other country can make this claim.

Therefore, when it comes to default risk, all investments are implicitly compared to U.S. Government Securities. Measuring default risk on a scale from low to high, U.S. Government Securities score a "none" — and it is the only asset class so ranked. Bank accounts, with their federal insurance protection, are a distant second.

> **Did you ever wonder why U.S. Government Securities are so safe? It's because the federal government has an unlimited source of capital:**
> **If it ever runs out of money, the government just prints more to pay its bills.**
>
> **I wish I could do that.**

The federal government issues many types of bonds, and we've already covered some of them in our discussion of cash reserves. In total, the federal government has issued securities worth $3.8 trillion, making the U.S. Government the largest issuer of bonds in the market (and the world's biggest debtor). In fact, nearly $360 billion worth of U.S. Government Securities trade on Wall Street *every day*, according to Wall Street Online.

Because of Uncle Sam's unconditional guarantee, it is impossible for U.S. Government Securities to default — unless there's a collapse of the entire federal system! And if you think that's going to happen, Chapter 50 will show you how to protect yourself.

THE WIZARD OF ID   PARKER & HART

By permission of Johnny Hart and Creators Syndicate, Inc.

ric's money quiz

Here's a chance to see how well you learned the information contained in
Part II – Understanding the Capital Markets. Don't worry if you get stumped —
just re-read this part until it sinks in. Remember, your financial
future depends on it.

The answers are at the end of the quiz. No peeking!

1. **If you buy a bond issued by Company ABC, which of the following is true?**

    - O a. you are a part owner of ABC
    - O b. if ABC loses money in any one year, they are not allowed to pay you interest for that year
    - O c. the interest rate could change
    - O d. none of the above

2. **If you buy stock in Company ABC, which of the following is true?**

    - O a. you are a part owner of ABC
    - O b. if ABC loses money in any one year, they are not allowed to pay you interest for that year
    - O c. the interest rate could change
    - O d. none of the above

3. **If you own stock in a company that goes bankrupt:**

    - O a. your original investment will be returned to you
    - O b. you must give back all dividends that had been sent to you
    - O c. your investment is worthless
    - O d. you will be repaid for the loss over time

4. **A bank CD is:**

    - O a. a stock
    - O b. a bond
    - O c. neither
    - O d. both

5. **Which of the following is *not* a criterion for cash reserves?**

    - O a. safety
    - O b. interest rate
    - O c. stability of value
    - O d. accessibility

6. **Which of the following is suitable for cash reserves?**

   O a. life insurance
   O b. fixed annuity
   O c. U.S. Treasury bonds
   O d. money market account

7. **One-year CDs:**

   O a. are very safe investments that typically earn high returns
   O b. are highly volatile and typically earn poor returns
   O c. will generally earn higher returns than investing in the stock market
   O d. if rolled over will produce a predictable income stream over many years

8. **FDIC:**

   O a. is funded by the U.S. Government
   O b. guarantees that your money is safe
   O c. is a private insurance company for banks
   O d. will completely pay off all deposi tors if a bank goes broke

9. **U.S. Savings Bonds are considered to be a member of which asset class?**

   O a. cash
   O b. bonds
   O c. government securities
   O d. stocks

10. **Which of the following investments are guaranteed?**

    O a. a bank savings account under $100,000
    O b. a U.S. T-bill
    O c. neither
    O d. both

Answers: 1-d (pg.53)   3-c (pg.53)   5-b (pg.56)   7-b (pg.60)   9-a (pg.57)
           2-a (pg.53)   4-b (pg.54)   6-d (pg.58)   8-c (pg.62)   10-b (pg.58)

Part III
Fixed Income
Investments

There's a quiz at the end of this part!

To see how much you already know, skip to the
end of this part and take the quiz now. Then, read
the part and take the quiz again. You'll discover
how much you've learned!

Part III — Fixed Income Investments

Overview - Income Before Growth

As explained in Chapter 5, all investments are designed to produce income or grow in value (sometimes both). Of the two, income is much more reliable than growth. After all, a company's management cannot make its stock price rise, but it can pay interest to its bondholders and declare stock dividends for shareholders. Therefore, income-producing investments are considered safer (in this case, safety is defined as *reliability*) than growth-oriented investments because investors can expect to receive their income more reliably than they can expect an investment to grow in value. Therefore, we'll look first at income-producing investments.

Of course, we're talking about bonds, and there are many issuers of bonds. We'll start with the safest issuer, which is the United States Government.

Chapter 8 - U.S. Government Securities

All federal securities can be placed into two categories:

Direct obligations of the United States:

- **Treasury bills, notes, and bonds.** *Treasuries* provide money for the general use of the government.

- **Government National Mortgage Association Pass-Through Certificates.** *Ginnie Maes* provide mortgages for home buyers.

Bonds backed by an agency of the United States, including:

- **Federal National Mortgage Association.** *Fannie Mae* provides money for mortgages.

- **Student Loan Marketing Association.** *Sallie Mae* provides money for student loans.

- **Federal Home Loan Corporation.** *Freddie Mac* also provides money for mortgages.

Understand Ginnie Maes Before You Invest

The Rules of Money Have Changed, and nowhere is this more true than with Ginnie Maes. Millions of investors across America buy these U.S.-backed certificates, and it's a safe bet that most have no idea how Ginnie Maes work. As a result, many are in for a shock when they look to get their money back, only to find out their investment is gone, even though it was government guaranteed.

Ginnie Maes are issued by the Government National Mortgage Association, a federal agency created by Congress in the 1960s in response to concerns that banks didn't have enough cash to provide loans to millions of would-be home buyers.

Here's how GNMA works: Wally borrows $100,000 from his bank to buy a house, at 6% interest for 30 years. His bank sells the mortgage to GNMA, freeing up its capital to provide more loans. GNMA assembles mortgages from banks throughout the nation into groups, or "pools," of $4,000,000. Each pool contains identical mortgages — the same face amount, interest rate, and maturity date. GNMA then divides each pool into $25,000 units and sells them to investors, taking half of one percent in fees.

So Wally's mortgage is now part of an investment paying 6% for 30 years. This is why Ginnie Maes are called "mortgage pass-through certificates."

Wally makes his monthly payment to the bank, which sends it to GNMA, which gives it to the investors who bought the pool in which Wally's mortgage is a part. GNMA payments to investors are issued monthly just like Social Security checks.

To protect investors against the possibility that Wally might default on his loan, GNMA promises to meet the obligation if Wally does not. Ginnie Maes, therefore, are direct "full faith and credit" obligations of the United States Government. The U.S. Treasury must satisfy the debt if Wally doesn't.

"There is nothing wrong with earning 5% or 6% on bonds; it just shouldn't take a year to do it."
—**Anonymous**

As every homeowner knows, Wally's monthly payment is part interest and part principal. Therefore, so is the monthly check that investors receive from GNMA. No other investment does this — not CDs, bonds, stocks, or mutual funds — and this unique feature is key to the confusion. While the interest portion will be relatively constant, the principal portion can fluctuate — sometimes dramatically. For instance, a Ginnie Mae investor who normally receives $150 a month ($125 in interest and $25 in principal) could suddenly get a check for, say, $3,400 — several thousand dollars more than usual.

This can occur whenever the mortgagees within the pool (e.g. Wally) increase their payments, since excesses are always applied to principal. This could happen if Wally sells his home or refinances, thus paying off his mortgage; if Wally dies, and his insurance company pays off the mortgage; or if he defaults, and GNMA pays off as required.

Because of the prepayments, the typical life of a Ginnie Mae is 12-15 years. Nowhere else can you obtain a 30-year bond that will return your money, plus interest, in a shorter period of time on a guaranteed basis. That's the good news. The bad news is that many investors don't realize their monthly check is a partial return of their own principal, so, believing it's all interest, they spend it. Ten years later they learn that because all the mortgages in their pool have been paid off, they will not get any more interest checks and, because their principal was being returned to them each month along with the interest, they are not about to receive a check for their principal, either. It can be quite a shock to discover that your principal is gone because you've been spending it unwittingly each month.

But for investors who understand how Ginnie Maes work, getting principal back monthly can be a big advantage. By reinvesting this monthly return of capital — not spending it — the compounding effect can boost the total return above that provided by the Ginnie Mae itself. Some advisors, in fact, can arrange for their clients to receive only the interest each month, keeping the principal portion in an interest-bearing account on behalf of the investor. Not all financial planners or brokers perform this service; you'll have to ask.

But if you're buying Ginnie Maes, that's the smart way to treat them.

Chapter 9 - Municipal Bonds

If bonds issued by the United States Government are the safest investment, then it follows that bonds issued by state governments are the second-safest. Known as *municipal bonds* (muni's) because they are issued by state and local municipalities, they have been a primary source of capital for state and local governments since colonial days.

There are two types: *General Obligation* and *Revenue*.

G.O. bonds are guaranteed by the government issuing the bond; revenue bonds are not guaranteed.

Typically, G.O. bonds raise money for schools, highways, and other public works which do not generate revenue, while revenue bonds normally are used for projects which do, such as toll roads, airports and hospitals. Revenue bonds rely on the revenue from the project to repay the bond's interest and principal. But if the project fails to raise enough revenue, you will not be paid. Thus, revenue bonds are subject to default risk, while G.O. bonds are not. If you're primarily concerned with safety, you should choose a G.O. bond over a revenue bond.

G.O. bonds never default? Well, that's not entirely true: Some G.O.s actually have gone broke. Can you name the states whose G.O. bonds have defaulted?

My seminar participants always guess Massachusetts, California, New York, and New Jersey. Yet none of these has ever defaulted.

If you haven't yet figured out which have, here's a hint: They lost the war. Yes, the states of the Confederacy defaulted on their G.O. bonds when they lost the Civil War. Remember: The only way a government-guaranteed bond can go broke is for that government to fail.

War aside, municipalities can't go broke because they have a never-ending revenue source. It's called (surprise!) taxes.

Municipal bonds are popular because the interest is free of federal income taxes. Of the four enemies of money, muni's beat one of them: You don't have to pay taxes to the federal government and, in 26 states, if you buy a bond from the state in which you live, you don't have to pay state income taxes, either.

Why is the interest earned on a municipal bond free from federal income tax? Why is Uncle Sam willing to give up the tax revenue?

The answer is provided by the courts. In the 1800s, Maryland sued the federal government, arguing that the feds were taxing the states on revenue the states were earning — in essence, an income tax on the states. The Supreme Court ruled (with one of my favorite quotes) that "the ability to tax is the ability to destroy." (Really? Gosh!)

The high court recognized that if the federal government taxed the states on their income, the states would retaliate by assessing property taxes against the fed for post offices and military bases. In other words, the two governments simply would tax each other endlessly.

To preserve our federal system, the Supreme Court ordered the two to stop. The federal government, said the court, may not tax state obligations and the states may not tax federal obligations. Since municipal bond interest is an obligation of the state (hence the name "General Obligation"), Uncle Sam cannot tax that revenue. Thus, there is a legitimate reason why muni interest is tax-free.

Now that you understand why muni interest is free from federal taxes, why do many states exempt muni interest from their own income taxes?

> *"The avoidance of taxes is the only intellectual pursuit that carries any reward."*
> —John Maynard Keynes

The answer is this: With 50 states plus a few U.S. territories all issuing bonds, there's a lot of competition. Thus, for Virginia to convince its residents to buy a Virginia bond instead of one from neighboring Maryland, Virginia residents demand an incentive. And what better incentive could there be than for Virginia to tell its residents that interest they earn from Virginia bonds will be free of Virginia income taxes, while interest from all other states will not be exempt? It's an effective sales tool used in 26 states. The others either do not have a state income tax, or most of their residents do not border other states. (Virginia residents, like most on the East Coast, are near four other states, and crossing state lines for goods and services is common. Other states, such as those in the Midwest, find that most residents never leave, so the "sales pitch" of local tax exemption is not deemed to be a necessary inducement.)

This also explains why the U.S. Government taxes you on interest you earn on its bonds. The U.S. Government, after all, doesn't have any competition, so if you want the supreme safety of Uncle Sam's Treasuries, you're going to have to pay federal taxes on the interest you earn.

One Important Tax Tip!

Focus for a moment on this last point: It provides an important tip you might have missed. Just as the courts require that muni interest is free of federal taxes, the courts also require that interest on a federal bond be free of state taxes. Therefore, if you live in a state which has an income tax, you make more money on a 3% U.S. Treasury than you do on a 3% CD, because the interest you earn from the Treasury is free of state income taxes while interest from a CD is not. Thus, the Treasury not only is safer, it's more profitable!

It drives me nuts when I hear that someone has been paying state income taxes on the interest they've earned from federal bonds — and that includes EE Savings Bonds! If you've been doing this, you need to file amended tax returns to get a refund of the excess taxes you've been paying.

In our planning practice, we often find that many people overpay their taxes needlessly because they fail to understand our tax laws and they don't obtain proper counsel.

The Call Feature, or Heads They Win — Tails You Lose

Most muni bonds are *callable*, which means that the government which issued the bond, at its option, can *redeem the bond* (i.e., give you your money back) before it matures.

Say the state government issues a bond at 7% and interest rates later drop to 3%. The government would save a lot of money if it were to cancel all those 7%'ers, return principal to the investors, and issue fresh bonds at the new current rate of 3%.

Which is exactly what has happened over the past decade. If you bought that 30-year bond in the early 1990s expecting to enjoy 7% interest for decades to come, you found yourself getting all your money back much sooner, forcing you to reinvest at the new lower rates. As a taxpayer, you'd be happy to see your government save money by refinancing its debt at lower rates, but as an investor, you'd be quite annoyed.

Of course, if interest rates had risen from 7% to 10%, the government would not have called the bonds. Thus, you would have been left with a bond that pays 7% while new investors would have been able to buy new bonds that pay 10%.

In other words, when it comes to callable bonds, heads the government wins — tails you lose.

Are Tax-Free's a Better Buy than Taxables?

Now that you understand how tax-free income works, answer this question: Which is better, a 5-year CD paying 4% or a 5-year tax-free bond paying 3%?

It's a tough question, because the CD's rate is *before* taxes, while the muni's rate is *after* taxes — an apples-to-oranges comparison. We need an apples-to-apples comparison, and that means we need to determine the muni's *taxable-equivalent yield*. Here's the formula:

$$\frac{\textbf{Muni Rate}}{\left(\textbf{100} - \textbf{\tiny Your Tax Rate}\right)}$$

When calculating the taxable-equivalent yield, be sure to include state income taxes. Figure 3-1 shows you the TEY you need to earn, depending on the current muni rate and your tax bracket.

The Triple Threat Against Muni's

It's worth noting that while the Supreme Court has upheld the tax exemption for muni bond interest many times over the past 150 years, the past 20 years have seen the federal government make small inroads against the tax-free status of municipal bonds.

Muni Tax Threat #1

The first occurred in the Tax Reform Act of 1986, when the federal government declared that certain tax-free bonds, known as Industrial Development Bonds, are not entitled to tax-free status. IDBs essentially are corporate bonds issued in the name of a state government, which states allow to induce big companies to do business in otherwise economically depressed areas. Since the proceeds of the bond offering are for the benefit of the company and not the state, the Supreme Court agreed with the federal government that tax exemption is not required. Although IDBs typically are offered to institutional investors, individual investors need to be aware of them...and steer clear.

TAXABLE EQUIVALENT YIELDS

If your Federal Tax Rate is... ▼	...and your municipal bond's tax-exempt rate is...					
	3%	4%	5%	6%	7%	8%
15%	3.53	4.71	5.88	7.06	8.24	9.41
25%	4.00	5.33	6.67	8.00	9.33	10.67
28%	4.17	5.56	6.94	8.33	9.72	11.11
33%	4.48	5.97	7.46	8.96	10.45	11.94
35%	4.62	6.15	7.69	9.23	10.77	12.31

...then this is what you must earn from a taxable investment in order to obtain the same after-tax return.

For an investor in the 33% federal tax bracket, buying a 3% muni is equivalent to buying a CD that pays 4.48%. The muni advantage gets even better when you factor in state income tax savings.

FIGURE 3-1

Muni Tax Threat #2

The second inroad came in 1991. That's when the federal government began requiring taxpayers to declare on their tax returns how much interest they receive from municipal bonds. Many are concerned that Uncle Sam wants this data for only one reason: So the feds can see exactly how much revenue they're losing from muni bonds. Until 1991, no studies had been done, so nobody was sure of the exact amount of interest paid by municipal bonds. There is concern that there will be renewed attempts to terminate muni's' tax-free status. While this situation is not something I'd lie awake at night worrying over, you should be aware of it because such a change would drastically reduce the value of muni bonds.

Muni Tax Threat #3 — The Biggest Risk of All

In June 1998, the U.S. House of Representatives passed a bill that would have eliminated the entire U.S. tax code (and the IRS along with it) by 2004. The legislation required Congress to create a new, alternative tax code as a replacement. Half a dozen proposals have since been offered: a flat tax, value-added tax, consumption tax, and more. Each of these proposals would have had the same effect on municipal bonds: They would eliminate the tax advantage that muni bonds enjoy, and if that advantage disappears, muni bonds could face losses of 20% or more.

Of course, none of that happened. Yet. But that doesn't mean that legislative threats to muni's are over. For example, the 2003 tax law changes allow some taxpayers to pay a tax of just 5% on dividends, making them much more appealing than before. This is a direct threat to muni bonds, and it's reasonable to expect other changes .

Remember that the primary benefit of owning muni bonds is based not on fundamental economic principles, but simply on tax law: Muni bond interest is free of federal and state income taxes merely because somebody says it is. And nowhere is it written that "somebody" might not change their mind. Indeed, if the tax advantages of muni bonds are legislated away, muni bonds stand to lose 20% or more of their value, almost overnight. Here's why this could happen:

Say 30-year muni bonds currently yield 5.5% and 30-year U.S. Treasuries yield 7%. The T-bond is more profitable — but only on a pre-tax basis. After paying taxes (assuming a 25% federal income tax bracket), the T-bond nets only 5.2%. That's less than the muni. So even though the muni rate is lower than the T-bond's rate, current tax law makes the muni the better buy.

This, again, is why muni bonds are so popular. But many of the tax proposals before Congress would remove the tax advantage that muni's enjoy. If that happens, muni's will lose their popularity as well.

> *"Taxes grow without rain."*
> —**Jewish proverb**

Tax Threats Aside, Might Municipal Bonds Make Sense For You?

The higher your combined federal/state income tax bracket, the more sense it makes for you to invest in muni's instead of taxable bonds. Or so the logic goes. Tax-free bonds are very popular because they have little default risk and, on an after-tax basis, they earn more than taxable bonds.

And brokers love to demonstrate that, on an after-tax basis, clients earn more in a 5.5% tax-free bond fund than in a 7% taxable bond. The higher your tax bracket, the more compelling this argument.

Thus, financial advisors routinely tell their clients to move from taxable to tax-free bonds and bond funds. This idea is so ingrained that no one challenges it.

Until now.

Even ignoring the major risk posed by recent tax law changes and proposals, I dispute the notion that municipal bonds are better for investors than taxable bonds. Consequently, it is my contention that municipal bonds and muni bond funds are among the most over-sold investments in America today.

The rationale for muni bonds goes like this: Interest paid by a 7% taxable bond is subject to tax; interest from a 5.5% muni bond is not. To fairly compare them, as we've seen, one must focus not on the taxable bond's 7% rate, but on its after-tax rate of 4.83% since the muni bond's rate of 5.5% is itself (being tax-free) an "after-tax" rate.

> *"The tax-exempt privilege is a feature always reflected in the market price of municipal bonds. The investor pays for it."*
> —**Justice Louis D. Brandeis**

Thus, it is easy to see that the muni bond's 5.5% beats the taxable bond's 4.83% (assuming a 25% federal income tax bracket and 6% state bracket). These results are illustrated in Figures 3-2 and 3-3: Figure 3-2 shows that $10,000 invested in a 7% taxable bond fund[4] for 20 years would be worth $25,687 after taxes, while Figure 3-3 shows that this same investment in a 5.5% muni bond would be worth $29,178. These results support the conventional wisdom that tells people to buy municipal bonds and muni bond funds instead of taxable bonds and taxable bond funds.

But the conventional wisdom is wrong. When you invest in taxable bonds, bond funds, and CDs, you owe taxes on the interest you earn. You report the interest on

TAXABLE BOND FUND
AFTER TAXES

year	start value	× yield 7.00%	− fed tax 25%	− state tax 6%	= net yield 4.83%
1	$10,000	$700	$175	$42	$10,483
2	10,483	734	183	44	10,989
3	10,990	769	192	46	11,520
4	11,521	806	202	48	12,077
5	12,077	845	211	51	12,660
6	12,660	886	222	53	13,271
7	13,276	929	232	56	13,912
8	13,917	974	243	58	14,584
9	14,589	1,021	255	61	15,289
10	15,294	1,071	268	64	16,027
11	16,032	1,122	280	67	16,801
12	16,807	1,176	294	71	17,613
13	17,618	1,233	308	74	18,463
14	18,469	1,293	323	78	19,355
15	19,361	1,355	339	81	20,290
16	20,296	1,421	355	85	21,270
17	21,277	1,489	372	89	22,297
18	22,305	1,561	390	94	23,374
19	23,382	1,637	409	98	24,503
20	24,512	1,715	429	103	25,687

Account Value: **$25,687**

FIGURE 3-2

STATE MUNI BOND FUND
TAX-FREE

year	start value	× yield 5.50%	− fed tax 0%	− state tax 0%	= net yield 5.5%
1	$10,000	$550	$0	$0	$10,550
2	10,550	580	0	0	11,130
3	11,130	612	0	0	11,742
4	11,742	646	0	0	12,388
5	12,388	681	0	0	13,070
6	13,070	719	0	0	13,788
7	13,788	758	0	0	14,547
8	14,547	800	0	0	15,347
9	15,347	844	0	0	16,191
10	16,191	891	0	0	17,081
11	17,081	939	0	0	18,021
12	18,021	991	0	0	19,012
13	19,012	1,046	0	0	20,058
14	20,058	1,103	0	0	21,161
15	21,161	1,164	0	0	22,325
16	22,325	1,228	0	0	23,553
17	23,553	1,295	0	0	24,848
18	24,848	1,367	0	0	26,215
19	26,215	1,442	0	0	27,656
20	27,656	1,521	0	0	29,178

Account Value: **$29,178**

FIGURE 3-3

---

[4] For simplicity's sake, this example assumes use of municipal bond mutual funds, with all interest reinvested at the same rate. A more complete discussion of mutual funds can be found in Part V.

Schedule B of your tax return, and this either simply reduces the refund you otherwise would receive, or increases the amount you owe.

If it reduces your refund, the IRS sends you a check smaller than what you otherwise would have received. But if you owe money, you simply (albeit grudgingly) write a check to the IRS for the amount due.

And that's the key: In our 250+ collective years of practice as financial planners and investment advisors, having worked with thousands of clients and with $2 billion in client assets, *we have never seen a client sell a bond or liquidate a bond fund in order to raise the cash needed to pay the taxes that Schedule B says are owed*. Instead, every client pays the tax from another source: either by offsetting the tax against other deductions on the tax return, or by using other assets, such as cash from a checking account, or both.

And by not turning to the bond fund itself, *the interest earned stays invested*, where it is allowed to compound, earning even more interest the next year. The results can be seen in Figure 3-4: By ignoring the tax implications, that 7% taxable bond fund in 20 years will be worth $38,697 — or 33% more than the muni fund!

The results are clear: In the end, you will have more money if you choose an investment that forced you to pay taxes than if you choose an investment that is more "tax efficient" — or in this case, tax-free.

TAXABLE BOND FUND
PAYING OUT OF POCKET

year	start value	X yield 7.00%	− fed tax 0%	− state tax 0%	= net yield 7%
1	$10000	$700	$0	$0	$10700
2	10700	749	0	0	11449
3	11449	801	0	0	12250
4	12250	858	0	0	13108
5	13108	918	0	0	14026
6	14026	982	0	0	15007
7	15007	1051	0	0	16058
8	16058	1124	0	0	17182
9	17182	1203	0	0	18385
10	18385	1287	0	0	19672
11	19672	1377	0	0	21049
12	21049	1473	0	0	22522
13	22522	1577	0	0	24098
14	24098	1687	0	0	25785
15	25785	1805	0	0	27590
16	27590	1931	0	0	29522
17	29522	2067	0	0	31588
18	31588	2211	0	0	33799
19	33799	2366	0	0	36165
20	36165	2532	0	0	38697

Account Value: **$38,697**

FIGURE 3-4

"The difference between death and taxes is that death doesn't get worse every time Congress meets."

—Anonymous

This phenomenon occurs because the notion of "taxable equivalent yield" ignores human nature. Muni bonds make sense if you pay the tax by liquidating your account, but in the real world, people don't do that. And all the financial planning formulas and testing models ignore the most important element affecting your personal finances: your lifestyle. Perhaps we should call this approach "real world yields."

Should you sell your muni fund and replace it with a taxable bond fund? This 4-question review will help you decide:

1) **Are you in the 15% federal income tax bracket or lower?** If you are, you are better off in Taxable's than in Tax-Free's.

2) **Do you have muni bonds or bond funds in an IRA or other tax-qualified account?** If you do, you're making a terrible mistake. (See Chapter 67 for more.)

3) **Do you reinvest the interest you earn from muni bonds?** If you do, then you should not invest in muni bonds or muni bond funds.

4) **Do you rely on your investment interest for current income?** Muni bonds are ideal for clients who need current income, so if you receive your interest or dividends in cash and if you are in a high tax bracket, owning muni bonds is probably the right strategy.

When it comes to successful money management, you must recognize that **The Rules of Money Have Changed**, and you cannot rely on the old way of doing things — no matter how ingrained those habits have become. If you bought muni bonds or muni bond funds, you need to reconsider that decision.

Insured Municipal Bonds

Some 55% of all the muni bond issues outstanding are insured. Many people feel buying insured bonds is smart investing, when in reality it's nothing more than smart marketing by Wall Street. Here's why:

When a stockbroker cold calls Mrs. Glidlick to pitch her a bond, his biggest challenge is to overcome her fear of default risk. Above all else, she wants safety. So, naturally, when he invites her to buy the muni, Mrs. Glidlick's first question is, "Is the bond *insured*?"

The fact that the bonds might be guaranteed is irrelevant to her, because she is not familiar with this concept (but you are!). So, she asks about insurance because she's been trained by the banks to seek FDIC coverage. After all, she can visit her money at the bank every day and see the gold FDIC sticker on the bullet-proof glass. To her, that's safety. So, Mrs. Glidlick wants to know if the broker's muni is insured like her bank account, and the broker, who knows that without insurance she'll refuse to buy, desperately wants to say, "Yes, it's insured!"

Enter the world of *insured municipal bonds*.

The broker can say, "Yes, it's insured!" thanks to outfits like Municipal Bond Insurance Association, which controls 26% of the insured muni market, and AMBAC, the second-largest insurer of muni bonds. In its sales literature, MBIA says if a muni defaults, it will reimburse investors, and the cost for this protection is about five dollars per thousand dollars of bond principal.

In other words, insuring a bond that pays 5% interest would cost you 10% of the total interest you are due from the investment. That's a pretty steep price to pay for insurance, especially considering that the only way the insurance can pay off is for the government that issued the bond to go broke first.

Even if MBIA was called upon to pay a claim, the payoff would not be what most investors would expect: MBIA does not promise to repay your principal. Instead, it will simply pay the interest the bond should have been paying; you'll have to wait until the bond's normal maturity date to get your money back — and that could take decades.

The whole idea of insured muni bonds is ridiculous. Not only are you cutting your interest rate from, say, 5% to 4.5%, the entire premise suggests that MBIA is stronger than the government that issued the bond! Now think about it: If Idaho went broke, what would that mean for the economy as a whole? Could any insurance company possibly be stronger and safer than a government? I don't think so, and neither should you. Avoid insured municipal bonds.

Chapter 10 - Zero Coupon Bonds

To understand zeros, let's look more closely at their name.

Coupon means "interest rate." The name derives from the 1800s, when coupons were attached to bond certificates. Each coupon represented six months' worth of interest, so twice each year the bond holder would clip a coupon from the certificate and take it to the bank, which would redeem the coupon for cash. Thus, "coupon" became synonymous with "interest rate."

Therefore, "zero coupon" means "zero interest." Why would anybody buy a bond offering zero interest? The answer is found in its price. Recall that all bond certificates feature a *face value*. Many people think the face value refers to the price of the bond when you buy it. Not true: The face value refers to the amount the issuer must pay when the bond matures (the maturity date also is displayed on the face of the certificate). Thus, a bond's *face value* is not necessarily the same as its *price*.

This is why people are willing to buy zeros, or bonds with "no interest": You buy them for a price substantially below their face value (this is known as a discount). At maturity, the issuer pays you the full face value, and the difference between what you paid and what you receive back is equal to the interest you should have earned during the life of the bond but didn't.

The Most Common Zero of All

You're more familiar with zeros than you realize, because the most common zero is a U.S. Savings Bond. EE Bonds, after all, do not pay any interest. Instead, you buy a $100 bond for $50 — half the face value — and when it matures, Uncle Sam pays you $100. The extra $50 that you get back at maturity is equal to what you should have earned in interest but didn't. That's all there is to zeros.

Despite their simplicity, many people are confused about how much interest they earn from Savings Bonds. That's because the rates vary, depending on when the bond was purchased. And the 1994 General Agreement of Tariffs and Trade, known as the GATT Treaty, made the biggest changes of all. Here's the truth about interest rates on U.S. Savings Bonds:

- Savings bonds you bought before GATT became law in May 1995 are not affected. That means you continue to earn a rate based on the rules that were in effect when you bought your bond.

- Savings bonds you buy now, but which you hold for at least five years, also are not affected by GATT.

- Only those bonds you bought since May 1995, and which you hold for less than five years, are affected by GATT. Under prior rules, bonds held less than five years received a minimum of 4% interest annually. GATT eliminated this floor and replaced it with a new market-based rate, similar to that which is in place for those who hold their bonds for more than five years.

Because there is no floor to this market-based rate, it is possible that savings bonds held for less than five years could pay no interest.

Four Reasons Why Zeros are Losers

Many financial planners (but not those at my firm) love to sell zero coupon bonds. Planners often will tell you that zeros are convenient and safe. Just buy a bond, toss it into your safety deposit box, and at maturity, it will be worth thousands — and in the meantime you don't have to fuss with certificates, interest checks, or other details. Because many zeros are government bonds, they also are safe from default risk.

But there are problems. Let's look at them.

Problem #1: The Return Is Roughly the Same as Treasuries

But on an after-tax, after-inflation basis, that return is not good enough. For a recap of this discussion, turn to Chapter 2.

Problem #2: Zeros Are Much More Volatile than Other Bonds

Prices for zeros are much more volatile than ordinary bonds because zeros don't pay current interest. Here's a horror story to illustrate: In the early '80s, an investor bought a 7-year zero coupon bond issued by Braniff Airlines. The bond's yield to

It's worth noting that although many people buy U.S. Treasury zeros, the U.S. Government does not issue them. Instead, they are created and manufactured by Wall Street broker-age firms. The brokers take ordinary Treasury Bonds and split them in two, giving the interest to one investor and the principal to another. The principal portion is the zero. You can buy such versions as LYONs (Liquid Yield Option Notes), TIGRs (Treasury Interest Grantor Receipts), STRIPS (Separated Treasury Receipts of Interest & Principal Securities), and ZEBRAs (Zero Equivalent Bond Rate Accumulators). By the way, you can also buy PIGs (Passive Income Generators), and Bunny Bonds (which pay interest in the form of more bonds instead of cash), but as you might expect, nobody on Wall Street has issued a BEAR.

maturity was 10%, about the same as other rates at the time. But in the 6th year, Braniff went broke, and the bond became worthless. Because the investor hadn't received interest each year, he not only lost his investment, he lost the interest that had been accumulating inside the bond as well.

You see, if you own an ordinary bond, you'll at least get a check for the interest on a regular basis. Had my client owned a regular Braniff bond, he'd have received checks during the six years equal to 60% of his investment. Instead he got nothing. This makes zeros much riskier than ordinary bonds.

Problem #3: Phantom Income

Even though you don't receive a check each year for the interest you've "earned," you must pay taxes as though you did. This is known as *phantom income*. Here's the IRS's rationale:

Say a zero-coupon bond is issued with a face value of $100 and a maturity date of 10 years from now. You pay $50 for the bond, and in 10 years you are to receive back the face value of $100. You earn $50 in interest, and it is paid to you at maturity in one lump-sum.

Since you are earning $50 in interest over a 10-year period, the IRS contends that you are earning $5 per year, even though you don't phys-ically receive the interest in cash each year. Thus, if you were to sell your bond after one year, you would receive $55, rather than the $50 you paid. The IRS therefore concludes that since the bond has grown in value, in effect you have earned interest, and therefore you must pay taxes on this interest. This is phantom income: You must pay taxes on income you didn't get.

Zeros are technical-ly known as OID bonds, for *Original Issue Discount,* and the tax you pay each year is based on *OID Interest.*

Let's go back to our Braniff investor. Not only did he lose his investment, he was paying taxes every year on the interest he never got. (In the year the bond became worthless, he was able to declare it as a loss on his tax return — small consolation!)

Problem #4: Zeros Are Callable

In itself, a zero that's callable doesn't seem to be any worse than any other callable bond. But because buyers of zeros toss their certificates into safety deposit boxes, they often aren't informed when the bond is called. One of my clients had a zero, which she bought in 1970. We quickly discovered that the bond had been called in 1984, and she never knew it. Since bonds stop paying interest when they are called, I had to inform her that her bond hadn't earned any interest for the last 19 years!

Six Reasons Not to Take Physical Possession of Certificates

This is why I discourage clients from taking physical possession of certificates. Had she allowed her broker to keep the certificate for her, the broker would have notified her when the bond was called. Clients who want possession of certificates think their investment is safer; not only is this *not* true, but by taking the paper, you're creating new headaches, to wit:

Possession Problem #1: You've Got to Keep Your Certificate Safe

Certificates are money and must be safeguarded like cash. They are very difficult to replace if lost or stolen.

Possession Problem #2: You Become Responsible for Monitoring Any Activity in the Bond

You must track receipt of interest checks as well as call actions and defaults. That's your broker's job, but he can't perform these services unless you let him hold the bond for you in your brokerage account.

Possession Problem #3: You Must Return Your Certificate to Your Broker When You Want to Sell or Redeem It, Anyway

Most advisors can't sell your bond until you deliver it to them. If the bond has been damaged (torn, stained, water damaged, or altered), your broker may reject it, forcing you to get a replacement certificate, which can take months. You can't sell the bond in the meantime.

To avoid worries that your broker might go broke or steal your bond, simply confirm that your broker is covered by the Securities Investors Protection Corporation. Coverage is provided up to $500,000 ($100,000 in cash and $400,000 in securities), and virtually all major securities firms carry supplemental coverage to protect each client up to $25 million, sometimes more. So, when it comes to the safe keeping of certificates, keep yours with your broker, not with you.

In fact, I predict that the government will abolish the production of physical certificates in favor of electronic transactions. All that paper is expensive to print and maintain, and it provides many opportunities for fraud. Soon, you'll be required to keep securities with your broker, so you might as well start now.

> SIPC, which is the brokerage industry version of FDIC, protects your account in case the brokerage firm collapses. SIPC *does not* protect you against investment losses, and many people have been fooled into buying investments they otherwise would not have bought because fast-talking brokers told them SIPC guarantees you against investment losses. It doesn't.
>
> And, yes, SIPC is about as well-funded as FDIC. (See Chapter 6 for more.)

Possession Problem #4: Losing the Certificate Will Cost You

If you can't find the document, you'd be wise to buy a "lost instrument" bond. This way, you'll be protected if someone else finds it and tries to cash it in. Downside: Bonding will cost you about 3% of the investment's value.

Possession Problem #5: Holding the Certificate Costs You Interest

Have you ever gotten an interest or dividend check in the mail? How long did the check sit on your dresser before you bothered to deposit it into your bank account?

Imagine how much interest you lose by doing this with every check you receive over many years!

By contrast, brokers who hold certificates for their clients are able to deposit interest and dividend checks into a money market fund the same day the checks are paid. And you never have to worry about misplacing those checks, losing them in the mail, or forgetting to go to the bank.

Possession Problem #6: Re-Registration Is a Pain

If the owner or co-owner of a certificate changes his or her name (say, due to marriage), dies or becomes incapacitated, you'll have to re-register each certificate you hold. That means each issuer's transfer agent must be contacted. You'll have to submit each certificate to the agents, and it's a very time-consuming process (and you can't sell the certificates in the meantime). If you hold everything with a broker, however, the entire re-registration process is vastly simplified.

Chapter 11 - Bond Ratings

There's never any question about the safety of U.S. Government Securities, but what about little county governments and corporations — and the bonds they issue? Several companies help investors evaluate the financial stability and default risks of companies and municipalities — and the bonds they issue. Standard & Poor's and Moody's are the two major bond rating agencies. Their scales are similar but do feature important distinctions between investment-grade and speculative-grade bonds.

First, when evaluating a bond, don't demand the highest rating (AAA from S&P and Aaa from Moody's). After all, even General Motors is only rated AA. In fact, only 21 companies that comprise the Fortune 500 are rated AAA.

That's why any company or bond rated BBB/Baa or above is considered investment-grade. Anything BB/Ba or below is speculative-grade (also known as junk bonds).

Just as you shouldn't overstate the importance of an AAA rating, don't overemphasize the ratings themselves, either, because companies and municipalities pay to be rated. (If you pay for your rating, you might cancel if you receive a poor grade. Maybe that's why the top rating is AAA instead of A: This way, to the uninitiated, an A rating sounds better than it is.)

Ratings affect prices; the lower the rating, the less investors are willing to pay for it (or, conversely, the more they demand to earn from it). For example, look at Figure 3-5. It shows two bonds, each with an interest rate of 8.4%, and each with a face value of $10,000. Bond A's price is the same as its face value. Therefore, the yield is the same as the rate: 8.4%.[5]

But Bond B is lower-rated. It too has a face value of $10,000. To compensate you for the higher risk of default, you demand a higher profit. To get it, you buy this bond for just $7,356, substantially below its face value. You still receive $840 in interest each year because that is what the certificate says it pays (8.4% on $10,000); the certificate doesn't know — or care — that you paid only $7,356 for it.

---

[5]For more on rate vs. yield, see Chapter 13.

In other words, the B-rated bond earns $840 on a $7,356 investment, and this translates to an annual yield of 11.4% — or 3% more than the AAA-rated bond. As you can see, the greater risk produces a greater return.

At least it's supposed to. This leads us to the story of RJR Nabisco.

BOND RATINGS

	Rating Descriptions	Standard & Poor's	Moody's	Face Value	Rate	Current Price	Yield	
I N V E S T M E N T **G R A D E**	Highest Score	AAA	Aaa	$10,000	8.4%	$10,000	8.4%	← **Bond A**
		AA+	Aa1					
	Very Strong	AA	Aa2					
		AA-	Aa3					
		A+	A1					
		A	A2					
		A-	A3					
		BBB+	Baa1					
	Adequate	BBB	Baa2					
		BBB-	Baa3					
S P E C U L A T I V E **G R A D E**		BB+	Ba1					
	Least Speculative	BB	Ba2					
		BB-	Ba3					**Bond B**
		B+	B1					
	Speculative large uncertainty or major risk exposure	B	B2	$10,000	8.4%	$7,356	11.4%	←
		B-	B3					
		CCC	Caa					
	In Payment Default	CC, D	Ca, C					

FIGURE 3-5

Chapter 12 - Event Risk

In 1988, Nabisco was one of the largest, best-known companies in America, makers of Oreo Cookies, Ritz Crackers, Lifesavers, and Camel cigarettes. Worth $22 billion with no debt, Nabisco was rated AAA and considered "too big" to be taken over by corporate raiders. After all, who could possibly raise enough money to buy the company? Thus, it was felt Nabisco could go about its business immune to the takeover artists of the '80s.

Until KKR came along.

Kohlberg, Kravits and Roberts decided to buy Nabisco in 1988. Based on then-current stock prices, KKR calculated that it could buy Nabisco for $22 billion, and then sell off the pieces of the company for a total of $26 billion — giving itself a profit of $4 billion in the process.

So, armed with $5 million of its own capital, KKR borrowed $26 billion from banks and investors around the world, using Nabisco itself as collateral for the loans. This is the same way you buy your home: With a little money down, you borrow a huge sum by posting the home as collateral; if you default on the loan payments, the bank becomes owner of your house.

"When a fellow says, 'It ain't the money but the principle o' the thing,' it's the money."
—Abe Martin

Of course, there were some interesting differences between what you do to buy your home and what KKR did to buy Nabisco.

If you are like most borrowers, your lender requires that you put down at least 5% of the value of your home. For KKR, this would have meant a down payment of $1.3 billion — yet they were able to get financing by putting down only $5 million. That's like buying a $400,000 house with a cash deposit of *fifteen hundred dollars*!

Also, KKR actually managed to borrow $4 billion *more* for Nabisco than it was worth — as though you could borrow $472,000 to buy a $400,000 house!

By posting Nabisco as collateral, Nabisco became obligated for the debt. In other words, KKR saddled a debt-free company with $26 billion worth of debt — $4 billion more than the entire company was worth!

When KKR announced the takeover on Monday, October 24, 1988, S&P and Moody's immediately cut Nabisco's rating to B from AAA!

Return now to Figure 3-5, and you'll see that AAA bonds (such as Nabisco's before the takeover) were trading at full face value, or $10,000 for a $10,000 bond. But B-rated bonds were trading for just 73 cents on the dollar, or $7,356 for a $10,000 bond. In other words, if you owned a Nabisco bond — which you bought for safety — you opened the newspaper on Tuesday to discover that your bond had lost 27% of its market value overnight!

KKR's takeover made Metropolitan Life Insurance Company very upset. MetLife had invested $117 million in Nabisco bonds. The takeover presented Met with a $32 million loss! MetLife sued KKR, but the New York Superior Court threw the case out, ruling in essence that when you pay your money, you take your chances.

This is *Event Risk*, defined as an occurrence within a company that is both unexpected and beyond the control of management, yet which produces an adverse effect on the value of the company's securities.

Can you think of other examples of event risk? How about:

- Johnson & Johnson's Tylenol poisonings

- Dow Corning & Silicon Breast Implants

- the beef industry & Mad Cow Disease

Note that an airline crash is not event risk. While such an event can and often does adversely affect an airline's stock, such an event is a known risk of that business and, therefore, does not meet the definition of event risk.

So as you consider any investment, think not only about the things you know can go wrong, but also about the things you haven't thought of, which could go wrong as well.

Chapter 13 - Rate, Yield, and Total Return

Say you put $10,000 into a 4% CD that matures in 10 years. How much money will you earn?

If you earn *simple interest*, the bank pays you $400 per year, and you'll have $14,000 in 10 years ($400 interest per year for 10 years is $4,000, plus your original $10,000). Thus, simple interest means there is no compounding, and therefore the *rate* and the *yield* are the same. In this example, both are 4%.

But what if the bank compounds your interest on an annual basis? If so, at the end of 10 years you would have $14,802 — not $14,000. Thus, a 4% CD compounded annually over 10 years *yields* the same as a 4.8% CD that does not compound. Therefore, the more often your interest is compounded, the more you will earn, as Figure 3-6 shows. That's why an investment's *yield* is more important than its *rate*.

THE MORE FREQUENTLY YOU COMPOUND THE MORE MONEY YOU MAKE

$10,000 Invested for 10 Years at 4%

Amount Invested	Annual Rate	Time	Compounding Frequency	Ending Value
$10,000	4%	10 years	simple interest	$14,000
$10,000	4%	10 years	annually	$14,802
$10,000	4%	10 years	quarterly	$14,888
$10,000	4%	10 years	monthly	$14,908
$10,000	4%	10 years	weekly	$14,915
$10,000	4%	10 years	daily[6]	$14,917

FIGURE 3-6

---

[6]Also known as "continuous compounding."

Therefore, don't assume one investment will earn more than another just because its rate is higher. Be sure to consider the frequency of compounding, for that will determine the *yield*, and yield is the true determinant of how much interest you will earn.

What's the True Yield?

So, fine, the yield is more important than the rate. But what exactly is a bond's *true* yield?

Say a broker offers to sell you a $10,000 bond that matures in seven years, pays 6.5% interest, and is callable in four years. The broker tells you the price of the bond is $11,284.

If you asked him, "What's the yield?," he could say the "nominal yield" is 6.5%. *Nominal yield* (also known as "coupon") is the stated rate of interest that is printed on the certificate itself.

Or, the broker could reply that the "current yield" is 5.8%. *Current yield* adjusts the rate of interest by the actual purchase price. Since you are paying $11,284 for a bond that pays $650 in annual interest, simple division shows you are earning 5.8%.

Less likely, the broker could say that the "yield to maturity" is 4.39%. *Yield to Maturity* is the effective interest rate you get if you hold the bond until it matures in seven years; it reflects the fact that you paid $11,284 but will receive back only the $10,000 face value at maturity, incurring a loss of principal of $1,284.

Least likely is that the broker will tell you that the "yield to call" is only 3.09%. *Yield to Call* recognizes that this bond could be called — meaning you might get your capital back in as little as four years. If that were to happen, you would get only four years' worth of interest payments instead of seven. And, like the yield to maturity calculation above, you will receive back only the $10,000 face value, not the $11,284 you paid. Yield to Call is the worst-case scenario for this bond — and the one most likely to occur.

So which is the true yield? Well, it depends[7] on your point of view.

---

[7] Aren't you getting tired of seeing this answer? And if you're just joining us, hi!

Technically, all these answers are correct. Therefore, the broker hasn't lied when he quotes a yield of 6.5% — he isn't telling you the whole truth, either. This is why, when buying an investment based on yield, it's difficult to determine the yield. It's dangerous to buy a bond based on yield, too, because yield says nothing about total return.

Yield vs. Total Return

We have learned that the same rate compounded at different intervals produces different yields, and that you should therefore focus on yield, not rate.

Now you can forget about yield, too.

Instead, favor *total return*. Here's why: In all our examples so far, both the rates and yields shown have assumed that your principal remains unchanged. This is the case for CDs, but what about investments where principal values can fluctuate? Indeed, for virtually every investment *except* bank accounts and CDs you must adjust the yield by any increase or decrease in the value of your original principal. Making such adjustments, known as a gain or loss, produces the *total return*, and that is the only figure that counts when trying to determine the return on an investment.

For example, suppose you invest $10,000 in a stock which pays a 3% dividend. After one year, your investment would be worth $10,300 (ignoring compounding). But suppose the stock's value increases by 5% during the same period, or $500. Therefore, your investment is really worth $10,800, and that means your *total return* — the dividends *plus* the increase in your principal's value — is 8%, far superior to the stock's 3% dividend alone. Likewise, if your investment had lost 1% of its value, your total return would have been only 2%.

Therefore, total return is your income (dividend or interest) plus or minus changes in the value of your original investment. Since CDs never change in value, its yield and total return always are the same, but that's not true for other investments. That's why you must never buy investments based on their yield, for those with the highest yields often have the lowest total returns, and since it's the total return that matters, a high yield is irrelevant.

Those who chase yields — meaning those who buy investments only because they offer high yields or rates of interest— do so out of greed, and greedy people get what they deserve.

Chapter 14 - Interest Rate Risk

So far, we've learned about a variety of risks: default risk, liquidity risk, inflation risk, tax risk, and event risk. Yet perhaps worse than any of these is interest rate risk. Without question, interest rate risk causes more people to lose money than any other type of investment risk. So pay particular attention to this chapter!

Harry is home having dinner when the phone rings. It's a cold-calling stockbroker. (They know when you're likely to be home!) The broker says, "Harry, instead of keeping your money in the bank at 1% interest, I can give you a bond issued and guaranteed by the U.S. Government, which pays 6% interest annually, pays that interest on a monthly basis — just like a Social Security check — is free from state income taxes, and is liquid at all times. Harry, what I'm offering you is safer than the bank, earns more interest than the bank, is as liquid as the bank, and lowers your taxes. What do you say? Can I put you down for $10,000?"

> *"Sometimes your best investments are the ones you don't make."*
> —Donald Trump

Pretty appealing pitch, isn't it? And as you've been learning, everything the broker has said is true: Government bonds are safer than banks, they pay higher interest rates, they are lower in taxes, and you can sell your bond whenever you want.

However, the liquidity part of that pitch is a bit weak — and is the cause of more investor losses than anything else on Wall Street. Here's how it works:

Say Harry accepts the pitch and invests $10,000 to buy that 30-year government bond with its 6% interest rate and $10,000 face value. Let's further say that two years later he decides to sell his bond, because he needs the cash to buy a car. Let's also say that during this time, interest rates have changed, and the government is now issuing new bonds with new 8% interest rates.

Enter Jane, another investor. She is interested in buying the same type of bond that Harry happens to be selling. This presents Jane with a choice: She can buy either Harry's government bond from Harry, or she can buy a brand new one from the government.

Since both have a face value of $10,000, which one will she buy: Harry's, offering a rate of 6%, or the new government bond which offers 8%?

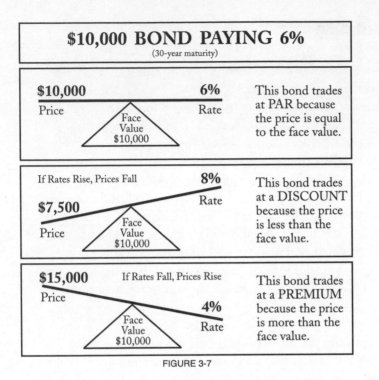

$10,000 BOND PAYING 6%
(30-year maturity)

$10,000 Price	**6%** Rate	This bond trades at PAR because the price is equal to the face value.
If Rates Rise, Prices Fall **$7,500** Price	**8%** Rate	This bond trades at a DISCOUNT because the price is less than the face value.
$15,000 Price If Rates Fall, Prices Rise	**4%** Rate	This bond trades at a PREMIUM because the price is more than the face value.

FIGURE 3-7

It should be obvious that Jane will buy the new government bond, which pays 2% more than Harry's bond. Simple enough.

But this next question is a bit more difficult: What must Harry do to convince Jane to buy his bond instead of the government's? He cannot change the interest rate of his bond. After all, that's set in stone — 6% is printed right on the certificate itself.

The answer: Since he can't increase the rate of his bond, *Harry must lower the price.* He must sell his bond for less than its $10,000 face value.

How much less? Well, in this example, for Jane to make as much money on Harry's bond as she would have earned on Uncle Sam's bond, she must buy it for $7,500. In other words, paying $7,500 for a $10,000 bond at 6% is equal to paying $10,000 for a $10,000 bond at 8%.

In this example, Harry must sell his bond for $2,500 less than what he paid for it! Try to explain to him how he managed to lose 25% of his money in a *government-guaranteed* investment!

This phenomenon is called *interest rate risk*, and as I said, it is the biggest cause of investor losses in the world. It is also very confusing to new investors, so follow this explanation carefully.

As interest rates change in the economy, the value of existing bonds will change as well — but in the opposite direction.

Picture a seesaw with interest rates on one end and bond prices on the other; as one side rises, the other falls. Therefore, had rates fallen to 4% instead of rising to 8%,

Harry would have been able to sell his bond to Jane for 50% more than he paid instead of 25% less. Thus, as a result of interest rate risk, bond holders can make a lot of money, or lose a lot of money. It all depends which way interest rates move.

You can use this advice the next time you take a cruise: Always rent a cabin near the center of the ship; since the bow and stern rock with greater severity, you're more likely to get seasick if you're out at the extremes. Investing can produce similar results: The further out (in time) you go, the more volatility and nausea you might experience.

Also, the longer a bond's maturity, the more extreme its swings in value. A 30-year bond fluctuates much more than a 1-year bond, as Figure 3-8 shows.

How to Beat Interest Rate Risk

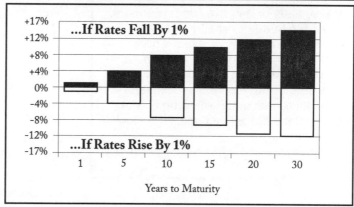

WHAT HAPPENS TO THE PRICE OF A 6% BOND

...If Rates Fall By 1%

...If Rates Rise By 1%

Years to Maturity

FIGURE 3-8

Have you been able to figure out how Harry can avoid losing $2,500? It's easy: All he has to do is *keep his bond*! He loses money only if he sells; if he keeps his bond to maturity, the government will pay him the full $10,000 amount.

Remember: The government's "full faith and credit guarantee" is only for the "timely payment" of interest and principal. That means Uncle Sam will pay interest *on time* to whomever owns the bond, and *at maturity* will return principal to whoever owns the bond at that time.

The government also says its bonds may be bought and sold prior to maturity, but is silent regarding the buy and sell prices, leaving investors to negotiate the price of

> **Bond buyers are never happy people. Consider Harry, golfing with his buddies, happy in the knowledge that he's earning 8% interest. Then his golf partner mentions he just bought a 10% bond. Suddenly, Harry's not happy. "Bert's getting 10% and I'm only getting 8%," Harry says to himself. So he goes home, calls his broker and says, "Sell my bond and get me one paying 10%!" His broker replies, "Okay, Harry, but if you sell your bond, you'll lose 20% of the value." Suddenly, Harry's not happy again.**
>
> **If he keeps his bond, he earns only 8%, or $800 on his $10,000 investment, while his buddy Bert earns 10%. If Harry sells his bond, he loses $2,000 — 20% of his investment — and if he reinvests the remaining $8,000 into that new 10% bond, his income will still be only $800 — exactly where he is today. No matter what Harry does, he's stuck.**
>
> **Bond buyers are never happy people.**

the security between themselves. This is where the phrase "negotiable security" comes from: All stock and bond prices are negotiable between buyers and sellers.

This also explains why the New York Superior Court ruled against MetLife in its suit against KKR. The court noted that the bonds, although reduced in market value, continued to pay interest as before, and if MetLife simply held the bonds to maturity, it would receive back 100% of its investment. Like telling the doctor your arm hurts when you "go like this," the court told MetLife, don't go like that! Keep your bond until maturity, and you don't have to worry about interest rate risk![8]

If you think Harry's predicament is merely hypothetical, recall the bond market of early 1993. Long-term interest rates had dropped to their lowest levels in 27 years, but in 1994 they rose 2.75%. That corresponded to a 27.5% *loss* for bond holders — the worst one-year loss in bond history; estimates put total investor losses at $1.5 trillion. In fact, it was the first time bonds posted a negative total return in modern times — all due to interest rate risk.

Conversely, the 13 interest rate cuts of 2001–2003 produced the largest increases in bond prices in two generations. But if interest rates rise later this decade, those gains will be replaced by equally massive losses.

This means you should buy only those bonds which feature a maturity date you can tolerate. Don't buy a 30-year bond for your child's college education, unless your kid plans to attend college in his or her 30s!

It is because of interest rate risk that bond yields don't tell the whole story. Follow Edelman's Rule #1: Never, never, never, never, never, never, never buy an investment

---

[8]MetLife had other concerns due to accounting rules affecting insurers, but that's not relevant here.

based on *yield.* Look at any personal finance magazine or the business section of any newspaper and you'll see ads proclaiming high yields, but none of these ads adjust their yields for any gain or loss in market value. Figure 3-9 shows that while a bond's income remains constant over time, its liquidation value fluctuates wildly.

> Institutional investors will buy a bond at 7.34% and sell it at 7.32%. Why bother trying to capture a measly two basis points ($^2/_{100ths}$ of 1%)? Well, if you were trading $300 million in principal, those two basis points would translate to $60,000 — or nearly twice the annual salary of the average U.S. worker. Not bad for a few minutes' work.

This volatility provides opportunity for high-risk speculators and gamblers to try to guess which way interest rates will move next. Thus, it is in the bond market that you'll find the biggest institutional players, not in the stock market. Indeed, while $72 billion worth of stocks trade each day in the U.S., according to the Securities Industry Association, $500 billion worth of bonds are traded. And bonds move by basis points; each basis point is just 1/100th of a percent.

IF YOU BOUGHT A 30-YEAR GOVERNMENT BOND IN 1972 FOR $10,000...

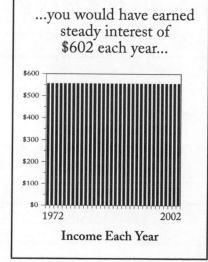

...you would have earned steady interest of $602 each year...

Income Each Year

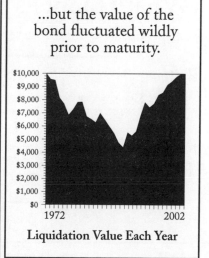

...but the value of the bond fluctuated wildly prior to maturity.

Liquidation Value Each Year

FIGURE 3-9

HEADS THEY WIN, TAILS YOU LOSE

What Happens to Bonds if...

	Your Bonds	Meaning	This is Known As
...Rates Fall:	will be called	You get your principal back, and are forced to reinvest at new, low rates.	Call Risk
...Rates Rise:	will continue to pay to maturity	You will continue to earn interest, but at less than currently available rates. If you sell, you will not get back 100% of your investment.	Opportunity Risk

What Happens to Ginnie Maes if...

	Then	Meaning	This is Known As
...Rates Fall:	The underlying borrowers will refinance early, speeding up return of capital to you.	You'll get your money back sooner than expected, forcing you to reinvest at new low rates.	Prepayment or Maturity Risk
...Rates Rise:	The underlying borrowers will delay or slow down repayment, extending the life of the security.	You won't get your money back as soon as you expected, and the delay could be decades.	Extension Risk

FIGURE 3-10

Should You Buy Bonds?

So before you buy bonds, ask yourself if you think interest rates are headed up or down over the next couple of years. After all, rates can do only one of three things:

- go up

- go down

- stay the same

If rates rise, your bonds lose value. If rates fall, your bonds grow in value. If rates stay the same, the bond's value stays the same. Thus, only one of these three scenarios — rising rates — places you in jeopardy.

If you believe rates are likely to rise, does this mean you should not buy bonds? Not at all. First of all, you're probably wrong (simply because most investors are; as *Barron's* put it, "If the majority were right, the majority would be rich."). Second, bonds are a cornerstone of any diversified portfolio (as we'll explore later), and besides, there are two very effective strategies you can use to protect yourself against interest rate risk.

The first strategy, as we've discussed, is simply to hold any bond you buy until it matures. But this forces you to keep a bond whose rate may be lower than those now available in the marketplace.

Using Gold to Beat Interest Rate Risk

The second strategy, although it might sound strange, is to buy hard assets, such as gold. Ordinarily, gold is a very silly investment. It is highly volatile and very speculative: The only reason investors buy it is because they think someone else will pay more for it in the future than they paid today. That's a foolish bet.

Furthermore, gold doesn't pay dividends, and while one share of stock can split, becoming two shares, your ounce will never become two ounces. Thus, gold is a silly investment. However, there is a demonstrated relationship between gold prices and bond prices.

Think about it: Gold hit its all-time high of $800/ounce in 1980, at the same time interest rates reached their all-time high. What caused gold and interest rates to be so high? Why, none other than our old nemesis, inflation.

Inflation makes gold prices rise. In fact, gold prices merely reflect inflation: A hundred years ago, a $20 gold piece (one ounce of gold) would have bought a fine quality man's suit. Today, that gold coin — one ounce of gold — is worth at this writing about $300, and it still buys a quality suit. Clearly, gold prices move with inflation: When inflation was high in the '80s, gold prices were high. When inflation fell, gold prices fell as well.

So gold and inflation are related, just as we have learned that interest rates and inflation are related. Do you see the connection? Both gold and interest rates have a positive correlation to inflation (meaning when inflation rates rise, gold prices and interest rates also rise).

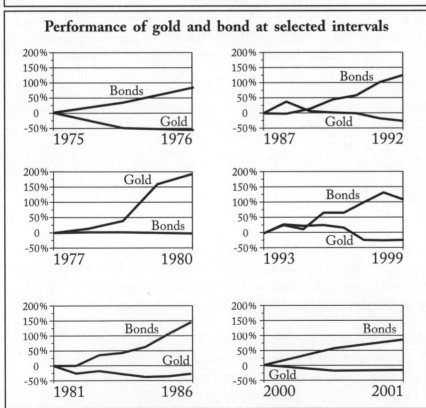

GOLD vs. BONDS
1975-2001

Performance of gold and bond at selected intervals

Now recall the relationship between interest rates and bond prices. That's an *inverse correlation*. When interest rates rise, bond prices fall.

Let's put it all together: When inflation rises, gold prices rise and interest rates rise. But as interest rates rise, bond prices fall. Therefore, infla-

FIGURE 3-11

106

tion causes gold prices to go up and bond prices to go down. Thus, we can see clearly the inverse relationship between gold prices and bond prices. And, it's again a 1 in 10 ratio: A 1% change in bond prices often reflects a 10% change in gold prices — in the other direction.

Therefore, when we buy bonds for a client, we often place one-tenth or so of that investment into gold. If we put $10,000 into bonds, for example, we might recommend $1,000 or so into gold. Note that we are not buying gold because we think it might go to $1,000 an ounce; rather, we buy gold because we're *afraid* it's going to $1,000 an ounce — for that would mean inflation has jumped and our clients' bond values are falling.

Reducing Risk Via Hedging Strategies

"A gold mine is a hole in the ground with a liar on the top."
—Mark Twain

Gold, therefore, is a *hedging strategy*, also known as insurance: I am protecting myself in case interest rates move against me. I don't care what happens to the price of gold, because that's not why I bought it. Rather, I am more concerned with the money I placed in bonds, because I have ten times as much in bonds as in gold.

Let's look at an example. Say I create a portfolio with a total investment of $99,000, consisting of $90,000 in bonds and $9,000 in gold. If rates rise 1%, my bonds should fall 10%, and if bonds fall 10%, then gold should rise 100%. Thus, my bonds would now be worth only $81,000, but my gold would be worth $18,000. Thus, the value of my portfolio would remain $99,000 — right where I started.

Why do this if my portfolio won't increase in value? *Because I don't want it to*. I'm buying bonds for the *income* they pay, not for their growth potential. If I want growth, I'll buy stocks; from bonds, I want the interest income without risk to my principal.

As with all hedging strategies, this one comes with a price. That price is the fact that I've placed 10% of my money into a hedge, which by design is not intended to make money for me (if it does, it's quite accidental — and would probably be negated by losses on the other side). By placing $9,000 into gold, I'm not earning any interest on that money, which means I'm diluting the rate of return I would have gotten had I placed my entire portfolio into bonds.

This is known as *opportunity cost*, and you could argue I'm throwing money away by hedging. But, do you earn interest on the money you spend on auto insurance? No. But you pay the premium anyway, in case you have an accident. I'm doing the same thing with my bonds: protecting them in case something goes wrong. Thus, this strategy means I will not earn as much money as I could, but then I am not taking as high a risk either. As with all investment strategies, there are tradeoffs, and you must decide which tradeoffs are worthwhile and acceptable.

Also, please note that since I'm buying gold only as a hedge for my bonds, I would sell the gold when I sell the bonds. I don't need one without the other.

It also needs to be stressed that this strategy is not a sure thing, although Figure 3-11 shows it has worked remarkably well since the U.S. left the gold standard in 1972. This prior success notwithstanding, gold is subject to a variety of non-inflationary factors, including political turmoil and the laws of supply and demand. Therefore, there can be no assurance that this strategy will work in the future as it has in the past. In fact...

> The fascinating part of this strategy is this most important principle: Introducing a risky asset into a portfolio lowers the overall risk of the portfolio.
>
> Bonds are safer than gold. Therefore, a portfolio of bonds is safer than a portfolio of gold. Thus, it would follow that a portfolio of bonds alone would be safer than a portfolio consisting of both bonds and gold, right?
>
> Wrong. A portfolio of bonds and gold is safer than a portfolio of bonds alone. So if you want to increase safety, buy a risky investment.
>
> Try explaining that to Harry.

...The Debate Continues: Is Gold Still an Asset Class?

It is important to note that the financial community has begun to debate whether gold still holds its luster. Some observers point to the fact that, since 1980, gold has steadily dropped from $800/ounce to around $300. But it's important to remember that, since 1980, we've gone from 15% inflation and 21% interest rates to 1% inflation and 2% interest rates. And in such an environment, you would expect the price of gold to be lower — and it is.

Therefore, gold's past performance validates its use as an asset class. You don't dismiss assets merely because they under perform; you dismiss them because they mis-perform, meaning they perform unexpectedly, given the economic environment. But gold has performed as one might expect, given the circumstances.

A Legitimate Argument

But the detractors offer a second argument, and I admit this one does hold greater legitimacy: In 1980, there were few ways to hedge a portfolio. "Hard" or "real" assets — meaning gold and real estate — were the only way to protect your portfolio from declines in "paper" assets (stocks and bonds). But this is not the case today. Innovation and modern technology — not to mention a new global economy and fewer restrictions in the financial community — have led to a vast array of new investment products. These vehicles — options contracts, forward currency trading, interest rate swaps, commodity futures and more, coupled with 24-hour availability due to always-open exchanges, enable institutional money managers to hedge their portfolios with greater ease and precision than ever before. Has the Brave New World supplanted gold (with its 5,000-year history) as the hedge vehicle of choice? If so, gold will fail to continue performing as you would predict.

> *"With money in your pocket, you are wise and you are handsome and you sing well too."*
> —**Yiddish Proverb**

While I acknowledge the validity of this premise, and ponder its notion with interest, I am not yet ready to concede that gold has lost its luster. For one thing, we haven't yet experienced the type of economic environment that would prove gold's demise and the newfangled hedges' ascent. Therefore, I remain committed to the use of gold and other hard assets (including other precious metals, minerals, commodities, and lumber, as well as the use of options and futures contracts) as a portfolio hedge.

> **How do you buy these assets? We use mutual funds, which we'll cover in more detail in Part V. If you prefer, you can buy bullion, gold coins, or shares of gold mining companies. But you'll discover that gold mutual funds do all of these, and much more conveniently than you could on your own. Also, owning gold via mutual funds alleviates the need for you to worry about safe-keeping.**

For more on hedging strategies, see Chapter 20.

ric's money quiz

Here's a chance to see how well you learned the information contained in Part III – Fixed Income Investments. Don't worry if you get stumped — just re-read this part until it sinks in. Remember, your financial future depends on it.

The answers are at the end of the quiz. No peeking!

---

1. **What does G.O. stand for?**

   - ○ a. Guaranteed Offering
   - ○ b. General Obligation
   - ○ c. Guaranteed Obligation
   - ○ d. General Offering

2. **If you own a bond that has a call date, it means:**

   - ○ a. the issuer will call you when the bond is about to mature
   - ○ b. the interest rate will change on the call date
   - ○ c. the issuer can redeem your bond prior to maturity
   - ○ d. the bond will be issued on that date

3. **What is the primary reason investors are attracted to municipal bonds?**

   - ○ a. the interest earned is always free of federal income taxes
   - ○ b. municipal bonds are safer than other bonds
   - ○ c. municipal bonds are cheaper than other bonds
   - ○ d. the interest earned is always free of state income taxes

4. **The calculation that an investor must perform in order to fairly compare a bank CD with a municipal bond is called:**

   - ○ a. yield-to-maturity
   - ○ b. taxable-equivalent yield
   - ○ c. PE Ratio
   - ○ d. yield-to-book

5. Zero Coupon Bonds are bonds that:

    - a. always mature in a "0" year, such as 1990 or 2000
    - b. do not pay current interest
    - c. are issued only by the federal government
    - d. pay tax-free interest

6. Bonds with which ratings would be considered "junk bonds"?

    - a. AA, BB, CC and D
    - b. BB, CC and D
    - c. CC and D
    - d. D only

7. Which of the following is *not* an example of "event risk"?

    - a. the hostile takeover of Nabisco
    - b. the Tylenol poisonings
    - c. a plane crash
    - d. the asbestos cancer link

8. Which of the following will *not* help you avoid losing principal due to interest rate risk?

    - a. buying gold
    - b. keeping bonds until they mature
    - c. buying government bonds only
    - d. do not buy bonds

9. Gold prices tend to move with:

    - a. stock prices
    - b. bond prices
    - c. inflation rates
    - d. tax rates

10. The relationship between interest rates and bond prices is as follows: As interest rates move up or down,

    - a. bond prices stay the same
    - b. bond prices move in the same direction
    - c. bond prices move in the opposite direction
    - d. bond maturity dates change as well

Answers: 1-b (pg.75)   3-a (pg.76)   5-b (pg.86)   7-c (pg.95)   9-c (pg.105)
              2-c (pg.77)   4-b (pg.78)   6-b (pg.92)   8-c (pg.100)   10-c (pg.100)

Part IV
Equities

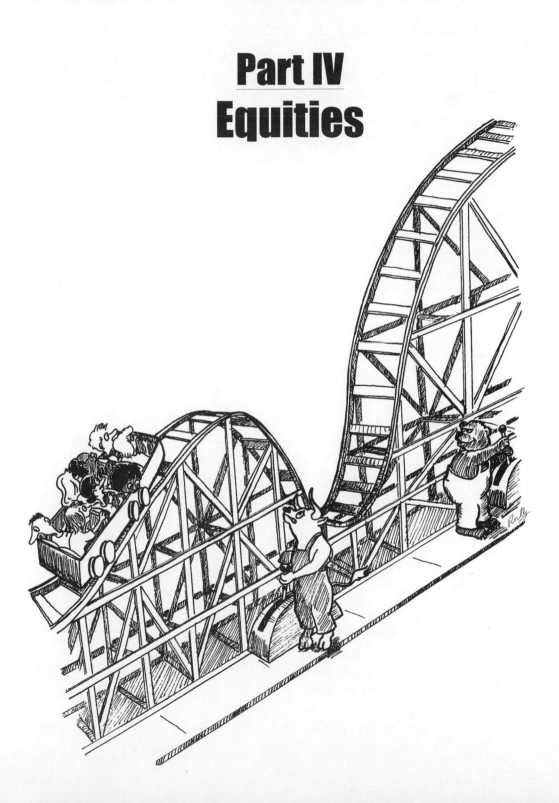

There's a quiz at the end of this part!

To see how much you already know, skip to the
end of this part and take the quiz now. Then, read
the part and take the quiz again. You'll discover
how much you've learned!

Part IV — Equities

Overview - Growth After Income

Equity means ownership. For example, if you own shoes worth $20, your equity in them is $20. Thus, when you own something, you have equity in it. When you have ownership in a company, your equity is your share of the company, which is represented by a stock certificate (those who lend companies money get bond certificates).

Thus, ownership = equity = shares = stock, and you'll find that the financial world uses these terms interchangeably.

As we've learned, stocks are higher in risk than bonds. With stocks, we don't know how much money we're going to earn (if any), and we don't know if we'll ever be able to sell the certificates (and doing so is the only way to get our money back).

"There is no security in this life. There is only opportunity."
—**Douglas MacArthur**

As Figure 4-1 shows, people are willing to take these risks because the odds are stacked in your favor: The most you can lose is 100% of your investment, but your gains are potentially unlimited.

WHY INVESTORS TAKE THE RISK

Potential Gain: *Unlimited!*

The best stocks of 2002

Company	2002 price change
Crown Cork & Seal	156%
MEMC Electronic Materials	119%
Cognizant Technology Solutions	88%
Corinthian Colleges	88%
Boston Scientific	87%
Dreyer's Grand Ice Cream	83%
Providian Financial	83%
Amylin Pharmaceuticals	79%
PacifiCare Health Systems	75%
Amazon.com	72%

Potential Loss: *Amount You Invested*

The worst stocks of 2002

Company	2002 price change
Williams Companies	-89%
Gemstar-TV Guide	-88%
Pegasus Communications	-88%
El Paso	-85%
Nvidia	-83%
Sprint PCS	-82%
AES	-82%
Lucent Technologies	-81%
Calpine	-81%
Andrx	-79%

FIGURE 4-1

Chapter 15 - Four Benefits of Owning Stock

Indeed, smart investors happily take the bad with the good. If you owned equal amounts of the 10 best and the 10 worst stocks of 2002, you'd be rich — despite the fact that 20% of the stocks you bought became virtually worthless.

But stock ownership goes beyond that. People invest in stocks for several reasons, so let's look at them in detail.

Benefit #1: Stocks Can Grow in Value

Figure 4-2 shows the capital appreciation of the S&P 500 Stock Index from 1926 through June 30, 2003. Based on this data, a $10,000 investment on January 1, 1926, would have grown to $763,958 as of June 30, 2003. That's an average annual rate of appreciation of 5.8%[9].

Benefit #2: Stocks Can Generate Income

As shown in Figure 4-3, that same $10,000 invested in 1926 earned dividends worth $263,015 through June 30, 2003. That's an average annual

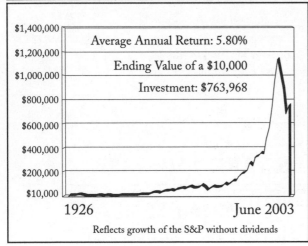

CAPITAL APPRECIATION OF THE S&P 500 STOCK INDEX
January 1, 1926 — June 30, 2003

Average Annual Return: 5.80%

Ending Value of a $10,000

Investment: $763,968

Reflects growth of the S&P without dividends

FIGURE 4-2

---

[9]Some cautions: Throughout this book, you'll see many references to the past performance of various investments over a variety of time periods. Often, these results are displayed graphically in a "mountain" chart like the one on this page. This information is intended for discussion only. Please remember that past performance is no indication of future results, and none of the charts you see here are intended to suggest that your experience will be the same.

Also, please note that although the S&P's average annual appreciation was 5.8%, in no year did it actually generate that exact return — just as no family in America has 2.3 children, although that's how many kids are in the "average" U.S. family. Choosing an investment because you expect it to earn a return based on its historical average almost certainly will lead to disappointment — or worse. So, please use all the "mountain" charts in this book solely for what they're intended: as discussion guides only.

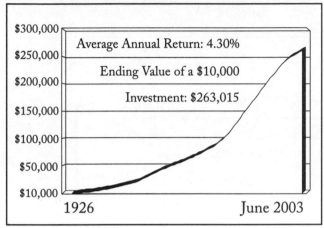

DIVIDEND INCOME OF THE S&P 500 STOCK INDEX

January 1, 1926 — June 30, 2003

Average Annual Return: 4.30%

Ending Value of a $10,000

Investment: $263,015

1926   June 2003

FIGURE 4-3

income from dividends of 4.3%. Notice how much more stable this mountain chart is compared to the first. That's because stock dividends are much more reliable than stock prices. That, in turn, is because companies control whether or not they pay dividends; they do not control their stock prices.

Therefore,

$763,958 from growth in value
+ $263,015 from dividends
$1,026,973 is your total return, right?

Wrong!

Instead of $1,026,973, you'd have $19,844,583.

How can the sum be greater than the two parts?

> **When banks pay income, it's called _interest_.**
>
> **When stocks pay income, it's called a _dividend_.**

The answer, of course, is due to the power of compounding. By reinvesting your dividends back into stocks, you own more shares, which generates more income, which generates more shares, and so on.

Thus, as we discussed earlier, the most important number is the total return, not just growth and not just dividends. No investment in this century has generated a higher average annual total return than stocks.

> **All mountain charts — those you see in this book and elsewhere — always assume dividends are reinvested, unless it says otherwise.**

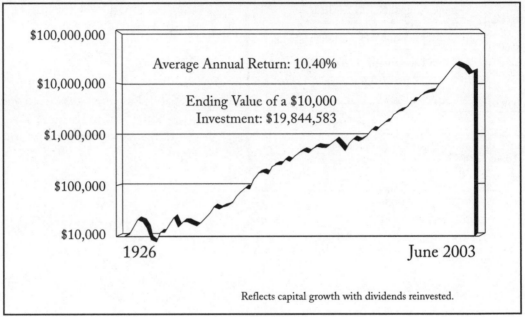

TOTAL RETURN OF THE
S&P 500 STOCK INDEX

January 1, 1926 — June 30, 2003

Average Annual Return: 10.40%

Ending Value of a $10,000
Investment: $19,844,583

$100,000,000

$10,000,000

$1,000,000

$100,000

$10,000

1926

June 2003

Reflects capital growth with dividends reinvested.

FIGURE 4-4

Benefit #3: Stocks Are a Hedge Against Inflation

By June 30, 2003, due to inflation, you would have needed $103,378 to buy what
you could have bought with $10,000 in 1926. If your money was in the stock mar-
ket, this would be no problem for you, for $10,000 invested in 1926 would have
been worth $19,844,583 by June 30, 2003, or 192 times as much as the rate of
inflation would have produced.

Benefit #4: Stocks Offer Four Tax Advantages

Let's compare the results of investing in stocks with that of investing in CDs.

Tax Advantage #1: The Tax on Stock Dividends Is Less Than the Tax on Bank Interest

If you earn interest from a CD, you pay taxes based on your ordinary income tax bracket, which could be as high as 35%. But thanks to the latest tax law change (called the Jobs and Growth Tax Relief Reconciliation Act of 2003), most stock dividends are taxed at a maximum of just 15%.

Tax Advantage #2: You Pay No Taxes on Growth Until You Sell

Interest income is taxable as ordinary income in the year it is earned. But if your stock rises in value, you pay no taxes on that growth (called a capital gain) until you sell the stock. If you hold the stock for decades, you pay no taxes for decades.

Tax Advantage #3: The Tax on Capital Gains Is Less than the Tax on Interest

Thanks to the 2003 tax law, the tax on capital gains for most taxpayers is just 15%, and for some, the rate is as low as 5%.

Tax Advantage #4: Capital Gains Pass to Heirs Free of Capital Gains Tax

Say you invest $10,000 in stocks and watch them grow to $25,000. Say you then die. Since you never sold the stocks, you never paid the capital gains tax. Say further that your kids (or other heirs) inherit the stocks. When they sell them, they will not pay a tax on the capital gains that were produced during your lifetime, either. So, the fourth break is that capital gains pass tax-free to heirs at death.

For more information on this tax break, see Chapter 63.

To summarize, the four tax benefits of owning stocks are:

1.   The tax on dividends is less than the tax for interest;

2.   you don't pay taxes on capital gains until you sell;

3.   when you sell, capital gains are taxed at a lower rate; and

4.   you can pass capital gains to heirs tax-free at death.

For more information on capital gains and other taxes, see Part IX.

Chapter 16 - Stocks: an Indication of the Nation's Financial Health — Sometimes

Buying stock is good for you, and it's good for the country, too, for it provides industry with the capital it needs to build business, which creates jobs. But owning stocks is risky, so Congress provides these tax benefits to encourage you to buy them. Still, what good are tax benefits if you lose your money in a stock that goes bust?

For example, look at Oracle Systems. In 1990, the day Oracle reported record revenues (up 54% from the previous year), Wall Street responded by knocking down the price of Oracle's stock by 31%. Why would the stock go down 31% the day the company reported a revenue gain of 54%?

The answer is that Wall Street had expected Oracle to do even better and was disappointed at the "meager" results reported by the company.

That might sound strange, but this is the most fundamental aspect of investing in the stock market, and it is in direct contrast to how you run your daily life. As individuals, we tend to focus on today. How was your day at school? When does the meeting start? How's traffic?

The TV news is great at telling us what happened today, but rarely does a news report tell us what's going to happen tomorrow.

B.C.   JOHNNY HART

By permission of Johnny Hart and Creators Syndicate, Inc.

The financial markets operate exactly the opposite. Rather than focusing on today, Wall Street looks to tomorrow. This is why the stock market is called a "leading economic indicator" as opposed to a lagging or coincident indicator.

The Three Types of Economic Indicators

Economic Indicator #1: Leading

A leading indicator tells you what is *going to happen*. For example, people who want to build homes first must apply for a construction permit. Therefore, the number of permit applications that are filed serve as a leading economic indicator, for this tells us how many homes *will be built*. If you own a lumber yard, a big increase in the number of permit applications would tell you to increase your inventory in preparation for an increase in lumber sales. Maybe you'd better hire more employees, too, to help you handle the new business. You don't need the extra inventory or staff today, but this leading indicator says you soon will.

Economic Indicator #2: Coincident

If you later learn that housing starts have increased recently, you know those homes *are under construction*, which means builders by now have bought all the lumber they need. Thus, you lumber yard owners had better stop ordering wood, for the recent wave of new business has reached its crest. Thus, construction starts is a *coincident indicator*, for it tells you *what is happening now*.

Economic Indicator #3: Lagging

And if you learned that sales of new homes have reached their seasonal high, you'd know that many homes *were built*. Thus, new home sales is a *lagging economic indicator*, for it tells you *what has happened*. If you owned that lumber yard, it's probably time to lay people off and hold a big sale to get rid of excess inventory.

It's important that you understand the concept of economic indicators, because that will help you understand the stock market. The market, as I mentioned, is a *leading* indicator. When you hear how the market "did" today, the stock market is not telling you how the U.S. economy *was*, nor how it *is*. Rather, the stock market is telling us how the economy is *going to be*, i.e., how much money Wall Street expects companies to make in the future.

These predictions generally are focused six to nine months in advance. Thus, a report that a company's stock is "up" (i.e., its price is higher than it was) doesn't mean the company is making more money today than it was yesterday. Rather, it means Wall Street expects that the company will be earning more money in six or nine months than it earns *now*. And if a stock goes "down" today, Wall Street expects the company to make less money in the future than it does today.

Because stock prices are based on the future, you cannot buy stocks based on what's happening today in business, politics, or society. Those who do soon discover they're too late. This is why you should ignore the "Buy Now!" tips often found in the personal finance press: They're constantly telling you what's hot now, but by the time you read it it's usually too late.

One of my favorite calls to my radio show occurred in mid-1991. Debbie was a sincere but thoroughly exasperated woman. "I just don't understand this!" she gasped. "When the economy was going strong in the 1980s, the stock market crashed, yet while we're in the midst of this terrible recession, the stock market is reaching new all-time highs!"

"What's going on?" Debbie demanded. "Has the financial world gone mad?"

Not at all. What Debbie didn't understand is that Wall Street talks in "future-speak." Stocks crashed in 1987, not because the economy had suddenly turned bad, but because Wall Street believed the economy was *going to become* bad.

And the recession in 1990 proved Wall Street right. Then, in 1991, as the recession reached its peak, the stock market reached new all-time highs, in direct contrast to what Debbie thought the market should do. After all, how could stocks make money in the middle of a recession?

The answer, of course, is that there's a big difference between a company's stock and the company itself. On

---

A client once called me, saying he wanted to buy stock in a certain company. When I asked why, he said the firm had just launched a new product. "I bet they're going to make a lot of money with this product," he said, "So I want to buy the stock."

I agreed with him. "You're absolutely right," I said. "You should buy the stock — last year!"

If you try to act on today's news, you're too late. Wall Street is way ahead of you, and there's little chance you'll catch up.

October 19, 1987, General Motors stock dropped 27%. But was GM any different from the day before? Of course not. Thus, you'll often discover that stock prices take on lives of their own — much to the consternation of a company's management.

I hope that by now you are beginning to understand how Wall Street prices stocks. I say "beginning" because you might have the impression, from what I've written, that the stock market works in an efficient, orderly manner. Unfortunately, it's not so simple, because Wall Street is sometimes (often?) just plain wrong, while at other times, it can't make up its mind.

In fact, an old joke says the stock market has predicted 18 of the last seven recessions — meaning that just because Wall Street *thinks* something is going to happen doesn't mean it *will* happen. Oracle is a perfect example. If Wall Street is always right, how could it have *overestimated* its projections of Oracle's profits by so much? And if Wall Street knew a recession was coming in 1991, why did it lower stock prices in 1987 — four years early? (Because its call was so premature, Wall Street was obliged to return prices to its pre-crash level, only to initiate a second price correction in the form of the mini-crash of 1989.) As a well-known money manager once told me, "I correctly called the Crash of '87, but I called it five years early."

Why aren't today's stock prices always in sync with a company's current value? Look at it this way: Say General Motors announces it is going to launch a new type of automobile — one that gets 1,000 miles to the gallon. Clearly, such a product would be fabulously popular — and GM would make a fortune. That means the value of the company would rise.

But to build this car, GM must construct a new factory that will take years and cost billions. For now, that means GM will not be making huge profits. No matter: Since investors are expecting profits to come in the future, they price the stock today as though those profits are already being realized. If GM later fails to earn that profit — say, if the technology proves faulty — GM's stock price will drop back to its former levels.

Thus, while it can take a company months or years to produce a profit, investors can price the stock today in anticipation of those profits. If investors do not believe the company will be profitable, that also will be reflected in today's stock price.

There were similar experiences occurred during the bear market of 2000-2002. During that period, there was little correlation between corporate profits and their stock prices.

Stocks Anticipate the Economy

Still, generally speaking, stock prices do anticipate both recessions and recoveries. As Figure 4-5 shows, the stock market has fallen as early as 12 months before the nation entered a recession, and regained its strength up to eight months before the rest of the nation.

While I've been using the phrase "Wall Street" both indiscriminately and in the singular, the financial markets actually consist of several hundred thousand analysts, researchers, statisticians, economists, mathematicians, computer scientists, physicists (yes, physicists), brokers, and traders from around the world — not to mention investors! So don't be lulled into a false feeling that "Wall Street" is a single unit. Not only is it not single, its players are not even homogenous. With so many people offering so many opinions, it's actually hard to believe that Wall Street is able to make any predictions with accuracy.

STOCK PRICES FALL FIRST AND RECOVER FIRST

The Dow Jones Industrial Average and Recessions

Recession Starts	Dow Peaked	Dow Lead (months)	Recession Ends	Dow Bottomed	Dow Lead (months)
Dec. 1948	May 1948	7	Dec. 1949	June 1949	6
July 1953	Jan. 1953	5	May 1954	Sept. 1953	8
Aug. 1957	July 1957	1	Apr. 1958	Oct. 1957	6
Apr. 1960	Jan. 1960	3	Feb. 1961	Oct. 1960	4
Dec. 1969	Dec. 1968	12	Nov. 1970	May 1970	6
Nov. 1973	Jan. 1973	10	Mar. 1975	Dec. 1974	3
Jan. 1980	Jan. 1980	0	July 1980	Apr. 1980	3
July 1981	Apr. 1981	3	Nov. 1980	Aug. 1982	3
July 1990	July 1990	0	Mar. 1991	Oct. 1990	5
Mar. 2001	Jan. 2000	14	Nov. 2002	Oct. 2002	1

FIGURE 4-5

Stock Market Indexes

To keep track of all these players, you need a scorecard, and Wall Street has produced lots of them. The best-known is the Dow Jones Industrial Average, which is a list (called an index) of 30 stocks, each representing a different industry. But there are more than 2,000 stocks listed on the New York Stock Exchange and more than 20,000 in the country.

If you wanted information about a group numbering 20,000, how accurate do you think your information would be if you only asked the biggest 30? Not very accurate, especially if you compared the results to a survey which asked 500, or 5,000. Obviously, the broader the base, the more accurate the data.

That's why many Wall Street professionals pay closer attention to the Standard & Poor's 500 Stock Index and the Wilshire 5000 than they do the Dow. The point is that you should not make buy or sell decisions simply because of what you hear about an index. Just because the Dow drops, for example, doesn't necessarily mean your stocks are down (unless, of course, you happen to own the same 30 stocks that comprise the index).

International Stocks

Everything we've discussed about stocks thus far has been focused on the U.S. But there's a strong case for investing in stocks internationally as well.

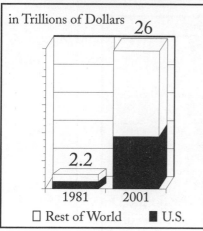

TOTAL VALUE OF STOCKS WORLDWIDE

in Trillions of Dollars

☐ Rest of World   ■ U.S.

FIGURE 4-6

In 1981, the value of all the stocks in the world was $2.2 trillion, and the United States accounted for about 50%. Today, world market capitalization is about $37 trillion, and the U.S. has only a 40% share, according to the United Nations.

Many view this as evidence of America's decline in power, but that's not the case. In 1981, the U.S. was worth half of $2.2 trillion, or $1.1 trillion. By 2001, the U.S. was worth 40% of $37 trillion, or about $15 trillion. In other words, the U.S. economy grew more than tenfold. Although its share of the world's wealth declined in percentage terms, we must keep in mind that the pie is much bigger than before.

It's because this pie is growing so rapidly that we need to place some of our investments internationally. While the U.S. economy has grown over 1,300% in the past 23 years and remains the largest in the

TOTAL VALUE OF STOCKS WORLDWIDE

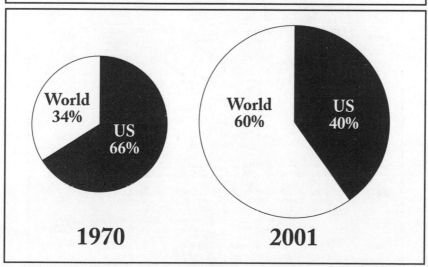

FIGURE 4-7

TOP PERFORMING MARKETS IN THE WORLD

Year	1st	2nd	3rd	4th	5th
1980	Italy +81%	Hong Kong +73%	Malaysia +63%	Austria +55%	U.K. +41%
1981	Sweden +38%	Denmark +25%	Malaysia +18%	Japan +16%	Spain +12%
1982	Sweden +24%	USA +22%	Netherlands +17%	Germany +10%	Belgium +10%
1983	Norway +82%	Denmark +69%	Australia +56%	Sweden +50%	Netherlands +38%
1984	Hong Kong +47%	Spain +42%	Japan +17%	Belgium +13%	Netherlands +12%
1985	Austria +177%	Germany +137%	Italy +134%	Switzerland +108%	France +83%
1986	Spain +123%	Italy +109%	Japan +100%	Belgium +81%	France +79%
1987	Japan +43%	Spain +38%	UK +35%	Canada +15%	Denmark +14%
1988	Belgium +55%	Denmark +54%	Sweden +49%	Norway +43%	France +39%
1989	Austria +105%	Germany +47%	Norway +46%	Denmark +45%	Singapore +42%
1990	UK +10%	Hong Kong +9%	Austria +7%	Norway +1%	Denmark 0%
1991	Hong Kong +50%	Australia +36%	USA +31%	Sing/Mal +25%	New Zealand +21%
1992	Hong Kong +32%	Switzerland +18%	USA +7%	Netherlands +6%	Netherlands +3%
1993	Hong Kong +116%	Malaysia +110%	Finland +83%	New Zealand +69%	Singapore +67%
1994	Finland +52%	Norway +24%	Japan +21%	Sweden +18%	Ireland +14%
1995	Switzerland +43%	Sweden +37%	USA +34%	Spain +28%	Netherlands +25%
1996	Russia +153%	Venezuela +131%	Hungary +107%	Poland +59%	Brazil +43%
1997	Turkey +118%	Russia +112%	Hungary +95%	Mexico +53%	Portugal +48%
1998	S. Korea +141%	Finland +123%	Greece +78%	Belgium +69%	Italy +53%
1999	Turkey +252%	Russia +247%	Finland +153%	Singapore +99%	Indonesia +93%
2000	Israel +28%	Switzerland +6%	Canada +6%	Venezuela +4%	Denmark +4%
2001	Russia +56%	S. Korea +49%	Colombia +46%	Sri Lanka +44%	Jordan +35%
2002	Pakistan +154%	Czech Republic +49%	Indonesia +43%	Sri Lanka +35%	Hungary +31%

FIGURE 4-8

world, the rest of the world has grown nearly 2,000% in the same period! As explained more thoroughly in Chapter 51, percentages are the key to your financial success, not *dollars*.

Look at Figure 4-8, which compares the percentage performance of the U.S. stock market against the stock markets of other nations. Since 1980, our market has been in the top five only four times — during the biggest bull market in our nation's history!

This is further evidence that **The Rules of Money Have Changed**, and we must respond by investing some of our money overseas.

Some people think I'm suggesting fly-by-night outfits. Quite the contrary. I'm not talking about tossing money into some jungle venture accessible by dirt roads. Rather, I'm suggesting that you invest your money in the biggest, safest, most successful, diversified, and technologically advanced companies in the world — the "bluest" of the "blue chip" stocks — the same kinds of companies you like here in the U.S. I merely suggest you do the same overseas.

It's easy to do. In fact, it's hard *not* to. For example, if you wanted to invest only in the safest, strongest, highest quality companies, and your search was limited to the U.S., you would omit:

- 7 of the world's 10 largest financial companies

- 7 of the world's 10 largest insurance companies

- 7 of the world's 10 largest utility companies

- 8 of the world's 10 largest appliance companies

- 8 of the world's 10 largest auto companies

- 8 of the world's 10 largest chemical companies

- 8 of the world's 10 largest electronic companies

- 9 of the world's 10 largest machinery companies

- 9 of the world's 10 largest banks

THE WORLD'S
LARGEST COMPANIES 2001

Only 37% are based in the United States

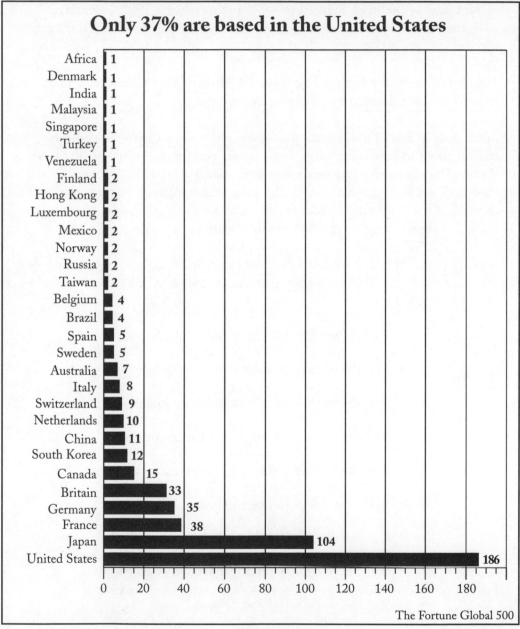

The Fortune Global 500

FIGURE 4-9

You've heard of the Fortune 500 — the largest companies in the United States. But have you looked at the Fortune *Global* 500 recently? Only 186 of them are U.S.-based companies (more than any other nation — but still only 37% of the total).

Let's talk in more practical terms. Do you use any of the products listed below?

DO YOU USE ANY OF THESE PRODUCTS?

- ❑ Alpo Dog Food
- ❑ Dannon Yogurt
- ❑ Glidden Paint
- ❑ Libby's Vegetables
- ❑ Mott's Apple Sauce
- ❑ Ponds Cold Cream
- ❑ Ball Park Franks
- ❑ Close-Up Toothpaste
- ❑ Dove Soap
- ❑ Hills Bros. Coffee
- ❑ Q-Tips Swabs
- ❑ Stouffers Dinners
- ❑ Contadina Sauce
- ❑ Frigidaire Appliance
- ❑ Ragu Tomato Sauce
- ❑ Vaseline
- ❑ Carnation Milk
- ❑ Cup-a-Soup
- ❑ Friskies Cat Chow
- ❑ Weed Eater

FIGURE 4-10

Each is manufactured by a foreign company. Don't get depressed that foreign companies sell lots of products in the U.S., though, because the U.S. does the same thing in other countries: 69% of Exxon/Mobil's sales occur outside the United States, as do 62% of Coca-Cola's, and 26% of General Motors. It is not a matter of whether you *like* being part of a global economy, only whether you'll *make money* from it.

The Risks of Investing Internationally

Say you want to own stock in Sony, the biggest consumer electronics company in the world. Sony's stock trades in Tokyo, not New York. Thus, to buy Sony stock, you must convert your U.S. dollars into Japanese yen before you can buy the stock on the Tokyo market.[10]

U.S. CORPORATIONS WITH BIG FOREIGN SALES

Company	Percent of Revenue Earned Outside the United States
Colgate-Palmolive	72%
Exxon/Mobil	69
Citicorp	68
Coca-Cola	62
Xerox	44
IBM	64
Dow Chemical	58
3M	53
Johnson & Johnson	44
Procter & Gamble	50
Goodyear	47
duPont	46
Sara Lee	42
General Motors	26

FIGURE 4-11

[10]And before some of you start yelling, "Hey! What about ADRs!", let me just say that (a) American Depository Receipts essentially make the currency conversion for you, and (b) keep in mind that this is an introductory-level book, not an intermediate-level one. So, shaaaaddup.

Therefore, you are subject not only to stock market fluctuation, which is perhaps the most well-known of all investment risks, you're also subject to foreign currency exchange rate fluctuation, which causes the value of the dollar to change relative to the yen. Should the dollar move against you at the same time the stock moves against you, your losses can be twice as bad as they otherwise would have been. Figure 4-12 shows the dual impact of changes in stock prices and currency prices. Thus, even if the stock makes money, you still could lose money if the dollar moves against you.

COMBINING CURRENCY CHANGES WITH INVESTMENT RETURNS

If the total return based on foreign currency is this...	...but the change in the foreign currency vs. the U.S. dollar is this...								
	20%	15%	10%	5%	0	-5%	-10%	-15%	-20%
	...then the total return for the U.S. investor (in U.S. dollar terms) is this:								
20%	+44%	+38%	+32%	+26%	+20%	+14%	+8%	+2%	-4%
15%	+38%	+32%	+27%	+21%	+15%	+9%	+4%	-2%	-8%
10%	+32%	+27%	+21%	+16%	+10%	+5%	-1%	-7%	-12%
5%	+26%	+21%	+16%	+10%	+5%	0	-6%	-11%	-16%
0%	+20%	+15%	+10%	+5%	0	-5%	-10%	-15%	-20%
-5%	+14%	+9%	+5%	0	-5%	-10%	-16%	-19%	-24%
-10%	+8%	+4%	-1%	-6%	-10%	-15%	-19%	-24%	-28%
-15%	+2%	-2%	-7%	-11%	-15%	-19%	-24%	-28%	-32%
-20%	-4%	-8%	-12%	-16%	-20%	-24%	-28%	-32%	-36%

If a foreign stock you own rises 15%, but that nation's currency falls 15% against the dollar, your total return would be -2%.

FIGURE 4-12

HOW TO CALCULATE U.S. RETURNS FROM A FOREIGN INVESTMENT

$$\text{Your Return} = \left[\frac{\text{Ending Value of Currency in U.S. \$}}{\text{Beginning Value of Currency in U.S. \$}} \times \frac{\text{Ending Value of Investment in Foreign Currency} + \text{Dividends, Interest, or Distributions}}{\text{Beginning Value of Investment in Foreign Currency}} \right] - 1.00$$

FIGURE 4-13

The Weak Dollar vs. Strong Dollar

You often hear that "the dollar is down" or "the dollar is up." What exactly does that mean, and is it good news or bad news?

The dollar going down against a particular foreign currency means that the foreign currency now buys more dollars than before. This makes it cheaper for foreigners to buy U.S. investments and products. The dollar going up is just the opposite: Like inflation, it causes foreigners to pay more for U.S. products and it lowers their returns from U.S. investments.

So is a declining dollar good or bad? Again, it depends.[11] If you are an American consumer buying a product made overseas, a declining dollar is bad, for it will cost you more dollars to buy that item. But if you are an American manufacturer who sells products overseas, the declining dollar is good, because your product is cheaper for foreigners to buy, and thus your sales are likely to increase.

This is why the government finds it so difficult to develop and execute monetary policy. If the administration supports a strong dollar, foreigners will not invest in the U.S. (which upsets U.S. business and Wall Street), but foreign goods become cheaper (which pleases U.S. consumers). That dynamic explains why the President (any president) cannot make everybody happy.

---

[11]Sorry.

Chapter 17 - Three Ways to Buy Stocks

You can buy a given brand of toothpaste at any number of retailers, but the stock of a given company is only available at one place — the stock exchange where it's listed.

And although you can go to any retailer to buy that toothpaste, you cannot buy the stock directly. Instead, you must ask someone who holds a federal securities license to buy it for you (with one exception we'll cover in a moment).

The first thing to understand is that all stocks have two prices, not just one. There's a price you pay to buy a stock, and a price you receive when you sell it. The difference is the "spread."

Understanding The Spread and Other Fees

The spread, which all stock investors pay, is the fee charged by the trader who executes the order that your broker placed for you.

Say you ask a broker for the price of a stock and he replies, "Ten, ten and a quarter." He means that someone who buys the stock will pay $10.25, while someone who sells the stock will receive only $10. The difference — 25 cents — is pocketed by the trader.

Most brokerage firms also have annual account fees, transaction fees, and other costs. At least one national firm charges a $4.50 fee each time you trade, while another levies a $50 charge when you close your account.

Investors are willing to pay these fees because they believe their profits will outweigh the costs. If you pay fees totaling 3% of your investment, you must earn 3% just to break even. Thus, you must consider costs as you invest.

Not long ago, I ran into an old friend of mine. He was one of the sharpest brokers I ever worked

> **In defense of brokers everywhere, please observe this rule of etiquette: Do not ask for advice from full-service brokers, then buy their recommendations from discount brokers to save money. It's rude.**

with — he once won the National Options Trading Championships — and he told me he had just created a new computer model for trading in options. Options are a (usually) speculative form of derivatives where huge trading costs usually require significant profits just to break even. (This is why most brokers who trade options do it for their clients instead of themselves. Clients may or may not make money, but the brokers are certain to profit from the commissions.)

Anyway, my friend told me that mathematical tests of his model, using historical market data, showed he would have made incredible amounts of money. Thus, my friend was now looking for investors to help him finance the further development of his model.

"What do you need investors for?" I asked. "Why don't you just start trading for real?" And he replied, "Because my model doesn't take commissions into consideration. Once I do, the trading costs are so high that I can't figure out how to make money with this thing!"

Remember that when people brag about how much money they're making, they're often not calculating their performance after fees. Remember, it's not how much you make, but how much you keep that counts!

Method #1:   Brokerage Firms

If you need help deciding what stock to buy, you need the services of an advisor. Brokers at the major national brokerage firms provide this service. They are paid commissions when you buy and sell shares — typically 1.5% of the investment amount. And that's each way, meaning you pay 1.5% when you buy a stock and another 1.5% when you sell it, for a total cost of about 3% (sometimes more, sometimes less, depending on how many shares you are buying, the price of each share and how frequently you trade; prices vary from firm to firm).

"The Broker's Creed: Never in doubt, sometimes in error."
—**Anonymous**

Method #2:   Discount Brokers

If you know what you want to buy and all you need is someone to get it for you (execute the trade), you can save money by turning to a discount broker, whose commission fees will be less — maybe a lot less. Discount brokers do not provide investment advice, nor do they provide you with a specific representative. Instead, you'll get a toll-free phone number or a web address for you to use when placing an order, like buying from a catalog.

Method #3:   Buying Stocks without a Broker

There's only one way to buy stocks without going through a licensed broker, and that's by buying your shares directly from the company that offers the stock.

It's called a Dividend Reinvestment Plan, and it's available from about 1,000 companies — typically large ones like IBM and General Motors. There are two advantages to DRPs: Buying shares is usually free or very low cost (because no broker is involved) and the company will reinvest your dividends into more shares, usually for a small fee. (Brokers generally cannot reinvest stock dividends for you.)

But DRPs have their problems, too.

Five Disadvantages of DRPs

If you know you want IBM stock, you can buy shares directly from IBM. There are disadvantages, however:

- Many DRPs still require you to execute transactions via U.S. mail, which takes time;

- restrictions usually apply, such as the amount you are permitted to invest;

- not all companies offer DRPs;

- many DRPs are beginning to charge fees, negating the primary benefit of using them; and

- you are forced to work individually with each company whose stock you buy, and the paperwork can become overwhelming. The same is true for the tax-reporting and record-keeping requirements, often making DRPs more trouble than they're worth compared to simply working with discount brokers.

There are many more problems with DRPs and DRP investing, which I cover more extensively in *The New Rules of Money*. Still, if you want to purchase DRPs, you can find information about the companies that offer them on the Internet and at your local library.

Chapter 18 - Real Estate Investing

Real estate allows you to diversify your investments beyond the "paper" markets of stocks and bonds into hard or "real" assets. There is one clear advantage, as you can see from Figure 4-14:

Real estate is much less volatile than stocks and bonds.

The reason is simple: It's easy to sell paper assets (just phone your broker), but selling real property takes a great deal more time. This reduced liquidity helps stabilize prices in the real estate market.

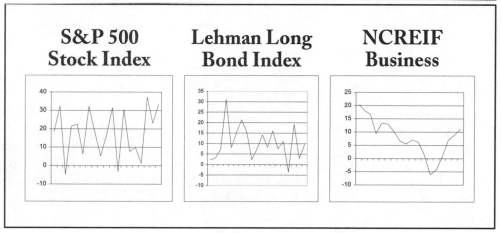

VOLATILITY OF ANNUAL RETURNS
1979 – 2002

S&P 500 Stock Index

Lehman Long Bond Index

NCREIF Business

FIGURE 4-14

But stability is a double-edged sword: While prices are more stable than stocks and bonds, your ability to get out of a bad investment is equally reduced. That means you could be stuck with a property you don't want, but which you can't sell — leaving you stuck with the carrying costs in the meantime (such as mortgages, taxes, utilities, maintenance, repairs, and security). All these negatives make real estate a very risky investment, and one to engage in only after you already own cash, bonds, and stocks (or mutual funds of bonds and stocks), and even then only if you have the financial (and emotional) resources to withstand a worst-case scenario.

So why buy real estate? Like stocks, real estate can produce income and grow in value, and those can be reasons enough to invest.

But forget about real estate's oft-cited third benefit: tax savings. The truth is that there aren't any long-term tax advantages to owning real estate that you don't also get from stocks. While it's true that owning investment real estate allows you to depreciate the property, depreciation only increases your ultimate capital gain. As for the deductions you get from all the expenses you incur from owning and maintaining the property, realize also that each dollar in deductions saves you only 20 or 30 cents in taxes. You're still losing 70 or 80 cents in the process. So if you're going to buy real estate, do so for income and growth, not tax benefits.

The biggest problem with real estate is that buying it is not a simple prospect. It takes a lot of time to select the right property, and the settlement process is cumbersome and time-consuming. Rental property also requires a large cash outlay, often beyond the ability of most investors. And let's not forget the Hassle Factor.

The Hassle Factor

You'll never get a phone call in the middle of the night because something went wrong with the stock you own, but people who own rentals face all kinds of management problems. You have to find tenants, which takes time and costs money, and then you must hope your tenant pays rent on time and doesn't trash the place. You'll get phone calls at odd hours because the heater's not working or the refrigerator has gone bad. So get ready, because buying a rental means you become a *landlord*.

You Need Strong Cash Reserves If You Own a Rental

Investors who own rental properties should maintain at least 12 months' worth of the rental's mortgage payments in cash reserves, in case the tenant fails to pay rent. Here's the worst case I've seen:

A client owned a rental property, and the tenant didn't pay rent. In his state, eviction couldn't occur for 90 days. On the 89th day, the tenant filed for bankruptcy, which stopped the eviction procedures. The bankruptcy lasted nine months, during which time my client was unable to evict the tenant (who still was not paying rent).

Finally, after a year and again facing eviction, the tenant vanished, and my client discovered that he had taken with him the washer/dryer, refrigerator, and dishwasher. There were holes in the walls, cigarette burns in the carpet, and broken doors. All told, my client had to spend $10,000 on repairs before he could rent the house again. This took two more months, for a total of 14 months with no rental income, plus $10,000 in repair costs.

I cite this story not to dissuade you from owning rental property, for many people do so with great success. My point, rather, is that bad things can happen, and as with all financial planning, you need to be prepared for the worst (and then hope it never happens!).

So, if you're going to invest in real estate, you need to buy several properties (for diversification). Make sure they are income-producing properties, to reduce your monthly cash outlays and to provide you a hedge against the risk that the properties might fall in value instead of grow. Don't buy raw land, and never borrow money to invest in real estate.

Your Home Is Not a Real Estate Investment

By the way, your home is not an investment. It's a place to live. Therefore, you should buy your home because you love the house, you can afford it, and it is close to schools, shopping, work, and relatives — not because you think the house will grow in value.

If your home's value does increase, that's only a coincidence, and you can congratulate yourself on your good fortune, not for your investment acumen. Homes are not *expected* to grow in value beyond the rate of inflation — unlike stocks, which are expected to grow faster than inflation. Besides, when you move, the next house you buy will cost more, so the fact that yours grew in value will be meaningless in real economic terms.

Think I'm wrong about the future value of your house? Look at Figure 4-15, which shows the average home value in the United States from 1982 to 2002. It shows that home values have grown an average of 4.4% per year, compared to inflation, which has averaged 3.7% during the same period.

Still, many a homeowner has been known to make the claim, "My house is the best investment I ever made!" What utter nonsense. Whenever I find someone who says that, I find that (a) their home is the *only* investment they ever made or (b) they don't live in any of the many parts of the country where real estate values have not enjoyed excellent growth.

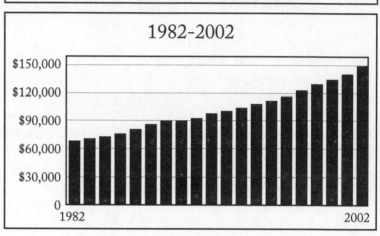

Average Home Values

1982-2002

FIGURE 4-15

Even if you were lucky enough to live in areas where homes have grown in value, your home has still failed to be "the best investment" ever.

Consider the facts: Say you bought your home in January 1990 for $250,000 and sold it in June 2003 for $600,000. Wow! That represents a gain of 140%. Anybody would have to admit that that's a pretty darn good return. But was it really? During the same period, the Dow Jones Industrial Average grew from 2590 to 9188 — a gain of 255%. Thus, the stock market performed even better than the real estate market.

So why does everybody think real estate is the greatest investment?

The answer is found not in the asset , but in the way it's financed. When you bought that $250,000 house in 1990, you didn't pay cash. Instead, you put down only $50,000 and borrowed the rest. Thus, you watched your $50,000 cash investment produce a profit of $350,000 — and *that's* a total return of 600% — far outpacing the measly 255% earned by the stock market.

But this is not being fair. You were willing to buy your house with borrowed money, but you would never buy stocks with borrowed money. Yet if you did, your stocks would have performed just as amazingly as your house!

In other words, it wasn't the real estate that produced those returns, it was the *leverage*. You borrowed somebody else's money, paid them a small amount for the privilege, and then invested it for huge profits. Lots of stock investors do that all the time (it's called a margin account) and it's highly speculative, because you must repay the loan even if the stocks go down in value.

As I explain in Chapter 59, I have no problem when clients borrow money to buy a home (except when buying rental property). Why? Because your home is not a real estate investment. Rather, it's a place to live.

Never Borrow Money to Invest in Real Estate

If you're going to invest in rental property, pay cash for it.

This is heresy to real estate investors, who know that fortunes are made through leverage. You buy a townhouse for $100,000 with only ten grand in cash. Then, after you get a tenant to pay rent equal to your mortgage payment, you wait for the property to appreciate. When the townhouse's market value hits $150,000, you borrow another $30,000 from the increased equity and use that money to buy three more $100,000 properties — using $10,000 as down payments for each one. Rent each as before, and after each property gains an additional $50,000 in value, you sell out, pocketing a cool $250,000 — on your original $10,000 investment!

Of course, that's assuming things go according to plan. But life has a way of not cooperating. Perhaps the best illustration comes by way of my client, Jason.

Jason bought a house for $150,000. As the market took off, he watched the value of his home grow in just two years to $300,000. Thus, Jason decided to buy more real estate to cash in on all the profits. "The money's just waiting to be made!" he gushed.

Jason, who had borrowed $120,000 to buy his first house, obtained a home equity loan for $100,000 more and used it to buy a $200,000 townhouse. Jason's monthly mortgage payment on the rental was $650; add taxes, insurance, and maintenance and repairs, and Jason discovered that he needed to charge $900 in rent just to break even on his costs. No problem; finding a tenant would be as easy as placing an ad in the classifieds.

Or so he thought. After six weeks, Jason finally rented his property for $700 — $200 less than his monthly expenses. (He didn't know that rental properties are routinely vacant 25% of the time.) He covered the mortgage out of his own pocket during this time.

But Jason was not worried about his "negative cash flow." He figured, "I'm getting tax benefits here, so I'll recover some of the losses on my tax return." Besides, he added, "with the house growing in value so rapidly, I'll more than make up the difference."

Then his tenant failed to pay rent one month, and the next month's check bounced — which caused Jason's mortgage check to bounce. Jason got rid of the tenant, but he remained liable for the rental's mortgage payments as well as those on his own home. He was fast running out of cash, so Jason found himself with a choice: Either sell the property or risk defaulting on the rental's mortgage. If the latter occurred, it would ruin his credit rating. Reluctantly, Jason chose to sell the property.

Unfortunately, the economy had turned. The result: Jason sold the townhouse for $180,000 — $20,000 less than he had paid. Factoring in his expenses (not to mention the 3 a.m. phone calls because the furnace was not working), Jason lost more than $25,000.

That's why you should buy investment properties for cash: If you lose your tenant, at least you have no risk of defaulting on a mortgage.

This is also why you must add and maintain at least 12 months' worth of rental income to your cash reserves for each property you own, just in case your investment doesn't go according to plan.

Chapter 19 - Collectibles

Collectibles include coins, stamps, artwork — even 1960s-era lunch boxes! One of my clients collects Japanese swords, another, comic books and baseball cards. Collectibles consist of all kinds of things (including the newest craze, SpongeBob SquarePants).

The most commonly discussed advantage to collecting is anonymity. With no government supervision or reporting mechanism, no one knows what you buy, the price you pay, or when you sell. This is quite different from dealing with registered securities: When you sell stocks and bonds, the IRS is informed about the transaction.

> **As a professional advisor, I remind you that tax law requires you to declare capital gains on the profits you earn when you sell collectibles. However, the burden of honesty is on you.**

The Four Problems with Collectibles

Assuming you do pay taxes on your profits, what's the big deal in owning collectibles? Sure, they can grow in value, but so can every other equity investment — stocks, real estate, even gold. And if growth is your sole motivation (excluding love for your collection), I challenge you to find any collectible that earned more money in any given time period than the best stock of that same period.

So don't kid yourself: You're not going to find instant wealth through collectibles. But what you will find are four problems.

Problem #1: No Buyer Protection

The anonymity of collecting can work against you. If you want to buy stock, you are guaranteed your trade will occur at the fair market value. But if you buy a piece of art, who's to

> *"I started out with nothing. I still have most of it."*
> —**Michael Davis**

say you're paying a fair price? And who's to say you're getting the original and not a worthless copy?

Indeed, the FBI estimates that 60% to 90% of all sports memorabilia sold to collectors are forgeries. One client of mine, an avid collector, told me that the only way to be certain your collectible is genuine is to watch the celebrity sign it.

But if everyone follows this strategy, you'll never find a buyer when you're ready to sell!

Problem #2: You Are Responsible for Safekeeping

If your collectible gets damaged or lost, the value is gone. You don't have to worry about that when you buy stock.

Problem #3: Lack of Liquidity

You can sell your stock virtually whenever you want. But who's to say you'll find someone to buy your record collection?

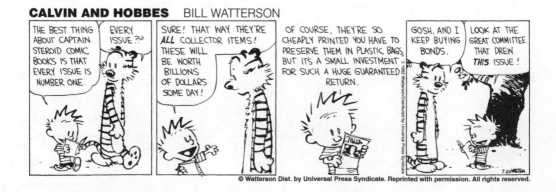

CALVIN AND HOBBES   BILL WATTERSON

Problem #4: You'll Never Sell

Yet the biggest problem with investing in collectibles is best demonstrated by one of my clients, a wine collector. At our first meeting, he gave me a list of his assets, including his $40,000 wine collection. When I asked, "When do you plan to sell your wine?" he replied, "Sell it? I'm going to drink it!"

Well, if he's going to drink it, it's not an investment! And that's the attitude I find among collectors. They fall in love with their collections. They won't sell any of it. People generally don't get too emotionally attached to their Treasury bills, but they do get attached to their Spiderman comic book signed by artist Sal Buscema.

Here's the bottom line: If you want to be a collector, recognize that it is a very high-risk venture. To succeed, you must approach it like a hobby. How do you know which coin is most likely to grow in value? Which baseball card is the best buy, or fairly priced? Like any hobby, you need to get immersed in the subject. You can't just go to a weekend card show and pick up something, or you could get ripped off: You'll pay $15 for something worth only $5. You must be serious about what you are doing.

And be especially wary of buying collectibles on the Internet. The Internet Fraud Complaint Center, established by the U.S. Justice Department, logged more than 75,000 complaints in 2002 — and 65% of those pertained to Internet fraud. These statistics represented a three-fold increase from the previous year, and the FBI says the frequency of fraud continues to rise.

Still, if you are serious — and careful — you can have fun with collectibles. But over the next 20 years, I'm not sure you'll make any more money than if you were to just buy stocks and stock mutual funds instead.

Chapter 20 - Hedge Positions

You may have noticed that this book is devoid of exotic investments, also known as speculation. That's because I'm not one to recommend that you engage in speculative trading activity, or that you buy overly risky investments.

However, as we discussed in Chapter 14, a speculative investment might succeed for the very reason a safer investment fails. Therefore, to protect the safer investment, we also should own some speculative ones. Let's examine the risks your investments could face and how speculative investments might protect you against them.

Risk #1: Inflation

We saw in Chapter 14 how inflation directly hurts bonds, because inflation causes interest rates to rise, and rising rates cause bond prices to fall. Gold, though itself a very speculative investment, tends to rise with inflation, and thus can be an effective hedge for your investment in bonds.

Risk #2: Deflation

The opposite of inflation, prices decline during periods of deflation. Why object to price declines? Because incomes and market values decline, too. So even though milk might cost less, making it easier to get by on your reduced paycheck, you'll still find yourself stuck with the same mortgage payment — because that fixed figure won't change. And if you think you'll just sell the house if your paycheck drops to the point where you can't afford the payment, think again: Due to deflation, the house might be worth less than what you owe on it.

> *"When you bet on a sure thing — hedge!"*
> —Robert Half

The most effective hedges against deflation are bonds, dividend-paying stocks and cash.

Risk #3: Recession

Another potential problem is recession, a period in which the economy is not growing. During recessions, stocks and bonds fall in price. However, some recessions have been brought on by shortages (real or perceived) in consumable goods. In those cases, while stock and bond prices fell, gasoline prices rose, as did the prices of many other commodities. Therefore, maintaining a position in natural resources — such as oil & gas, minerals, forest products, and others — makes sense. You can buy these types of investments in a variety of ways, such as through mutual funds, stocks of companies that operate in these industries, and even directly through commodities trading.

Risk #4: Lack of Confidence

In Chapter 5, you learned that consumers believe issuers when they say that stock and bond certificates have value. But if consumers were to lose that faith, paper assets would not be worth the, uh, paper they're printed on. Therefore, it makes sense to possess hard assets as a hedge against paper ones. The most common hedges are real estate, gold, and other precious metals.

> **Sorry, jewelry doesn't count. The markup prohibits you from selling at a profit, and most jewelry is not investment grade. Like a home, buy jewelry because you love it, not because it's protecting your Treasuries.**

Risk #5: Collapse of the Dollar

When the dollar dumps, you'll be glad you own foreign stocks and currencies, which you can do directly or through mutual funds.

Risk #6: Stock Market Crash

If you think the stock market is going to go down — or if you just want to protect yourself in case it does — consider two strategies: selling short (defined in Chapter

23) or options trading (discussed below). Although a complete discussion of options is beyond the purpose of this book, you should be aware that options can be defensive. Following is one such example.

How to Boost Your Stock Returns While Lowering Your Risk

Options are derivatives, which most people think are highly speculative. While many derivatives gamble fortunes in all-or-nothing stakes, there are some that actually increase safety. Such is the case with an options strategy called Covered Call Writing.

CCW is a conservative strategy designed to reduce risk and increase income when investing in stocks. Briefly stated, stock options are contracts in which you buy or sell the right to buy or sell. (Read that again; it sounds redundant, but it isn't.)

Although there are eight types of options contracts, we're interested here in low-risk "Covered Call Writing." Here's how it works: Say it's August and you buy 300 shares of XYZ stock at the price of $48 per share. XYZ pays a quarterly dividend of 50 cents per share. Therefore, if the price never moves, you'll earn 4.2% per year.

At the same time, you would participate in Covered Call Writing. To do so, you would "write three January 50 Calls." This means you are selling ("writing") the right for someone else to buy the stock from you (they can "call" it away) between now and the third Friday of January at the specified price of $50. (All contracts expire the third Friday of the month.)

Each contract represents 100 shares, hence three contracts. The buyers pay you a fee (called a "premium") of $3.50 per share, or $1,050. (The premium is based on the amount of time until expiration and the spread between the current price and the "strike price," in this case $50. Therefore, the premium changes constantly.)

> *"There are two times in a man's life when he should not speculate: when he can't afford it, and when he can."*
>
> —Mark Twain

Assuming you don't cancel, only two things can happen next: The contract will get exercised (meaning your stock will be sold as agreed for $50) or it will expire worthless in January. Either way, you keep the $1,050.

Let's look closer at what happens in each case.

If the option is exercised:

Naturally, no one would exercise an option to buy your stock at $50 if the price stays at $48. Therefore, the buyer of the option is betting XYZ will rise above $50 by late January. If it does rise, say to $53, he can buy your shares for $50 and immediately sell them for $53, profiting $3/share.

If this happens, you've sold them for $50, $2 per share more than what you paid for them. That's a gain of $600, or 4.2%. Add the $1.00/share in dividends you received, plus the $3.50/share premium, and you've made 13.5% in less than six months. Total annualized return: 27%.

If the option expires:

If the price fails to climb above $50, the options will not be exercised. Therefore, you will still own the stock in February. Then you sell another option, and earn another $1,050. Keep repeating this process and, including dividends, your total annual return will be 18.75%.

Clearly, this strategy can yield big rewards. Among the advantages are: 1) you are establishing a profitable sell price the day you buy the stock. If exercised, you are guaranteed a profit; 2) you reduce risk because the premium in effect reduces the price you paid for the stock; and 3) your annual yield is boosted far above that of the dividend alone.

However, there are other considerations. For one, you are limiting your potential profits. No matter how high the stock rises, you won't sell for more than $50. You can solve this problem by buying your option back, in effect canceling it out. You would do this if you later think the stock will dramatically rise and you don't want to miss the gains to be made. (This is "buying a January 50 call.")

Also, you have not reduced the risk that your stock may drop in price. The only certainty is, should XYZ drop $25, your option will not be exercised — a small consolation. To protect yourself, you may "buy a January 45 put" giving you the right to sell your stock for $45 ("put" it to someone else). This is the opposite of what we've reviewed here, and is designed to minimize losses, rather than protect gains.

Because of the potential for price drops, you should choose a high quality, blue-chip stock that fits your budget, and which offers a stable trading range, solid fundamentals, high dividends, and good growth potential.

Keep in mind the figures shown exclude commissions, which will reduce your total return. Also, dividend and option income is taxable.

Covered Call Writing is not a reason to own stocks, but the strategy might be of help if you already own them. Prior to opening an account, you must receive and are urged to read "Characteristics and Risk of Standardized Options," which is published by the Options Clearing Corporation in cooperation with the NASD and all major U.S. stock exchanges. The booklet is available from any broker or financial advisor.

ric's money quiz

Here's a chance to see how well you learned the information contained in Part IV – Equities. Don't worry if you get stumped — just re-read this part until it sinks in. Remember, your financial future depends on it.

The answers are at the end of the quiz. No peeking!

1. **You should pay close attention to the performance data provided in this book because:**

   ○ a. that's how you'll learn to make money in the future
   ○ b. past performance is the best way to judge investments
   ○ c. the data helps explain concepts under discussion
   ○ d. there is no reason to focus on performance data

2. **The stock market is a:**

   ○ a. leading economic indicator
   ○ b. lagging economic indicator
   ○ c. coincident economic indicator
   ○ d. none of the above

3. **People invest in stocks despite the risks because stocks:**

   I. can grow in value
   II. often pay dividends
   III. offer a hedge against inflation
   IV. offer tax advantages
   ○ a. I only
   ○ b. I and II
   ○ c. I, II and III
   ○ d. I, II, III, and IV

4. **$10,000 invested in the S&P 500 Stock Index back in 1926 would be worth this amount by June, 2003:**

   ○ a. $2,000,000
   ○ b. $6,000,000
   ○ c. $12,000,000
   ○ d. $20,000,000

5. In the past 10 years, how many times has the performance of the U.S. Stock Market ranked among the top 5 world-wide?

- ○ a.   once
- ○ b.   four times
- ○ c.   seven times
- ○ d.   all 10 times

6. Of the 500 largest companies in the world, what percentage are based in the U.S.?

- ○ a.   76%
- ○ b.   37%
- ○ c.   12%
- ○ d.   95%

7. If the dollar weakens (goes down), the value of foreign investments owned by U.S. investors:

- ○ a.   goes down
- ○ b.   goes up
- ○ c.   stays the same
- ○ d.   there is no direct correlation

8. To be successful buying collectibles:

- ○ a.   you must be a hobbyist
- ○ b.   you need lots of money
- ○ c.   you must hire a broker
- ○ d.   you need no special knowledge

9. Investors who own rental properties should maintain at least how many months' worth of mortgage payments in cash reserves?

- ○ a.   6
- ○ b.   12
- ○ c.   3
- ○ d.   18

10. Hedge investments can protect you against which of the following risks?

I.   recession
II. collapse of the dollar
III. stock market crash
IV. inflation

- ○ a.   I and II
- ○ b.   II and IV
- ○ c.   I, II and III
- ○ d.   I, II, III, and IV

Answers: 1-c (pg.116)   3-d (pg.116)   5-b (pg.128)   7-a (pg.134)   9-b (pg.140)
           2-a (pg.122)   4-d (pg.117)   6-b (pg.131)   8-a (pg.147)   10-d (pg.149)

Part V
Packaged
Products

There's a quiz at the end of this part!

To see how much you already know, skip to the
end of this part and take the quiz now. Then, read
the part and take the quiz again. You'll discover
how much you've learned!

Part V — Packaged Products

Chapter 21 - The Four Problems You Encounter When Buying Investments

In Parts III and IV, we learned about the many types of investments that are available to you. In this part, we're going to revisit those investments, but in a slightly different way. Why? Because although many of the investments we've discussed are neat ideas, buying them is sometimes easier said than done. Let's examine why.

Problem #1: Lack of Affordability

Many of us don't have $10,000 to invest — let alone a quarter million. You might have only $25, and try finding investments you can afford with that amount — or a broker willing to help you.

Because of what investments often cost, millions of people avoid the investment world. By not buying stocks and bonds, though, companies have trouble raising the cash they need to build factories, which in turn would create jobs and boost the economy. Thus, lack of affordable investments not only is a problem for investors, it's a problem for our nation.

Problem #2: Limited Liquidity

Perhaps you like the idea of investing in a Ginnie Mae,[12] and you've got the $25,000 needed to buy it. But say you later need $2,000 unexpectedly. This would present you with a problem, for you can't sell a piece of your Ginnie Mae; you'd have to sell the whole bond. So, although investments are liquid, they're not as flexible as savings accounts.

---

[12]See Chapter 8.

Problem #3: Inability to Achieve Diversification

It's a lot safer to own dozens of stocks instead of just one or two, but buying many stocks requires lots more money than you might have to invest.

Problem #4: You Have Little or No Assistance

Even if you do have the money to buy shares of many stocks, which will you choose? With more than 20,000 stocks and hundreds of thousands of bonds available, which should you buy? And once bought, when should you sell? If you're like most people, you'd be better off hiring a professional money manager to make those decisions for you — if you could afford one.

Chapter 22 - How to Beat the Four Problems

In the Crash of '29, the problems cited in the previous chapter became so overwhelming that millions of investors fled the markets, leading to the Depression. To bring individual investors back, Congress needed to fix the four problems, cited in Chapter 21, and it did so with the Investment Company Act of 1940.

> **Be sure you read the previous chapter before you read this one.**

The Act allowed Wall Street to create new kinds of companies. The sole purpose of these new companies was to allow consumers to invest — in other companies! Individuals buy shares in these investment companies, which then hire managers to buy dozens of stocks and bonds. The profits (or losses!) of each company are then distributed to their respective investors on a pro-rata basis. So, if an investment company has assets of $1 million, of which $5,000 is yours, you would receive 5,000/1,000,000^{ths} of the profits or losses. That's all there is to it.

INVESTMENT COMPANIES ARE POOLS OF MONEY

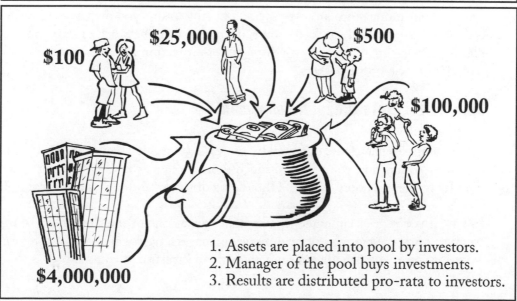

$100

$25,000

$500

$100,000

$4,000,000

1. Assets are placed into pool by investors.
2. Manager of the pool buys investments.
3. Results are distributed pro-rata to investors.

FIGURE 5-1

The Four Benefits of Investment Companies

Thus, you can beat the four problems cited in Chapter 21 by investing in investment companies. By doing so, you'll enjoy these benefits:

Benefit #1: Affordability

You can join most investment companies with as little as $100, and you can add to your account whenever you want, with amounts as little as $25. Investing in stocks and bonds is now within reach of almost everyone.

Benefit #2: Your Money Is Liquid

Since you own shares of the investment company instead of owning individual stocks or bonds, you can sell pieces of your investment any time you wish, simply by selling your shares of the investment company. Thus, if you've invested $5,000, you can sell, say, $200 if that's all the cash you need at the moment. You can't do that with individual securities.

Benefit #3: Diversification

Placing your money into an investment company means you own a small piece of hundreds of individual stocks or bonds instead of just one stock or one bond. Like placing 12 eggs in 12 baskets, you have better protection against something going wrong with one of the baskets.

Benefit #4: Professional Management

Investment companies are operated by professional money managers, and if you are like most Americans, you will earn much more money by relying on their expertise than by trying to choose from the thousands of stocks and bonds all by yourself.

In fact, if you've ever lamented the fact that you, as one of the "little guys," can't compete with the big institutional money managers, now you can: Just hire one to work for you — by placing your money with an investment company.

Chapter 23 - The Most Common Type of Investment Company

You're a lot more familiar with investment companies than you may realize. Although the Act created three types of investment companies, the most common is an *open-end fund*, which you know under its more familiar name, "mutual fund."

That's right: Plain ol' mutual funds are really investment companies, and this explains why mutual funds have become the most popular way Americans invest. (It also explains why the previous chapter's description of investment companies sounded so familiar.)

When the law was created in 1940, 68 funds existed, with a total of $400 million in assets. Today, more than 8,200 funds hold more than $7 trillion in assets, according to the Investment Company Institute. Yet, the irony is that nobody reading this book owns a mutual fund. In fact, no investor anywhere owns a fund. No one has, and no one ever will.

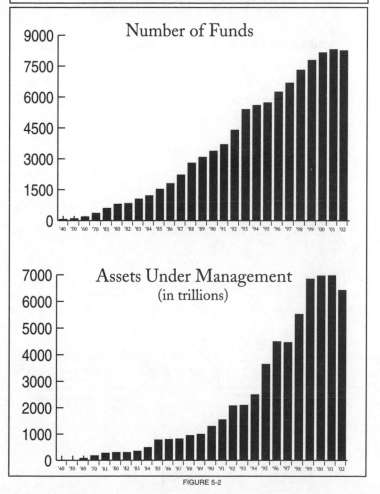

THE SOARING POPULARITY OF MUTUAL FUNDS

Number of Funds

Assets Under Management
(in trillions)

FIGURE 5-2

Mutual Funds Are Not Investments

Rather, mutual funds simply are a *method through which people invest*. People call my firm all the time asking, "What are your mutual funds paying?" The truth is that mutual funds don't "pay" anything!

People also say, "I don't like mutual funds because they're risky." But there's no such thing as a "risky" fund. Nor has anyone ever lost money in a mutual fund. Mutual funds are not good, and they're not bad.

A mutual fund, in fact, is merely a mirror — a reflection of something else. Thus, if you invest in a mutual fund that invests in stocks, you own stocks, and you are as likely to make money or lose money as any other person who invests in stocks.

In fact, you can use mutual funds to buy virtually any kind of investment: stocks, bonds, government securities, real estate, gold and other precious metals, international securities, foreign currencies, natural resources, hedge positions, even CDs and money markets. You can find funds that engage in virtually any type of trading activity, including options and futures contracts, derivatives, and even selling short.[13]

Technically, mutual funds are called "open-end" investment companies because they forever buy and sell their shares. In industry jargon, mutual funds "sell" shares to the public (and they will do so forever, because they have an unlimited supply of shares to offer), and when you want your money back, the fund will "redeem" them for you (and they will accept redemptions forever — or, rather, for as long as there are shares to redeem).

---

[13]Short-selling is a bet that a given stock will decline in value rather than rise. When selling short, the potential gain is limited, but potential losses are unlimited — making short-selling extremely speculative.

© Tribune Media Services, Inc. All Rights Reserved. Reprinted with permission.

The price of a fund always equals the value of whatever it owns.

The price is called the NAV, for net asset value. (If it seems obvious that the fund's NAV[14] would equal the value of the fund itself, stay tuned; you'll later discover another type of investment company where this is not true.)

The Biggest Myth About Mutual Funds

When you mention the words "mutual fund," most people think of stocks. But the truth is that mutual funds do not always invest in stocks. In fact, many mutual funds invest in government bonds — either U.S. or municipal. If this surprises you, revisiting our earlier manufacturing lesson (Chapter 5) should help you understand.

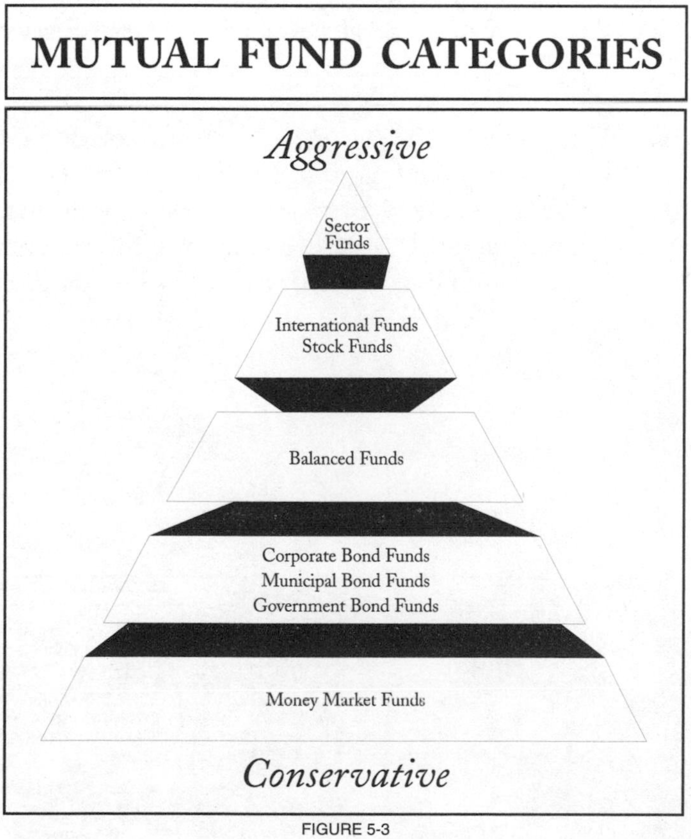

MUTUAL FUND CATEGORIES

Aggressive

Sector
Funds

International Funds
Stock Funds

Balanced Funds

Corporate Bond Funds
Municipal Bond Funds
Government Bond Funds

Money Market Funds

Conservative

FIGURE 5-3

---

[14]That's en-ay-vee, not nah-v.

Like any manufacturer, Wall Street seeks to make products that consumers will buy. Above all else, what do most people want from their investments? *Safety*. Since government bonds are the safest investment, consumers seek them above all others — which is why Wall Street manufactures so many government bond mutual funds.

Yet you rarely hear about government bond funds. All those financial magazines and investment newsletters brag about the "Hot Mutual Funds to Buy Now," but only the riskiest of investments (stocks, gold, real estate, international securities, and other equities) can achieve such lofty returns. And sure enough, when you look at the lists of top performers, the riskiest funds are almost always the ones listed. Thus, for many people, mutual funds have become synonymous with stocks, even though stock funds represent only a portion of the mutual fund universe.

Today, more than 400 companies, called *fund families*, sponsor mutual funds. Each family typically offers 20 or 30 funds, although the largest families offer 200 funds or more. In most families, the choices range from very conservative to very speculative. Let's look at these basic fund categories one by one, starting with the lowest risk category.

The charts that follow represent the average performance of all mutual funds in the category, for the 10-year period ending June 30, 2003, according to Morningstar as reported by Ibbotson Associates, and assuming reinvestment of dividends and ignoring taxes. In keeping with my goal of teaching you fundamental concepts rather than trying to get you to buy a specific fund, this book will not recommend any fund by name.

NON SEQUITUR   WILEY

U.S. Government Securities Funds

There are 313 U.S. Government Securities Funds that have at least a 10-year track record, according to Thomson Financial. For the 10 years ending June 30, 2003, the average annual return of these 313 funds is 5.96%; $10,000 would have grown to $17,478. Look closely at Figure 5-4: Can you see the Bear Market of 2000–2002?

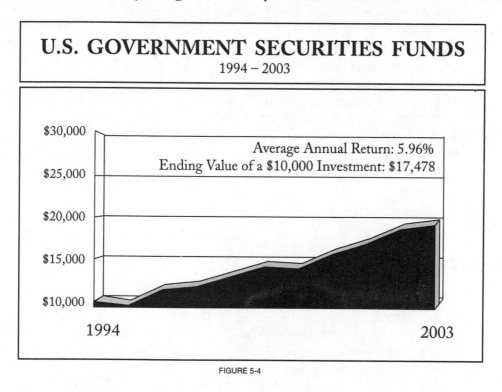

U.S. GOVERNMENT SECURITIES FUNDS
1994 – 2003

Average Annual Return: 5.96%
Ending Value of a $10,000 Investment: $17,478

$30,000
$25,000
$20,000
$15,000
$10,000

1994   2003

FIGURE 5-4

Of course not — the stock market's decline did not hurt government bonds!

Just as there are several types of government securities, there are several types of government securities funds as well, including:

- **Ginnie Mae funds**. Ginnie Maes are the most popular of all government bonds, so it follows that Wall Street would offer funds that invest exclusively in them. These are typically the highest yielding government funds, with equally high volatility due to interest rate risk.

- **Adjustable Rate Mortgage funds**. These feature lower yields and lower volatility.

- **Zero-Coupon funds** (also known as "Target Maturity" funds). These funds only buy zero-coupon bonds.

- **Intermediate funds**. Treasuries bought by these funds typically mature in three to seven years.

- **Short-Term funds**. These buy Treasuries that mature in less than three years.

- **Ultra-Short funds**. These buy high-grade securities that mature in less than one year, and often in less than six months.

- **Global Government funds**. These funds buy bonds from governments around the world. If rates are rising in the U.S. but falling in England, the British bonds could be the better investment, and these funds can buy accordingly. Watch out for currency risk in addition to interest rate risk.

"If you put your money where your mouth is, you will look very funny to other people."
—Winston Groom

Municipal Bond Funds

The next step up in risk takes us to municipal bonds. The average rate of return for the 257 muni bond funds that existed for the 10 years ending June 30, 2003, was 5.14%; $10,000 would have grown to $15,870. Like before, the collapse of the dot-coms is invisible on this chart.

Muni funds include:

- **Money Market funds**. These funds are a tax-free alternative to bank savings accounts.

- **Single-State funds**. These funds invest exclusively in the bonds from one state, so that investors who live in those states can avoid state income taxes as well as federal income taxes. (Other muni funds buy bonds from many states, forcing investors to pay state income taxes on their interest. Single-state funds avoid this problem — but their yields often are less. You must calculate the taxable equivalent yield [Chapter 9] to determine which is best for you.)

- **Puerto Rico funds**. As a territory, not a state, obligations of Puerto Rico are obligations of the federal government. Thus, the interest is free of state income taxes as well as federal income taxes, and all Puerto Rico G.O.s carry a AAA bond rating. But Puerto Rican bonds are burdened with an unfair reputation, which forces Puerto Rico to offer higher interest rates — to entice investors to buy what are perceived to be "riskier" bonds than those available from the states. It's silly (maybe sad), and smart investors can take advantage of this discrepancy — especially those who live in states which do not exempt the interest on their own bonds.

- **Insured Muni funds**. All the muni bonds in these funds carry insurance from MBIA, AMBAC, or another insurance carrier.

- **High-Yield Muni funds**. It's almost an oxymoron that a government-guaranteed bond can be considered "junk," but Wall Street frowns on states which are not prudent with their finances. Most of the bonds in these funds are revenue bonds, which carry no government guarantees. Still, defaults are rare, and the extensive diversification helps further to reduce the risk.

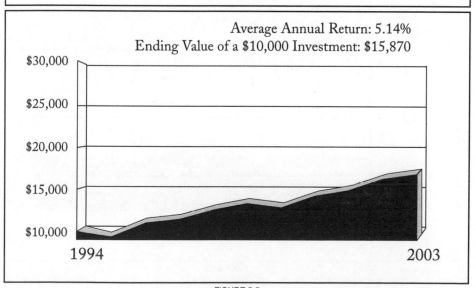

FIGURE 5-5

High-Yield Corporate Bond Funds

Next, we find 100 high-yield corporate bond funds with a 10-year track record; the average annual return is 5.1%, meaning $10,000 would have grown to $15,572. There are three kinds of corporate bond funds:

- **Short-term** and **Intermediate funds**, both of which buy high quality bonds; and

- **High-Yield funds,** which buy long-term bonds of low quality (i.e., junk).

In my opinion, junk bond funds were created for only one reason: so Wall Street can make money selling them. Their primary selling point is the yield, but this contradicts Edelman's Rule #1: Never, never, never, never, never, never, never chase yield.

Those who chase yields *always* get what they deserve.

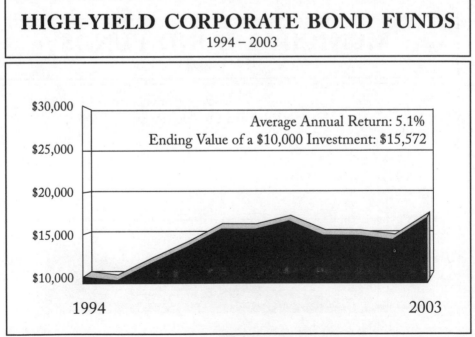

FIGURE 5-6

The History of Yield-Chasing

Ever since your granddaddy was a little boy, bank accounts never paid more than 5%. In fact, for most of the 20th Century, banks paid only 2% or 3%. There was virtually no difference in rate from one bank to another, and thus few options for savers.

Until 1974, that is, when Congress deregulated money rates and allowed the securities industry to create money market funds. (Banks were prohibited from offering these new products.)

As interest rates climbed with inflation in the late '70s, these new money funds began to offer rates as high as 14%, and consumers flocked to them. For the next six or seven years, savers enjoyed the high rates and safety offered by these money funds, and Americans slowly became spoiled — even dependent — on them.

By the early '80s, as interest rates started back down, so did the money fund yields. As rates dropped to 8% (only half as good as before but still much higher than banks), yield-addicted consumers longed for the "good old days" of the inflationary '70s.

> **For millions of investors, Ginnie Mae funds were a lesson learned too late. For others, it was a lesson not learned at all.**

Seeing the demand, Wall Street offered the first U.S. Government Securities mutual fund. By investing primarily in Ginnie Maes, the highest yielding government security, investors were dazzled with yields once again around 13%. Thus, as money fund yields dropped, investors switched their assets into Ginnie Mae funds. What could be wrong with that? These savers had been using money funds ever since they were created, and nobody had lost money. (Like bank accounts, money funds feature a stable NAV of $1; since the share price never moves, all the fluctuation is in the yield, which changes daily.)

While there was little practical difference between savings accounts and money funds, this was not true when savers moved from money funds to Ginnie Mae funds. And few were prepared emotionally or financially for what was about to happen.

As we learned in Chapter 14, Ginnie Maes (like all bonds) rise in value when interest rates are falling. And that's what happened in the early- to mid-'80s. Interest rates fell from 1980 to 1986. To restore their fallen yields, owners of money funds switched to Ginnie Mae funds, where they got back their higher yields, along with the added bonus of capital gains (which occurred because interest rates continued to drop). Thus, everyone was happy.

Until 1987.

By then, long-term rates, which had reached their low of 7%, began climbing upward. As rates went higher, so did the yields on Ginnie Maes. But as you know by now, yield doesn't tell the whole story. So although the yields grew, the value of Ginnie Maes fell. By 1988, U.S. Government Funds were facing negative total returns — investors actually were losing money in what they thought were "government-guaranteed" investments!

To boost this declining performance, some funds began trading in options in a futile effort to artificially boost the yield, but as rates continued to rise, this only increased their losses. Thus, the fun and easy profit of government bond funds was gone, and having realized the limitations of these investments, Wall Street stopped trying to make them something they weren't.

Government bond funds became dull, boring investments, with good but not great yields, and a new emphasis on maintaining a stable NAV. That was fine for savvy investors who knew how to separate good investments from bad, but what about the yield-hungry neophytes?

Never one to pass up a sale, Wall Street came through once again, this time with corporate bond funds. As we learned in Chapter 11, yields on AAA-rated bonds are similar to the yields of government bonds, while junk bond yields are much higher to compensate investors for the higher risk.

Thus, Wall Street didn't bother creating funds that consist of bonds issued by Ford and General Electric. What would be the point? With little risk of default, yields on those bonds were about the same as Treasuries. Since investors weren't happy with the yield available from government paper, they certainly wouldn't be interested in the yield of high-grade corporates, either.

But junk bonds were another story. Because these companies had one foot in bankruptcy court, they offered investors obscenely high yields — 18% was common. Armed with these great yields, junk bond funds hit the market in 1987 (with euphemistic names like "High-Yield" instead of "junk") and attracted huge amounts of money in very short periods. Once again, everything went well — until interest rates started rising again in 1989. But this time, it was worse than the two earlier episodes of rising rates.

In the past, losses were incurred only because of interest rate risk. This time, though, investors had to contend with credit risk in addition to interest rate risk. When interest rates rose, the increased borrowing costs forced many companies out of business, and investors found themselves holding worthless bonds. While a holder of government bonds can ride things out until rates come back down or until the bonds mature, owners of junk bonds enjoy no safe harbor. When the companies went broke, the bonds defaulted and investors discovered their money was gone. That had never happened with their bank accounts or their government bond funds.

Needless to say, the yield-chasers fled junk bond funds, most of them never to return. But where did they go?

You can find the yield-chasers hanging around one of Wall Street's latest enticements: *collateralized mortgage obligations*. CMOs, at one point the hottest product on the Street, are *derivatives*, because they owe their existence to (are "derived from") something else. In a CMO, Wall Street literally "invents" a security, much the same way the government invented mortgage bonds in the '60s.

It's one thing to create a bond backed by mortgages (since the mortgage itself is backed by a house — an appreciating asset), but it's quite another to create a bond where the collateral is of less certain value. Indeed, some amazing things have been collateralized over the past decade. Like automobile loans.

NON SEQUITUR WILEY

Did you see the *60 Minutes* report a few years ago about Denver's default on some industrial development bonds? *60 Minutes* interviewed a retired widow who had invested her life savings — $40,000 — in these bonds. The bond's yield was 18% (at a time when bank accounts were paying 8%) before they went bust. So *60 Minutes* put this teary-eyed widow on TV, and she won the sympathy of everyone watching.

Except me, for this lady didn't always have tears in her eyes. Earlier, her eyes were filled with dollar signs. When her broker offered those high-yielding bonds to her, her only question was, "How many can I get?"

Well, she got all she wanted — and as much as she deserved.

I know this sounds cruel. I know there's a lot more to the story, such as the fact that the broker should not have let her place such a high percentage of her net worth

It works like this: A bank issues thousands of auto loans, holding each car's title as collateral (if the borrower fails to pay, the bank repossesses the car.) A bank packages together thousands of these loans, then sells the package to Wall Street. Since the interest rates for auto loans typically are higher than mortgage rates, Wall Street can re-sell them to investors at higher yields than mortgage bonds.

That sounds okay in theory, but these products are so new that nobody knows for sure what will happen if borrower defaults exceed expectations. You could find mutual funds owning a lot of cars.

Even more bizarre are derivatives that secure credit card debts. By doing with credit card balances what they did with auto loans, this version of a Wall Street CMO touts the highest yields available (since credit cards charge 18% to 21%), but look out below!:

- there's no collateral to go after, should cardholders default on their debt and

- nobody knows what will happen when interest rates rise (will it force a new wave of defaults?)

The bottom line: Stay tuned for a replay of the junk bond market.

Those who spent the last 15 years chasing yields have had a rocky ride — far rockier than their counterparts in the stock market. And that's the irony: The yield chasers wanted safety above all else, and safety is the one thing they never got. But investors in the stock market, who gave up the holy grail of safety, enjoyed higher returns and much less volatility — even considering the Crash of '87 and the bear market of 2000–2002.

Remember, if you chase yield, you deserve what you get.

into one investment; that the city of Denver had a responsibility to bring to the market only bonds that were viable; and that inflation and its attendant higher costs of living forced her to seek higher returns so she could pay her bills.

I'm aware of all that. But I'm equally aware, having worked with thousands of individual investors, of two other points:

First, *she was greedy*. Nothing else can explain why she would place all her money into those bonds. Investing some money, even a lot of money, was the fault of an overly aggressive salesman. But all her money could only be her own greedy fault; and

Second, *it's your money, honey*. Despite the promises a broker might make, you are ultimately responsible for your actions, and you are the one who must live with the results.

Like I said, I know this sounds cruel. But sometimes, life is.

If you insist on buying junk bonds, please at least buy them through mutual funds. When the widow's story broke on *60 Minutes* (see sidebar), my colleagues and I (naturally) reacted with the same horror as the rest of America.

We quickly analyzed our clients' mutual funds to learn if any of them owned these bonds, and we discovered that one of the funds we'd recommended to clients did own these bonds. However, our initial shock quickly evaporated. Why? Because the fund had $8 billion in assets, with several thousand bonds in the portfolio. The Denver bonds represented two-tenths of one percent of the portfolio, which meant that when the bonds defaulted, a given client's account which had been worth $10,000 was now worth $9,980.

And that's not all. Despite the default, the fund's dividend had remained intact because all the other bonds in the portfolio were unaffected by the Denver bonds' collapse. Thus, the fund earned in the month of the default only two-tenths of a percent less than it should have earned. Thus, our clients who owned this fund didn't notice that they owned the Denver bonds, nor that the bonds had defaulted, because they owned a highly diversified bond fund instead of just one bond.

Thus, while the widow should not have bought junk bonds in the first place, life would have been much kinder if she had at least put her life savings into a fund of junk bonds. That way, if one bond were to default, she would have been insulated.

By the way, can you see the dot-com blowout in Figure 5-6? Not yet! We're still dealing with the bond market, and it was the stock market that fell.

Balanced Funds

Of all mutual fund categories, the next is the most unique and the least understood of all — and a favorite of mine and my colleagues. Unlike mutual funds that invest exclusively in one asset class or another (such as government securities funds or stock funds), a balanced fund invests a portion of its assets into each of the four major asset classes: cash and cash equivalents, government securities, corporate bonds, and corporate stocks. Thus the name "balanced": The theory is that if one asset class were to fall in value, another would rise to compensate, thus giving you a "balanced" rate of return.

Because balanced funds do not place all their assets into any one asset class at any one time, they generally are considered to have the lowest level of risk of all mutual funds. But be careful when selecting a balanced fund: Fewer than 400 exist, although many more claim the title. Funds similar to balanced funds are:

- **Asset Allocation funds**, which allow the fund manager to move between asset classes, often without limitation. Some invest in foreign stocks, bonds, currencies, and precious metals, in addition to the four traditional asset classes of a balanced fund. (True balanced funds, by contrast, must maintain certain minimums in the basic four asset classes at all times.) Asset allocation funds can be surprisingly volatile, for the manager is able to make aggressive "bets" as to which asset group is poised to do best. If he bets wrong, you've got a problem.

- **Growth and Income funds**, which split the assets between only two assets groups (stocks and bonds) instead of all four. Generally, these funds make more money in good times and lose more in bad times than balanced funds, but their average returns over long periods are not very different.

- **Equity Income funds** create the most confusion. People often choose these funds for diversity, thinking they are getting stocks (*equity*) and bonds (*income*). Actually, that's not what the title means; "Equity" indeed means "stock," but "income" in this case means "dividends," not "bonds." Thus, these funds buy stocks which pay dividends (as opposed to stocks which do not pay dividends). These funds are not nearly as diversified, or as low in risk, as you might think.

For the 10 years ending June 30, 2003, balanced funds averaged 7.6%; $10,000 would have grown to $20,143. Take a close look at Figure 5-7. You can see the bear

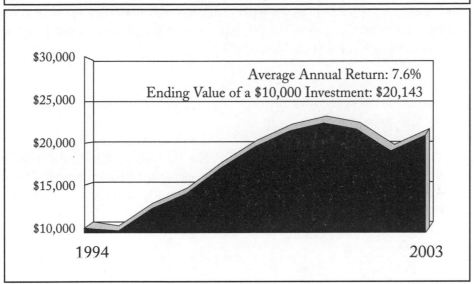

BALANCED FUNDS
1994 – 2003

Average Annual Return: 7.6%
Ending Value of a $10,000 Investment: $20,143

$30,000

$25,000

$20,000

$15,000

$10,000

1994

2003

FIGURE 5-7

market of 2000–2002, because balanced funds have a portion of their assets in stocks, and that portion got walloped.

Stock Funds

The average rate of return was 8.4% for the 1,250 stock funds that existed for the 10 years ending June 30, 2003; $10,000 would have grown to $21,977. On Figure 5-8, the 2000–2002 bear market is easy to spot, isn't it?

The Crash's dramatic effect on stock funds forces us to recognize that most well-known of all risks: market risk. As you know, and as the chart confirms, stocks and stock funds are very sensitive to this risk.

Types of stock funds include:

- **Large Cap (for capitalization) funds** buy stocks of large companies (those that are worth a lot of money). Companies such as General Motors and Colgate-Palmolive are unlikely to go broke, and that makes them safer than other stocks (at least in terms of default risk), but they are less likely to score huge percentage increases in profits in short periods.

- **Small Cap funds** buy stocks of smaller companies. Such lesser-known firms have a greater risk than large caps of going broke, but they have greater potential for profit, too.

- **Dividend Yield funds** (also known as Equity Income Funds, discussed earlier) buy stocks which pay dividends. Close cousins are Rising Dividend funds, which buy stocks whose dividends are expected to increase.
- **Option Income funds** sell option contracts against the stocks they buy. This strategy boosts the fund's income above that generated by dividends alone, but

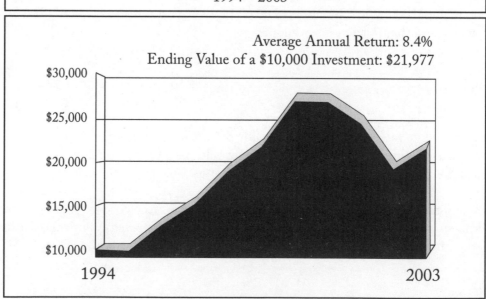

FIGURE 5-8

it also places a ceiling on the potential gains the fund can earn in any particular stock. (See Chapter 20 for a description of how these options work.)

- **Sector funds** buy stocks of only one industry, such as airlines, health care, or the Internet. These are extremely speculative, for Wall Street can be very harsh to individual sectors even when the overall market is rising.

- **Index funds** attempt to replicate a market index such as the Dow Jones Industrial Average or the S&P 500. (To learn why I hate index funds — and especially those modeled after the S&P 500, read Rule 36 of *The New Rules of Money* and Chapter 13 of *Discover the Wealth Within You*.) A new breed of index fund — Exchange Traded Funds — trade on a stock exchange. These let investors buy and sell during the day, to capture intra-day prices.

International Funds

The 284 international stock funds have averaged 5.0%; $10,000 would have grown to $16,288.

Types include:

- **Global funds** buy stocks from nations throughout the world.

- **International funds** buy stocks from all nations except the United States. Choose these (instead of global funds) when you also buy a U.S. stock fund, to avoid creating redundancy in your portfolio.

- **Single Nation funds** buy stocks from only one country.

- **Regional funds** buy stocks from a single continent or region, such as Europe, the Pacific Rim, or Latin America.

- **Sector funds** buy stocks of specific industries from foreign nations.

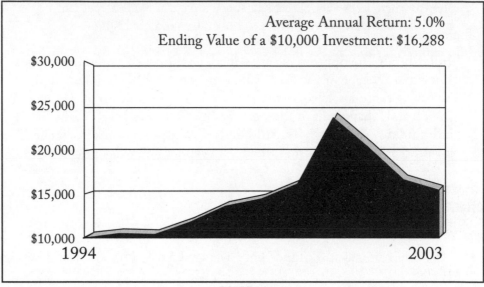

INTERNATIONAL FUNDS
1994 – 2003

Average Annual Return: 5.0%
Ending Value of a $10,000 Investment: $16,288

FIGURE 5-9

Never Invest in Funds That Exclusively Buy Foreign Bonds

Although you also can find international funds that buy bonds, they are a bad bet. Bonds are supposed to be safer than stocks, but buying foreign bonds subjects you to the same foreign currency risk as foreign stocks. Thus, if you're willing to expose yourself to foreign currency risk, you might as well give yourself the opportunity to enjoy the potential gains, and that means you should choose stocks when investing overseas, not bonds.

Indeed, some of the most ironic investments in the market are international government bond funds. With the pitch of buying bonds issued only by the strongest governments in the world, these funds appeal to conservative investors, yet they gyrate wildly in the foreign currency markets.

Chapter 24 - Closed-End Funds

The second product created by the Investment Company Act of 1940 was a *closed-end fund*. Unlike open-end funds, which offer an unlimited number of shares forever, closed-end funds sell only a certain number of shares, like seats in a stadium. Shareholders who wish to sell cannot return their shares to the fund like mutual fund owners. Sellers instead must seek buyers on the New York Stock Exchange.

This accounts for the most fundamental difference between open-end and closed-end funds: Because you sell your shares to another investor instead of the fund, the price is determined by negotiation. And that means the price agreed upon could be different from the fund's actual NAV.

And, in fact, it usually is. Closed-end funds routinely trade 10% to 20% below their NAVs. This is not a criticism of such investments, simply a fact. But what is a criticism is the sales pitch that I've heard brokers use to get people to invest in closed-end funds.

"You can get $10,000 worth of stock for just $8,000!," is how the pitch goes, with the implication that one day the fund will trade at the net asset value of $10,000, giving the investor a profit of $2,000.

The pitch would be fine if it was true, but it's not. It's normal for closed-end funds to trade at discounts, and because it is unlikely for them to rise to their NAV, it is unethical for brokers to suggest otherwise. It is also foolish to buy these funds on such assumptions.

Many closed-end funds invest in foreign countries, which means they face more risks than open-end stock funds, including both currency risk and — because they invest in only one country — sector risk.

Chapter 25 - Unit Investment Trusts

The final product created by the Investment Company Act of 1940 was the *Unit Investment Trust*. UITs were created to solve a problem faced by the Act's other two types of funds: the absence of a maturity date.

Remember that those who own individual bonds can avoid interest rate risk simply by holding their bonds until maturity, at which time they will receive back 100% of their investment, regardless of the current level of interest rates.

But owners of the Act's first two investments (mutual funds and closed-end funds) do not have that luxury. Because they own funds containing hundreds of bonds instead of individual bonds themselves, there is no single maturity date. Thus, when one of the bonds in the portfolio matures, the portfolio manager uses the money to buy another bond. Therefore, open-end and closed-end funds never mature, and the only way to get your money back is to sell your shares. This means you are always subject to interest rate risk.

This problem is solved by UITs. Here, the manager buys hundreds of bonds, as do its fund cousins. But here, each bond is selected for similar maturity dates and interest rates. Thus, when a given bond matures or is called, your pro rata share of the proceeds is returned to you. Thus, while you can sell at any time (subject to interest rate risk as with the others), you also have the ability to wait for the UIT to mature.

That's the good news about UITs. The bad news is that while mutual funds and closed-end funds offer the triple benefits of diversification, professional selection, *and* professional management, UITs feature *only* diversification and professional selection. There is no professional management, for once the bonds are purchased they simply are held until maturity.

Chapter 26 - Wrap Accounts a.k.a. Private Money Management

Wrap accounts are an attempt to solve the conflict of interest problem that pervades Wall Street. After all, since your broker earns a commission every time you trade, is he telling you to sell XYZ and buy ABC because it's good for you, or good for him? Investors lie awake at night fretting over this question.

Wall Street's first solution was private money management. Instead of taking recommendations from your broker, your broker would take instructions from a professional money manager, to whom you would pay a flat fee of 3% per year. The manager would issue buy/sell recommendations to your broker, who would execute the transactions as before.

This eliminated conflict of interest because the broker did not order trades but merely executed them, and since the money manager earned the same fee whether he ordered many trades or few, he had no incentive to trade unnecessarily.

But this solution created a new problem: In addition to paying your broker 3% per year for executing trades, you were now also paying 3% to your money manager. You had to earn 6% just to break even!

Enter the *wrap account*.

Introduced in the early 1980s and now routinely available from every brokerage and financial planning firm in the country, wrap accounts offer the same private management and trade execution as before — but for much less cost. (Typically, the manager gets 60% of whatever fee is charged, and the brokerage firm shares the remaining 40% with the broker.) The minimum account size is usually $100,000, although some require $500,000 or $1 million. Often, investors with larger amounts can negotiate lower fees.

Wrap accounts make sense for the same reason that mutual funds do: Most investors would be foolish to try investing on their own because of their lack of experience, knowledge, or the time that's required to achieve success. It's often equally foolish to blindly accept the recommendations of a stockbroker, who often is little more than a salesperson on commission. (Remember, stockbrokers are hired by brokerage firms to *sell*, not to *analyze*, and asking most brokers to manage a stock portfolio is like asking a car salesperson to repair a transmission.)

But asking your broker to help you find qualified managers, whether they work at a private money management firm or a mutual fund, makes perfect sense. In fact, placing your money with a mutual fund is the same as using a private manager. After all, who do you think manages a mutual fund? A money manager, of course! And just as private managers give part of their fees to brokers and planners, funds do as well.

Of course, there are differences between funds and private managers. For one thing, you can't brag to your friends on the golf course that you, *humph*, "hired" a mutual fund. After all, any soul with a hundred bucks can do that. But most private managers require a minimum of $100,000, so the mere mention that you've hired a manager carries with it the implicit statement that you're, *ahem*, RICH!! And while mutual funds simply send you quarterly statements in the mail, private managers often give you a gold-embossed leather binder with your name on it. *Wah hoo*! If you're lucky, they may even buy you dinner. *Hubba Hubba*!

But aside from these differences, you'd be hard pressed to find any other material differences between so-called "private" managers and those who manage regular ol' mutual funds.

The Wrap vs. Fund Debate

If there's little difference, why are firms encouraging their brokers to sell wraps instead of funds?

The answer can be traced to the Crash of '87. Before then, wraps were little used. But investors in the Crash's aftermath, worrying whether stocks will continue to fall, *simply stopped trading*.

And when investors stopped trading, brokers and their firms stopped earning commissions! This soon plunged the nation's brokerage firms into a severe recession, well ahead of the rest of the country.

But brokers who had placed clients into wrap accounts were sitting pretty. Although trading activity was reduced dramatically, the wraps were still earning their daily fee of 0.008219% (that's 3% per year).

Soon, all brokerage firms saw the light: By moving clients into wrap accounts, they were assured of collecting management fees whether clients traded or not, whether markets crashed or not. Indeed, fees have proved to be a much more stable source of revenue than commissions, and Wall Street is jumping on the bandwagon.

If you don't believe me, try this little test: Call a brokerage firm and ask the receptionist to connect you to the best broker in the firm. He'll say okay, then connect you to the *Broker of the Day* (the one randomly assigned to receive all incoming calls that day). When the Broker of the Day answers, say, "I have $10,000 to invest in stocks for the long term. What do you suggest?"

Odds are high she'll recommend a stock mutual fund, since you can't buy many individual stocks with just ten grand. Ask her to mail you information, then hang up.

Thirty minutes later, ask a friend to do the same thing with the same firm. When they get connected to the same broker, have your friend say the following: "I have $100,000 to invest in stocks for the long term. What do you suggest?" Odds are high that this same broker will now suggest a wrap account.

The push toward managed accounts, as wraps are technically known, is being endorsed by Wall Street regulators. Long concerned by the conflict-of-interest issue, regulators have made it clear that they prefer a compensation model that does not reward brokers for trading.

Despite this well-intentioned attitude, there are many reasons why wrap accounts are of questionable value.

11 Reasons to Avoid Wrap Accounts

If a fund was good enough for the client with $10,000, why is it not good enough for the one with $100,000? "Because mutual funds are for little investors," the broker will answer. "You don't need them when you've got large assets."

Yet just the opposite is true, because the more you invest, the less mutual funds cost (as we'll see a few pages from here). Therefore, it can be argued that *small* investors are the ones who are ill-suited for funds, not *large* investors, because small investors pay higher fees.

Proponents of wrap accounts also claim that investors can influence a wrap manager's selection decisions. Thus, if you don't want to invest in tobacco companies, you can tell your manager to avoid those stocks. In a mutual fund, since your money is commingled with everyone else's, you do not have this opportunity.

But I don't see this as an advantage. After all, you're hiring the manager to buy stocks for you because you lack the expertise. Why, then, would you want to tell the manager what to include or exclude? It doesn't make sense!

If these reasons aren't enough to make you reconsider the use of wrap accounts, here are nine more reasons why wraps are not preferable to mutual funds:

1. **You can't easily track your performance** until your manager sends you a statement, something most do only four times a year. But mutual fund prices are published in newspapers every day, and all are available via the Internet 24/7, making your monitoring efforts much easier.

2. **Wrap accounts incur huge paperwork and tax reporting requirements**. Every time your manager buys or sells a stock, you get a confirmation in the mail. This makes for one massive IRS Schedule D when you prepare your tax return. Mutual fund owners do not have these problems, for the trading is an internal function of the fund and does not require paperwork to the client.

3. **The wrap fees you pay are rarely tax-deductible.** To try to get a tax break, you must itemize wrap fees as a miscellaneous deduction on Schedule A, and deductibility is allowed only to the extent that total Schedule A expenses exceed 2% of your Adjusted Gross Income. As a practical matter, this means most investors cannot deduct their wrap fees. Mutual fund owners do not have this problem, though, because fund fees are built into the NAV. Therefore, fund fees automatically translate 100% into lower capital gains taxes when you report sales on Schedule D. Wrap account holders get nothing without a lot of work — and even with the work, they still often get no tax benefits.

4. **There are no standard reporting requirements for wrap accounts.** Although managers are supposed to comply with AIMR Performance Measurement Standards, they are not legally required to do so. Some managers report their performance before fees are deducted, while others report performance for only certain portfolios or clients. Both tactics distort the truth, and investors can find it difficult to compare one manager with another. This problem does not exist

for mutual funds, which must comply with Securities and Exchange Commission rules regarding value and performance calculations.

5. **The SEC has found that most wrap account managers do not seek "best execution" on behalf of their clients.** By law, money managers have a fiduciary responsibility to the client, meaning they must place the client's interests ahead of all others. One obligation is to execute trades via brokers who offer the lowest commissions. But this rarely happens; managers almost always place their trades with the broker who brought them the account.

   The SEC also has noted that many wrap accounts are nothing more than "unregistered mutual funds," and it has proposed rules that will force many wrap accounts to either substantially change the way they operate or get out of business.

6. **You get one heckuva lot of mail,** as your broker sends you paperwork every time a trade is executed in your account. You'd better keep, sort, and organize all of it if you hope to be able to prepare your taxes accurately.

7. **You must sign a contract** that could be difficult to terminate if you decide to cancel. Many contracts require you to pay hefty fees if you cancel, or levy other restrictions you usually don't find with mutual funds.

8. **Wrap accounts earn no more than mutual funds.** No less, either. That's because most wrap accounts are managed by the same folks who operate mutual funds — it's all the same product in a different wrapper (no pun intended); and

9. **Wrap accounts are expensive.** Paying 3% per year is an exorbitant cost for professional advice — especially compared to mutual funds, as we'll see next.

For more on this issue, see Chapter 9 of *Discover the Wealth Within You*. And, please, think carefully before you invest in a wrap account.

Chapter 27 - Mutual Fund Charges and Expenses

There are two types of charges assessed by mutual funds: the *annual expense ratio* and the *sales charge*. Most investors don't notice these fees because they never write a check to pay for them, and the costs do not appear on statements. Instead, fund share prices are reduced by the fee(s). To see what the fees are of your fund, read page two of the fund's prospectus.

The Annual Expense Ratio

All mutual funds charge an annual fee to their shareholders, called the annual expense ratio. It is through this fee that funds recover their operational, administrative, and management costs. The fee ranges from 0.2% of assets to 12%, but most funds charge 1.5% to 2.5% each year. Like all fees, the annual expense ratio is assessed daily. Thus, if the expense ratio is 2% per year, the fund will deduct 0.005479% from the share price each day.

Because of the fee, funds actually earn more than they say they earn. That's because they report the results after they deduct the annual expense ratio. All funds operate in this manner.

The Four Types of Mutual Fund Loads

In addition to the annual expense ratio, many funds also feature a sales charge, or "load." There are four kinds:

Sales Charge #1: Front-End Load

Also known as Class A shares, or up-front load, you pay a fee when you invest. Unlike the expense ratio, which is paid every year, a front-end load is paid only once, when you invest money. There is no fee for reinvesting dividends or capital gains, and you can withdraw your money at any time without charge (at the then-current value, which may be higher or lower than when you invested). Although the legal maximum is 8.5%, virtually all equity funds charge 5.75% or less, and almost all bond funds charge 4.75% or less.

If you invest $100 in a Class A fund, you pay the load, and if you invest another $100 next month, you pay another load — but only on the new deposit; the money already in the account is not charged a second time.

So don't bother trying to invest $100 today and $10,000 tomorrow, hoping to avoid the fee on the second deposit. That trick won't work. In fact, on Wall Street, no trick ever works — so please forget about trying to out-clever the system. You won't succeed.

Furthermore, front-load funds offer several discounts:

- **Breakpoints** essentially are volume discounts; the more you invest in one fund family, the lower the load. While an equity fund's maximum charge might be 5.75%, discounts often start at $25,000. Big discounts typically apply if you invest $100,000, $250,000, or $500,000, and most funds waive their loads entirely for those who invest $1 million or more.

- **Letter of Intent.** If you open an account today with a small amount but plan to invest more within the next 13 months, you are entitled to the breakpoint today, thus giving you a discount on today's investment even though you have not yet invested enough money to actually qualify for it. (If you fail to fulfill your LOI, the fund will retroactively collect the higher fee from your account.)

- **Rights of Accumulation** give you a discount based on the total amount of money you invest — and not just in that fund, but in any fund in the same fund family. Thus, if you are investing $15,000 in a fund but previously have invested $35,000 in other funds of the same family, you are entitled to the $50,000 discount level on the $15,000 investment you are making today. You also are permitted to add together all the investments made by members of your household for purposes of calculating the biggest ROA discount.

- **Free transfers.** All fund families allow investors to move money between funds with no additional load, provided the money stays in the same family. Note that a small transfer fee might apply, and unless it's a retirement account, the transfer will be considered a taxable event.

Five Common Broker Tricks

Federal rules require all front-end load mutual funds to automatically award the above discounts to investors. However, the higher the load, the higher your broker's commission. Therefore, make sure you're working with an ethical broker.

Trick #1: Splitting Registrations to Avoid Breakpoints

Instead of opening a joint account with husband and wife for $250,000, the broker opens two accounts, one in each name, for $125,000 each. This avoids the $250,000 breakpoint, meaning you pay a higher load and the broker gets a higher commission. *It's illegal.*

Trick #2: Failing to Award Rights of Accumulation

An investor who already has a large account in a fund family opens a new, small account for her children, but the broker fails to apply the discount to the new account, which she's entitled to by virtue of the existence of the larger account. *It's illegal.*

Trick #3: Failing to Disclose Letter of Intent Availability

A broker allows a client to open an account with a small amount, knowing that the client intends to add to the account within 13 months, but does not execute the trade with the proper LOI discount. *It's illegal.*

Trick #4: Recommending an Investment Amount Slightly Below a Breakpoint Level

A broker tells a client to invest $95,000 into a fund, failing to disclose that if the client were to invest just $5,000 more, the entire investment would receive the $100,000 discount level. (Quite often, due to the discounts, investing $100,000 can cost less than investing $95,000.) *It's illegal.*

Trick #5: Churning

This is when a broker encourages a client to sell a fund from one family for the purpose of buying a second fund from another family, without any economic or fundamental justification to support the recommendation. The broker simply wants the client to incur a second load, so he can earn a second commission. *It's illegal.*

These tricks are all illegal — and also far too common. A 2003 NASD review of A Share mutual fund trades at the nation's largest brokerage firms revealed that clients failed to receive the proper breakpoints 30% of the time.

So if you think any of these tricks have been played on you, inform your broker of the error and your account will be quickly corrected. If your broker is slow to cooperate, notify the branch manager or the fund directly. The law is on your side, and you'll have no problem getting it fixed. The last thing your broker wants is for you to contact the federal regulators, for any of the above violations could cost brokers their licenses.

When Tricks are Really Treats

Also note that there can be very good reasons why it might appear you have overpaid when in fact your broker actually is working for your best interests. Indeed, as an NASD arbitrator, I can assure you that what might appear to be a rule violation often turns out to be a generally accepted practice which is in the best interests of the client and therefore acceptable to regulators. Two common examples include offering funds from several families and recommending that a client move assets from one fund family to another.

Such recommendations make sense when the advisor determines that a client needs to place some assets into, say, both a bond fund and a stock fund. No one fund family offers the best funds in all asset classes, so most advisors recommend funds from several families when recommending several funds.

Although this might deprive you of the discounts that otherwise may be available through Rights of Accumulation, the recommendation nonetheless might be acceptable, for it emphasizes *performance* over *fees*. After all, higher costs certainly are worthwhile if it reasonably can be expected to produce greater safety, lower volatility or higher returns. If your broker or planner instead placed primary emphasis on the *family* instead of the *fund*, you might wind up with second-best (or worse) funds.

"The most dangerous untruths are truths moderately distorted."
—Georg Christoph Lichenberg

Just as Ford gave us both Mustangs and Edsels, fund families have their winners and losers. No single fund family has the best funds in every category. So to get the best funds, you often must choose funds from different families, and while this strategy might increase cost, it also can result in higher profits.

Sales Charge #2: Back-End Load

Also known as rear-load, reverse load, or Class B shares, these funds don't charge you when you invest. Instead, reverse loads assess a withdrawal fee, also called a surrender fee. The amount is typically 5% or 6% in the first year, declining 1% per year until it vanishes after the 6th or 7th year. Each deposit receives its own "clock."

Technically called a *Contingent Deferred Sales Charge*, reverse load funds offer several features to minimize the surrender fee. For example:

• You are permitted to withdraw dividends and capital gains at any time with no charge.

• Many funds allow you to withdraw each year up to 12% of your investment at no charge.

• For liquidations beyond these amounts, the fund assumes you are withdrawing the oldest shares first, thus paying the lowest fee possible.

• You may move money between funds with no surrender fees, and without restarting your clock, provided the money stays in the same family. As with A Share transfers, a small transfer fee might apply, and unless the money is held in a retirement account, the transfer will be considered a taxable event.

Also, note that the expense ratio for B Shares is usually 0.75% higher than for A Shares, but only for the first six or seven years. After that, B shares convert to A shares. Thus, the expense ratio is reduced to that of the A Share.

> **Here's an example of how the CDSC might work: Say you invest $1,000 and after three years the fund has grown to $1,100.[15] If in that third year you were to withdraw $600, the first $100 of the withdrawal would be at no charge, because the surrender fee does not apply to profits. The remaining $500 would be subject to a 3% fee (the surrender charge in the third year). Thus, your total cost for withdrawing $600 in this example is $15.**

Sales Charge #3: Level-Load

Known as Class C shares, these also do not charge a front-end load, and the back-end load is usually just 1% on surrenders that occur in the first 12 months.

The expense ratio for C Shares is usually the same as that for B Shares, but whereas the B Share expense ratio will drop after six or seven years, the C Share's ratio will remain at this higher level.

Sales Charge #4: No-Load

In these funds, you don't pay a front-end, reverse, or level-load. You do, of course, pay the annual expense ratio, and many no-load funds feature higher annual expenses than A, B and C Share funds.

Comparing Loads

Many funds which claim to be "no load" are not. Ignore the advertising and look carefully at the prospectus to see if loads exist.

For comparison, figures 5-10 and 5-11 on the next pages ignore taxes and assume equal annual expense ratios and a 10% annual return for 10 years.

---

[15]Okay, that would be a lousy fund. But work with me here, people.

COMPARING FEES

No-Load Method

Year	Amount	Sales Charge NONE	Net Invested	10% Growth	12(b)1 Fee (none)	Ending Value	Surrender Fee (if applicable)
1	$10,000	-	$10,000	$1,000	-	$11,000	-
2	$11,000	-	$11,000	$1,100	-	$12,100	-
3	$12,100	-	$12,100	$1,210	-	$13,310	-
4	$13,310	-	$13,310	$1,331	-	$14,641	-
5	$14,641	-	$14,641	$1,464	-	$16,105	-
6	$16,105	-	$16,105	$1,611	-	$17,716	-
7	$17,716	-	$17,716	$1,772	-	$19,487	-
8	$19,487	-	$19,487	$1,949	-	$21,436	-
9	$21,436	-	$21,436	$2,144	-	$23,579	-
10	$23,579	-	$23,579	$2,358	-	$25,937	-

Front End-Load Method

Year	Amount	Sales Charge 4.75%	Net Invested	10% Growth	12(b)1 Fee (none)	Ending Value	Surrender Fee (if applicable)
1	$10,000	($475)	$9,525	$953	-	$10,478	-
2	$10,478	-	$10,478	$1,048	-	$11,525	-
3	$11,525	-	$11,525	$1,153	-	$12,678	-
4	$12,678	-	$12,678	$1,268	-	$13,946	-
5	$13,946	-	$13,946	$1,395	-	$15,340	-
6	$15,340	-	$15,340	$1,534	-	$16,874	-
7	$16,874	-	$16,874	$1,687	-	$18,562	-
8	$18,562	-	$18,562	$1,856	-	$20,418	-
9	$20,418	-	$20,418	$2,042	-	$22,459	-
10	$22,459	-	$22,459	$2,246	-	$24,705	-

FIGURE 5-10

COMPARING FEES

Rear-Load Method

Year	Amount	Sales Charge NONE	Net Invested	10% Growth	12(b)1 Fee (0.75%)	Ending Value	Surrender Fee (if applicable)
1	$10,000	-	$10,000	$1,000	($83)	$10,918	($500)
2	$10,918	-	$10,918	$1,092	($90)	$11,919	($400)
3	$11919	-	$11,919	$1,192	($98)	$13,013	($300)
4	$13,013	-	$13,013	$1,301	($107)	$14,207	($200)
5	$14,207	-	$14,207	$1,421	($117)	$15,510	($100)
6	$15,510	-	$15,510	$1,551	($128)	$16,933	-
7	$16,933	-	$16,933	$1,693	($140)	$18,487	-
8	$18,487	-	$18,487	$1,849	-	$20,336	-
9	$20,336	-	$20,336	$2,034	-	$22,369	-
10	$22,369	-	$22,369	$2,237	-	$24,606	

Level-Load Method

Year	Amount	Sales Charge NONE	Net Invested	10% Growth	12(b)1 Fee (0.75%)	Ending Value	Surrender Fee (if applicable)
1	$10,000	-	$11,000	$1,000	($83)	$10,918	($100)
2	$10,890	-	$11,979	$1,089	($90)	$11919	-
3	$11,859	-	$13,045	$1,186	($98)	$13,013	-
4	$12,915	-	$14,206	$1,291	($107)	$14,207	-
5	$14,064	-	$15,470	$1,406	($117)	$15,510	-
6	$15,316	-	$16,847	$1,532	($128)	$16,933	-
7	$16,679	-	$18,347	$1,668	($140)	$18,487	-
8	$18,163	-	$19,980	$1,816	($153)	$20,183	-
9	$19,780	-	$21,758	$1,978	($167)	$22,035	-
10	$21,540	-	$23,694	$2,154	($182)	$24,056	-

FIGURE 5-11

As you can see, the results are as follows:

Year	Value After 10 Years
No-Load	$25,937
Front-Load	$24,705
Rear-Load	$24,606
Level-Load	$24,056

WHICH TYPE OF LOAD PRODUCES THE HIGHEST PROFITS?

Year	The Most Profitable	Middle	The Least Profitable
1	Level	Front	Rear
2	Level	Front	Rear
3	Level	Rear	Front
4	Level	Rear	Front
5	Level	Rear	Front
6	Rear/Level (tie)		Front
7	Rear/Level (tie)		Front
8	Front	Rear	Level
9	Front	Rear	Level
10	Front	Rear	Level

FIGURE 5-12

It's clear from this example that, all other factors being equal,[16] the no-load fund is the most profitable choice. But of the remaining three, which is best?

Clearly, there's not much difference among them, but if you think the front load fund is best, beware: We're looking at 10-year results. If you examine different time intervals, the answer changes.

As you can see, "best" is determined by how long you stay invested. Since we don't know how long that will be (despite your intentions), it is impossible to tell which share class (A, B, or C) will prove best for you. Because the differ-

[16]And they never are.

ences are so small, and because you really can't be sure how long your money will stay invested, simply choose the version you like best; the economic difference between the three versions is so slight you needn't worry about making the "wrong" choice.

> It is inappropriate to ask a stockbroker for advice regarding no-load funds. By doing so, you're asking the broker to work for free, and that's rude: If you ask a waiter to bring you food, you had better be prepared to pay for the service — regardless of how the food tastes. (If you don't want to pay the service charge, go to a fast food joint and save the 15%.)

Why Pay a Load at All?

But let's return to the bigger question: Since the no-load clearly is best, regardless of how long you invest, how can you explain the fact that 78% of all mutual fund owners buy load funds?

Many people think — and lots of brokers argue — that paying a load is worthwhile because load funds earn higher returns, which more than compensate you for the fees you incur.

Nice theory, but dead wrong.

The truth is that *loads have absolutely no effect* on investment performance. For example, the book "The 100 Best Mutual Funds You Can Buy" contains 34 no-loads and 66 loads.

Loads do not affect performance because the load is merely a marketing expense.

Remember we talked about the manufacturing process in Chapter 5? All products must be sold — even (especially?) mutual funds — and funds accomplish this in various ways. Some families distribute their funds through stockbrokers, whom they compensate by paying commissions. Such funds charge loads — front, reverse, or level — which they in turn give to the broker. (You could bypass the broker when buying A, B, or C shares by going directly to the fund, but you'll still pay the fee because it is assessed by the fund, not the broker.)

No-loads sell their products via advertising in newspapers, magazines, direct mail and the Internet. This is why they do not charge a load: By selling directly to investors, they skip the broker and hence the load they would have paid him or her.

Buying a load fund from a broker is the same as buying an airline ticket from a travel agent. Whichever way you buy your ticket, the price is the same. When you let a travel agent place the order for you, the airline rebates a portion of the ticket price to the agent, just as load funds rebate a portion of the load to the broker.

Since air fares are the same, it makes sense to work with a travel agent. He knows you like aisle seats and non-smoking hotel rooms near the elevator. He'll help you find the best route, handle reservations, and even courier your tickets to you — all for free! Hotels, car rental companies, and airlines pay travel agents to perform these services — so you don't have to! But either way, using or not using a travel agent will have no effect on your air fare, nor on whether your plane leaves on time.

Just as tickets bought from travel agents can't determine the quality of the flight, paying loads won't get you a better fund. There is, in fact, only one legitimate reason for paying loads: to provide compensation to the person assisting you.

In accepting this compensation, your advisor (whether a stockbroker, financial planner, or other advisor) cannot promise performance. But she can promise — and you should demand — a high level of service. In addition to helping you select funds that are appropriate for you, your broker should monitor them for you and advise you when you should sell due to changes either in the economy or in your personal circumstances. Your advisor should handle all record-keeping and tax-reporting for you as well.

In fact, the Forum for Investor Advice, a trade organization representing load mutual funds, says a professional advisor will:

* understand individual financial needs and help investors formulate long-term investment goals and objectives;

* help the investor develop realistic expectations by discussing the risks and rewards of investing;

* match individual goals and objectives of the investor with appropriate mutual funds;

* continually monitor the individual's mutual fund portfolio and keep the investor apprised of any pertinent changes;

* conduct a regular review of the investor's financial status to ensure proper positioning of the mutual fund portfolio; and

- help investors "stay the course" of their long-term investment programs.

If you are not receiving these services, then you're not getting what you're really paying for. (For more on choosing an advisor, see Part XIII.)

Thus, if you know how to analyze and select funds, and if you have the time and ability to monitor them and handle your own tax reporting, then you probably should buy a no-load fund. In fact, that's who no-loads are for: the do-it-yourselfer, because in practice, "no load" really means "no help."

Assuming you work with an advisor, it doesn't really matter whether you choose Class A, B, or C, for the economic difference is statistically insignificant over time. The choice basically is whether you want to pay when you buy, pay (maybe) when you sell, or pay a little bit annually.

This is why loads are irrelevant to investment performance: Funds hire portfolio managers to manage their assets, and these managers are not concerned about whether a given fund is load or no-load. Such issues are marketing decisions, not investment management issues.

As Michael Lipper of Lipper Analytical Services, a major mutual funds rating organization, told *Business Week*: "If it's a period shorter than five years, I'd pay attention to the sales charge. If it's beyond five years, I would look at it but not be terribly influenced."

Chapter 28 - Annuities

How would you like to invest in mutual funds without paying taxes each year on the profits you earn? And how would you like to own an investment that guarantees you won't lose money? Enter the *variable annuity* — the best product since mutual funds.

Here's how it works: Instead of opening a mutual fund account, you turn to an insurance company, which sponsors variable annuities. Each annuity offers "sub-accounts" managed by a mutual fund family. These sub-accounts closely mimic the fund family's mutual funds, and you can choose the ones you want.

Variable annuities derive their name from the fact that the return you earn *varies* with the performance of the sub-accounts you choose.

If you choose a stock sub-account, your account will rise and fall with the stocks in that portfolio; if you invest in the bond sub-account, your account will reflect the performance of those bonds.

The Power of Tax-Deferred Growth

Why bother inserting an insurance company as middleman? Because under current tax law, money placed in an insurance contract grows *tax-deferred*, meaning you don't pay taxes on your earnings until you withdraw your money. And money that grows tax-deferred grows more quickly than money that is taxed annually, as Figure 5-13 demonstrates.

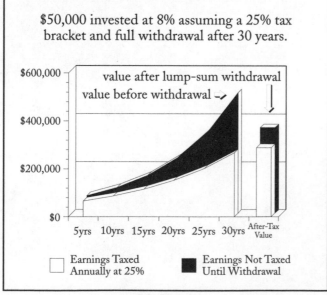

THE POWER OF TAX DEFERRED GROWTH

$50,000 invested at 8% assuming a 25% tax bracket and full withdrawal after 30 years.

value after lump-sum withdrawal
value before withdrawal

$600,000
$400,000
$200,000
$0

5yrs 10yrs 15yrs 20yrs 25yrs 30yrs After-Tax Value

☐ Earnings Taxed Annually at 25%
■ Earnings Not Taxed Until Withdrawal

FIGURE 5-13

Annuity marketers love to produce charts like 5-13, but there's a big difference between theirs and the one you see here: They always compare the tax-deferred's high point of $503,132 with the taxable's end value of $287,174. But this is an apples-to-oranges comparison, for the taxable investment is net of taxes while the tax-deferred is not. They like to brag that the tax-deferred investment produces a net profit 906% higher than the taxable investment, but that's not true. After paying the taxes that have been deferred, the after-tax profit is $339,849, meaning that the true increase in profit is 680%, not 906%.

Still, this remains a solid improvement and confirms that annuities are worthy of investment, but it's not quite as dramatic as annuity marketers would lead you to believe. That's why you must never take charts and statistics at face value (even those in this book!). Be sure to examine who's behind the numbers, and what their agenda might be.

Now That Capital Gains Taxes Have Been Cut, is Tax-Deferral Still a Good Idea?

Many are questioning the viability of tax-deferred strategies, given today's low capital gains tax rates (Chapter 60). Should you pay low taxes now or higher taxes later?

That's a valid question, and the answer is ... well, I think you know what the answer is: It depends[17] — on how you receive the money at retirement. Look at Figure 5-14, which assumes $100,000 invested at 10% annual interest for 10 years. To exaggerate the point, I've made two key assumptions: First, that 100% of the profits in the currently taxable investment will enjoy the 15% capital gains rate. This is unrealistically favorable, to make the currently taxable investment look as good as possible. Second, I've assumed that the tax-deferred investment will be taxed at the highest rate, to make tax-deferral look as bad as possible.

---

[17] See footnote 7.

CATHY CATHY GUISEWITE

WHY TAX-DEFERRAL SEEMS TO FAIL...

$100,000 invested at 10% for 10 years

TAXABLE			TAX DEFERRED		
Year	Tax Rate	Value of Taxable Account	Year	Tax Rate	Value of Taxable Account
1	15%	108,500	1	0%	110,000
2	15%	117,723	2	0%	121,000
3	15%	127,729	3	0%	133,100
4	15%	138,586	4	0%	146,410
5	15%	150,366	5	0%	161,051
6	15%	163,147	6	0%	177,156
7	15%	177,014	7	0%	194,872
8	15%	192,060	8	0%	214,359
9	15%	208,386	9	0%	235,759
10	15%	226,098	10	0%	259,374

If you withdraw a lump sum:

Gross Value of Tax Deferred Fund	$259,374
Original Principal	$100,000
Taxable Profit	$159,374
Less 35% Tax	($ 55,781)

Net Value of Taxable Fund $226,098 | **Net Value of Tax-Deferred Fund $203,593**

... But Why it Really Succeeds

If you take a 10% income stream:

Net Value	$226,098		Net Value	$259,374
Income	x 10%		Income	x 10%
	22,610			25,937
Less 25% Tax	(5,653)		Less 25% Tax	(6,484)
Net Annual Income	**$16,958**		**Net Annual Income**	**$19,453**

FIGURE 5-14

200

Variable annuities are a great deal — so great, in fact, that the IRS loses tens of millions of dollars in tax revenue, because many who otherwise would invest in mutual funds buy annuities instead. For this reason, President Clinton in June of 1998 tried to get Congress to severely restrict their use. But the House rejected the president's request, by a vote of 419-0.

This wasn't the first time tax-favored investments have been targeted: Single premium whole life was outlawed in 1982 and significant restrictions were placed on IRA contributions in 1986. In both cases, Congress allowed existing accountholders to keep their accounts; new accounts simply were forbidden (this is called grandfathering).

It's likely that further attacks against annuities will be made. Therefore, if they are right for you, you should buy them while you still can.

Here are the results: After ten years, if you liquidate both accounts, you'll have (after-taxes) $226,098 from the tax-as-you-go account, vs. $203,593 from the tax-deferred account. Thus, it appears that tax-deferral (and thus annuities) is no longer a good idea.

But appearances are deceiving.

In reality, it is highly unlikely that you would ever liquidate 100% of your investment in one lump sum. You are more likely instead to withdraw a monthly income from the account — and if you do, the annuity wins. As the chart shows, your income from the taxable account would be $16,958 (after taxes), vs. $19,453 from the tax-deferred annuity (also after taxes). Thus, you get from the tax-deferred annuity nearly 15% more income than you get from the taxable account.

Thus, despite today's lower capital gains tax, tax-deferral makes a lot of sense, and the power of tax-deferred annuities can't be ignored.

How Variable Annuities Can Help You Overcome Your Fear of a Stock Market Crash

If tax-deferral isn't enough, how would you like to invest knowing that you won't lose any money, even if the stock market declines in value?

As a result of the bear market of 2000–2002, many investors have become conflicted. If you're like them, you know that the only way to grow assets effectively over long periods is to invest in stocks. But you also know that stocks can lose much of their value, as evidenced by the early 2000s.

To convince investors that it's okay to invest, insurers have begun offering performance guarantees. They come in two parts, living benefits and death benefits. Let's examine them.

Guarantee Against Market Losses #1 - The Living Benefit

When offered, in the typical design, the annuity promises that you won't lose money. This guarantee is either an income guarantee or a principal guarantee.

Living Benefit #1 - The Income Guarantee

Via the income guarantee, the annuity promises to pay you an income stream that is based on your original investment, even if the value of that investment has declined. The guarantee is usually up to 7% per year.

Here's an example: Say you invest $100,000. The annuity will pay you up to 7% per year, or $7,000, until you receive back your original $100,000. The annuity will do this even if the account value itself becomes worthless. Thus, regardless of market performance, you will receive 7% per year for a minimum of 14.3 years. And if the value of your account rises, two good things happen:

- first, the period during which you can receive income extends beyond the original 14.3 years, and

- second, every five years, the annuity resets its income calculation to reflect the new higher value. Thus, if the account grows to $200,000, you'll be able to begin receiving 7% of $200,000, or $14,000 per year.

You are not required to begin taking income immediately. Instead, you can defer doing so until such time as you need the cash flow. This guarantee is ideal for those who will use their annuity to produce income at some point.

Living Benefit #2 - The Principal Guarantee

Some annuities promise to return 100% of your original investment, even if the account value is less, provided that you don't withdraw the money for 10 years. If you do make a withdrawal during this time, the guarantee is reduced by any amount withdrawn.

As with the living benefit described above, annuities typically re-set the guarantee every five years or so, to reflect the new higher value. Thus, if the account grows, the new higher value becomes the minimum guarantee, but if the account value falls, the original, higher value remains guaranteed.

This feature makes it easy to invest in something ordinarily considered risky, like the stock market. Assuming you are a long-term investor, this guarantee enables you to invest with the confidence that your principal is not at risk. This guarantee is ideal for those who will not need their capital for 10 years or more but who ultimately plan to spend the principal (say, on college costs) rather than receive periodic payments from it.

Why Insurance Companies Are Willing to Offer These Guarantees

There is a simple reason why insurers offer these guarantees: They make money doing so. In exchange for the guarantee, annuities charge a fee (often 0.35% per year).

Does that fee seem too small for the insurer to make a profit? It's not, and here's why: The insurer knows that some of its customers won't keep their money intact for the entire period, and others will die — both cases voiding the guarantee — but the insurer keeps the fees it's been collecting.

Second, insurers have history on their side: not since the Great Depression did the stock market ever end a 10-year period lower than when it started. In other words, the insurance companies are charging you a fee to protect you from losses even though losses over such long periods are highly unlikely, with or without a guarantee.

So, clearly, these features represent a smart business move for the insurance companies. But they still represent a smart move for investors, too. It's like homeowner's insurance: We know that companies make a profit selling it, but that doesn't mean consumers are dumb to buy it.

By that notion, I firmly believe that these "living benefits" are worthwhile. A 0.35% fee is just $350 per year for a $100,000 investment, and I'm worried about the hundred grand, not the three hundred fifty bucks. Stated another way, by buying this guarantee, an investment that otherwise would have grown 10% would return to you only 9.65%. But if that same investment loses money, you would lose nothing. Considering that the S&P 500 Stock Index lost 45% from 2000-02, I conclude that a 0.35% annual charge is well worth the price to protect one's life savings.

Guarantee Against Market Losses #2 - The Death Benefit

Say you place $100,000 into a variable annuity. Let's further say your timing isn't exactly wonderful: The day after you invest, a market crash cuts the value of your account to $75,000.

If you were to withdraw the $75,000, you'd lose $25,000. Therefore, you should instead withdraw $74,000, leaving $1,000 in the account. The reason: The annuity's death benefit usually guarantees to give your beneficiaries:

what you invested minus withdrawals,

or

the current value, whichever is greater.

Your investment ($100,000) minus withdrawals ($74,000) is $26,000. The current value is $1,000. Therefore, the insurance carrier owes your beneficiary the greater of the two, or $26,000, should you pass away.

Variable annuities also usually periodically reset the minimum value of your investment for purposes of calculating the above. In other words, every five or seven years or so, the annuity carrier will set the *current value* as the *new minimum* below which you cannot fall.

Thus, if you invest $100,000 and it later grows to $150,000, the latter amount becomes the basis for the minimum guarantee. If the account later falls to $125,000, the contract guarantees you the $150,000 value.

One Piece of Fine Print

Remember: This is a death benefit. That means the only way to enjoy (?) this feature is to **DIE**!

Actually, the guarantee is from an insurance company! So although this guarantee is excellent, it comes with, um, a fairly significant piece of fine print. Thus, most folks should not be impressed with this "no-loss" guarantee, but for some people it is worthwhile. Take elderly retirees with lots of money in CDs, for example. Such

Check out these ads (I've hidden the names), which appeared in trade magazines read by insurance agents. In both cases, agents earn higher commissions than the investors earn in interest! This annuity pays agents a 10% commission; while another pays 13.25%! Variable annuity sponsors don't play these ridiculous games.

WHICH WAY

FIXED INTEREST
6.09%*

EQUITY INDEXED INTEREST

100% Participation No Cap**

DON'T KNOW ?

Wondering Which Way to Steer Annuity Clients?
Give Them a Choice With The Confidence Index 2000 Annuity.

- 3% Premium Bonus (6.09%*) Added to Funds Deposited in Years 1-5 (Style 1)
- Option to Transfer Between Fixed Interest **OR** Equity Indexed Interest <u>Every</u> <u>Certificate</u> <u>Year</u>!
- 100% Participation Rate with NO CAP!**
- Flexible Premium ($100 additional deposits)
- Up to 60% Loan Availability (of fixed Account Value)

13.25% **8.50%**
Commission   Commission
Ages 0-80   Ages 81-85

For Agent use only - This document has not been approved under the advertising laws of your state for dissemination to individual purchasers.

Product not available in all states. *6.09% first year yield on initial premium for fixed account. 3.00% first year base rate is not guaranteed and subject to change. 2.50% minimum guaranteed interest rate on fixed account **100% first year participation rate 20% guaranteed participation rate (0.0% n CA)

folks are not spending all their money and they know they never will. Rather, they intend to leave their money to their grandchildren for college.

Because they want nothing to happen to their money, the grandparents put everything into CDs. They should consider an annuity's stock sub-account instead: Because of the no-loss guarantee, the worst thing that could happen is that the account will be worth at their death exactly what it is worth today, even if the stock market crashes in the meantime. But assuming stocks perform as well in the future as they have in the past, the account should be worth substantially more than if they invest the money in CDs.

What if the Insurer is Unable to Pay?

The living and death benefits are only as good as the insurance companies offering them. If the insurer goes broke, the benefits become worthless. That's the bad news. The good news, though, is that the money invested in the annuity would remain unaffected, because the assets are segregated away from the insurer. So, even if the account falls in value and the insurer is unable to pay, you're no worse off than if you were invested without the guarantees; all you'll have lost is the 0.35% annual fee.

Fixed Annuities

Some people don't like the "variable-ness" of annuities, although the guarantees described above reduce much of this concern. Regardless, some people want the tax-deferral but they also want a fixed rate of return, like they get from CDs. To meet this demand, insurers offer *fixed annuities*.

Under the law, fixed annuities are considered insurance products, while variable annuities are considered securities products. This subtlety makes a big difference, because fixed annuity assets are commingled with the general assets of the insurance company. Thus, if the insurance company goes broke, your money is lost with it. But variable annuity assets are segregated from the assets of the insurance carrier. Thus, even if the insurance company goes broke, your money remains safe, as described above.

> **If you insist on buying a fixed annuity, buy a variable annuity instead and select the fixed sub-account. You'll get the fixed return you want and the safety you need.**

Remember when Executive Life of California Insurance Company went broke? People who owned its fixed annuities received letters saying they might never get their money back. People who owned Executive Life's variable annuities, however, were not affected by the carrier's troubles. That's a big difference in safety.

If you own an annuity and want to know whether it is fixed or variable, try one of the following:

- Call your agent and ask.

- Call your insurance company and ask.

- Look at your contract for the word "fixed" or "variable." You'll find one or the other.

- Look at your most current statement. If it says you will earn a specific rate of interest over the next several months or year, you have a fixed annuity.

Equity Indexed Annuities

Most fixed annuities offer fixed rates of interest, like bank CDs. Some, however, offer interest rates that are tied to the stock market. These equity indexed annuities, or EIAs, typically offer a minimum interest rate with the promise to pay a higher return if stock prices rise. Typically, the formula used means you'll get, at best, only a fraction of the market's returns.

How to Move From One Annuity to Another

You easily can transfer money from one annuity to another with no tax consequences by executing a *Section 1035 Exchange*. This section of the tax code allows tax-free exchanges between annuities, provided the assets are transferred directly from one insurance company to another.

"There is nothing more demoralizing than a small but adequate income."

—Edmund Wilson

To execute a 1035 exchange, simply sign a form available from any annuity carrier. Be aware that although 1035 exchanges avoid tax liabilities, you might incur a withdrawal fee for leaving the annuity you currently own. Contact your annuity carrier to be certain, or ask the advisor who sold it to you.

Annuity Charges and Expenses

Virtually all annuities are offered on a Class B or Class C basis, as discussed in Chapter 27.

The IRS has a say, too. In exchange for not taxing you each year, any withdrawals you make prior to age 59½ are subject to a 10% IRS penalty. Thus, annuities are intended as long-term investments.

Variable annuities also incur the following expenses:

- **an annual contract fee** which ranges typically from $30 to $75 per year, depending on the size of your account;

- **the annual expense ratio** of the sub-account. Since variable annuities are managed by mutual fund families, you'll incur their annual costs as well (see Chapter 27); and

- **an annual mortality charge** of 1% to 2% per year to compensate the insurer for the death benefit guarantee it provides.

Because of the additional costs, many assume they will earn more in mutual funds than in annuities. But consider the following:

- **You must pay taxes annually** on the profits you earn in a mutual fund, but you don't with the annuity. This tax-deferral can more than compensate for the additional cost, as long as you keep the variable annuity long enough.

- **You can lose money in the mutual fund**, but the annuity offers performance guarantees. Thus, you receive benefits in exchange for the additional cost.

- **Perhaps most importantly, the assumption itself has not always proven valid**. Several studies have found that, net of all costs, average variable annuity stock sub-accounts gained more than average stock mutual funds for various time periods. There are several theories as to how this occurrs. I favor the theory that people who invest in annuities, considering their surrender fees and tax penalties, do so for the long term. Thus, redemption requests are minimal, and the sub-account managers know it. Therefore, while mutual funds must keep a portion of their assets in cash to handle redemption requests, annuity managers can invest a higher percentage of the annuity's assets. By putting more of the money to work, they can earn more — thus helping to compensate for the higher costs.

Warning: Annuities Contain Two Tax Traps

There are two tax traps with annuities that you must beware:

Annuity Tax Trap #1: Withdrawals are Income

If you liquidate an annuity or receive income from it, the proceeds are taxed at ordinary income tax rates, not more favorable capital gains rates. However, a portion of each withdrawal is often considered to be a return of principal and thus tax-free.

Annuity Tax Trap #2: No Step-Up in Basis

This will affect your children more than you: Annuities do not enjoy a stepped-up basis at death, which we discussed in Chapter 15. This means your children could incur significant tax liabilities — equal, in fact, to the tax savings you enjoyed during your lifetime. The bottom line is that the tax break provided by annuities is *deferral*, not *exemption*. Someone (eventually) will pay taxes on the profits you earn in your annuity — if not you, then your heirs.

In my experience, most clients are unconcerned by this, or rather, they are more concerned (and rightfully so) that they have sufficient income throughout their lifetime. Possible adverse tax implications for heirs are a secondary consideration.

Chapter 29 - Real Estate Limited Partnerships

As discussed earlier, real estate should be part of your overall investment mix. Unfortunately, it requires a lot of cash and can cause considerable headaches from The Hassle Factor (see Chapter 18).

These concerns led to the creation of limited partnerships. It has been said that limited partnerships consist of investors who have the money and the general partner who has the experience. Later, the general partner has the money and investors have the experience.

Well, maybe not always. Certainly, a lot of people lost a lot of money through partnerships in the 1980s. This has led to the bad name given these products. But blaming investment losses on partnerships is like blaming the bottle for killing you instead of the poison you drank from it. The truth is that partnerships have been known to be profitable.

Partnerships are similar to closed-end funds: Rather than buying property on your own, you pool your money with other investors (known as limited partners), and a manager (the general partner) buys property, then manages and eventually sells the property, returning to investors their pro-rata share of the proceeds. Limited partnerships can be formed to buy any type of investment, such as oil wells or railroad cars, but most deal with real estate.

How did this simple concept cause so many people to lose so much money? As with most strategies, there was nothing wrong with the concept. It was the *implementation* that ruined the deal. To see how partnerships work, and what went wrong, let's return to the late 1970s.

A Trip Through Time

Have you ever noticed that physicians often work in the same building? Here's why: Doctor Billem needed office space. So, he formed a partnership with 19 other physicians, each putting up $50,000 ($1 million total); Each owned 5% of the partnership.

The partnership is *limited* because Dr. Billem's liability is limited to his $50,000 investment. (Unlike a *general partnership*, where all partners have unlimited personal liability for any losses the partnership incurs.)

Actually, the doctor didn't put up $50,000 in cash. Instead, he got a bank loan at 10% interest (a $5,000 annual cost). The partnership, flush with $1 million raised from the doctors, then borrowed an additional $1 million from the bank. With $2 million, the partnership bought land and erected a building, and the doctor, with only $5,000 cash-out-of-pocket, now owns a 5% interest in the partnership, valued at $100,000.

During the two years it takes to complete the building, the partnership spends most (maybe all) of its money in construction costs. These losses pass through the partnership to the partners (including Dr. Billem), who claim the losses on their tax returns. Thus, over two years, he spends $10,000 in loan interest payments but gets perhaps $70,000 in tax deductions. At his 70% marginal tax bracket, this saves him $49,000 in federal income taxes. Not bad for a $10,000 investment.

And it gets better. When the building is complete, Dr. Billem moves in. As a tenant, he pays rent to the partnership, and since rent is a routine office expense, it is tax-deductible. Furthermore, as one of the building's owners, he receives his rent back as a cash distribution from the partnership — tax-free due to interest and depreciation allowances.

Thus, Dr. Billem pays rent and gets a tax break on one hand, and gets his money back — along with a second tax break — on the other hand. Not too shabby!

But, the Tax Reform Act of 1986 killed all these games. But in doing so, the Act didn't simply tell partners such as Dr. Billem that they weren't allowed to build more buildings in this fashion. No, the Act changed the rules *retroactively*. Thus, the tax deductions Dr. Billem had previously taken were reclaimed, so that back taxes were due in full — with interest and penalties. Dr. Billem went from owning a shrewd investment to owing hundreds of thousands of dollars!

And all the other real estate investors got skinned with him. Before TRA, developers who wanted to borrow billions to erect buildings (not knowing if anyone would move in, and not caring either, since the tax savings were worth five or six times their investment), found money readily available from banks. Tenants were irrelevant in this game, and the banks knew it.

But when the tax law changed, these builders found themselves with buildings they couldn't fill — and losses they couldn't deduct. With no tenants, the builders had no rental income, and with no income, they couldn't make their loan payments. The banks foreclosed.

But banks don't want buildings. They're in the banking business, after all, not the real estate business. They want cash so they in turn can pay interest to their depositors. Forced to foreclose on defunct developers, the banks became reluctant owners of see-through buildings (so-called because without any tenants you could see in one window and out the other side), and banks started to lose money themselves.

This (admittedly oversimplified) explains the S&L crisis of the '80s.

The problem was not the partnerships, nor was it real estate. Rather, the problems were caused by investors borrowing too much money and relying too heavily on tax benefits instead of pure economics. Through leverage, Dr. Billem borrowed $100,000 he didn't have, and his profits were dependent on tax law.

Unfortunately, as he learned too late, there is nothing natural about tax law. *What Congress giveth, Congress may taketh away.*

As with all packaged products, the key to success is not found in the product packaging but in the underlying asset. If you want to own real estate but don't have enough money to buy your own, partnerships can be acceptable alternatives — if done correctly.

What To Do If You Own a Busted Partnership

If you own a partnership that has gone bust, guess what you need?

Another partnership! Ever since the Tax Reform Act of 1986, partnership losses are considered *passive*, which you cannot deduct against active income, such as income from your job. So, you need to buy another partnership that generates *passive income*, to use to offset your passive losses. Such partnerships are called PIGs, for *passive income generator*.

Try telling people who've lost money in one partnership that what they need is another one! It's not the sort of recommendation that usually goes over very well.

Chapter 30 - Real Estate Investment Trusts

REITs (pronounced reets) are similar to partnerships, with one major difference: REITs trade on the New York Stock Exchange, allowing investors to buy and sell whenever they want. Investors in limited partnerships can't do this; once you invest in an LP, you can't get your money back until the general partner sells the properties (which won't happen for 10 years or more).

So the good news is that REITs are liquid. But that's also the bad news. For being able to sell means investors do sell. The result: Shares in REITs trade with the same volatility as stocks.

If you think about it, it's illogical for REITs to rise and fall like stocks. After all, they are real estate investments, not stocks. But when investors are panicking, logic has no place. So investors who choose real estate to divorce themselves from the volatility of the stock and bond markets quickly discover that REITs fail to achieve that objective.

The bottom line is that while you should invest in real estate, we have found no truly efficient, effective way to do so. Be aware of the problems of each method, choose the version that you regard to be the "least evil" and invest only a small percentage of your total assets in this asset class.

ric's money quiz

Here's a chance to see how well you learned the information contained in Part V – Packaged Products. Don't worry if you get stumped — just re-read this part until it sinks in. Remember, your financial future depends on it.

The answers are at the end of the quiz. No peeking!

---

1. **More mutual fund assets are invested in the following asset class than in any other:**

   - ○ a. stocks
   - ○ b. derivatives
   - ○ c. government securities
   - ○ d. international securities

2. **Which of the following is *not* true about mutual funds?**

   - ○ a. mutual funds are more liquid than individual stocks and bonds
   - ○ b. when bought through banks, mutual funds are insured
   - ○ c. mutual fund investment decisions are made by private money managers
   - ○ d. mutual funds offer extensive diversification

3. **Net Asset Value refers to:**

   - ○ a. the difference in a mutual fund's value between the beginning of the year and the present
   - ○ b. the annual hidden fees that mutual funds charge investors
   - ○ c. the value per share of a mutual fund
   - ○ d. what it costs to buy a front-load mutual fund

4. **Balanced funds invest in which of the following major asset classes?**

   I.   cash and cash equivalents
   II. corporate bonds
   III. corporate stocks
   IV. government securities

   - ○ a. I and III
   - ○ b. II and III
   - ○ c. I, II, III, and IV
   - ○ d. IV and I

5. **Of the following choices, which offers both extensive diversification and relatively low volatility?**

    ○ a. asset allocation funds
    ○ b. equity income funds
    ○ c. balanced funds
    ○ d. growth and income funds

6. **The phrase "no load" means:**

    ○ a. no fees of any kind are charged
    ○ b. no up-front commissions are charged
    ○ c. no surrender fees are charged
    ○ d. both b and c

7. **The Investment Company Act of 1940 created:**

    I.   mutual funds
    II.   unit investment trusts
    III. closed-end funds
    IV.   fixed annuities

    ○ a. I only
    ○ b. I and II
    ○ c. I, II and III
    ○ d. I, II, III, and IV

8. **A closed-end fund has the following attributes:**

    I.   only a limited number of shares are available
    II.   shares trade on the New York Stock Exchange
    III. when selling shares of a closed-end fund, the price is equal to the net asset value
    IV.   closed-end funds are sold commission-free

    ○ a. I
    ○ b. I and II
    ○ c. I, II, and III
    ○ d. I, II, III, and IV

9. **A mutual fund which features a 4% contingent deferred sales charge is known as a:**

    ○ a. front-load fund
    ○ b. no-load fund
    ○ c. rear-load fund
    ○ d. level-load fund

10. **Variable annuities are popular because profits are:**

    ○ a. tax-free
    ○ b. tax-exempt
    ○ c. tax-deferred
    ○ d. tax-deductible

Answers: 1-c (pg.164)   4-c (pg.174)   7-c (pg.159, pg.179 and pg.180)
           2-b (pg.160)   5-c (pg.174)   8-b (pg.179)
           3-c (pg.163)   6-d (pg.191)   9-c (pg.190)   10-c (pg.198)

Part VI
The Best Investment Strategies

There's a quiz at the end of this part!

To see how much you already know, skip to the
end of this part and take the quiz now. Then, read
the part and take the quiz again. You'll discover
how much you've learned!

Part VI — The Best Investment Strategies

Overview - Combining Growth and Income

Up to this point, I've focused on teaching you how different kinds of investments work, including their risks and fees. Now we're going to focus on how to develop successful investment strategies using those investments. By the end of this part, you'll be able to answer the two most difficult questions all investors ask: Where should I invest my money, and when is the best time to invest?

Chapter 31 - Safe or Risky?

If you were to put your six-year-old's education fund entirely into one asset class, knowing that your child will not be able to attend college if you lose the money, would you invest it entirely in the stock market?

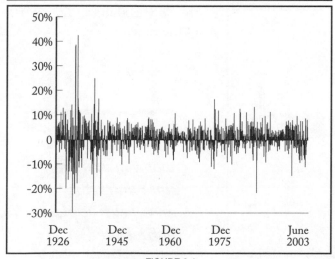

MONTHLY RETURNS OF THE S&P 500

FIGURE 6-1

Most people (including you, probably) would say "no" because the stock market seems so uncertain, risky, and volatile.

This attitude is supported by Figure 6-1, which displays the monthly performance of the S&P 500 Stock Index from 1926 to June 30, 2003, according to Ibbotson Associates. During those 77½ years (919 months), the market made money in only 62% of the months. Although these are good odds from a gambler's perspective, few parents would take such a "gamble" with their kid's college education.

ANNUAL RETURNS OF THE S&P 500

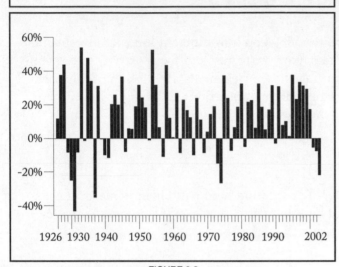

FIGURE 6-2

But see in Figure 6-2 how the stock market did over one-year intervals: Stocks now made money 70% of the time — even including the bear market of 2000-2002. Still, is this success rate high enough for you to invest in stocks?

5 YEAR RETURNS OF THE S&P 500

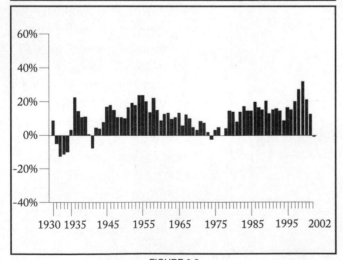

FIGURE 6-3

How about five-year intervals? In the 73 rolling five-year periods since 1926, shown in Figure 6-3, the S&P 500 made money 90% of the time.

"If you don't know who you are, the stock market is an expensive place to find out."
—George Goodman

10 YEAR RETURNS OF THE S&P 500

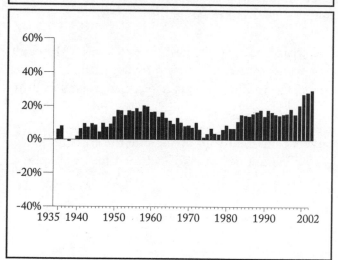

FIGURE 6-4

15 YEAR RETURNS OF THE S&P 500

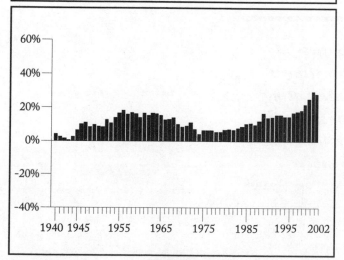

FIGURE 6-5

In every 10-year interval, the S&P 500 made money 99% of the time. In fact, in every 15-year interval and beyond, the stock market made money 100% of the time.

Yet most people don't see it this way. They fret over what the market is doing today, even though the market is focused on tomorrow. "Should I get in now or wait?" the multitudes ask. "If things are going well, I'll get in, but if things are going bad, I'll stay out." That attitude will cause you to lose lots of money, because as we will learn in Chapter 32, the stock market is focused on the future, not the present. Therefore, your investments must be based on where you're *going*, not on where you are.

Thus, the key is not *when* you invest in the stock market, nor *which* stocks you buy. The key is *how long* you invest. We can convert something as risky and uncertain as stocks into a safe, predictable investment.

Chapter 32 - World Events Will Not Destroy Your Investments

Those who focus on today's headlines always make bad investment decisions. The news is filled with doom and gloom, and as we hear about today's crisis, we develop a pessimistic attitude. That discourages us from investing.

Yet it can be argued that a time of crisis is exactly the best time to invest. Although this is the opposite of when people want to invest, history proves it is the best time. And since our nation is always suffering from one major crisis or another, it's always a great time to invest!

Indeed, as Figure 6-6 shows, markets consistently go up, despite the crisis du jour. In fact, from 1940 through 2002, the market went up 75% of the time — despite some pretty awful problems.

Yet most investors dismiss this logic and instead act emotionally. It's a recipe for investment disaster.

"Successful investing is anticipating the successful anticipations of others."
—John Keynes

WORLD EVENTS DO NOT DESTROY STOCKS

The S&P 500 Went Down in Only 16 Years Since 1940

Year	Event	S&P 500
1940	Germany invades France	-9.78%
1941	Pearl Harbor	-11.59
1942	Gas rationing begins	+20.34
1943	War escalates	+ 25.9
1944	Consumer goods shortage	+19.75
1945	Roosevelt dies	+36.44
1946	Labor strife	- 8.07
1947	Cold War begins	+ 5.71
1948	Berlin blockade	+ 5.5
1949	Russia explodes A-bomb	+18.79
1950	Korean conflict begins	+31.71
1951	Korean conflict	+24.02
1952	Government seizes mills	+18.37
1953	Russia explodes H-bomb	- 0.99
1954	McCarthy hearings	+52.62
1955	Eisenhower falls ill	+31.56
1956	Suez Canal crisis	+ 6.56
1957	Russia launches Sputnik	-10.78
1958	Recession	+43.36
1959	Castro seizes power	+11.96
1960	Russia downs spy plane	+ 0.47
1961	Berlin Wall erected	+26.89
1962	Cuban missile crisis	- 8.73
1963	Kennedy assassinated	+ 22.8
1964	Gulf of Tonkin	+16.48
1965	Civil rights unrest	+12.45
1966	Vietnam War	-10.06
1967	Race riots	+23.98
1968	USS Pueblo seized	+11.06
1969	Japan is new economic power	- 8.5
1970	N. Vietnam invades Cambodia	+ 4.01
1971	Wage and price freeze	+14.31

Year	Event	S&P 500
1972	Record US trade deficit	+18.98
1973	Mideast oil crisis. Long gas lines	-14.66
1974	Deep recession in US & Europe	-26.47
1975	Recession deepens	+ 37.2
1976	Gold prices plunge	+23.84
1977	Trade wars loom	- 7.18
1978	Interest rates surge	+ 6.56
1979	Inflation & oil prices skyrocket	+18.44
1980	American hostages in Iran	+32.42
1981	High unemployment	- 4.91
1982	Worst recession in 40 years	+21.41
1983	Interest rates fluctuate	+22.51
1984	Deficit goes over $200 billion	+ 6.27
1985	Record number of S&Ls fail	+32.16
1986	Tax Reform Act of 1986	+18.47
1987	Stock market tumbles	+ 5.23
1988	Fear of recession	+16.81
1989	Invasion of Panama	+31.49
1990	Iraq invades Kuwait	- 3.17
1991	The Gulf War	+30.55
1992	Civil War in the Balkans	+ 7.67
1993	The Great Flood of 1993	+ 9.99
1994	Worst bond market ever	+ 1.31
1995	Oklahoma bombing	+37.43
1996	Olympic park bombing	+23.07
1997	Inspection crisis in Iraq	+33.36
1998	Asian currency collapse	+22.58
1999	Y2K	+21.04
2000	Presidential Election Controversy	- 9.10
2001	September 11 attack on America	-11.80
2002	Threat of war with Iraq	-22.10

FIGURE 6-6

Chapter 33 - Focus on the Hill, Not the String

People fear the stock market because stock prices are volatile. Prices can fall, and people fear falling.

Yet, this fear is misguided. By focusing on the daily ups and downs of the market, people forget the more important point: Stocks rise more than they fall. Imagine a boy walking up a steep hill while playing with a yo-yo.

If you focus on the yo-yo, you'll become obsessed with its wild gyrations — while ignoring the fact that the boy is steadily climbing higher. True, the yo-yo will always reach a low point, but each low point will be higher than the last low point, because the boy is now on higher ground. So it is with the stock market.

BORN LOSER   ART SANSOM

Reprinted by permission of Newspaper Enterprise Association, Inc.

Chapter 34 - Understanding Volatility

Risk is the basis for volatility: Indeed, in its most elementary definition, "risk" simply refers to the degree to which the future value of your money may differ from the present value of your money. The greater the difference, the greater the risk. This difference is expressed by the term *volatility*.

A 30-day T-bill carries no volatility: One dollar invested in a T-bill always is worth one dollar. But one dollar invested in stocks can rise or fall dramatically. Therefore, stocks are considered to be much riskier than T-bills.

However, volatility is not a reason to avoid stocks any more than it is a reason to *own* them. Rather, volatility is merely a *characteristic* of stocks. Prices go up, and prices go down. And they do that a lot. As Figure 6-7 shows, the average spread since 1940 between the S&P 500's highest prices of the year and the lowest is 23%. That's extreme volatility. Yet all these gyrations have occurred on an upward slope. So, you need to focus not on the daily activity of the market, but on its long-term trend.

"According to my calculations, the stock market should go up, down, up, down, up, down, up, down, up, down, then up."

If you think 23% is a lot of fluctuation, remember that's just the *average*. For truly extreme volatility, look at the S&P during and after a *crisis*. As Figure 6-8 shows, in the five weeks following every major crisis since the Korean War, stocks dropped an average of 16%. At that rate, stocks would be completely wiped out in just eight months.

That's enough to scare anyone.

But if those crises caused you to sell in a panic, you'd have made a big mistake. Because in the six months following each crisis, those same stocks gained an average of 14% and 18% in the year afterward.

ANNUAL MARKET VOLATILITY
OF THE S&P 500

1940	35%	1962	31	1984	14
1941	26	1963	18	1985	26
1942	27	1964	13	1986	22
1943	25	1965	13	1987	40
1944	14	1966	25	1988	16
1945	29	1967	19	1989	27
1946	31	1968	21	1990	22
1947	17	1969	17	1991	29
1948	21	1970	30	1992	11
1949	21	1971	15	1993	9
1950	20	1972	16	1994	9
1951	14	1973	26	1995	32
1952	14	1974	46	1996	21
1953	16	1975	31	1997	25
1954	37	1976	17	1998	34
1955	29	1977	17	1999	21
1956	14	1978	21	2000	21
1957	23	1979	15	2001	42
1958	31	1980	35	2002	21
1959	13	1981	20		
1960	14	1982	33		
1961	23	1983	22		

Avg: 23%

FIGURE 6-7

STOCKS DURING AND AFTER A CRISIS

Crisis	Change in S&P 500	Next Six Months	Next Year
Korean War	-15% in 5 weeks	+31%	+36%
Sputnik	-10% in 3 weeks	+ 8%	+30%
Steel Price Roll Back	-20% in 8 weeks	+11%	+24%
Liquidity Crisis	-12% in 4 weeks	+16%	+42%
Arab Oil Embargo	-17% in 9 weeks	- 1%	-28%
Nixon Resignation	-19% in 5 weeks	+30%	+27%
Hunt Silver Crisis	-12% in 4 weeks	+26%	+29%
Crash of '87	-26% in 3 weeks	+ 7%	+16%
Gulf War	-12% in 3 weeks	+11%	+25%
September 11th	-12% in 2 weeks	+ 7%	-17%
Average	**16% in 5 weeks**	**+14%**	**+18%**

FIGURE 6-8

Remember, the stock market is like a yo-yo. It drops fast and hard, and it rises equally so. Ignore the short-term or momentary fluctuations, for they have little impact over long periods.

So if you want to achieve investment success, all you need to do is think of stocks the same way you do puppies.

Why Do People Love Puppies?

After all, most people don't like stocks, but almost everyone loves puppies. Yet all puppies pee on the rug. While this is not something people enjoy, it's not a reason to avoid buying puppies either (okay, maybe it is).

You should have the same attitude regarding stock market volatility. You are not buying stocks because you like volatility, but rather *in spite of it*.

Don't let volatility scare you away from stocks. If you do, you'll miss wonderful opportunities.

Chapter 35 - Following Your Emotions Is a Sure Path to Failure

Investor losses almost always begin with emotions. To illustrate, let's return to 1972.

The Dow is at 700. Over the next 10 years, America will face runaway inflation, Watergate, the resignation of the President, two recessions, an oil embargo, 18% interest rates, and hostages in Iran.

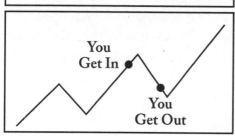

CHART OF EMOTIONS

You Get In

You Get Out

FIGURE 6-9

Let's move forward to 1982. The Dow is still at 700! Not only is nobody making money in stocks, it's hard to remember the last time anybody did. All this gloom and doom led *Business Week* to publish its now-infamous cover story entitled "The Death of Equities."

As we move further into the 1980s, we find big differences from the '70s. Our hostages come home. Interest rates come down. The recession comes to an end. And everywhere you turn, people are talking about stocks again: On the bus, at the water cooler, during dinner parties, people are talking about the money they are making in the market, and each evening's newscasts announce "yet another all-time high" for stocks.

All of which lead you to a new emotion: **Hope.** Hope that the market will keep going up. By 1986, after the Dow reaches its all-time high of 2700, hope is replaced by yet another emotion: **Greed.** "Look at all the money they're making," you say to yourself. "I've got to get in on this."

> It sort of makes you ask the question, "Should I stay out of the market and watch it go up, or should I get in and make it go down?"

So you invest in stocks in early 1987, just in time to catch the market's peak in August. By September, with the market down 5%, your greed is replaced once again by **hope**: This time saying, "I hope it goes back up!"

But on October 19th, stocks drop 12% in a single day (they're now down 35% from their August 22 high) and hope quickly converts into the strongest of all emotions:

FEAR. In a panic, you sell, leaving you to ponder how you managed to lose money during the biggest bull market in the history of the United States.

An identical story could be told from the 1990s. In 1990, you hadn't even heard of the Internet, and it wasn't until the mid '90s that you began to hear stories of incredible profits from Internet stocks like Microstrategy, America Online and Priceline.com.

By the time you invested in these and other dot-com stocks, they already had gained 1,000% or more — and you hoped the gains would continue. Then, as we entered the new millennium and these stocks began to fall, you began to forget about dreams of fast profits and instead hoped for a fast recovery so you could get your money back. Just as in the aftermath of 1987's crash, you find yourself wondering how you managed to lose money during the biggest bull market in U.S. history.

Apparently, the Crash of '87 taught you nothing. Did you also learn nothing from Internet Mania?

The lesson is to quit drawing conclusions from the evening news. All they do is report on what has happened, and you can't make money after you hear the news, because the news will elicit an emotion from you, and that emotion is certain to send you in the wrong direction. After the stocks rose, the news encouraged you to buy, and after the stocks fell, the news led you to sell. Both were the exact opposite of what you should have done.

Indeed, if we follow our emotions, we're going to do the exact opposite of what we're supposed to do, for the simple reason that half of all the people who invest in the stock market are dead wrong.

The Odds are 50/50 That You're Dead Wrong

Don't believe me? Ask yourself: If you wanted to sell a stock, to whom would you sell it? To *Somebody Else*, right? Well, one of you is dead wrong — we just don't know which one! After all, the stock is going to go up or down — so one of you has to be wrong!

In other words, the proper way to buy stocks is completely opposite from the way you buy everything else. For example, have you bought a TV lately? How about a car, dishwasher, or other major item?

When you made that purchase, did you buy from the same manufacturer as you did before? If so, no doubt the reason was because you had great success with it. And you fully expect your future experience to match your past experience.

But did you select your new car *only* because your last one was good? No, not you. You're too smart for that. No, you spent a weekend at the library reading *Consumer Reports*, and you interviewed all your friends and co-workers to learn their experiences. Then, once you settled on the brand and model, you shopped all over town looking for the best deal — eventually driving 200 miles to save thirty bucks.

Does this sound familiar?

Sure it does. Yet, you'll throw five grand at a stock because you overheard some guy who, you don't even know — on TV or at the water cooler — talk about it.

Admit it. When it comes to investing, you act emotionally.

You must recognize that relying on past performance and product reviews — which is how you buy ordinary products — does not apply to the stock market. In fact, so basic is this principle that the U.S. Securities and Exchange Commission requires every mutual fund prospectus to proclaim in bold print that:

"PAST PERFORMANCE IS NO INDICATION OF FUTURE RESULTS."

It doesn't say "*not much indication*" or "*sometimes not any indication*" or "*just a little indication*." It says **NO INDICATION**. The past is completely irrelevant: Just because money did well when invested in one way at one particular time does not mean money invested in that same way at another time will perform as it did before. In fact, you can guarantee yourself that it won't, for the simple reason that the economic circumstances of the past are not the same as those of today — and those of today will not be the same tomorrow.

Ohmigawd, It's Snowing!

While in the midst of a crisis, one frantic client called me. "The market's down 12% in just this month!" she cried. "At this rate, I'll be broke in a year!" True, I calmly explained to her, if stocks continued to go down at their current rate, she'd soon lose all her money.

"Let me remind you that past performance is no guarantee of future results."

But I also noted that it was February, and a large snow-storm had dumped two feet of snow on the ground in less than a week. At this rate, I told her, she could expect to be buried under 35 feet of snow by July. "That's silly," she replied. "It'll be done snowing by then. Things will have changed a lot by July."

My point exactly.

Yet the market's snowstorms cause people to panic. In a panic, people throw away all their goals but one: safety. Forget about college, forget about retirement, the heck with taxes, *I want my money to be safe*!

As I've shown you throughout this book, any time you focus on safety instead of performance, you are sure to fail financially. In fact, people who focus on safety are at the greatest risk of being bamboozled. Witness *Money* magazine's March 1994 cover story, "8 Investments That Never Lose Money." The stock market had recently plunged, rising interest rates had sent bonds plummeting, the dollar was fading against the yen, so *Money* came to the rescue with a list of eight investments that "never lose money."

By the end of the year, six of the eight did.

Beware those who make claims about safety. Investing is about performance, not safety, and volatility is your traveling companion.

"8 INVESTMENTS THAT NEVER LOSE MONEY"

Money Magazine's March 1994 Cover Story

	Subsequent Performance March 1 – December 31
CGM Mutual	-9.85%
Dominion Resources	-6.55%
Gillette	+22%
Hershey	-3.17%
Investment Co. of America	-2.5%
Merrill Lynch Capital A	-4.89%
Sentinel Balanced	-2.98%
Unilever NV	+5.76%

FIGURE 6-10

Chapter 36 - Standard Deviation

Say an investment's rate of return fluctuates, or *deviates*, each year. If its rate of return were to *routinely* deviate, this deviation would become *standard*. Hence the term "standard deviation."

The standard deviation is the amount of swing in performance that an investment can be expected to have from year to year. The standard deviation is an investment's "average variation from the average return." The higher the standard deviation, the greater the volatility, and therefore the greater the risk.

> **If you want to get rid of a cold-calling broker, ask, "What's the standard deviation?" They'll never call you back, fearing you know more than they do!**

This is a difficult concept, so let's try an example. Say Fund ABC has earned an average of 8% per year over the past 10 years, with a standard deviation of 6. Statistically, there is a 67% probability that returns will fall within 1 standard deviation, and a 95% probability that returns will fall within 2 standard deviations. Thus, 67% of the time, Fund ABC earned between 2% and 14%, and 95% of the time, the fund earned between -4% and 20%.

This explains why neophyte investors so often get what they don't expect. The amateur, who expects Fund ABC to earn 8% (since that's the average annual return), is shocked when the fund loses 2%. But the astute investor knows such a result in any one year is quite possible, based on knowledge of standard deviation.[18]

To carry it a step further, it is highly unlikely that a fund's return in any one year will be exactly the average. Rather, it always will be either higher or lower than the average.

Thus, standard deviation teaches us to look beyond the "average annual return" figures that are touted by stockbrokers and mutual fund advertising.

---

[18]Standard deviation is not without its flaws. The biggest problem is that it punishes funds for *overperformance* just as much as for *underperformance*. Yet, most investors don't mind making money nearly as much as they hate losing money. This introduces *semivariance*, a variation of standard deviation which places greater emphasis on downside volatility than upside volatility. But that, and its offspring *lower partial moment*, is rather complex stuff, not suited for a basic book like this. Forget I mentioned them.

The Tortoise and the Hare

Compare the two investments below. Assuming you knew in advance that they would perform as shown, which would you choose?

Year	Tortoise	Hare
1	+10%	+18%
2	+10%	+32%
3	+10%	+11%
4	+10%	-17%
5	+10%	+10%

FIGURE 6-11

Most would choose the hare, believing it produces a higher rate of return, and indeed, that's exactly how most people choose their investments: by focusing on returns and ignoring risk. Such a strategy usually fails, as it does here, for the tortoise makes more money than the hare.

I know you don't believe me, so get a calculator to prove it to yourself.

Not only does the tortoise make more money, it does so with far less risk: The hare's standard deviation is 17.85, while the tortoise's is zero. That means you can be 95% certain that the tortoise in any one year will earn 10%, while the hare could lose 25%!

Since we don't know when real losses will occur, it's better to invest like the tortoise. Yet, if these were two mutual funds, personal finance magazines and the hare itself (in advertisements and direct mail) would brag about the year when it gained 32%, and investors would have been enticed to buy it. The tortoise, meanwhile, would have gotten little or no press attention.

Is 20% Really Better Than 10%?

In fact, it's the funds you don't hear about — the ones that don't make it to #1 — that really are the best choices.

For example, given the one-year performances of two funds below, which would be ranked #1?

Year	Fund A	Fund B
1	+20%	+10%

The answer is Fund A, of course. But what if the following occurs in the second year?

Year	Fund A	Fund B
1	+20%	+10%
2	+0%	+10%
Total	+20%	+20%

Both A and B now display a two-year total return of 20%, but as you can see below, an investor would have made more money in Fund B.

	Fund A	Fund B
Initial Investment	$1,000	$1,000
Value After Year 1	$1,200	$1,100
Value After Year 2	$1,200	$1,210

Yet, you would have been more likely to invest in Fund A, because its marketing literature would have bragged about its performance in Year One.

Thus, there is a big difference between investment returns and investor returns.

Standard deviation reveals a fund's true level of risk. Look at Figure 6-12: It clearly shows the volatility of international stocks. Because of this volatility, my colleagues and I rarely recommend that clients place more than 15% of assets into this asset class, and depending on the client, we may recommend much less (maybe even zero). Yet investors who fail to examine standard deviation often place too much money in risky investments, with correspondingly disastrous results.

STANDARD DEVIATION
1994–2003

U.S. Government Securities Funds	3.6
Municipal Bond Funds	4.4
Corporate Bond Funds (High Yield)	7.8
Balanced Funds	10.4
Stock Funds	16.6
International Stock Funds	19.1

FIGURE 6-12

Chapter 37 - Why Funds Make Money But People Do Not

Although most stock funds have made a lot of money over the years, many of the people who bought those funds actually managed to lose money. Let's examine how.

Morningstar analyzed the asset growth and total returns of 219 stock funds, tracked over a five-year period ending May 31, 1994. It compared each fund's average annual return, which it called the *investment return*, with the return on the average dollar that was actually invested, which it called the *investor return*. The investment return, then, is the total return of the fund while the investor return is the return that people actually earned based on when they bought and when they sold.

The study's average annual investment return over the five years was a positive 12.5%, but the average annual investor return was a negative 2.2%. How could investors have lost money when the investments themselves made money?

The answer is simple. Investors bought their shares after hearing that the funds did well (meaning they bought when the price was high) and then panicked during market declines, thereby selling when the prices were low. When the market picked up again, investors jumped back in.

Buying high and selling low is the exact opposite of what you're supposed to do: You need to stick it out, for that is the only way to earn high consistent returns. Panicking only causes you to lose.

And the longer you hold your investment, the more time you have to catch up to the average investment return. The secret to investment success, then, is to buy quality investments and hold them for many years — especially through bad or declining markets and periods of uncertainty.

Intellectually, that's easy. The challenge is to control your emotions, which tempt you to buy or sell at exactly the wrong time.

One of the most successful mutual fund managers in the business once told me, "My goal is to place in the top 25% each year, because if I do that, my 3-year ranking will place me in the top 10% and my 5-year ranking will be in the top 5%. That's because so few funds are consistently in the top 25% each year." Yet, he lamented, many investors pass his fund by because each year he's only in the top quartile, and there's nothing glamorous about that. Smart investors know better.

The year 1991 provides an excellent illustration. The S&P 500 gained 25.8% that year, but it's a fair bet that few investors enjoyed those profits. Why? Take a look at the figure below.

As you can see, the market gained 13% in the first six weeks of the year. Imagine! Thirteen percent in just six weeks! At that rate, the market would be up 112.7% for the year!

And by mid-February, that's exactly what the TV newscasters and financial press were telling us. Upon hearing this news, lots of folks cashed in their CDs, and bought stocks and stock mutual funds. Then they just sat back and waited for the profits to come rolling in. And they waited. And waited. And waited.

They waited for 10 months. And virtually nothing happened.

Indeed, by mid-December the S&P 500 stood at 377.70, barely higher than mid-February's level of 369.02. That represented a dismal gain of just 2.4% — well below what investors could have earned virtually anywhere else — even in dull CDs. Disgusted, investors sold their shares and returned to the bank. Hey, at least they'd get 5% in a certificate of deposit.

And sure enough, no sooner had the masses given up hope, the stock market took off. From December 11 to the end of the year, the market skyrocketed, with the S&P gaining 10.4% in just two weeks. For the year, the market posted a gain of 25.8%, one of the most impressive yearly performances in Wall Street history. But while the market made tons of money, many investors didn't, for almost all of the gains for the entire year occurred in just eight weeks — the first six and the last two. The masses, desperately trying to catch the wave, weren't even in the water when the tide came in.

Some people, though, did enjoy all the profits of 1991. They were the folks who had invested in 1990 and were still invested in 1992.

FIGURE 6-13

Chapter 38 - Beta

Another tool Wall Street uses to evaluate mutual funds is *beta*, which is the amount of volatility a mutual fund experiences relative to the stock market as a whole.

A fund with a beta of 1 is deemed to have the same risk (i.e., volatility) as the S&P 500. Thus, a fund whose beta is 2 is twice as volatile as the S&P, while a fund whose beta is 0.5 is half as volatile. In practice, this means if the S&P rises 10%, a fund whose beta is 2 would be expected to rise 20%, while if the S&P falls 10%, the fund would be expected to drop 20%.

> If you know the Greek alphabet, you must be figuring, hey, if there's a beta, there's gotta be an alpha. After all, would you start a list with the letter "B"?
>
> *Alpha,* also called the Jensen index, measures the return produced by the fund's manager, as opposed to the return produced by the overall market. A positive alpha means the manager brought value to the fund.

Know Beta for What It Isn't

Although beta is a popular tool, it is often misunderstood. Here are two points to remember about beta.

Point #1: Beta Does Not Predict Fund Profitability

Just because higher-beta funds rise faster in up markets than lower-beta funds, don't be fooled into thinking higher-beta funds always make more money than lower-beta funds. Beta does not predict future circumstances. Rather, it merely suggests how a given fund is likely to perform if those circumstances exist. It could very well be that actual circumstances will favor low-beta funds.

Point #2: Beta Compares Fund Performance to the U.S. Stock Market

Betas are available for all mutual funds, including bond funds, international funds, even gold funds. However, be careful to use beta only when comparing funds that invest in U.S. stocks. Otherwise, you could draw the wrong conclusion. For example, the beta of the average international stock fund is .64. This suggests that international stock funds are very low in volatility, but you know that's not true.

R-Squared *(R²)*

To determine whether a fund's beta is reliable, examine the R-Squared (R^2). An R^2 of 100 means all movements of the fund are due to movements in the market. The lower the R^2, the less impact the market has on the fund's movements, and the less relevant are beta and alpha.

> If that cold-calling cowboy wasn't scared off when you asked about standard deviation, start talking about R^2. You'll hear a dial tone real quick!

One Beta I Really Like

As you'd expect, research shows that the average beta of all stock funds is 1 (after all, the average of all stock funds is by definition the market average). However, the average beta of balanced funds is only .53, according to Morningstar.

As you saw in Chapter 23, for the 10 years ending June 30, 2003, balanced funds produced an average annual return of 7.6% and stocks returned an average of 8.4%. In other words, balanced funds earned 91% of the return of stock funds but took only 53% of the risk to do it!

This strikes me as an excellent risk-to-reward relationship and explains why I'm such a big fan of balanced funds.

Chapter 39 - Portfolio Optimization vs. Maximization

A maximizer's primary goal is to earn as much as possible. To her, any risk is acceptable. Optimizers, by contrast, want to earn as much as possible *relative to the risk they must take to get there.*

My firm's planners are optimizers. Our clients might be able to earn higher returns elsewhere, but it's unlikely they'll do so on a risk-adjusted basis. Still, for those who are purely performance-motivated, our style may be too boring.

This is not a right-or-wrong issue. That's why, when you're interviewing planners or brokers, you should ask if they consider themselves to be maximizers or optimizers, and you need to make sure their answer matches your attitude.

For more on developing an Optimal Portfolio, see Chapter 45.

> *"Money isn't everything, as long as you have enough."*
>
> —Malcolm Forbes

Chapter 40 - The Rankings Trap

All this explains why you must never invest in a mutual fund simply because of the rankings published in some personal finance magazine. Yet many investors do. But if you misuse the rankings, you could wind up with disastrous results.

Indeed, when reviewing recently published performance statistics, many fund owners ask, "Why aren't the funds I own listed as the best?"

This question implies that you should be able to choose the one fund out of thousands that will produce the highest return. Such a feat not only is impossible, it's the wrong reason for choosing a fund. Still, used properly, rankings can be helpful in monitoring and comparing funds. Here, then, are tips about rankings.

Tip #1: Last Year's Winners Rarely Repeat Their Performance

How mutual funds perform in one year has little to do with how they'll perform the next, which is why every prospectus states:

"PAST PERFORMANCE IS NO INDICATION OF FUTURE RESULTS."

Yet, millions of investors ignore this advice and dump huge amounts of money into funds simply because the fund was at the top of some magazine's list.

Witness the Oakmark Fund. It had a mere $8 million in assets when it was introduced in 1991. After it was ranked #1, investors started pouring money in. By December 1992, assets had ballooned to more than $320 million, and by December 1993, assets had skyrocketed to more than $1 billion (that's *billion*).

The same thing happened to the Lexington Strategic Investment Fund, named the #1 fund of 1993, with a whopping 263% profit. The fund had assets of only $8 million in January 1993, but had $90 million just one year later — an 11-fold increase. What happened?

Hearing of the fund's great performance, investors rushed in, expecting Lexington to make as much money in 1994 as it did in 1993.[19] But was that a reasonable expectation? Hardly: Lexington had one of the worst track records in the industry! Indeed, an investment of $10,000 in 1983 was worth only $409 in 1993 — even including 1993's outstanding performance!

Indeed, Lex's average annual return for the 10-year period of 1984-1993, at 14%, sounds fine, but the average annual return from 1983-1992 (which omits 1993's huge return) was *negative* 11.9%. That's why the fund, which had $173 million in assets in 1984, only had $8 million by January '93!

These stories are not isolated. Rather, they are the norm. Another example is the Janus Fund, which bet heavily on tech stocks. It earned 23% in 1997, 39% in 1998 and 47% in 1999, giving it a three-year average of 36%. With that great track record, investors began pouring money into the fund — just in time for the fund to experience a 15% loss in 2000, followed by a 26% loss in 2001, and a 28% loss in 2002. So much for past performance.

Clearly, just because a fund is "tops" at one time does not mean it will be "tops" at another. The reason is because the time periods themselves are completely arbitrary.

Why Do Rankings Always Track the Calendar?

Do you only invest on the first day of a month and sell on the 31st? Rankings always assume you do. After all, they have to choose some start and stop dates, and besides, what difference does it make which dates are used?

If you think it makes no difference, think again. Take the Bull & Bear Special Equities Fund, for example. The fund's average annual return over the five-year period ending October 1, 1995, was an impressive 18.3%. But look at its five-year

---

[19]It's true. Lex started the year with $8 million. Based on its 263% gain, Lex should have ended the year with $29 million. Instead, it had $90 million. Where did the other $61 million come from? From new investors, of course.

record ending August 1, 1995, instead. By starting and stopping the five-year clock two months earlier, the fund's average annual return drops from 18.3% to a dismal 5.2%. That's a pretty incredible difference.

So you tell me: Is that a great fund or a terrible one? Think about that the next time you pick up the current copy of some consumer magazine. Maybe you'll catch the August issue and buy the fund; maybe you'll read the October issue and avoid it.

Be a smart investor and ignore the fact that somebody happens to rank a fund #1 for some arbitrary period of time.

Tip #2: Do Not Focus on the Rate of Return

If last year's winner (Fund ABC) earned 100%, but this year's winner (Fund DEF) earned only 50%, that means ABC is a better fund, right?

Wrong. This year's economy is different from last year's; thus, you should expect fund performance to mirror those differences.

Therefore, what matters is how a fund does in a particular time period as compared to similar funds *in that same period*. Relativity is the key, not isolated statistics.

Tip #3: Disregard Short Periods

The longer the period, the more accurate the ranking. Not only is quarterly performance data meaningless, few professionals make decisions based on even one-year periods. Statistically, the most meaningful data is derived from 10-year intervals or longer.

This is why the SEC requires funds to advertise 10-year performance data; left on their own, funds certainly would promote shorter intervals if it made them look better (and it often does). Yet, although 10-year data is more important, the personal finance press usually tout one-year and three-year data; many even list 90-day results (a notable exception is *Forbes*, which displays readings not merely by years but also by up-markets and down-markets, which transcend the calendar).

As a former journalist in the financial trade press, I can tell you that many publishers tout 90-day returns merely because they have subscriptions to sell. They need something new to say in each issue just to stay in business. Thus, what's important to the media is not necessarily important to investors. (This also supports the argument against buying last year's winners: Every quarterly list contains names that are different from before. The names on each list constantly change, proving the impossibility of predicting next quarter's winning funds.)

Tip #4: Be Sure You Use Valid Rankings

More than two dozen publications rank funds, and many are flawed. Some forget that mutual funds have different objectives, which will produce different rates of return. It is ridiculous to compare stock funds to bond funds, yet many rankings do. Be certain you are comparing apples to apples, as a review of *risk* is as important as one of performance. Others rank only a few hundred funds — sort of like saying the Washington Redskins had the best record in '02, which is true if you ignore the 21 teams that did better.

Used properly, rankings can help you select funds that:

- demonstrate consistent long-term performance that is competitive with other funds in the same category;

- offer volatility equal to or below that of others; and

- are based on your outlook, positioned to perform favorably over the next five years or beyond, interim fluctuations notwithstanding.

Keep these points in mind the next time you review the rankings, and you'll be a happier, more successful investor.

Chapter 41 - Do You Need to Pick the Best Fund?

Although I've given you valuable tips in using rankings, I really believe that the whole concept is somewhat flawed. People turn to rankings with the false hope (expectation?) of finding the "best" fund, because both fund advertising and the personal finance press give the impression that you had better choose the best fund or risk losing all your money.

That's nonsense, and I'm here to tell you that you can relaaaaax. Although it's always desirable to pick the "best" fund, don't be overly concerned about the need to do so. Because, in fact, picking the best fund is really not that important. Not only is it nearly impossible to do, even picking the worst isn't so bad.

Look at Figure 6-14, which shows the average annual return for the best, worst, and average funds in each category for the 10 years ending June 30, 2003, according to Thomson Financial. In the balanced fund category, for example, even the worst earned 7.5%, while the best averaged 12.9%. So if you're worried that you'll never be able to pick the best fund, relax: It's not a winner-take-all contest. The truth is you don't have to pick the best fund, for even picking the worst — in any category — produced returns over the last 10 years that were similar to the 5% average annual return that CDs provided.

IS CHOOSING THE WORST REALLY SO BAD?

Performance of Mutual Funds by Category
1984-2003

	Best	Worst	Average
U.S. Government Securities Funds	9.7	7.7	8.0
Municipal Bond Funds	8.9	4.9	7.5
Corporate Bond Funds	10.2	2.6	7.9
Balanced Funds	12.9	7.5	10.3
Stock Funds	15.7	4.9	10.4
International Stock Funds	12.8	4.0	10.5

Average Annual CD Rate for Period: 5%

FIGURE 6-14

"It is better to be approximately right than precisely wrong."
—**Warren Buffett**

Chapter 42 - The Computer vs. The Money Manager

In a study of money manager performance, researchers asked managers to program a computer with their investment style, and then they compared the performance of the computer's buy/sell decisions with that of the managers themselves. Guess who won?

The computer, every time. Why? Because the computer didn't wake up in a bad mood or second-guess itself. To understand this, say you're buying a stock at $20 a share. At what price will you sell?

...

I bet you haven't thought of a price. So, go ahead and think of a price before continuing. I'll wait.

...

Okay, now you have a price in mind. I'll bet your price is *higher* than $20. Am I right?

Hasn't it occurred to you that maybe, *just maybe*, the price might go *down*? That's the first problem with investors: They never think their stock will go down. After all, they say, "Why would I buy it if it's going to lose money?"

That's why you must establish *two selling prices* whenever you buy a stock: one that's higher than your buy price, and one that's lower.

You Greedy Pig

By the way, I bet your sell price was $30, wasn't it? That's a 50% gain over your buy price! You greedy pig![20] You've lived with a 2% return from your bank account, but you now demand 50% from the stock! That doesn't make any sense! Remember: Bulls and bears both make money, but pigs get slaughtered.

---

[20]I don't even want to comment on those of you who set $40 as your sell price.

Let's be reasonable about this. Let's establish $18 and $24 as our sell prices; that would be a 20% gain while limiting losses to 10%. Thus, when your broker calls to say your stock has hit your sell price of $24, guess how you will respond?

You'll say, 'It's doing great! I don't want to sell now! It's going to $30! Hold on to it!' Greed has taken over.

And indeed, the stock will go to $27, then $28, back to $22, and you'll end up selling at $18. You'll manage to lose 10% of your investment — and then complain that stocks are too risky.

Stocks are not the problem — you are the problem, because you let your emotions get in the way.

When you buy an investment, determine when you're going to sell — either a price (such as $50 per share) or a time (when my son goes to college). And when your sell point is reached, **_SELL!_** And the simple way to avoid driving yourself crazy is to follow Edelman's Rule #2: Once you sell an investment, _you no longer may look at the price in the newspaper_. Observe this rule or you will drive yourself crazy.

I often get questions on my call-in show from people thinking of refinancing their mortgage. "The rate is 8.5%," they say. "Should I take it or wait for the rate to drop to 8%?" I have no answer because they're asking the wrong question!

The right question is: Are you happy with the rate currently available? If you are, take it. If you're not, don't take it. Trying to catch the top or bottom of any market is a fool's game.

Chapter 43 - The Theory of Market Timing

The stock market's century-long upward curve is filled with many short-lived peaks and valleys. Rather than holding stocks for decades (which forces you to experience the market's declines as well as the surges), wouldn't it be smarter to be in stocks only when prices are moving upward?

Market timers say yes, you should invest at the low, ride the wave up and get out at the top, before the market goes down. Then, simply wait on the sidelines (in cash) for the market to hit another low, then jump back in, and ride the next wave to the next high. Simply repeat this process of buying low and selling high, and you'll become fabulously rich.

Very appealing pitch, isn't it? Don't worry if you don't know how to do it, for lots of Wall Streeters will do it for you — for a fee, of course. According to *Forbes*, one million people spend $500 million a year subscribing to newsletters which offer market timing advice, and millions more have invested billions in accounts managed by money managers who buy and sell stocks based on timing strategies.

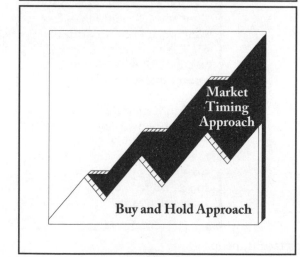

THE THEORY OF MARKET TIMING

Market Timing Approach

Buy and Hold Approach

FIGURE 6-15

There's only one problem with market timing: *It doesn't work.*

Why not? *Because nobody knows how to do it!*

For example, if you had invested in the S&P 500 on March 31, 1993, and sold 10 years later, you would have earned an average of 8.5% per year. But if you were out of the market for just 10 days — the 10 days in which the S&P made the most money — what do you think your 10-year average return would have been?

Just 3.5%. That's right: 59% of the S&P's total 10-year profit was earned *in just 10 days*. If you missed those 10 days, you would have earned 3.5% per year instead of 8.5%.

And if you skipped the 20 biggest days, you actually would have *lost* money! That's right: Your average annual return would have been -0.3%.

If this shocks you, read on, for this is not an aberration. In the 919 months from January 1, 1926, to June 30, 2003, a period where stocks averaged 10.3% per year, just 61% of those months were profitable. Yet, if you took away the top 71 months — just 8% of the total — your total return would have been *zero*. *Removing 8% of the time eliminates 100% of the profits.*

Think about it. How often does the nightly television news start with a story about "today on Wall Street?" Rarely, because on a typical day, the stock market is quite boring. But when the market does move — watch out! Market moves are rare but dramatic, and that's why the stock market is news only a few times each year.

> *"God created economists to make weather forecasters look good."*
> —**Anonymous**

That's why market timing fails. Prices move so rapidly — often for no apparent reason and with no warning — you can't react in time.

Hundreds of articles and studies over the past century, from economists and money managers, in government, academia, and business, *unanimously agree that market timing does not work*. In fact, the only people who endorse the concept are those newsletter writers, stockbrokers, financial planners, and money managers who make money by convincing you to try it.

And this raises another major point about taking advice from people: Are they telling you to do something because it's good for you or good for them? What exactly is their motivation? All too often, sellers of financial advice make more money getting you to do something than if they had done that very thing themselves.

I assure you: Rarely do the brokers who pitch market timing actually do it with their own money, and if they do, they certainly are not making very much money at it — for if they were, they'd be so busy managing their own money they wouldn't waste time trying to get your money from you.

There can be no other conclusion. Let's face it, people in my profession are not exactly known for their charity. They're in this business to make a buck. And once enough bucks are made, they're off to the Hamptons.

Thus, if market timing really worked, these guys certainly would have made enough money from their own account by now that they could kick back and relax. Yet they're still plying their wares to an unsuspecting public.

Forget about the argument that market timing is so new that timers haven't had enough time to earn the millions they fully expect to earn — suggesting that you need to get in now before the rest of the world finds out about their success. This argument is nonsense because market timers have been around as long as the markets themselves — like fleas on a dog.

"Wall Street's graveyards are filled with men who were right too soon."
—**William Hamilton**

In fact, if you were a market timer, and you knew your system worked, how much money would you put into your strategy?

All you've got, I'm sure.

Say you were around in 1926 and you had a system that you *knew* would correctly time the market. How much money would you have invested? Ten dollars? A hundred? A thousand?

The truth is, if you began in 1926 with one hundred dollars, and were shrewd enough to be in the market each month stocks made money and were out of the market each month stocks lost money — so that your account only went up, never down, every month over 77 years — guess how much money you'd have had by June 30, 2003?

Your $100 would have grown to more than $407 billion — that's *billion* with a "b." If you started with $10,000, you'd now have $41 *trillion* — far more than enough to pay off the national debt. Microsoft's Bill Gates would look downright poor by comparison, with his measly $.058 trillion (that's $58 billion, okay, not so poor).

The awesome power of this number is so enticing, so compelling, that market timers use it as an inducement to sell their services. Imagine! If your timing efforts produced only a fraction of these results, you'd be fabulously rich beyond your wildest dreams! So, c'mon! Let's give it a try!

Yeah, right.

The problem is that market timing is not like the lottery. At least with the lottery, you know someone is going to win — maybe even you, although with odds of 4 million to 1, you're more likely to get hit by lightning. But market timers offer no such odds. *Nobody* wins with market timing — except the con artist selling it to you. After all, if they were so sure about their abilities, why don't they do it with their own money instead of trying to collect 3% in annual fees from you?

Indeed, the Forbes 400 — a list of the wealthiest people in America — features no market timers. Not on the current list, nor any previous list. You'd think that with all the people selling timing services, *somebody* by now would have amassed billions. So the fact that no timer has ever made the list ought to tell you something.

> *"An economist is an expert who will know tomorrow why the things he predicted yesterday didn't happen today."*
> —**Laurence J. Peter**

By contrast, though, #2 on the Forbes 400 (right behind Bill Gates) is none other than Warren Buffett, the most successful investor in America, and arguably in American history. How did he amass his $32 billion? By buying stocks such as Coca-Cola, GEICO Insurance, Gillette, American Express, Dairy Queen, The Washington Post Company, and Disney, and holding onto them for decades.

Yep, the timers are absent from the Forbes 400, but the buy-and-holders are well- represented.

Why Market Timing Fails

Market timing fails for the simple reason that you must be right twice in order for it to work: You not only must know when to get ou, you also must know when to get back in (At least with lottery tickets, you need to be right only once.) Indeed, one wrong will undo many rights.

Even the experts can't get it right. Consider the economists at the Federal Reserve Board? Certainly the forecasts issued by the Fed each February and July ought to be pretty darn good. After all, because it controls interest rates, the Fed (theoretically at least) is in the position of being able to influence the very events it is predicting. So it would follow, then, that the best predictions ought to be coming from the Fed's own forecasts.

Yet, according to a study of the accuracy of Fed predictions of Gross Domestic Product from 1980 to 2002, conducted by the Fed itself, the Fed never made a correct prediction. Yup, they scored a big fat zero. Nada. Nothing. Zilch. If the Fed itself can't make accurate predictions, would you care to try?

Would an Advance Score Card Make Any Difference?

For the sake of argument, let's assume for the moment that market timing works. In fact, let's go the timers one better and pretend we know in advance what will happen in the short-term. Would it make any difference in the long-term?

> *"All you need is to look over the earnings forecasts publicly made a year ago to see how much care you need to give to those being made now for the next year."*
>
> —Gerald M. Loeb

Let's say it's August '87, three months before the Crash, and you're about to invest for five years. You must choose a money manager and stick with whomever you choose. Which group of managers will you choose:

(a) those who are destined to make money in the Crash of '87, or

(b) those who not only will lose money in the Crash, but will lose more than the average.

Although those in group (a) clearly make more money over the next three months than those in group (b), that's not the case over the next five years. According to the Hulbert Financial Digest, money managers who made money in the Crash of '87 earned an average of just 1.4% in the five years following the crash, while managers who lost money during that period earned, as a group, an average of 5.1% in the following five years. Thus, even picking the right group in the short-term would have led to failure in the long-term. Which is more important to you — long-term or short-term?

What If You Switch Managers Every Year?

Okay, you say, the prior example is fine, but it's pretty unrealistic. After all, who says you've got to stick with the same manager every year? Why not just move from manager to manager each year based on their track records? After all, the above example demonstrates that at least one group of managers did manage to prosper in the Crash.

True, but the above example also assumes you were able to identify that group of managers before the fact — which is as impossible as picking next year's Super Bowl winner. But the point is well taken anyway. So let's try another example.

Here's the story of a broker who attracted new clients by demonstrating his ability to pick winners every time.

How did he do it? Each month, he'd mail letters to 100 prospective clients. Fifty of the prospects would receive a letter saying they should sell a particular stock; the other 50 would get a letter advising they buy that same stock. Naturally, one of the letters would prove correct. So, the next month, to whichever group had received the "correct" letter, the broker would mail a second letter. These 50 letters would again contain a recommendation pertaining to a specific stock, and again, 25 would be told to buy and 25 would be told to sell.

In the third month, the 25 prospects who had received the second 'correct' letter got one more, half again containing buy recommendations and half touting sells. In the fourth month, the broker would call the dozen remaining "correct" prospects, and tell them the following:

"Look, I've told you to do something three times in a row. I was right every time, but you didn't listen to me. Now, I'm giving you another recommendation right now, and if you don't take it, you'll never hear from me again." Every prospect would sign up.

This sales pitch is illegal, and when he was found out, the broker was barred from the securities industry.

Since we can't predict who will do well in the coming year, we'll do the next best thing: Each January 1, we'll switch our account to the #1 money manager of the previous 12 months. After all, this is how millions of investors pick their mutual funds. They buy some magazine, check the rankings for last year's winners, and promptly buy those funds.

Let's say we do the same thing. According to Thomson Financial, for the 10-year period ending June 30, 2003, switching annually to the best manager of the previous 12 months would have produced an average annual loss of 12%.

On the other hand, if we had switched each year to the worst manager of the previous 12 months, we would have produced an annualized loss of 3.7%. Meanwhile, if we had just bought the S&P 500 itself and held on, our annual gain would have been 9.5%. The correct conclusion, then, is that nothing beats the buy-and-hold strategy. Even making the right timing choice is not as good as making no timing choice. Invest your money into a broadly diversified group of mutual funds and leave them alone.

When the Pros Try Timing

I'm not saying you shouldn't engage in active trading or market timing just because you can't do it as well as the typical Wall Street pro. I'm saying they can't do it, either.

If you want proof, look at the Financial Trading Association. This now-defunct group (which kinda says it all) used to stage the U.S. Trading and Investing Championships. Although open to all investors, most entrants were professional stockbrokers. The contests challenged these pros to see how much money they could make in short periods of four months to one year. Since the pros traded for their own account (not for their clients) and since they invested real money (not computer models), there was no doubt everybody tried their best.

> *"I don't have a clue which direction the next 10% or 15% price movement will take the market. But I know with certainty which direction the next 100% movement will take it, and that's all that really matters."*
> —Nick Murray

Yet, according to the last published data I saw, of the 3,500+ entries from 1983–1990, only 22% made any money at all. Only a handful managed to keep pace with or exceed the S&P 500.

> *"Even when the experts all agree, they may well be mistaken."*
> —Bertrand Russell

These results are not a phenomenon. Rather, they're quite common. As Mark Hulbert, editor of the *Hulbert Financial Digest*, has written in *Forbes* magazine: "Most active traders are losers ... trading is costly. It is so costly that the average investor is almost guaranteed to lag the market unless he or she follows a long-term investment strategy."

Please pay attention to this. Don't trade actively. Instead, change your investments as often as you change televisions. When properly selected, your TV ought to last years — and when you finally do replace it, odds are good it's because your circumstances have changed, not because the TV broke. So, pick your investments like you would a TV — with a lot of care and a plan to hold on for a long time.

Chapter 44 - Diversification: The Key to Your Investment Success

Am I saying all your money should be in stocks or stock funds? Of course not. Nobody should subject all their money to just one risk.

While it's easy to understand why people don't like risk, in truth there's nothing wrong with placing your money at risk; in fact, it's impossible *not* to, for even bank accounts place you at risk, if only due to taxes and inflation. Thus, every investment choice involves risk. The key, then, is knowing which risks are appropriate.

Most people are willing to gamble small amounts of money, as the popularity of lottery tickets, casinos, and football pools attests. Gamblers know they can't earn big money unless they're willing to take big risks. The secret, then, is to learn how to take risks properly.

So let's learn how to do that. Say you have $25,000 to invest for 25 years. If you choose a 3% CD, your account would grow to $52,344 (ignoring taxes).

On the other hand, let's say you split your $25,000 evenly into five piles as follows:

- With the first pile, **you buy 5,000 lottery tickets**, and like almost everyone else who plays the lottery, you lose it all. Thus, after 25 years, the ending value of this $5,000 is zero.

- With the second pile, **you bury it all under your mattress**. Thus, by earning no interest for 25 years, this $5,000 remains $5,000.

- With the third pile, **you open a bank savings account at 2% interest**, where it grows to $8,203 over the next 25 years.

- With the fourth pile, **you buy a U.S. Treasury** earning 3%. This pile grows to $10,469.

- And with the fifth pile, you invest in the stock market, earning 10% per year. At that rate, your $5,000 will grow to $54,174.

In total, you have $25,502 *more* than if you had invested the entire amount in a CD — even though you lost *all* of the first pile, earned *nothing* on the second, invested in bank accounts with the third, super-safe government bonds with the fourth, and "gambled" in the stock market only with the last fifth. How can this be?

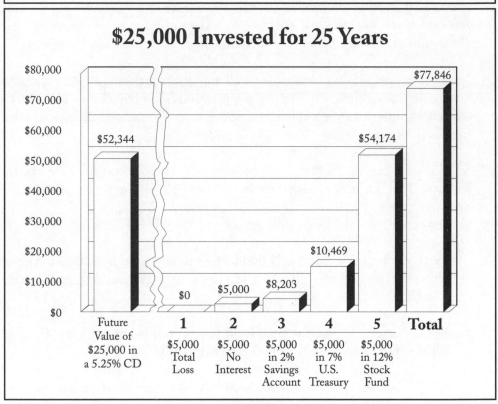

DIVERSIFICATION vs. BANK CDs

$25,000 Invested for 25 Years

FIGURE 6-16

This result is possible thanks to *diversification*. This simple principle recognizes that the maximum loss of any investment is limited to the amount you invest, but the maximum gain is unlimited — as shown in Chapter 3. Thus, the profits from earning $54,174 on the fifth pile more than compensate for the losses incurred in the first pile. Even though part of your money might go down in value and other parts may earn less than acceptable returns, only one small part of your money needs to earn above-average returns to make your overall return far higher than if all your money had been placed into just one mediocre (but safe!) investment.

> Do not make the mistake of Mr. Anderson. He came to my firm as the unhappy owner of five mutual funds, into each of which he had placed 20% of his money for diversity. Yet, each one had lost money. Not only that, each had lost roughly the same amount of money. Upon inspection, we discovered that all five funds were invested in U.S. government bonds! That's not diversity — that's redundancy! Naturally, when interest rates went up, his funds all went down. And this guy couldn't figure it out. "How could all five funds lose money?" he demanded. "Mutual funds are awful!"

And that's the key: Diversification allows to you take small, calculated risks, and the key to achieving personal financial success is in knowing how to do this. As General George Patton put it, "There's nothing wrong with taking risks. That's quite different from being rash."

But successful risk-taking means you must be *willing* to take financial risks. Most Americans are unwilling to do so. By emphasizing safety, they lock themselves into low returns, which leads to financial failure. In fact, many people fail financially not because they take too much risk with their money, but because they take *too little* risk with their money.

Note: This example, which uses five categories invested in equal amounts, is not intended to serve as an actual investment model. My firm, for example, routinely creates portfolios using eight or nine major asset classes with different amounts placed in each, and we don't use mattresses or lottery tickets.

Asset Allocation

How do we create proper diversity? Through *asset allocation*. This concept focuses on the forest, not the trees, and its premise is supported by a landmark study published in *Financial Analysts Journal*. By examining the performance of 82 large pension plans over a 10-year period, the study sought to explain why one institutional money manager makes more money than another.

The study found that 93.6% of the difference in volatility from one plan to another was due to asset allocation, not investment selection. Thus, what matters is not which stocks you buy, but what portion of your total assets you place into stocks. That's why investors who devote all their attention to figuring out which stocks or funds to buy are missing the point — as are the magazines and newsletters that proclaim with each issue, "Hot Stocks to Buy Now!"

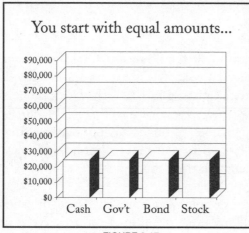

ASSET ALLOCATION

You start with equal amounts...

FIGURE 6-17

...so that your pie looks like this:

Stock · Cash · Bond · Gov't — 25% / 25% / 25% / 25%

FIGURE 6-18

Here's how asset allocation works, using a hypothetical example solely to demonstrate the concept, as shown in the figures below.

This model uses four major asset classes: cash, government securities, bonds, and stocks, and to keep things simple, we're splitting our assets equally into each of the four categories.[21]

Asset allocation acknowledges that higher-risk asset classes are expected to grow more quickly than lower-risk ones. On that premise, we would expect stocks to be our fastest-growing group. If this happened, we would later find that we no longer have equal amounts in each asset class: Since our stocks made more money than the other investments, stocks now hold 38% of our total assets instead of the original 25%, and the weightings of other asset classes have changed based on their performance as well.

---

[21]This example is not intended to serve as an actual allocation model. In a real model, we might add real estate, international investments and foreign currencies, natural resources, precious metals, and other hedge positions, placing more money in some categories than in others based on the client's circumstances, objectives, liquidity needs, and risk tolerances.

As Chapter 51 explains, think in percentages, not dollars: While the pie's value changes with time, the percentage is always 100%. With stocks now 38% and cash only 15%, we find that our model has fallen out of balance. Thus, to restore the pie to its original shape, we need to rebalance the portfolio. We do this by reallocating the assets: We sell enough of the stocks and bonds to bring them each back down to 25%, and use those dollars to buy more of the cash and government bonds to bring each of them up to 25%. This will return the model to its original proportions.

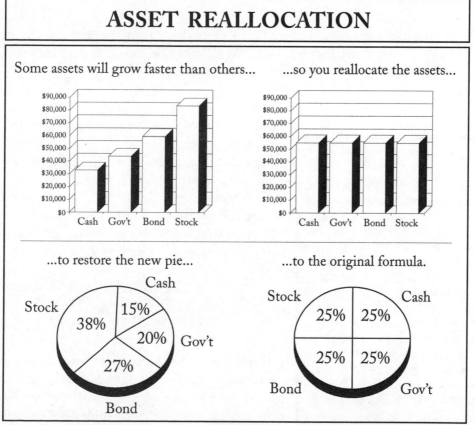

FIGURE 6-19

In other words, asset allocation requires that you sell your winners — the ones that made the most money — and buy your losers — the ones that made the least money (or perhaps even lost money).

I'll bet you're thinking, "Is Edelman crazy?"

Not at all. Think about it: If you spend your investing career "selling winners" and "buying losers," you will become very, very wealthy.

Asset allocation succeeds because it forces you to do the very thing you don't want to do. Emotionally, you want winners, not losers. If stocks are doing much better than bonds, you'll want stocks. After all, you ask, why on earth would you want to sell the great stocks and put the money into the rotten bonds?

Because you *don't want to buy winners*.

If you're buying winners, that means they've already made money, and you thus would be buying after the fact. But *selling* a winner means you made money with it — and that's the whole point to investing, isn't it?

Thus, *you want to buy losers*, or more accurately, it doesn't matter if it was a loser *before* you bought it. All that matters is that it becomes a winner before you sell it. But if you act emotionally, you'll fail. You'll buy more stocks — "They're making so much money!" — and you'll sell your government securities — "Those dogs! I want to dump them!" In other words, you'll want to buy and sell based on past performance, even though

PAST PERFORMANCE IS NO INDICATION OF FUTURE RESULTS.

Please realize that in this example, my concern is not that I think stocks are no longer a good investment. Instead, my concern is that having 38% of the money in stocks is too high a percentage (according to our hypothetical example's circumstances, risk tolerance, and financial objectives). Thus, the decision to reduce exposure to stocks is a financial planning issue, not an investment outlook issue.

There is no "is."

When people tell me they love their investments, it always is because those investments have made money (nobody ever loves an investment that has lost money). This creates a trap, for there is no present tense in the world of investing.

At no time will you ever own an investment that is doing great. You might have an investment that has done great, or one that will be great, but that's it. This is very different from one that is great.

And just because it has been great doesn't mean it will be great. Remember: on Wall Street, there is no "is."

You see, if you don't reallocate, eventually you will own nothing but stocks. You'll find that you have 100% of your money in just one asset class, and you will have abandoned the concept of diversification.

> Of course, in the real world, you might not want to reallocate your assets back to the original model. Over time your health, income, marital status, and other circumstances could change, and these changes could require a change in your model portfolio.

How Often Should You Reallocate?

Aside from changes in your personal circumstances, this does raise an interesting question: How often should you rebalance your portfolio? Many academicians have tried to answer this question, using computer models back-dated to 1926. Researchers have focused on chronology (meaning you rebalance the portfolio at certain time intervals); weightings (you rebalance whenever any asset class gains or loses a certain percentage); or a combination of the two.

The conclusion is that there is no conclusion: Like the search for Pi, no one has been able to determine the most effective and efficient rebalancing program. (If someone had found the formula, you'd have heard about it by now.) Instead, researchers have discovered that different methodologies produce similar results, provided each methodology is applied consistently. In other words, the key to successful rebalancing is to establish your parameters and stick with them.

For example, you might choose to rebalance your portfolio every two years. Or perhaps, whenever one asset class increases or decreases 20% from its initial weighting. Or perhaps some combination of the two. The design is not as important as the implementation: Changing your methodology or failing to execute it on schedule will reduce the effectiveness of this strategy.

Chapter 45 - Developing an Optimal Portfolio

Most neophytes think they must choose between investments that are safe but which earn low returns, or those that are risky but which can earn high returns. Broadly speaking, this means investors often feel they must choose between stocks and bonds.

As you've learned in this book, bonds are safer and, on average, earn less than stocks. Therefore, it holds that Portfolio A, consisting of 100% bonds, is safer than Portfolio B, which is 100% stocks. It also holds that A makes less money than B. Thus, a chart of these facts would look like Figure 6-20.

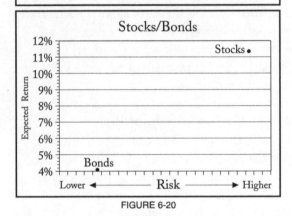

PORTFOLIO OPTIMIZATION

FIGURE 6-20

Therefore, you would conclude that any portfolio containing a combination of stocks and bonds must fall somewhere between these two points.

But it doesn't work out that way. As you see in Figure 6-21, which reflects market performance from 1926 to 2002, a blended portfolio of 20% stocks/80% bonds actually is lower in risk than a portfolio of 100% bonds — and it earns more money, too. How can this be?

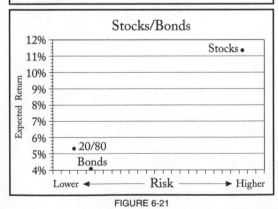

PORTFOLIO OPTIMIZATION

FIGURE 6-21

The answer lies in the fact that all investments contain risks. But not all investments face the same risks.

For example, the biggest risk facing bonds is interest rate risk (Chapter 14). Stocks are not as sensitive to this particular risk as bonds. Therefore, if you owned a portfolio that was 100% bonds, and you wanted to reduce interest rate risk, you could do so by moving some of your money, say 20%, away from bonds. Moving that money protects that 20% from interest rate risk, and if you moved that money to stocks, you'd be increasing your return at the same time, since stocks earn more than bonds. Therefore, a portfolio that contains some stocks is actually safer than a portfolio that does not.

> **This is the same principle as that used in Chapter 14 to demonstrate that gold can reduce the risk of owning bonds.**

PORTFOLIO OPTIMIZATION

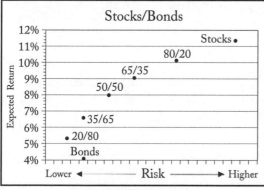

FIGURE 6-22

OPTIMIZING BETWEEN U.S. AND INTERNATIONAL STOCKS

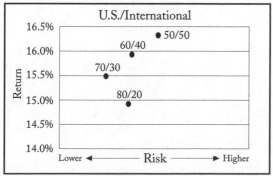

FIGURE 6-23

Figure 6-22 shows the risk/return of a variety of portfolios, based on their holdings of stocks and bonds. As shown, a portfolio of 20% stocks/80% bonds is lowest in risk. But which is the optimal portfolio? Recall that an optimal portfolio is one which earns the highest returns relative to risk.

The answer is the portfolio containing 35% stocks/65% bonds. Why? Because it has virtually the same risk as the portfolio of 100% bonds, but its return is nearly 75% higher.

Similar results can be found comparing U.S. stocks with international stocks, as Figure 6-23 shows.

This discussion is not intended to suggest that you should build a portfolio consisting of just two asset classes. The point is that you can build a portfolio that is safer and more profitable by investing in many asset classes than you can by investing in only one asset class. Indeed, *introducing a risky asset into your portfolio reduces the overall risk of that portfolio*. Put another way, if you want to lower your overall investment risk, invest in something risky.

And you don't have to be a rocket scientist to do it, either. Although professional advisors like me and my colleagues are experts at Modern Portfolio Theory and other sophisticated concepts, and can help you build more efficient allocation models than you'll create on your own, even simple models you create yourself can do wonders for your portfolio.

After all, there are four types of portfolios...

- low risk/low return

- low risk/high return

- high risk/low return

- high risk/high return

...and the best one is low risk/high return. Indeed, as seen in Figure 6-24, simply splitting your assets equally among cash, bonds, and stocks goes a long way toward achieving that goal, and using five asset classes, again just evenly split, does even better. With expert guidance, you can obtain even better results. So hire someone to show you how to do it, or do it yourself — but do it.

DIVERSIFICATION PROVIDES HIGHER RETURNS WITH LESS RISK

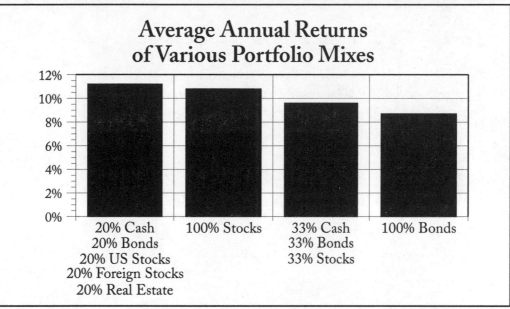

Average Annual Returns of Various Portfolio Mixes

20% Cash
20% Bonds
20% US Stocks
20% Foreign Stocks
20% Real Estate

100% Stocks

33% Cash
33% Bonds
33% Stocks

100% Bonds

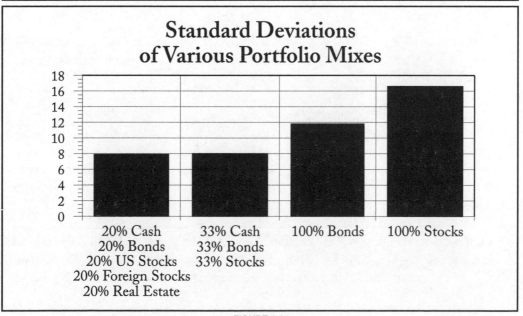

Standard Deviations of Various Portfolio Mixes

20% Cash
20% Bonds
20% US Stocks
20% Foreign Stocks
20% Real Estate

33% Cash
33% Bonds
33% Stocks

100% Bonds

100% Stocks

FIGURE 6-24

267

Chapter 46 - Dollar Cost Averaging

So far, we've been talking about investing as though you had a large sum of money to invest right now. Maybe you don't. Instead, maybe you have only a few dollars to put away each month.[22]

Your answer: dollar cost averaging. Here's how it works.

Say you have $100 and you buy a stock mutual fund which costs $10 per share. That means you buy 10 shares. Next month, you save another $100, which you place into the same fund, only now the shares are just $5. Thus, you buy 20 shares. What's the average price of all your shares?

Month	Amount Invested	Price Per Share
1	$100	$10
2	$100	$5

If you said $7.50, you're wrong.

You invested $200 ($100 per month over two months) and you own 30 shares (you bought 10 shares, then 20). Divide $200 by 30 shares and you'll find that the answer is $6.67.

Why did you think the answer was $7.50?

Because you used the *arithmetic mean* ($10 plus $5 divided by 2 = $7.50.) But I used the *harmonic mean*[23] ($200 by 30). Thus we're both right — the average price is $7.50, but the average *cost* is $6.67. Since the harmonic mean always produces a lower number than the arithmetic mean, *you have a built-in profit*!

Dollar cost averaging works because it acknowledges that we're all dummies when it comes to the stock market. Should we buy at its high of $10 a share? Of course not, but we're too dumb to know that the current price is destined to be the high,

---

[22]If you don't think you can even manage that, see Chapter 49 to learn how.
[23]Don't get too excited — you learned about both of these in grade school.

so we buy it. Thus, dollar cost averaging protects you by saying, "Okay, you dummy, if you insist on buying at $10 a share, I'm not going to let you buy very much."

Later, when the price goes down to $5 a share, DCA says, "Hey, you dummy, now's the time to buy!" so it forces you to buy lots of shares. In other words, DCA has you buy relatively few shares when the price is higher and more shares when the price is lower, thus giving you the average lowest cost. And since the average lowest *cost* is lower than the average lowest *price*, you're in a great position to enjoy a profit.

> Investors are a funny lot. When the price of their favorite ice cream drops 50%, they load up, but if the stock market cuts the price on their favorite stock — in essence, putting it on sale — they figure there's got to be something wrong, so they return the shares they previously bought!

Thus, dollar cost averaging succeeds because you buy fewer shares at higher prices and relatively more shares at lower prices. To make it work for you, simply invest a specific amount of money at a specific interval. Perhaps $100 per month, $25 per quarter, or a $3,000 IRA each year. It does not matter as long as you are consistent. Be sure to invest at each interval regardless of what the stock market is doing at the moment.

In fact, dollar cost averaging helps you overcome your fear that you'll invest at the top of the market. If you had invested $1,000 in the S&P 500 on January 1 of every year from 1965 through 2002, you'd have earned an average annual return of 10.2%. But if you got really lucky and were able to make your investments on the one day each year when prices were at their lowest, you'd have averaged 10.9% instead. But, knowing your luck, it's more likely that you'd have picked the worst day to invest each year. If so, your average annual return would have been 9.8%.

As you can see, it doesn't much matter when you invest when you dollar cost average. It only matters that you do invest and that you stay invested. "Timing" doesn't matter — "time in" does.

> *"Common sense is genius dressed in its working clothes."*
> —Ralph Waldo Emerson

Two Problems and Two Tips with Dollar Cost Averaging

There are two problems with trying to implement dollar cost averaging correctly — and you're the cause of both of them (what else is new?).

Problem #1: When the Price Goes Down, You Won't Want to Buy More

"Why should I keep buying this dog?," you'll ask, allowing your emotions to defeat you. Therefore, when dollar cost averaging, follow Edelman's Rule #2: Never follow the price in the newspaper; it will only upset you and prevent you from doing what you need to do to achieve financial success. Just buy your shares and ignore the rest.

Problem #2: You May Fail to Follow Through

It is vital that you stick to your plan. Too often, people simply forget to keep it up, what with life's everyday hectic schedules and all. Don't let anything stop you from fulfilling your DCA obligation on schedule.

To help you establish a successful DCA strategy, be sure to follow these two important rules:

Tip #1: Use Stock Mutual Funds, Not Individual Stocks

Do not use individual stocks or you run the serious risk of mistakenly engaging in the dangerous practice of *dollaring down* instead of dollar cost averaging.

Case in point: On a tip from his uncle, one of my clients once bought a stock at $6/share. When the stock later dropped to $4, he bought more. ("If I liked it at six," he figured, "I ought to love it at four!") When it dropped to $2.50, he bought

> Like everybody else, our clients too have difficulty keeping up with dollar cost averaging. To help them, we created a free service called The S.M.A.R.T. Plan.™
>
> Through The S.M.A.R.T Plan,™ we mail an invoice each month to our clients. It's not an actual bill, but it looks like one. The invoice reminds them to send money to their mutual fund account. Each client chooses the amount to be displayed on the invoice, but they are not required to respond, although of course, it's in their own best interest to do so!
>
> Thus, when our clients are busy paying their phone bill and sending in their mortgage payment, seeing this invoice reminds them to "pay themselves first." Our clients love this service, because it helps them stick with their financial plan. After all, Saving Monthly Accumulates Rewards over Time.

> You don't need my firm's S.M.A.R.T Plan,™ to enjoy the benefits of dollar cost averaging. Just sign up for Automatic Checkbook Debiting with your favorite mutual fund. Through ACD, the fund each month will withdraw a pre-authorized amount from your bank checking account and deposit that money into your fund account. All you need to do is remember to record the transaction in your checkbook.

more, and more still when it dropped to $1. Soon after the stock became worthless, *Forbes* ran a story disclosing that the stock was an alleged front for the Mafia. By that time, my client had lost $33,000.

You see, when a given stock begins a significant sustained downward spiral, there's often a good reason — with no assurance that the price will ever recover.

Yet for dollar cost averaging to succeed, the price must recover. This is why you'll have better success with DCA via a mutual fund instead of via specific stocks, because if a given stock is on a permanent downward trend, the fund manager can dump the stock and replace it with another. Thus, although a given stock might never recover, the fund can, preserving DCA's effectiveness.

Tip #2: Choose the Most Volatile, Speculative Investment You Can Find

The best choice for DCA, and this might surprise you, is a fund whose price tends to swing to great highs and lows. Ordinarily, we'd dismiss funds with such high betas (Chapter 38) as too risky, but when you're using DCA, this risk plays to your advantage.

Why? Because DCA's success is based on the efficient accumulation of shares. That means you need an investment which can drop in price, for the bigger the drop, the more shares you accumulate and the better your efficiency. After all, if you use a bank account, dollar cost averaging won't make any difference.

> Why do so many people fail financially? Because they fail to follow successful strategies like dollar cost averaging. The president of one of the largest mutual fund companies in the nation once told me that of his fund family's four million shareholder accounts, only 65,000 were adding money to their fund on a regular basis.

Thus, you should choose an investment (such as a U.S. or international stock fund) which experiences dramatic swings in value. If you are using DCA in such a fund, you'll actually celebrate when the stock market crashes! My clients who were dollar cost averaging during the Crash of '87 certainly did: Since these investors were buying each month anyway, the 30% drop in stock prices gave them the chance to buy on sale! When the market later recovered, they made a bundle. (Remember, the only people who get upset during market crashes are those who are selling — not those who are buying!)

Two Other Forms of Averaging

There are two other ways you can average your investments: income averaging and value averaging.

Taking Risk with Income, Not Principal

Some people just can't bring themselves to invest in stocks. If that describes you, consider income averaging. Through this method, you invest your money in super-safe U.S. Government Securities. Then, simply invest the monthly interest into a stock mutual fund. This way, your principal remains safe and sound, and your income will be invested in stocks via dollar cost averaging.

Naturally, this strategy is not as effective as investing the principal itself in stocks, but it's a good compromise for safety-conscious investors.

Value Averaging

This is actually a more effective strategy than dollar cost averaging, at least on paper, but I don't emphasize value averaging because most people cannot stick with it.

Unlike dollar cost averaging, where you invest a *specific amount* at a specific interval, value averaging has you buy a *specific number of shares* at each interval. The goal is to have your investment grow by a specific amount over each interval.

For example, you might plan to invest $300 per month, or you might want your account to increase in value by $300 per month. The former is dollar cost averaging; the latter is value averaging.

With value averaging, you add only enough money to achieve your goal. In other words, if your account grew by $200 in the month on its own (thanks to capital appreciation or dividends), you'd add only $100 (to bring the monthly increase to $300).

Value averaging works because you invest less money when prices rise but more when prices fall. With dollar cost averaging, on the other hand, you invest equal amounts regardless of what the stock market is doing — and this is not as efficient as value averaging.

If you run some models of value averaging on a computer spreadsheet, you'll see that it produces more efficient returns than dollar cost averaging. The problem, though, is that you may be required to invest a sum that exceeds your ability at any given interval, and if you can't fulfill the obligation, you destroy the strategy. For example, if the share price falls in a short period, you might not have the money that's suddenly required. Another problem is that although you're able to invest $50, you only invest $25 one month because the share price dropped. Not investing when you have the ability to do so is a waste of opportunity.

Therefore, I and most planners tend to favor dollar cost averaging, for you can more likely fulfill its requirements than you can those of value averaging. Dollar cost averaging also is easier because you send in the same amount each month. With value averaging, you have to track your investment to determine how much money you are supposed to send in.

So if you're a diehard, try value averaging. If you're a scaredy-cat, use income averaging, but if you're just like me, you'll use dollar cost averaging.

Chapter 47 - When Is the Best Time to Invest?

Given $100,000 to invest, should you slowly invest that money over a period of time or simply invest all at once as one lump sum?

To understand the answer, realize that dollar cost averaging (Chapter 46) is intended for the *accumulation of assets*, not the *distribution of assets* already accumulated. Studies have shown that the investor who invests all at once makes more money than investors who DCA their way into the market.

> *"The only absolute safe way to double your money is to fold it once and put it in your pocket."*
> —Frank McKinney Hubbard

This should be no surprise to you; after all, the entire benefit of *averaging* means that by default, you are guaranteed *not* to receive the *lowest* cost available, which in turn means you will not receive the highest returns, either. Since stock prices historically have an upward bias, the *sooner* you invest, the more money you will make, and dollar cost averaging delays that effort.

People who try to DCA large sums into the market soon learn why their strategy doesn't work: By investing $100,000 over a one-year period, they invest just $8,333 in the first month. That means they *didn't* invest $91,667. What will they do with that block of cash in the meantime?

It sits in cash, earning 1% interest — hence the problem. Although you lower your risk by dollar cost averaging, you also lower your return. Therefore, the best time to invest is when you have the money! (After all, if you don't have any money, it's a pretty lousy time to invest, eh?)

This also means you should invest *as soon as you do have the money*. People sometimes tell me they're saving $25 per month in a bank account. "As soon as it grows to $5,000, I'll buy a mutual fund," they say. If your money is sitting in a bank at only 1% per year, do you realize how long it will take $25/month to grow to $5,000? Don't wait: Invest your money effectively *now*.

Though all this sounds fine, you're probably unconvinced, because you know that with your luck, the stock market will crash the day after you invest your life savings.

So please don't misunderstand me. I said to invest all your money at once, not invest all your money *into stocks* at once. The proper way to invest a lump sum is to invest it all at once — but into a highly diversified portfolio. Revisit Chapter 44.

Chapter 48 - Investing for Current Income

You may have noticed that all my strategies thus far assume you are investing for the future. But what if you need income now? This is a common problem for retirees, and here's your answer.

If you are retired, or about to be, keep in mind you still need to diversify because you still need at least some growth. In fact, a big mistake investors make is to focus too much attention on retirement. As a financial planner, I really don't care that you might be nearing retirement, and neither should you.

After all, retirement is a lifestyle issue, not an economic one (unless you have failed to make the proper preparations). Indeed, entering retirement doesn't mean you will stop eating.

My point is that being retired does not mean your life is over — although it once did. For most of our nation's history, people never retired. Instead, they died. Of course, this is no longer true: When you retire at 65, you can expect to live another 20 or 30 years. That means if you're 60, you need to be just as concerned about inflation as someone who is 30.

Yet most retirees and pre-retirees believe their only worry is *safety*. Wrong! You should be worrying that you'll be able to afford food after inflation erodes your income in the years to come. You don't want to run out of money before you run out of life.

Yet most people don't see it this way: By focusing exclusively on safety and their need for *current* income, they ignore — even sacrifice — *future* income by placing all their money into CDs.

Recall the retirees we described in Chapter 6. Over 15 years, their CD income was cut 85% while the cost of living doubled leaving them with an income of $155 when they needed $3,041. Indeed, inflation and a large drop in interest rates have created a true crisis for Americans who depend on investment income.

The solution to this crisis is a *Systematic Withdrawal Program*, and it's available with virtually every mutual fund. Here's how it works:

Invest in a fund (balanced funds are my favorite for this strategy) and reinvest the dividends and capital gains. Believe me, you don't want them: They come only occasionally, and the amount changes frequently with fluctuations in interest rates and the fund's performance.

Instead, tell the fund you want to make withdrawals on a systematic basis each month, equal to the rate of 5% per year (or any rate you choose; you can increase or decrease the rate at any time, although clearly the more you withdraw, the higher the risk that you may begin to withdraw your own principal).

> *"The difference between rich people and poor people is where they sign their checks. Poor people sign the front. Rich people sign the back."*
> —Ric Edelman

On $100,000, a 5% income stream would be $5,000, or $416 a month, and your check will arrive like clockwork every month, just like a Social Security check.

Figure 6-25 shows the results of a Systematic Withdrawal Program using the average balanced fund from January 1993 to June 2003. (This hypothetical example relies on the average results of the universe of balanced mutual funds in existence as of June 30, 2003, according to Thomson Financial. There is no assurance these results will be repeated.)

The $100,000 investment distributed $5,000 per year, yet ten and a half years later, the value of this hypothetical account had grown to $154,438.

Not only did you get a stable income, but at the end of the period, you would have been able to adjust your income to begin taking 5% from the current value of $154,438. Thus by boosting your annual income to $7,722, *you would have kept pace with the cost of living*.

Contrast this to a series of 1-year CDs: They would have paid only $51,600 during the 10 years, the ending value would have remained $100,000, and the income in 2003 would have been just $1,100.

Two important points about this strategy: First, note that during this period, the account value fluctuated dramatically. In this example, the account fell in value three times — in 1994, 2001 and 2002. But so what? Your income remained stable (which is the primary concern of retirees), and over the entire period, the account grew. Second, the tax implications are confusing. Although you received checks totaling $5,000 per year in our example, this is not necessarily the amount on which you paid taxes. Instead, taxes are due on the fund's dividend and capital gain distributions, which you voluntarily reinvested, and this figure might have been higher or lower than the income stream you received. (Remember: You always pay taxes on dividends and capital gains, whether you receive them in cash or reinvest them back into the account.) For more on taxes, see Part IX.

If you — or your parents or relatives — are upset that today's CD rates are only a fraction of what they used to be, consider this outstanding alternative. And also take a look at the income guarantees offered by variable annuities in Chapter 28.

SYSTEMATIC WITHDRAWAL PROGRAMS

Assuming a $100,000 investment through June 30, 2003

Year	...invested in a 1-year CD:		...invested in the Average Balanced Fund receiving monthly income equal to 5% per year on a systematic basis:	
	You would have received annual interest income of...	...and the Year-End Value of your CD would have been:	You would have received annual income of...	...and the year-end value of your fund would have been:
1993	$3,390	$100,000	$5,000	$105,800
1994	$4,570	$100,000	$5,000	$98,049
1995	$6,300	$100,000	$5,000	$117,856
1996	$5,680	$100,000	$5,000	$128,766
1997	$5,830	$100,000	$5,000	$148,618
1998	$5,770	$100,000	$5,000	$164,425
1999	$5,400	$100,000	$5,000	$180,964
2000	$6,670	$100,000	$5,000	$181,755
2001	$4,850	$100,000	$5,000	$170,575
2002	$2,040	$100,000	$5,000	$146,812
2003	$1,100	$100,000	$5,000	$154,438
Total Income:	**$51,600**		**$55,000**	
Ending Value:	**$100,000**		**$154,438**	

FIGURE 6-25

Chapter 49 - Four Ways to Create Savings

Maybe you're finding it hard to save. That's not uncommon, for even those who are free of debt sometimes find it difficult to save money. Many people spend all their money each month, and they can't (or won't) change their spending. If that describes you, the following strategies will help.

Savings Creator #1: Pay Yourself First

Let's begin by accepting two facts. Fact One: You spend all your money every month, and have nothing left to save. Fact Two: You can't change Fact One.

Fine. I won't argue with you.

Instead, let's just make a subtle change in *how you pay your bills*. Currently, you deposit your paycheck into your checking account, and then you start writing checks. If you're like most, you pay the mortgage first, then car payments and other loans, followed by the phone bill and utilities. You save the credit cards (if any) for last, because the amount you pay to them is directly related to how much is left in your checkbook after all the other bills are paid.

> *"A billion dollars doesn't go as far as it used to."*
> —J. Paul Getty

So, you send minimal amounts to each credit card company and by the time you're done, your checkbook balance is at or near zero. And while you promised yourself that you'd save some money this month (like you promise yourself every month), you now discover (as always) that there's nothing left to save. In fact, you barely had enough to pay the bills themselves.

Without realizing it, you are treating yourself as a creditor — albeit a benign creditor. You want to pay this fellow named Yourself, but you know Yourself will never hassle you for the money, so it's okay to miss a few payments — or ignore Yourself altogether. Thus, you pay Yourself last each month, which all too often translates into not paying him at all.

To fix this, you must pay Yourself first — before you pay any other bills. By writing a check to Yourself for $25 or $50 (or whatever), you are certain that you will have paid Yourself — before your checkbook runs out of money.

And if you're concerned that you will run out of money, don't fret — because you're going to run out of money anyway (you always do, right?). At least, this way, you'll run out of money after you've paid Yourself. And that's the point.

Savings Creator #2: Your Future in a Peanut Can

Try using a trick my big brother Brad taught me when I was eight years old: Stop spending coins; spend only paper currency.

It's easy: Just put the change you collect each day into a piggy bank (I still use the Planters Peanuts can that Brad gave me) and you'll save $20 a month or more — and double the savings if your spouse does likewise, even more if you get the kids involved. Then deposit the money into your mutual fund account.

Who says saving money is hard?

Savings Creator #3: Spend Your Way to Wealth

Many people fail to save because they simply don't want to stop spending. Fine. Keep spending. In fact, I want you to.

Just change what you spend your money on:

- Instead of buying a bottle of ketchup, buy Heinz stock.
- Instead of buying a gallon of gas, buy stock in Exxon.
- Instead of a six-pack of soda, buy shares of Coca-Cola.
- That new lawnmower? Try stock in John Deere instead.

So go ahead and spend your money. Spend as much as you want. But instead of buying things that later will have no value (like an empty ketchup bottle or a vacation), or virtually no value (like costume jewelry, clothing, or furniture), make sure the things you buy will retain and even grow in value. Remember: Life is a series of choices. I'm not telling you to stop spending money, merely to choose *how* you spend it.

Once you get into this habit, you'll develop as much excitement buying investments as you currently do buying clothes. The reason that this is a foreign concept for you is that you have never bought anything that has retained its value — except maybe your house.

But once you start to buy things that rise in value, you'll never look back. If you think shopping is fun, wait until you start shopping for things that make money for you. Now, that's shopping!

Savings Creator #4: The Right Way to Use Supermarket Coupons

If you're like most people, you clip coupons. And you redeem them at your local supermarket.

And if you're like most people, you're doing it wrong.

Think about it: The coupon in your pocket says SAVE ONE DOLLAR.

Well?   Did you?

"Take care of the pence, for the pounds will take care of themselves."
—**Philip Dormer Stanhope**

I mean, *did you save that dollar*? Or did you merely spend that dollar on something else?

Maybe you don't get my point. Say you're headed to the grocery store to buy $50 worth of food and household goods. You have $50 in your pocket or purse, along with a "dollar off" coupon that you can redeem against an item you need to buy. When you leave the store, you will have either:

- fifty dollars' worth of items, and one dollar in your pocket or
- $51 worth of stuff, and *no money left because you spent it all!*

Although the former is how you're supposed to handle coupons, the latter is more likely how you are handling them. If you're smart, you'll spend $49 and SAVE ONE DOLLAR by placing it into your peanut can before you even leave for the store! (See Savings Creator #1.)

Chapter 50 - How to Prepare for Economic Collapse

You may have noticed that all the advice in this book is based on the simple premise that the world is not going to come to an end. But for all the pessimists, doomsayers, conspiracy theorists, and other party poopers who disagree with me, for those who truly believe (or who merely occasionally ponder the notion) that our entire economic system is about to collapse, let me offer you the steps you should take to prepare:

1. Immediately sell all investments: stocks, bonds, government and municipal securities, mutual funds, company retirement plans, IRAs, and stock options. Close all bank accounts and empty any safety deposit boxes. Cancel all insurance policies and obtain any cash values from such policies now.

2. Quickly sell your home and all other real estate.

3. Place one-quarter of your assets in cash (U.S. currency), using small denominations — nothing larger than twenties. Keep substantial amounts of cash with you at all times. Bury the remainder in several geographically distinct places, each at least 10 miles from one another.

4. Place one-quarter of your assets in the currencies of the Euro, England and Japan. Keep a substantial amount of these currencies with you at all times. Bury the remainder alongside your U.S. currency.

5. Place one-half of your assets into gold coins (using the American Eagle, Canadian Maple Leaf, or South African Krugerrand) or bullion (using coins, wafers, and kilobars [32.15 ounces]. Avoid bars [at 400 ounces, they're too big]). You also can use silver ingots if you wish. Keep a substantial amount with you at all times. Bury the remainder alongside your cash.

6. Quit your job. The paycheck you get will be no good anyway.

7. Buy a house with surrounding property in the mountains, selected with the following criteria:

    *   difficult to find, more difficult to see, most difficult to reach
    *   at least 100 miles from any government office or military base
    *   reliable, independent water source on the property
    *   easily defended

8. Build several escape routes and hidden entrances/exits/hiding places on the property, along with traps and mines to keep intruders and trespassers at bay.

9. Buy at least one all-terrain four-wheel drive vehicle, one motorcycle for each person in your group, and two German shepherds (male and female). Stock lots of fuel and spare parts for the vehicles and biscuits for the dogs.

10. Load up on survivalist gear: clothing, weapons and ammunition, dry-packed foodstuffs; electrical generators, lamps, two-way and ham radios, emergency medical kits, tools, and rations. Also: complete reference books covering the fields of botany, medicine, mechanical engineering, warfare, construction, farming, psychology, pharmacology, and sociology. Also almanacs, encyclopedias, and while you're at it, novels, too, for leisure time might be high. Books on tax law will not be required. A Bible, Koran, or Torah is highly recommended.

11. Hope to hell you're right, for if you're not, you'll look awfully silly.

BROOM HILDA   RUSSELL MYERS

© Tribune Media Services, Inc. All Rights Reserved. Reprinted with permission.

ric's money quiz

Here's a chance to see how well you learned the information contained in Part VI – The Best Investment Strategies. Don't worry if you get stumped — just re-read this part until it sinks in. Remember, your financial future depends on it.

The answers are at the end of the quiz. No peeking!

1. **The higher the standard deviation of a fund:**

   - O a. the greater the volatility
   - O b. the greater the risk
   - O c. both a and b
   - O d. neither a nor b

2. **Beta:**

   - O a. predicts fund profitability
   - O b. compares fund performance to the international stock market
   - O c. compares fund volatility to the U.S. stock market
   - O d. measures the return produced by the fund's manager

3. **Introducing a risky asset into a portfolio can _____ of that portfolio.**

   - O a. reduce the risk
   - O b. increase the risk
   - O c. reduce the fees
   - O d. increase the fees

4. **One factor has been shown to account for 93.6% of the difference in volatility between large institutional investors. This factor is:**

   - O a. which stocks they buy
   - O b. the percentage of total assets they place into stocks
   - O c. the timing of when they buy stocks
   - O c. none of the above

5. **For asset allocation to be successful, you must:**

   I. invest in a variety of asset classes
   II. invest primarily in aggressive asset classes
   III. reallocate your assets periodically
   IV. sell winning investments to buy losers

   - O a. I, III, and IV
   - O b. I and II
   - O c. II and III
   - O d. I and IV

6. An "optimal" portfolio is one which:

    ○ a.   makes the most amount
            of money
    ○ b.   takes the least amount of risk
    ○ c.   minimizes expenses, including
            transaction costs, carrying costs,
            and tax effects
    ○ d.   balances return against risk

7. When buying a mutual fund, you should plan to:

    ○ a.   switch each year to whatever
            fund made the *most* money in
            the previous year, and switch like
            this annually for 10 years
    ○ b.   switch each year to whatever
            fund made the *least* money in
            the previous year, and switch
            like this annually for 10 years
    ○ c.   hold your fund for 10 years
    ○ d.   switch into other funds as often
            as you see fit for 10 years

8. Which of the following is an example of Dollar Cost Averaging?

    ○ a.   placing 100% of your company
            retirement plan contributions
            into the stock fund
    ○ b.   buying U.S. savings bonds
            via payroll deduction
    ○ c.   placing equal amounts of money
            into four different kinds of
            mutual funds
    ○ d.   buying 100 shares of a given
            stock every time the price
            changes by $10

9. Dollar Cost Averaging works best with:

    ○ a.   bank CDs
    ○ b.   IRA accounts
    ○ c.   stock mutual funds
    ○ d.   individual stocks

10. Systematic withdrawal plans:

    ○ a.   are available from virtually every
            mutual fund
    ○ b.   will send you a set amount of
            money from your fund each
            month
    ○ c.   reinvest your dividends
            and capital gains
    ○ d.   all of the above.

Answers: 1-c (pg.234)   3-a (pg.265)   5-a (pg.261)   7-c (pg.256)   9-c (pg.271)
           2-c (pg.240)   4-b (pg.259)   6-d (pg.242)   8-a (pg.269)   10-d (pg.275)

Part VII
The Best Financial Strategies

There's a quiz at the end of this part!

To see how much you already know, skip to the end of this part and take the quiz now. Then, read the part and take the quiz again. You'll discover how much you've learned!

Part VII – The Best Financial Strategies

In this part, you will learn:

- How to get out of debt

- Whether to buy or lease your next car

- How to pay for college

- Whether parents of young children should work

Chapter 51 - How to Get Out of Debt

I'm going to show you how to get out of debt and increase your ability to save. But first, let's see how people get themselves into debt in the first place.

Is money a problem for you? Here are some warning signs, courtesy of the Consumer Credit Counseling Service:

- **an increasing amount of your net income is going to debt payments**

- **you pay only the minimum amount on loans and credit cards**

- **you've reached your limit on credit cards**

- **you pay bills with money that was intended for other things**

- **you use credit cards to pay for things that you used to pay for with cash**

- **you often pay bills late**

- **you delay or omit visits to the doctor or dentist because money is tight**

- **you get calls from collection agencies regarding unpaid bills**

- **you work overtime or a second job to raise cash to pay bills**

- **losing a job would create instant financial trouble**

- **money is a constant concern to you**

If any of these hit home, you need to read this chapter.

Don't Spend Tomorrow's Income Today

Nobody intends to become debt-ridden, but at some point in your life you may turn around and say, "Gee, how did I accumulate all this debt?" It starts very innocently.

You see, none of us are born in debt. We start life with a clean slate. But then we make bad decisions, or we fall into traps, and the most common trap people fall into is committing themselves to a future lifestyle that is based on their current income.

> *"A family budget is a process of checks and balances; the checks wipe out the balances."*
> —Arthur Langer

Here's a great example. Debbie is 23 and lives with her parents. She earns $23,000 a year. Her parents cover her basic living expenses, although Debbie chips in $500 every month.

Recently, Debbie's old clunker died and she needed a new car to get to work. She intended to buy a Ford Escort for about $14,000, but the salesman talked her into buying a hot new Mustang for $28,000. Well, we can't really blame the salesman — Debbie loved sitting behind that wheel. And considering her income and expenses, as the salesman showed her, Debbie easily was able to afford the 'stang. So she bought it, financing $20,000. Her payment is $445 a month for five years.

By committing herself to this payment for the next five years, she will not be able to move out of her parent's house. Consider the figures: Her after-tax income is about $17,000, or $1,400 per month. From this, Debbie has obligated herself to $445 for the car payment, plus another $150 per month for insurance, gas, and

BABY BLUES   KIRKMAN & SCOTT

© Baby Blues Partnership. Reprinted with Special Permission of King Features Syndicate.

maintenance — a total of 43% of her income! That leaves her with only $805, and that's not enough to rent an apartment and pay for food, clothes, furniture, and utilities — plus entertainment expenses.

Today, Debbie doesn't mind. But what about three years from now? She has made a decision today that commits her income for the next five years. This not only means she must continue to earn at least as much in the future as she earns today, she must actually *increase* her earnings if she wants to improve her lifestyle.

And since she has already committed $595 per month toward her automobile expenses for the next five years, and another $500 to her parents in lieu of rent, her discretionary income is reduced to just $305 per month. So guess what happens when she decides to rent a house at the beach for a week with her girlfriends next summer? Debbie runs out of money — not because she doesn't have any money, but because she has already committed the money she has.

> *"Just as soon as people make enough money to live comfortably, they want to live extravagantly."*
> —Anonymous

So, to get by, Debbie starts to pay for gasoline with a credit card. When it is time for fall clothes and Christmas shopping, she uses the credit card some more. Soon, she discovers that she's built up thousands of dollars in credit card charges. When the bill arrives each month, she finds herself unable to pay it off because her money already has been spent.

It's very easy to fall into this trap, and newly-weds are caught all the time. My clients Darren and Barbara asked me if they could afford to buy a $225,000 house, and after reviewing their situation I told them they could, but only if they were willing to become "house poor." They'd have to use all their current savings and investments to get into the house, and then, even after considering both incomes, they'd be stretched each month to pay for the mortgage and related costs. Thus, I told them, they could afford the house if they both continued to work and *if* their future expenses and income both remained unchanged.

Because I didn't say "no" outright, they were excited. "But," I was quick to remind them, "you don't have children yet."

Too often, I have seen couples experience radical changes when a baby comes. But by purchasing such an expensive home — by committing such a large amount of their income to maintaining that home — they essentially were making decisions today that would affect (haunt?) them in the years to come.

Therefore, I advised them to buy a less expensive home, one that did not place such financial restrictions on them for the next 30 years. I cautioned that by doing it their way, in the best case they'd be house poor and in the worst case they'd lose their home. They rejected my advice. Six years later, after two children, they lost the house and divorced. (For more on the notion of working while raising young children, see Chapter 54.)

Expenses Should Be Adjustable Over Time

If you want to avoid the debt trap, keep your fixed expenses as low as possible. Don't obligate yourself to long-term expenses, such as "buy now, pay later" deals. That way, if your income or lifestyle changes, you will be able to handle the change financially. Debbie and Darren & Barbara failed to do this.

But let's say you have succeeded on this point. Let's say you haven't made commitments for income you haven't yet earned. Thus, when your expenses go up or your income goes down, your lifestyle can change accordingly. Congratulations — but don't skip the rest of this chapter yet.

There's still one more trap awaiting you: You must be willing to make that lifestyle change when the time comes. Being *unwilling* to change is as deadly as being *unable* to change.

> *"Budgeting: A method of worrying before you spend instead of afterward."*
> —**Anonymous**

The best example I can offer is Lon and Gretta. When they married, Lon was 42 and Gretta was 39, and she became (rather unexpectedly) pregnant at 41.

From the time she was 18 until her marriage, Gretta had been on her own. She owned a condo, and enjoyed an excellent career. She earned $60,000 and, with no family, was able to live quite comfortably.

Lon was in research, with an income not as high as Gretta's. He too owned a home, and after the wedding, they sold their houses and together bought a bigger, more expensive home. Still, not much

> *"Money is better than poverty, if only for financial reasons."*
> —**Woody Allen**

changed for them financially. Their joint income allowed them to live pretty much as before.

Then they had the baby, and six months later, Lon was let go after his firm lost a big grant. This forced the family to rely solely on Gretta's income for a time. Soon, Lon was back at work, although at a lower salary. Although things should have worked out, by the time they came to my office, Lon and Gretta owed $30,000 to credit cards.

Although they had not fallen into the trap of spending money they hadn't yet earned, they had fallen victim to the second trap: They each continued to spend as they always had, without regard for their new and different circumstances.

Indeed, they acted as though they were still "single and free." Gretta would think nothing of spending Saturday at the mall. Lon, too, regularly indulged himself. A car buff, he was forever under the hood, installing some new gizmo or other he bought at the local speed shop.

Yet they never adjusted their spending to reflect their new family obligations. So while they incurred new expenses with the house and the baby, they still maintained their *previous* spending habits. And while they easily could have paid for their new lifestyle or their old one, they couldn't afford both simultaneously.

Thus, Lon and Gretta continued to use their credit cards as each had done for the past 20 years. But now, instead of being able to pay them off each month as they'd always been able to do, balances started accumulating. At thirty thousand, it occurred to them that something was wrong. But they weren't sure what. After all, they hadn't been doing anything new or different. They had always spent money, and their incomes had always been enough to cover it. So *spending* couldn't be the problem. What, then, could it be?

This is the trap many people get into. We are so used to supporting only ourselves that we become used to instant gratification. We don't have to worry about feeding or clothing others, and since we earn our own money, we don't have to ask others for permission before we spend it. We've got ready access to cash that we're not afraid to spend. And since all our friends are just like us, it seems both easy and right.

Then one day you find yourself in your mid-40s with a spouse, a house, and kids — and lots of debts. Make sure you don't commit tomorrow's income today, and when your life changes, make sure your spending habits change with it.

Getting Out of Debt is Like Losing Weight

Now that you understand how people get into debt, let's focus on how to get out of it. In fact, it's a lot like losing weight.

The problem with trying to lose weight is that nature abhors a vacuum. Most people who eliminate (or sharply reduce) eating from their daily activities don't replace it with anything. That goes against nature, for if you don't fill the void, nature will fill it for you.

You know the drill: People who lose weight focus all their attention on *the food they're not eating*. So as soon as they reach the weight they wanted, guess how they celebrate? By going out to dinner!

I find the same problem with clients who are trying to get out of debt. Many people who want to eliminate their debt or save money try to do so by *not spending* — and as soon as they reach their goal, they reward themselves by, you guessed it, *shopping* — putting themselves right back where they started.

So if you want to get out of debt, the first thing you must realize is that "getting out of debt" is the wrong goal. For one thing, it's not fun. Getting out of debt means you can't spend money, and that's no fun for the same reason dieting is no

SALLY FORTH   HOWARD & MACINTOSH

Reprinted with special permission of King Features Syndicate.

fun (for dieting means you can't eat, or at least you can't eat the stuff you want to eat, or in the quantities you want to eat it).

So we need to set the right goal. And that means we must learn about goal-setting.

The Four Steps to Properly Setting Goals

First, set a positive goal for yourself. "I will save to buy a home" is a positive goal, while "I will not spend money" is a negative goal. By focusing on the positive, you'll quit spending money because you'll be so focused on your goal that you won't notice you've stopped spending money.

Second, set a date for achieving your goal. A goal is not a goal until you set a date for it. Having lived in the Washington, D.C., area for 23 years, I've always planned to go inside the Washington Monument. But I never have, just as New Yorkers never visit the Statue of Liberty! Why not? Because I have never set a date. We have too many things to do in our lives, and therefore only those with deadlines ever get accomplished.

So set a date for achieving your goal, and make sure your date is attainable. If it's not, you'll become discouraged and quit. But don't set a date so far away that achieving it is pointless. "I want to be debt free by the time I die" is a silly deadline, because you won't be able to enjoy the benefits of achieving that goal.

And don't worry about missing your deadline, either. One of my clients is 35 and a self-made millionaire. When I congratulated him on his success, he replied, "What success? I failed miserably! My goal was to be a millionaire by age 30 — I didn't make it until I was 34!"

If you aim at the eagle, you'll bag the pheasant, and you won't eat crow.

Third, write it down. Until you see your goal in front of you, it's not real. Tape your goal onto your bathroom mirror, your refrigerator door, your car's steering wheel, and your PC's monitor. Keep reminding yourself of your goal. One client of mine kept a picture of his dream house above his television. Another, who wanted to buy a Jaguar, bought a Matchbox version for five bucks and kept it in his pocket. His co-workers regularly saw him playing with it at his desk. (Today, he drives the real thing.)

And fourth, stay focused. Keep your goal in front of you. If your goal is to buy a home, tour model homes. Read *House and Garden*, *Architectural Digest*, and similar magazines. Design your own floor plan. By immersing yourself in your goal, you'll find it easy to stop spending money, because you won't regard it as "not spending." You'll regard it instead as "preparing to spend my money on something really special."

Focus on the benefits you'll derive by reaching your goal, not on the sacrifices you're enduring. If you can't perceive the benefits, you won't achieve your goal, and even if by some chance you do reach your goal, you won't sustain your victory.

> *"Whoever says money can't buy you happiness doesn't know where to shop."*
> —Gittel Hudnick

Keep all this in mind as I show you the mechanics of getting out of debt, for if you simply follow the steps I outline for you, you won't do yourself any good. Oh sure, following my plan will get you out of debt — but it won't keep you out of debt. Only you can do that.

Set your goal, give yourself a deadline, write it down, and stay focused. You'll be amazed how far this will take you. And for more on goal setting, read **Discover the Wealth Within You**; half of that book is devoted to this topic.

Where to Start Your Journey

What's the first thing you do when driving to a place you've never been? *You look at a map.* And where's the first place you look? *Where you are.* Only after finding your current location do you then seek the place you're trying to reach. By comparing the two, you can figure out how to get there.

> *"Obstacles are things a person sees when he takes his eyes off his goal."*
> —E. Joseph Cossman

And that's the first thing you've got to do with your debts: You must become an expert on *where you are*. Do you know *exactly* how much money you owe and to whom you owe it? Can you tell me the cost of that debt — the interest rate and minimum payment?

Too often, people in debt have no idea how much they owe. If you don't know the details, you can't fix the problem. Telling your mechanic that the car doesn't work is not much help. He's got to know exactly where the problem is — before he starts repairs. Similarly, if you don't have a firm grasp of exactly what you owe, to whom you owe it, and what the payment terms are, forget about trying to eliminate your debts. So let's start there.

It's simple to do. Just take a sheet of paper and make four columns. In the first column, list the name of each creditor (who it is you owe). In the second column, list the amount you owe to that creditor. Third, state the interest rate each is charging you, and fourth, state the minimum payment you must make each month. Do this before continuing. I'll wait.

...

Now that you have your list, I'll bet you wrote them down as you thought of them, in random order. So let's do it again, this time in order. Which creditor will you place at the top of your list? When I ask that question in my debt management seminars, most participants think the first debt to list is the one with the highest balance.

Wrong.

When making your list, show first the creditor which charges you the *highest interest rate*. Place the 21% credit card above the 18% credit card, which appears above the 14% card and so on — even if you owe more to the 14% card than to the 21% card.

I hope seeing all your debts listed on a sheet of paper makes you realize that you need to pay off those debts. If you keep going into debt, you might set a new record. In our firm, that record is held by a client who has $170,000 in credit card debts. His minimum payment is $12,000 per month!

Management Before Elimination

How long will it take you to become debt-free? For most people, at least as long as it took to accumulate the debt. So if you've been increasingly in debt for five years, plan on taking five years to get out of debt.

If that surprises you, remember that you can jump into a hole faster and easier than you can climb out of one, and if that discourages you, remember to focus on the benefits, not the costs, and forget about quick fixes. There is no such thing.

And you can forget about "credit doctors" or other marketers who claim they can "fix" your credit record for you. Such pitches are a scam. There is nothing anybody can to do repair a bad (but accurate) credit record — except you, by following the methods I'm outlining for you here. No quick fixes, no magic solution.

I'm addressing these credit repair outfits in a sidebar because that's all the attention they're worth.

I emphasize the rate instead of the balance because we have to stop the bleeding before we can cure the patient. You're not going to get rid of your debt overnight, and until you do, additional interest charges are accruing. Therefore, you must reduce the speed with which interest charges are accumulating, and that means we have to focus on the debt that's charging you the highest interest.

And, in case I need to say it: While we're working on eliminating your debts, do not add to them.

Now that you have listed all your debts in the proper order, look at column four: the minimum monthly payment. Each month, make certain you pay the minimum payment to each creditor. Never skip a payment and always send at least the minimum. If you don't, the creditor will make a note in your credit file, and this will haunt you when you try to buy a house or a car. Make sure you stay current. I cannot overemphasize the importance of this.

After you pay the minimum to each creditor, devote all your remaining money exclusively to the creditor that charges you the highest rate. Do not spread this money evenly among all the debts. Instead, send whatever you have left entirely to the most expensive creditor. After you finish paying off that creditor, go down your list to the next-highest creditor, again devoting all resources (beyond the minimum payments) to that creditor until that debt too is gone, and keep repeating this process until they're all gone.

Empty Your Bank Account

To accelerate this process, withdraw any money you have in the bank and send it off to the creditor at the top of your list.

If this advice shocks you, please understand that it makes absolutely no sense to have money in the bank earning 3% while you have debts that cost 18% or 21%. While you're at it, liquidate any other assets you have, such as savings bonds, stocks, mutual funds, even baseball cards.

> **Liquidate all your assets, with one exception: Do not liquidate your IRA or company retirement accounts. The tax penalties would be so high and you would be jeopardizing your future retirement to such an extent that it's not worth it.**

"But if I close my bank account, I won't have any money," you might be complaining. Well, I've got news for you: *You don't have any money now!* You just don't realize it. And if you're worried about needing cash in the event of an emergency, let me ask you: What do you think a credit card is for?

Why bother paying more than the minimum to *any* card, when paying the minimum is so much easier? Besides, paying the minimum will eventually pay off the balance, right?

Right. But the key word there is *eventually.* Say you've got an 18% credit card with a balance of $1,800. If you pay only the minimum each month, it will take you nearly 14 years to eliminate the debt. But if you pay just $10 more per month, you'll get rid of the debt in less than four years — saving you 10 years and $1,400 in interest!

CLOSE TO HOME   JOHN MCPHERSON

Yet another example of the credit card companies' aggressive attempts to attract new card-holders.

Love Your Credit Card

I love credit cards. What I don't like is credit card debt. Credit cards are wonderful cash management tools, and I encourage you to obtain one and keep it with you. If the car breaks down during a road trip, you can pay for repairs and overnight lodging. If Aunt Ida needs you to care for her, you can buy a plane ticket to see her right away.

> *"I had plastic surgery last week. I cut up my credit cards."*
> —Henny Youngman

So I have no problem with credit cards. What I have a problem with are people who don't pay them off every month, and with people who own assets that produce lower returns than the cost of the debt, when they should be selling the assets to eliminate the debt.

Get Out of Debt By Getting Into Debt

Next, go borrow some more money.

And get as much as you can — provided that (a) the amount of money you are now borrowing is not more than the total amount of debts you already have and (b) the interest rate you'll have to pay on this new debt is less than the rate you're currently paying.

See how this trick works? Say you owe $5,000 to an 18% VISA card. Maybe you can get a new VISA card from another bank that charges only 14%. Take $5,000 from the new card to pay off the balance on the old card — and in essence, you'll cut your interest rate to 14% from 18%. Do this as often as you can to reduce your interest charges while you're working to eliminate the debts themselves.

> *"Practice economy at any cost."*
> —Anonymous

Keep in mind that this is just a temporary solution. The real goal is to eliminate the debts, not merely reduce their cost. And be sure you understand the terms of your new card: Many card issuers offer introductory rates to get you to switch, but these "teaser rates" often last only a few months, after which time the rate rises dramatically — perhaps to a rate even higher than the rate you're currently paying. In other cases, the low rate applies only to new purchases, not to existing balances that you transfer from another card. Execute this strategy carefully, or you'll defeat the purpose.

Next, Focus on the Cause

Now that you've stopped adding to your debts, reduced their interest charges, and begun a plan to eliminate them, we can focus on what caused all this debt in the first place.

And guess what the cause is? *It's you*. You are the cause. You are the problem. Remember the Newmans from Chapter 1, and how they were spending their money? Like them, too many of us let our spending habits get us into trouble.

The most astonishing aspect about the Newmans is that their daily spending represented 3% of their total annual income. To understand the importance of this, consider John D. Rockefeller. When he died in 1937, how much money did he leave behind?

All of it!

Do you get the point? You were trying to guess how much money he had in dollar terms, because that's how you're used to dealing with money. But where money is concerned, *dollars* are irrelevant. To succeed financially, you must think in terms of *percentages*.

Thus, when Rockefeller died, he left "all of it" behind, or 100%. Rockefeller had 100% of his money, just as you have 100% of yours. The reason this is so important: *Amounts* constantly change, but percentages never do. The amount of money varies from day to day, but the percentage never does: You always have 100% of your money.

> By the way, Rockefeller had $900 million when he died in 1937, the equivalent of about $13 billion today.

This is why you have the same assets as Rockefeller: He had 24 hours a day, just as do you, and he had 100% of his money, just as you have 100% of yours.

If you don't earn interest on your money today, you've given that day away forever. And if you earn a lower interest rate today than you should have earned, you have given that away as well — forever.

If you want to make your finances very simple, just think of all of your money as 100 *per cent*. Through your entire life, you will have only 100 of these cents, and you will never get more, so spend them with care.

> *"My problem lies in reconciling my gross habits with my net income."*
> —**Errol Flynn**

Where Does Your Money Go?

So start thinking about it. What will you do with your 100 pennies? The first thing you do is something you'd rather *not* do: pay taxes. That costs you about a third of your pennies, leaving you with 67.

Finished with the taxman (or should I say he's finished with you), you first need shelter. Lop off 28% of your income for housing. That leaves you with 39 pennies.

Next comes food, on which the average family spends about 18% of income. You're down to 21 pennies — and you're still naked!

So let's buy some clothes. Seven pennies ought to cover that. Now, you need to get around town, so siphon off 11 pennies for transportation-related expenses. You've got three left.

What's going on here? You've got only three pennies left and you haven't had any fun yet! (You also haven't paid for insurance, utilities, or your kids' education, either, but I won't mention those because I don't want you to get discouraged.)

SALLY FORTH   HOWARD & MACINTOSH

Reprinted with special permission of King Features Syndicate.

And with their precious three pennies left, the Newmans chose to buy candy bars and coffee! So, the next time you think spending fifty cents on a soda won't make any difference, think again.

You Make Plenty of Money

Please don't try to tell me you're in debt because you don't make enough money. You already make as much money as it takes to become financially successful. You simply are not using your resources wisely. Life is all about choices, and if you are in debt, I'm willing to bet it's because you made some bad choices. You spent every tax refund you ever got — often before you got it. Every time you got an increase in salary, you upgraded your lifestyle. And while it's true that this new income allowed you to handle the new payments, it also did two more things: It forced you to maintain your income stream so you could keep paying for these new financial obligations, and since the new income was pre-allocated, you were prevented from saving it or from using it for other purposes in the future.

If you think you're not rich because you never had the opportunity to become rich, look elsewhere for sympathy. Why do I say this? Because in a study by the Employee Benefit Research Institute, 70% of non-retired Americans say they could reduce their expenses in order to save for retirement, but only 18% say they are very likely to do so. Apparently, living well today is more important to most of us than living well tomorrow.

Indeed, say you go out for dinner and a movie twice a month, spending $75 each

> **Just to prove I'm not totally heartless, I will admit that there is one legitimate cause of indebtedness that is beyond one's control: huge medical bills resulting from health problems.**
>
> **But that's about it. Being out of work doesn't qualify, which will annoy those reading this who have been downsized in the past few years. While I agree that a person might be facing some serious economic challenges after being let go rather unceremoniously, that's not an excuse to be in debt. You should have been accumulating savings while you were working, and maintaining cash reserves to tide you over (at least for a time), and your lifestyle should not have been relying on your full income stream. In other words, loss of your job should be a difficulty — not a disaster.**
> **If this scenario has happened to you, I'm sorry. And if it hasn't (yet), be forewarned so you can be prepared.**

time. That's $1,800 a year. If you instead saved that money over 30 years at 10% per year, you'd have $325,698! Yet, according to EBRI, restaurant meals "are no longer considered luxuries, but a standard part of the middle-class lifestyle."

So, please, don't tell me you don't make enough money. The truth is you simply *spend* too much money.

Track Your Expenses

What all this leads to is the need to track your expenses. You've got to determine where you are spending your money, because until you know where your money is going, you won't be able to stop it from going there.

I want you to track your expenses so that you can see how you are spending your money. I am convinced that once you see how you are spending your money, you will quickly and easily fix the areas that need improvement. And you'll be able to do all this without having to create — or live with — a budget.

There are two ways to track your expenses. One way is fast but hard; the other is slow but easy. The choice is yours. The fast/hard way is to spend a weekend going backward in your checkbook and through your credit card statements for the past six months. It's hard, because you'll work all weekend, and you'll have gaps, particularly regarding the cash you spent, but by Sunday night you'll be ready to go to the next step.

> Forget about budgeting, for you won't do it even if I tell you to. There's probably nothing more tedious, or less effective, because budgets only reflect how you think you'll spend your money, not how you really do spend your money. After all, how often does life go according to plan? So forget the dreaded "B" word.
>
> See? There's good news after all!

The other way is slow/easy, and here you start to track all your expenses for the *next* six months. It's very easy to do, for you just record expenses as they occur. It takes very little effort, but it's slow: It'll take you six months to complete the process. The choice is yours.

PC or No PC

If you have a computer, you can do this with Quicken, Managing Your Money, Microsoft Money, or any similar software package. You also can use a spreadsheet program. *This is not an excuse to buy a personal computer, nor does it dismiss those who don't have one.* Tracking expenses is just as easy with an ordinary pencil and paper, so don't think you need to spend two grand on a PC to get started, or that you can't get started because you don't have a PC.

If you have a PC, follow the instructions provided by the software. I'll explain how to do it here for those using paper, which is how my wife Jean and I did it when we started to get our financial life in shape.

But first, starting now, you may no longer spend cash. To effectively track spending, your money must leave a paper trail, and cash leaves no trail. Therefore, you must use checks and credit cards only. I'll talk more about how to properly use credit cards later in this chapter.

To begin, draw on your paper a series of columns (you'll probably need 20 or so, maybe more).

TRACKING YOUR PERSONAL EXPENSES

Paid To	Amount	Food	Clothes	Gifts	Auto	Travel/ Enter.	Phone
Grocery Store	157.99	157.99					
AT&T	21.21						21.21
Ford Motor Credit	236.49				236.49		

FIGURE 7-1

In the first column, list to whom you wrote each check. In the next column, write down the dollar amount of the check. For each of the next 20 columns (or more if needed), assign a spending category — one each for FOOD, CLOTHES, AUTO, UTILITIES, and as many other categories as you wish. Then list the amount shown in column two under the appropriate category.

For example, say you spent $157.99 at the grocery store. In the first column, you'd write the name of the store. In the second column, you'd write "$157.99" and then you'd move to the FOOD column, where you'd again write "$157.99." See Figure 7-1.

I don't care what your categories are, provided that each is meaningful to you, and that you use the category consistently. For example, where will you show money spent on dinners at restaurants? Will you list it under FOOD or ENTERTAIN-MENT, or perhaps DINING OUT or something else? For some people, UTILITIES is sufficient, while others set separate categories for TELEPHONE, ELECTRICITY, WATER, and GAS.

The choice is yours; just make sure you are consistent with where you place the expense. Also try to ensure that each category is not so broad that it is used too often nor so limited that it is seldom used. For example, CLOTHING is fine, but

EXPENSE CATEGORIES

Household
Mortgage/Rent
Association Fees
Utilities
Phone/Cable
Food
Child Care
Private School
Clothing
Maintenance

Charitable
Church Dues
Tithe
Donations

Transportation
Auto Loan/Lease
Fuel/Oil
Public Transit
Parking/Tolls
Repairs/Maintenance
Registration Fees

Health Medical
Professional Fees
Drugs/Medicine
Parental Care

Debt Service
School Loans
Personal Loans
Credit Cards

Insurance
Life
Health
Disability
Long-Term Care
Auto
Home
Personal Property
Umbrella

Gifts
Birthdays
Anniversaries
Holidays
Graduations
Special Occasions

Savings/Reserves
Auto
Home
College
Retirement
Special Events

Recreation
Club Dues/Fees
Movies
Vacation
Dining Out
Lessons/Camp
Hobbies

Legal & Accounting
Retainers
Tax Preparation

Miscellaneous
Barber/Beautician
Professional Dues
Subscriptions
Pet Care
Domestic Help
Child Allowances
Dry Cleaning
Alimony
Child Support
Toiletries

FIGURE 7-2

creating three categories   CLOTHING HIM, CLOTHING-HER, and CLOTHING-KIDS might enable you to determine more easily where the money is really going. But I once had a client who showed a category of "Clothes, William, Socks, Blue." Another client not only listed ENTERTAINMENT, she showed the name of the movie, gave a review, and listed that she bought a Kit Kat and Junior Mints. Both of these people are a little nuts.

Okay, they're a *lot* nuts. Don't go crazy with this. Just make sure your categories make sense to normal people. Figure 7-2 lists categories to help you get started.

What to Do When an Expense Extends to More Than One Category

Often, you'll need to itemize your spending. Say you spend $300 at a department store, buying a variety of items. Write the name of the store in column one, "$300" in column two, then split the total among the various categories appropriately. See the example in Figure 7-3.

TRACKING YOUR PERSONAL EXPENSES

Paid To	Amount	Food	Clothes	Gifts	Auto	Travel/Enter.	Phone
Grocery Store	157.99	157.99					
AT&T	21.21						21.21
Ford Motor Credit	236.49				236.49		
Macy's	300.00		225.00	75.00			
Cash	190.07	18.76			46.31	125.00	

FIGURE 7-3

Do this for all your spending each month, and then total each column at the bottom. This will show you not only your total spending for the month, but how much you spent in each category.

Once you have produced dollar totals for each column, you need to convert the dollars to percentages, so you can see what percentage of your total spending occurred in each category. To do this, divide each column's dollar total by the total dollars you spent (the figure at the bottom of column two). See Figure 7-4.

TRACKING YOUR PERSONAL EXPENSES

Paid To	Amount	Food	Clothes	Gifts	Auto	Travel/ Enter.	Phone
Grocery Store	157.99	157.99					
AT&T	21.21						21.21
Ford Motor Credit	236.49				236.49		
Macy's	300.00		225.00	75.00			
Cash	190.07	18.76			46.31	125.00	
Total	905.76	176.75	225.00	75.00	282.80	125.00	21.21
Percent	100%	20%	25%	8%	31%	14%	2%

Example: $\dfrac{176.75}{905.76} = 20\%$

FIGURE 7-4

When you're done, all the percentages should add up to 100% — and this is how the Newmans discovered that 3% of their income was going to coffee and candy bars. And you'll be just as shocked about how you're spending your money as the Newmans were shocked about how they were spending theirs, and that's how you'll fix it.

You'll see that you are spending incredibly high percentages of your income in completely foolish places, and you won't tolerate it. Instead, you'll stop. But until you go through this process, you won't know whether the amount you're spending in a given area is too much or too little.

Where Americans Spend Their Money

According to the federal government's Consumer Expenditure Survey:

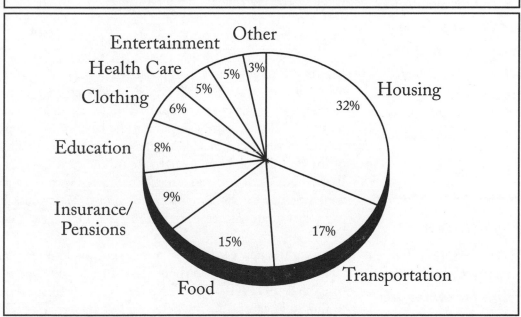

WHERE AMERICANS SPEND THEIR MONEY

FIGURE 7-5

How to Handle Credit Card Purchases

Most of us use credit cards often. Although you write a check to "VISA" or "DIS-COVER" or whatever, that obviously doesn't reflect what you bought. Therefore, you must break down the invoice, itemizing the bill across the many categories you've established.

> Yes, go get another card. How many debt counselors advise people that they need to get *more* credit cards to help them get out of debt!

"Never borrow money except for a primary residence, education, or emergency health problems."
— **Old South saying**

"It takes time to succeed because success is merely the natural reward for taking the time to do anything well."
— **Joseph Ross**

But what if you're only making a minimum payment, or if you already had a balance, added to it, and now are making only a partial payment? It can get confusing, and here's how to solve that problem: Go get a new credit card.

I want you to get a new card because I want you to stop using all your existing credit cards. By placing all your new charges on the new card, you'll be able to track them each month. And make sure you pay off the balance in full every month. If you won't be able to pay off the balance at the end of the month, you have no right to use the card now. Remember, a credit card is merely a way for you to use the bank's money for 28 days instead of your own. If you can't pay for an item with cash, then you can't use the card, either.

By using the new card, you're not using the old ones - but you still have balances on them. That means you need a category called DEBT SERVICE. And as you make payments to those old cards, this is where you list the payment. This way, you can ignore what the money was used to buy. Those purchases are ancient history; all that matters now is paying off the debt.

Two Tricks to Help You Pay Off Your Cards Each Month

If you are concerned that you don't have the discipline to pay off the balance in full each month, get a charge card, not a credit card. With a charge card, you do not pay interest. Instead, you MUST pay the full balance every month.

> **The truth is, if you don't have the self-discipline to pay off your credit card every month, I'm not sure this chapter will help you very much. You know carrying a monthly balance is stupid, and if you do it anyway...well, there's not much I can do for you if yer gunna ackt stoopid.**

Here's another trick that might help you pay off the balance each month: Every time you use your new credit card, immediately write a check payable to VISA (or whomever) for the amount you just charged. If you spend $35 at a store and put it on VISA, write a check for $35 to VISA right away. Then put the check in your drawer, and when the bill shows up, just slip the check into the envelope. You will have already recorded the check in your checking account, so the money is already there to cover the bill when it arrives.

If You Must Spend Cash

Sometimes spending cash is unavoidable, so if you must spend cash, get a receipt so you can remember what to record later. Just write "cash" in column one (like when you wrote a check to "VISA") and itemize by category where the money went. Thus, if you withdraw $100 from the ATM machine, you'll need to record what you spent that money on — whether it was a pack of gum (FOOD), a parking meter (AUTO), beer with the gang after work (ENTERTAINMENT), or all three.

CALVIN AND HOBBES BILL WATTERSON

Two "Unexpected" Expenses You Must Expect

When I ask participants in my debt management seminars to list categories of spending, they're real quick to offer food, shelter, clothing, transportation, education, travel, entertainment, and a few others. But there are two categories no one ever mentions, and I think this helps explain why you're in debt.

Unexpected Expense #1: Repairs

When I see that people have credit card debts, I ask why. And they often reply with something to the effect of, "Well, the car broke down. It cost $800 to fix. As soon as I get out from under that, I'll be okay."

And they work real hard and they pay off $100 a month until they get rid of that bill, and guess what happens next? The roof leaks. Or their son falls on the playground and breaks his arm. Or the washing machine dies. Let's face it: Life happens. Yet when things happen, people feel shocked, as though they didn't know things happen.

If you think occurrences like these are unexpected, you're deceiving yourself. Things are great until the car breaks down. Things are great except you owe $500 in taxes. Things are great until the basement floods. *Things are great until the next thing happens.* Time, a great physicist once said, is just one damn thing after another.

You just bounce from one crisis to another, like the guy who's always losing 10 pounds. He loses 10 pounds but then it's Thanksgiving. So in January he loses 10 pounds again, then it's Easter. Afterward, he loses 10 pounds, and it's Father's Day. He loses 10 pounds and goes on vacation. It's just a vicious circle, and we find our debt clients running round and round all the time. They're constantly going from "I paid off my credit cards" to "I owe $2,000" because they don't recognize that expenses in the UNEXPECTED category occur all the time. While it's true we don't know what the expense is, when it will occur, or how much it will cost, we should acknowledge that something will occur — and it's going to cost us money.

> *"Earn a little, and spend a little less."*
> —John Stevenson

This is why you can't track your expenses for just one month. You must do it for six months because you might go several months without an incident. And if you have a crisis that costs you several hundred dollars every four or five months — and you do, as tracking your expenses will reveal for you — you'll learn that you must set aside enough money on a monthly basis to prepare for it. So set a new category for yourself called UNEXPECTED.

Unexpected Expense #2: Gifts

Haven't you heard of Christmas or Hanukkah? Every December, people are overwhelmed by the money they spend on presents. Then they get to January and say, "Thank goodness that's over," and they spend the next six months paying off the bills. Come November, they get shocked all over again.

It's easy to prepare for the costs of gift-giving: Just look at last January's credit card bills and checkbook — because you're going to do it again this year!

And while we're on the subject, does anybody you know have a birthday? If you're not anticipating birthdays, anniversaries, graduations, confirmations, weddings, births, and other milestones in the lives of those you love, you're just adding to the "repair bill crisis" that is certain to hit you.

Control Yourself

After completing their six-month review, many people show me their results and lament all the money they spend on gifts. "But I've got no choice," they say. "I've got a large family and we're very close," implying they are forced to spend hundreds or thousands of dollars every year.

FRANK & ERNEST BOB THAVES

WHILE MY LEFT BRAIN WAS WORKING OUT A SENSIBLE BUDGET FOR THE MONTH, MY RIGHT BRAIN ORDERED A GIANT PIZZA!

THAVES 10-11
© 1994 by NEA Inc.

E-mail FandEBobT@AOL.COM

Nonsense. If you are deep in debt, you have no business spending money you don't have on gifts that people don't need. You can bake cookies or rely on a hobby to make them a gift. Write a check to the American Cancer Society and tell the family that you've done so in their name.

Do you think I'm being cheap? Hey, I'm talking about survival here. If you were rich, yes, I'd say you were cheap. But since you're broke, I'd say you are prudent. And if your family — the people who know you best and love you most — can't support you in your efforts to improve yourself financially, then shame on them.

Have you ever heard the phrase "the rich get richer and the poor get poorer?" It's true, because the rich keep doing the things that got them rich, while the poor keep doing the things that got them poor.

Indeed, being "poor" is a state of mind. But being "broke" is just a temporary financial condition. People who are poor stay poor; they won't bother to read this book or seek to improve their lot in life. But you're not poor, you're just broke — as evidenced by the fact that you are reading this chapter. And although you're broke at the moment, that will change because of your desire and your effort.

Don't be SNIOP

And frankly, you shouldn't care if your sister thinks you're cheap. Because if that's what she thinks, then she's not much of a sister.

Don't let the attitudes of other people drag you down or dissuade you from achieving your goals.

Don't be SNIOPed. Don't be Susceptible to the Negative Influences of Other People. Think about it the next time your co-workers invite you out for a drink after work. You know that if you go, you'll spend fifteen or twenty dollars. You want to go with everyone, it's fun, it helps with office politics, and so on, but you also know you'll spend twenty bucks you don't have.

You need to excuse yourself from going. "I'm really tied up. I have other plans." (Your "other plan" is to become wealthy.)

But they'll use peer pressure. You know what I'm talking about. So you give in, telling yourself you won't spend much. But the night goes on, and sure enough, you've spent $20. Congratulations: You've been SNIOPed.

You need to put a steel rod in your back and say "I CAN'T MAKE IT." If they criticize you, or talk about you, or hassle you about not joining them, please realize that this is their problem, not yours. If you allow yourself to be caught up in their game, you'll never get anywhere financially. This is often hard to do, but it's a critical element to eliminating your debt.

> **If you're wondering how it is that your friends, neighbors, and co-workers can afford to go out for dinner, buy fancy cars, take frequent vacations, dress their kids in the latest fashions, and decorate their home so extravagantly, here's the answer: They can't.**
>
> **These people are seriously in debt. Look, you know what they earn — about the same as you. And you know you can't afford it. That means they can't afford it, either. But your neighbors are so busy keeping up with each other that it's hard to tell. Remember: You can see their clothes, their house, their car, and their vacation photos, but you haven't seen their credit card statements or bank accounts. Don't assume that since they're doing it, (a) it can be done, and (b) you ought to be doing it, too.**
>
> **Why? Because the truth is, (a) it can't be done, (b) they shouldn't be doing it, and (c) you shouldn't be trying, either.**

Without question, you will experience the feeling of being SNIOPed. "No way," you're saying. "Not from my friends." Wanna bet? You'll find it's like crabs in a barrel. As soon as one crab starts to crawl out, another will reach up and pull it back down. If you're not prepared psychologically for this to occur, you will get SNIOPed for sure.

Virtually All Your Expenses are Optional

George and Monica came to me several years ago. At the time, they had a combined annual income of $120,000, yet owed $22,000 to credit cards, and they were adding debt at the rate of $2,000 per month (they were obtaining a new card every month). Despite their high income, they were spending considerably more than they were earning.

When we reviewed their situation, I discovered that a lawn service visited their home twice a month, at $85 per visit. I told them to cancel the service, and George replied, "But our lawn will look terrible if we do that! We must keep this expense."

I also noticed that they subscribed to cable TV, including every premium channel — a monthly cost of $97! I told them to cancel cable. Monica gasped. "There will be nothing for us to watch! We can't cancel cable!"

I'm sure you'll agree with me that a lawn service and cable TV are optional, yet neither George nor Monica understood this. Both these expenses are optional, just as — pardon me for shocking you — virtually *all* your expenses are optional.

Health club membership? Optional.

Entertainment? Optional.

Telephone? Optional.

Clothes? Most of it — or more accurately, the total money you spend on it — is optional.

Food? Again, mostly optional. Oreos, I regret to inform you, are not mandatory.

Are you getting my point? Almost everything you spend money on is optional! So don't tell me, "I gotta do this, I gotta do that." Sometimes, though, you'll find that you've been spending money on a certain item or in a certain way for so long that by now, not only can't you remember when you *didn't* spend money like that, now you think you *must*. Again, let me repeat: *Cable TV is optional*. Hard to believe, but true.

You *can* stop spending your money on things that in the bigger picture really don't matter. You *can* change it. You *can* fix it. You *can* stop it.

Don't feel locked in or trapped, because you are not. True, there are some expenses that you cannot change easily or quickly. Once you buy a car, you're stuck with the payments. But most of your spending is much more flexible than you might think at first. You are in more control of what's happening around you than you realize. But you've been SNIOP'd for so long you've forgotten that you do have a choice about how you spend your money.

The bottom line is that you got into debt because of your attitude, not your income. And it is your attitude about money that must change first, or changes in income won't matter.

As it didn't for George and Monica. By refusing to change how they spent money, they sought other solutions for their debt. And they found one: the equity in their home. They owed $150,000 on their $200,000 home, so from the $50,000 in equity, they borrowed $25,000 and used that money to pay off their credit cards. Problem solved, right?

Wrong: Within a year, their credit card balances were back up to $24,000, only this time they no longer had $50,000 in home equity to rely on. Within two more years, unable to keep up with the payments on their house, they sold it and rented an apartment (at least that ended the lawn service). Still, it wasn't enough, and they later filed for bankruptcy. It will be 10 years before they are able to buy another house — if ever.

I got a call one day from a viewer to my TV show. "I have $15,000 to invest and need your advice," he said. "By the way, I'd really like to talk with you about our debts." He explained that he and his wife owed about $40,000 to credit cards, so I told him to use the $15,000 to help pay down the debt. "No, I don't want to do that with this money. I want to invest it," he said. "I want to handle my debts separately."

I asked him about his income. "My wife and I both sell real estate," he answered.

"Oh," I replied. "I guess the recent softness in the real estate market has hurt your income."

"Not at all," he said. "We made about $225,000 last year and $165,000 so far this year. We just can't seem to get rid of these debts."

He asked for an appointment to come in and talk about it. "But we have to see you as soon as possible," he said. I wondered why. "Are you facing some deadline?" I asked.

"No," he said. "It's just that we're leaving for a two-week vacation to Cancun and I'd like to get started on this debt thing before we go."

Like I said, people get into debt because of attitudes, not incomes.

Focus on the Future

Although you must deal with your debts, don't beat yourself up over them — and don't let anyone else beat up on you, either. Not your spouse, not your parents, not your friends. No matter what your debt scenario, how you got into debt is relatively unimportant. The past cannot be changed, so focus your energy on what you can change: the future. Determine what you need to do from here forward, and then do it.

> Once, while I was presenting this information in a seminar, a woman asked, "Isn't there a shorter way to do all this?"
>
> I just stared at her.
>
> If there was a shorter, easier, faster, less painful way to accomplish your goal of becoming debt free, don't you think I'd have told you by now?

Simple Does Not Mean Easy

Everything I've described in this chapter is fairly simple to understand, but that doesn't mean it's easy to do, and I know this from personal experience.

Back in 1982, before Jean and I launched our financial planning practice, we were in another business, and it was several years before we admitted failure, ending up about $6,000 in debt.

To solve that problem, we decided to kill the business (before it killed us) and start over, rebuilding from scratch. With no income and no assets, we moved out of our three-level, 3,000 sq. ft. townhouse and into a one-bedroom, 900 sq. ft. ground-floor apartment.

We placed an ad in the paper which read, "Moving family must sell everything," — which we did, except for the kitchen table my best friend, Andy, built for me in high school, the bedroom suite that once belonged to my parents, and a sofa. We sold all our other furniture, the TV — everything.

If you've never had a bunch of strangers walk through your home, offering you ten bucks for a desk that got you through college, or $15 for your stereo, you can't imagine what this experience is like.

We accepted all offers and raised $2,000 that day, because we needed $600 for a security deposit on the new apartment, $200 to rent a truck to move our few remaining items, and to buy food and gas for the next few weeks while we got ourselves re-established. For three weeks, we spent $25 per week on food — mostly fruit and vegetables. If you think it can't be done, think again, for we proved it's possible. People who are eating peanut butter to save money are fooling themselves: We discovered that processed foods are so expensive we couldn't afford them. But you can eat well enough to survive on very little money.

The manager of a nearby store let us have some boxes he planned to throw away, and we used them to pack our clothes and dishes. I didn't want to pay $30 a month for a self-storage place, and since we had no furniture anyway, we stacked the boxes in our new apartment, creating a mountain in the living room. But I told Jean not to worry. "It'll only be for three or four months. We'll be out of here by then," I said.

We ended up living there for four years. During that time we did not own a television, nor did we buy a newspaper, because I refused to spend 25 cents each day when I knew I could get a copy at the office after someone else finished reading theirs.

Entertainment was the library and public parks. Years later, when we eventually bought a TV, we discovered how smart we were to sell our old one. By not having a TV, we were not constantly bombarded with messages to buy, buy, buy. By avoiding television's influence, we didn't feel the need to spend money. Perhaps you can control the TV shows you watch, but you can't control the commercials that air during them.

To rebuild income as fast as possible, Jean and I both had several jobs, working seven days a week, often leaving one job to arrive at another.

After living so frugally (made all the more difficult because life wasn't always like that for us) one day we splurged on dinner, spending $7 at a nearby Roy Rogers. We knew we shouldn't spend the money, that we'd regret it later, but we needed the release, and, boy, did those burgers taste good! That meal reminded us of the things we had given up and it increased our resolve to be able to return to a life that would allow us such luxuries. It was a year before we visited Roy's again.

Despite the challenge, we knew we weren't going to have to live that way forever, and for sure, we don't live that way any more. By denying ourselves the little pleasures, setting goals, and focusing all our energy on achieving them, we paid off those debts and in four years had saved enough to buy a townhouse. We've since sold that and built a single family home, which we later sold to move into an even bigger one. Indeed, Jean and I are able to enjoy our lifestyle now because we were willing to sacrifice it all for a time, something most people will not do. We give each other a "knowing glance" whenever people comment on the success we've achieved. "You're both so young," people tell us. "It's amazing how successful you've both become in such a short time." If they only knew. You might say it took us years to become an overnight success.

You, too, can become an "overnight success." You will be on this Earth for 40, 60, or 80 more years. You can choose to live month-to-month as you have been living, or you can choose to live better. Give up your materialism for a few years, reduce your needs for now, and one day, you'll be able to exceed your current lifestyle. All it takes is a little effort each day, and a lot of days.

There isn't any magic to this, no get-rich-quick scheme. And while you may be afraid of how much time it will take to succeed, that's nothing compared to how much time is really left in your life. So what if it takes you 10 years to get out of debt? You'll still have 30 or 50 or 70 years to enjoy after that.

Take advantage of this information. I know you can do it. The mere fact that you've read this far tells me that you've got the interest. I've given you the direction, so all you need is the initiative! Find it within yourself and as W. Clement Stone, the great motivational trainer, said, **Do It Now**.

> *"Nothing lasts forever —*
> *not even your troubles."*
> —**Arnold H. Glasow**

Chapter 52 - Should You Buy or Lease Your Next Car?

It'd be easy for me to tell you to take the bus or keep your junker for another 140,000 miles, but that's not realistic. Besides, you know all that stuff anyway. So, since you're going to get a new car no matter what I say, let's answer the question: Should you buy it or lease?

Let's take the example of a car whose sticker price is $34,000. To buy it, with a 7% four-year loan and a down payment of 20% ($6,800), your payment would be $650 a month.

However, if you were to lease instead, you would pay a one-month refundable security deposit and your payment would be $450 a month.

Thus, leasing would save you $200 a month, and you would need only $450 down, not $6,800 (plus, in both cases, sales tax). This is why leasing is so popular.

Why Lease Payments Are So Cheap

Economically speaking, cars consist of three parts: equity (ownership), depreciation (loss in value over time), and interest expense (on the loan, if any). If you finance the purchase of a car, you pay for all three parts, and you will own the vehicle in, say, four years. But if you lease, you are paying only for use of the vehicle. Therefore, you pay for the car's depreciation and interest, not the equity, and you return the car at the end of the lease term. This is why monthly lease payments are lower than purchase payments. Leasing, quite simply, is the difference between owning a car and renting one.

Why would a car dealer want you to rent (i.e., lease)? It's simple: If you lease the car, you pay $450 a month for four years. Then you give the car back, giving the dealer the chance to resell it. In other words, the dealer gets to sell the same car twice!

This means the dealer doesn't have to charge you (the first buyer) the full $34,000; you pay only the difference between what the car is worth today ($34,000) and what it will be worth four years from now. The second buyer pays the rest at that time.

Say the dealer expects this $34,000 car to be worth $15,200 in four years. He would therefore want you to pay $18,800 and the second buyer to pay $15,200. Thus, your lease payments would be based on just $18,800, whereas your payments to buy would be based on the full $34,000. That's why your monthly lease payments are $450 instead of $650. When the dealer resells the car in four years, he'll get the other $15,200.

The Key Factor: Residual Value

Leasing, then, features lower monthly payments because dealers expect the car to retain a certain value. In reality, though, lease rates are not based on what the car's residual value will be, but on what the dealer *pretends* it will be.

That's why lease payments often are so attractive. If, according to industry standards, a $40,000 car will be worth only $12,000 in four years, the dealer would have to base your lease on $28,000 worth of depreciation. That would make the lease payment absurdly high, and no one would take the deal. So the dealer pretends that the residual value will be $30,000, leading to lower, more attractive, lease payments. This game is dangerous for the dealer, but a bargain for you.

The key to the cost of leasing, then, is the "residual value," or what the dealer says the car will be worth at the end of the lease. Expensive cars tend to offer better lease deals than cheaper cars, for they retain more of their value, and the higher the residual value, the lower your lease payments.

"When you think no one cares if you're alive, try missing a couple of car payments."

—Anonymous

Three Money-Saving Tips When Leasing

As with most financial transactions, success or failure is found in the fine print. Here are three items to keep in mind:

Money-Saving Tip #1: Make Sure You Have Gap Insurance

This is perhaps the single most important — and most overlooked — element of leasing.

Say your contract says the car's residual value at the end of the lease will be $15,200, but the car's actual value will be only $10,000. If you wreck the car three months before your lease expires, guess how much your insurance company will pay in settlement?

The insurer will pay the dealer (who owns the car) the actual market value, which is $10,000. But your contract says the residual value is $15,200. That means you are responsible for the other $5,200.

This "gap" between the lease contract's stated residual value and the car's actual value has caused many lessees to incur huge losses due to accidents.

The solution: Make sure your lease contract includes "gap insurance" — even if you have to pay extra for it, for being without it is like driving without insurance.

Money-Saving Tip #2: Avoid the Cap Cost Reduction

When someone buys a car, the more money he puts down, the less his monthly payments. Similarly, to lower your lease payments, you can make a cap cost reduction, which is a large, one-time payment made at the start of the lease. And as with a down payment, the more you pay in cap (short for capitalized) cost reductions, the lower your monthly payments. However, this is where the similarity ends.

Remember that when leasing, you do not own the car. Thus, if you make a cap cost reduction, you are making a down payment on property that is not yours. Never do that — no matter how much the dealer wants you to, and no matter how much it reduces your monthly payments — for in the long run, you are throwing your money away. And the run might not be so long, either: Steve leased a $25,000 car and paid $3,000 in cap costs. Two months later, he totaled the car. Since he didn't own the car, his insurer repaid the dealer $22,000; Steve lost his $3,000.

Paying cap costs is a waste even if you don't wreck the car. Why? Because the only reason dealers want you to pay it is so they can offer you a monthly payment that sounds really low.

Would you visit a dealer who advertised a $20,000 car for just $199 a month? You bet! But would you get excited about having to pay $263 per month for the same car? Not likely. And that's why dealers want you to pay a cap cost reduction. You see, in one recent ad, a car dealer offered a $20,000 car for $199 per month for 24 months with a cap cost reduction of $1,525. But paying $199 per month with $1,525 down is the same as paying $263 per month with no cap cost reduction. If $263 doesn't sound so hot (and it's not), then the other deal isn't so hot, either.

Instead of paying a cap cost reduction to lower your payments, ask the dealer to let you make additional security deposits. This will have the same effect as a cap cost reduction, except you'll get the deposit back when you return the car.[24]

Money-Saving Tip #3:   Never Buy Optional Equipment in a Car You're Not Buying

When leasing, you must keep in mind that you don't own the car. That means you must be careful when agreeing to options that the dealer offers you. Take Carmen for example. She worked out a fine deal on a car — $250 per month for 36 months, with no cap cost reduction. But then she decided to have the dealer install mats, fancier hubcaps, a 10-disc CD changer, and a telephone. The cost of all these items came to $1,800, so the dealer added $50 to the monthly payment. This not only made sense to Carmen, since $50 per month for 36 months is $1,800, she thought it was a heck of a deal — because although she would be paying for the options over three years, the dealer did not add in any interest.

It was a deal all right — but for the dealer, not Carmen. When the lease expired three years later, Carmen returned the car — and with it, the mats, hubcaps, CD changer, and telephone. Carmen paid the full cost of owning those items, but she only rented them. Dumb move, Carmen.

---

[24]Unless, of course, you wreck the car or return it with excessive wear and tear.

What she should have done is incorporated the cost of the options into the overall price of the car, and then negotiated the lease price. That way, she'd be renting the options along with the rest of the car.

Remember: When you lease, you are renting the car and everything in it. Don't pay the costs of ownership when you lease.

Leasing and Taxes

When leasing, you are liable for sales tax even though you do not own the car. If your state levies a personal property tax, you'll have to pay this, too. But to entice you to lease, many dealers offer to pay the property tax for you. Shop around for the best deal.

To Lease or Not to Lease: Here Is the Answer

To determine whether you should buy or lease, answer these two simple questions:

1. How many miles do you drive per year?

In most leases, you are allowed to drive only 10,000 to 15,000 miles per year, 40,000 to 60,000 miles on a four-year lease. Anything more will cost you up to 25 cents per mile. Therefore, leasing works best for people who drive less than 10,000 miles per year, and if you know you'll drive significantly fewer miles than 10,000 to 15,000 per year, you can negotiate a lower lease payment.

2. How long do you generally keep your car?

Leasing is best for people who keep their cars for four years or less. Remember that when leasing, you never enjoy a payment-free month. At the end of the lease, you must turn in the car and get a new one, with a new lease or purchase contract.

Thus, if you like to keep cars for seven or eight years, you'll find that, over the long run, leasing is much more expensive than buying.

Don't Lease Beyond the Car's Warranty

If you choose to lease, don't lease for a term beyond the car's warranty. If the car comes with a two-year bumper-to-bumper warranty, for example, get a two-year lease. By opting for a three-year lease, you could be stuck with huge repair bills in year three — on a car you don't own!

Leasing for Business

Leasing makes great sense for business, regardless of how many miles you drive, because you are allowed to deduct the cost as a business expense. (If you buy a car for business, you must depreciate it instead.)

Since cars are one of the largest purchases you'll make, talk with your financial advisor before you decide whether to buy or lease, how much to put down, and whether or not you should finance. The right decision can save you thousands!

"Drive-in banks were established so most of the cars today could see their real owners."

—E. Joseph Cossman

Chapter 53 - How to Pay for College (Really!)

The first seminars I ever presented were to PTA groups on "How to Pay for College." But rather than presenting them to parents of high school sophomores and juniors, I would speak to parents of elementary-age schoolchildren.

Why? Because if you wait until your child is 16, you won't have enough time to prepare for the costs of college. You've got to focus on this subject while your kids are still in grade school.

> Heck, you need to work on this before the kid is born. Most who think about college costs already have children. And planners routinely advise their clients to plan for college (as this chapter suggests) while their kids are still young.
>
> But if you think you've got at most 18 years to plan for college, think again: Nobody says you have to wait for the baby to be born before you start saving. If you know you'll have children one day, you might as well start saving for college now. That way, you give yourself 20 or 25 years to save instead of just 18, 15, 10 or 3. And the more time you have to save, the easier it is to achieve your goal.

CURRENT COSTS OF THE IVY LEAGUE

School	2002-2003 Total Cost	Change Since 1988
Yale	$35,370	+68%
Tufts	$36,465	+50%
Harvard	$35,950	+65%
Princeton	$37,960	+58%
Brown	$36,356	+47%

FIGURE 7-6

The cost of college for today's newborns will be more than $180,000. That's tuition, room, and board for a four-year education at a typical state college. The Ivy Leagues will be more than $300,000. That's *per child*. Get used to it: It's like buying several houses simultaneously.

Too often, parents either don't think about future college expenses until their kids register for the SAT test, or their "plan" is a simple one: My kid will win an athletic or academic scholarship. *Voila…! Zee Crisis, she eez solved!*

If it were only that easy. The truth is that nationally, less than one-third of students receive any form of financial aid, and of those who do, the average aid meets only one-third of the need. Thus, if you're assuming your third-grader will be a football star because he's the fastest kid in his class, or that your child will be valedictorian because she always gets straight A's, think again. Educators will tell you there is no way to predict whether your young child will be a star when he or she is seven years old (funny things happen to kids when they hit puberty — remember?), and it's a foolish financial plan that relies on such a premise.

A better idea is to start saving now. And how will you come up with the hundreds of thousands of dollars it will take to get your kid through college? Well, let me ask you this: How do you eat an elephant?

One bite at a time.

To accumulate the savings needed to send a six-year-old to college, you'll need to start saving anywhere from $600 to $1,500 per month, depending on your rate of return and the cost of the school your child will attend.

Those are absurd numbers, and they lead parents to do absurd things, including the biggest of all absurdities, *doing nothing*. "I'll never be able to save that much, so I might as well not save anything." Like most attitudes, this one will become a self-fulfilling prophecy.

Another dangerous strategy is to rely on the equity in your home.

This is an extremely common tactic among parents of today's college students, because today's 50-some-things have been caught totally off-guard by the costs of college. During the 1960s and 1970s, a four-year college education cost under ten grand, and often under five grand. It was no particular financial struggle — either for the students or their parents. So, based on that experience, they assumed it would be the same when their kids reached college age.

"The 'birds and bees' I know about, Dad. I need to know more about the 'bulls and bears'."

But **The Rules of Money Have Changed** and college costs have skyrocketed, far outpacing the rate of inflation.

The result is that Mom and Dad are shocked when they attend College Night at their 17-year-old's high school. Where will we get the money, they ask each other? They quickly scan their assets: They have some savings, but not nearly enough for even one year, let alone four. They have the money in their company retirement plans, but that can't be touched without severe tax penalties. And they have their house, which they bought a few years before their daughter was born and which now has substantial equity. Thus, the answer is clear: They will take out a home equity loan to pay for college.

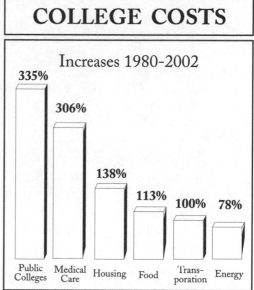

FIGURE 7-7

Bad Idea #1: Using Home Equity to Pay for College

This strategy will work: The child can attend college. However, this tactic all but destroys Mom and Dad's retirement plans and creates a ticking time bomb.

Think about it: Mom and Dad bought their home in their early 30s for $25,000. With a 30-year mortgage, they knew the house would be paid off in their early 60s — around the same time as they plan to retire. (After all, this is how their parents did it.) The mortgage balance is now down to $12,000 — but the house also is now worth about $100,000 — allowing the parents to pull out not just the original $13,000 they've repaid over the past 20 years, but $70,000 more. Indeed, Mom and Dad are able to send their kids to college, but they find themselves three or four times deeper in debt than when they bought their house, and 66% closer to retirement.

The result: Mom and Dad will not pay off their home until they are in their 80s — 20 years *after* they had planned to retire!

Thus, using equity in the home is a fine solution for your college plan, but it creates havoc with your retirement plan. Still, all too many of today's parents feel they have no choice if they're to give their kids a college education.

Bad Idea #2: Using Student Loans to Pay for College

The second solution, commonly used when parents don't have home equity to rely on, or not enough to cash cover the college costs of all their children, is to seek student loans.

But reality soon hits. Under current federal rules for Stafford loans, first-year students can receive a maximum of $2,625. Even college seniors are eligible for only $5,500 — and these figures are a far cry from the actual costs of college.

The qualification rules are perverse: Federal rules say parents who have managed to save just a little money must spend all of it on college, while parents who have amassed large assets are not so obligated.

For example, take two families, both earning $80,000 per year. The Smiths have saved $20,000 vs. $40,000 for the Browns. Under current rules, the Smiths are required to contribute $15,600 per year before becoming eligible for aid, while the Browns must contribute the same amount! On a percentage basis, that means the Smiths contribute 78% of their assets per year, while the Browns must contribute only 39%!

> *"A major problem these days is how to save money for your children's college education when you're still paying for yours."*
> —Doug Larson

It really doesn't matter, of course, because both will eventually run out of money. Assuming the annual cost of college is $15,000, the Smiths will run of out money in the second year, while the Browns will run out of money in the third year. Thus, the federal loan rules are telling parents to save a lot — so some of your savings can survive college — or save nothing. For if you save only small amounts, you'll have nothing left after college, anyway. Since many parents find it impossible to save a lot, the system encourages them to save nothing.

Those who follow this strategy live to regret it. Many college graduates are saddled with tens of thousands of dollars in student loan debt, which will haunt your kids for 10 years or more after they graduate. Try buying a house or even a car with such a debt load.

EXPECTED PARENTAL CONTRIBUTION TO YEARLY COLLEGE COSTS

Based on Assets and Income

Total Income	Net Assets				
	$20K	**$40K**	**$60K**	**$80K**	**$100K**
$20,000	0	4,000	12,000	20,000	30,000
$40,000	0	4,000	12,000	20,000	30,000
$60,000	200	5,000	13,000	22,000	31,000
$80,000	700	6,000	14,000	23,000	32,000
$100,000	1,200	7,000	15,000	24,000	33,000

Figures provided are for a family of four, with one child attending college. These figures also assume one working parent per family.

FIGURE 7-8

Bad Idea #3: Using College Tuition Prepayment Plans

Sponsored by both individual schools (the first was Duquesne) and most states, these programs all work basically the same way: You send in a certain amount of money now (normally the current cost), and they promise that college will be paid for when your child turns 18.

There's lots of fine print, though, to wit:

- These programs cover tuition only — not room and board, which constitutes 40% to 60% of the cost of college.

- There is no guarantee your child will be accepted to the school.

- Your child might not want to go to that particular school, to a school in that state, or to any school, and in some programs, refunds are limited only to the amount you paid, with no interest.

- There is no guarantee the program will succeed. Colorado, for example, cancelled its program and returned all the money to parents because it was unable to keep up with the cost increases of its own colleges. Ohio, Florida and dozens of other states are considering similar action, while still others are hiking the cost of their plans as much as 30%.

- There are tax liabilities if you join a college's private plan. Say you invest $15,000 now to avoid having to pay $75,000 when your child goes to college. The IRS considers this to be a capital gain of $60,000, which means you'll owe roughly $9,000 in federal taxes. Under current law, this tax is waived for state-sponsored tuition pre-payment plans — but only until 2010.

> **If you're wondering why I haven't discussed the notion of kids getting a job, it's not because I don't believe in it. I do. The problem, though, is that kids working a few hours a week at some minimum wage job will not enable them to earn and save the $10,000 or $20,000 annual cost of college.**
>
> **So, sure, putting the kids to work can help, but it's not a real solution to the problem.**

A better idea is to put your money into a good investment where the odds are high that it will perform at least as well as any prepayment plan, yet allowing you to maintain full control over the assets in the meantime.

Bad Idea #4: The Coverdell Education Savings Account

Provided that you have an adjusted gross income of less than $190,000 (if married, or $95,000 if single), you can contribute to this new college-planning account up to $2,000 per child per year.

Don't.

Why not? Because if you use an Education Savings Account, you could be prohibited from using the Hope Scholarship Tax Credit or the Lifetime Learning Tax Credit — and both of them offer far better tax benefits than the ESA.

> **In case you haven't noticed, I've been talking about college as though your child will attend for four years and then enter the workforce.**
>
> **Think again. With increasing frequency, today's college graduates go on for post-graduate degrees. So while you're figuring out ways to pay for the B.A. degree, make sure you or your child have resources left for graduate school.**

Three Reasons Not to Save Money in Your Child's Name

Parents trying to save for college often save money in the child's name. Don't do it, for three reasons:

Reason #1: There Is Little Benefit Under Current Tax Law

In the old days, putting money in your kids' names made great sense, because the parents were in tax brackets as high as 70%, while children were in 0% brackets. That huge spread created a tremendous financial advantage.

But the Tax Reform Act of 1986 closed this loophole by creating the Kiddie Tax. Today, Mom and Dad are likely to be in the 25% tax bracket, or maybe 28% . Few Americans are in the 33% bracket, and even the highest is just 35% — a far cry from the 70% top marginal bracket in the old tax code.

And worse, kids today earn little money tax-free: Until age 14, the first $750 they earn is not taxed, income between $750 and $1,500 is taxed at 10%, and everything above that is taxed at their parents' rate. After 14, they pay taxes at their own rate, but by then — if Mom and Dad are saving regularly in the kid's name — the child could be in the 25% bracket anyway.

Since Mom and Dad are paying 25% and their young kids are paying 10%, the spread is only 15% — and this is too narrow a margin to make saving in the child's name worthwhile, especially when you consider the next two points.

Reason #2: Kids Take Legal Control of Their Money at Age 18

When saving for a child, the account must be registered in the child's name under the Uniform Gift to Minors Act. In a UGMA, an adult (usually a parent or grandparent) serves as Custodian and is responsible for investing and managing the assets. But the child is the "beneficial owner," meaning the assets really belong to the child, not to the adult. At age 18, the assets must be turned over to the child.

> **All states offer UGMAs or the Uniform Transfers to Minors Act. The former allows children to own stocks, bonds, mutual funds, and other securities; the latter allows them to also own real estate. Also, under UTMA, you can delay giving the assets to the child until age 21.**

Picture handing $50,000 to your 18-year-old. If he wants to spend the money on a trip to Europe or a car instead of college, you can't stop him (short of your parental influence). A better strategy, then, is to save the money in your name, perhaps in a separate account, and to know in the back of your mind that the account is intended for college. (Hey, if your child decides not to go, or wins a scholarship, you get to keep the money!)

Reason #3: Saving in the Child's Name Hurts Your Ability to Qualify for College Financial Aid

All other factors being equal, a family whose child has assets is less likely to qualify for aid than a family whose child doesn't have assets. Because virtually all of the child's expenses are college-related (while parents have additional financial obligations), federal financial aid rules require that students spend a larger portion of their assets than parents. Therefore, putting money in the parent's name rather than the child's will increase the family's eligibility for financial support.

What To Do If You Have a UGMA

Unfortunately, many parents — perhaps including you — already may have established a UGMA for your child. Creating such an account constitutes an irrevocable gift, and legally you cannot cancel the account and return the money to your own name. (Doing so would annoy the IRS, so don't do that.)

What, then, can you do?

Here's the solution: Remember that under a UGMA, the assets belong to the child, and the law requires that the assets be used for the benefit and welfare of the child. Most parents think this means the money can be used only for college expenses, but that's not so. In truth, money in a UGMA can be used for almost anything — provided "anything" is for the benefit and welfare of the child.

After all, your child needs clothes, food, shelter, education, and medical care, and there's nothing in the UGMA rules that say you can't use the child's assets to pay these expenses. For example, say you take your child to the doctor for her annual check-up and the bill is $200. Instead of paying for that yourself, withdraw $200 from the UGMA account and use that money to pay the bill. Simultaneously, send $200 of your own money into an investment (in your name) that is similar to the one used by the UGMA.

In this manner, you'll slowly erode the value of the UGMA, while building assets in a new account in your name. If you pay for all of the child's expenses through the UGMA, such as private school, camp, music lessons, clothing, even their portion of food, shelter, utilities, and insurance costs, you ought to have no problem eliminating that account well before the child is 18.

Keep good records and maintain receipts to show the IRS (if they ask) that the money you withdrew from the UGMA was used for the direct benefit of the child.

And don't get carried away: Liquidating a UGMA to buy yourself a new car "to chauffeur the child to soccer practice" is unlikely to win IRS approval. If in doubt about the validity of any expense, ask your tax advisor.

One Case for Using a UGMA

All the above notwithstanding, there is one circumstance where I regularly recommend the use of UGMA accounts: When a grandparent wants to save for a grandchild's college costs. I am unconcerned that a UGMA will hinder the family's ability to qualify for aid when the source of the UGMA assets is someone other than the parents, because this money is a gift. What does it matter if college is paid for by gifts or financial aid?

If a relative or family friend wants to give the child money for a birthday, holiday, or other celebration, that money must go into a UGMA for the child. After all, the donor is making the gift to the child and they want to know the child will indeed be the ultimate recipient of the money. They don't want the money to be used for the parents' financial problems (if they did, they'd have given the money to the parents, not the child).

So don't fret, Mom and Dad, that gifts to UGMAs will hurt your college financial aid eligibility.

Beware of IRC Section 2036(c)

But grandparents and other donors need to be aware of Section 2036(c) of the Internal Revenue Code. This section of the code holds that transfers to minors are considered void if the donor acts as custodian of the account.

Thus, if Grandpa gives $1,000 to the child, he should not serve as the custodian to the child's UGMA account. A parent of the child or other adult should serve as custodian instead.

Congress created 2036(c) to close an estate tax loophole. Remember that the custodian decides how to invest and manage the assets, so if a grandparent gives money to the grandson but serves as custodian, the grandparent retains control over the asset — almost as though the gift was never made. Yet if the grandparent dies, the asset would be excluded from his estate, avoiding or reducing estate taxes.

Congress rightfully concluded that lots of folks were making "sham" gifts in this manner, so the law was amended to say if you make gifts to an account for which you serve as custodian, the value of your gifts will be included in your estate for purposes of calculating the estate tax.

You can avoid this problem simply by naming someone else as the custodian. For more on estate taxes, see Chapter 64.

Section 529 Plans: The Best Way to Save for College

So far I've shown you the four ways not to save for college. Now you'll learn the *best* way to save. It's called a Section 529 Plan, based on Section 529 of the Internal Revenue Code (duh).

Technically, Section 529 grants the states permission to establish college savings programs, giving special tax benefits to consumers who participate in those programs. And, as part of that technicality, Tuition Pre-payment Plans are also part of Section 529, but nobody refers to them as that, so I won't, either.

Instead, I'll call Tuition Pre-payment Plans exactly that, and I'll refer to College Savings Plans as 529 plans, even though both CSPs and TPPs are part of Section 529.

And that's just the beginning of the silliness surrounding the creation of 529 plans. The other silly part is that the law permits states to create these programs, instead of the private sector. (Hey, the law creates IRAs too, but you don't see states operating those programs, now do you?)

The result is that although each of the states has created its own 529 plan, almost all of them subcontract the effort to mutual fund companies. And some states operate two plans, which explains why there are more than 70 available even though there are only 50 states plus the District of Columbia.

So, despite the fact that 529 plans are established by states, they are almost all operated by mutual funds. Consequently, consumers tend to select plans based more on which fund company is involved than on which state is the sponsor. And that's smart, because the fact is that your money is invested with, and managed by, the funds you select, not the state.

Thus, even though these are state-based programs, the investments are plain ol' everyday mutual funds. And you can join any state program you want, regardless of where you or the child lives (although a few states offer a small tax incentive to entice you to join the plan where you live, but this enticement is so small it's usually irrelevant).

So, even though the 529 programs are state-based, they all operate under the same IRS rules. And those rules are terrific. To wit:

- When investing in these plans, you can set aside huge amounts of money. Although the limits per child are set by each state, they are all well into six figures, and as much as $250,000 per child — all with no gift tax problem (see Chapter 63). Thus, if you have the means, every state's limits are high enough for you to easily set aside in these programs more than enough to meet even the highest college education costs. (That actually poses a potential problem, which I'll explain later.)

- By investing your contributions into mutual funds, you'll earn market-based returns, rather than the inflation-based return offered by tuition pre-payment Plans.

- All the profits earned in the account grow tax-deferred;

- When you need to withdraw money for college, the withdrawals are tax-free (at least until 2010; Congress will need to pass legislation extending this date — something I fully expect it to do).

- If the child wins a scholarship or grant, you can withdraw a similar amount without losing the above tax benefits.

- The money withdrawn can be used for virtually all college expenses — including room and board (TPPs cover tuition only).

- You can use the money for any college in the country — (your state's TPPs offer full benefits only for state schools in that state).

- If the child doesn't use all the money in the account, you can redirect any remaining monies to another child in the family or a parent, grandparent, sibling or cousin of the child. You can even keep the money invested and later name a child of the child — someone who won't be born for perhaps 40 years — creating literally decades of tax-free growth! Because of this flexibility, we often recommend that our clients establish only one 529 plan, for their oldest child, instead of one for each child. This is easier and cheaper, and the excess balances can be redirected to the younger children at any time.

- There is no age limit for use, and the money can be used for graduate school. Thus, the money can be used by a 50-year old who's returning to school for an MBA (including you!). In contrast, the Education Savings Account must be used by age 30.

- Once you open the account, anyone can contribute to it. This way, grandparents who like to make gifts to the kids don't have to establish their own 529 plans. Instead, they can just add money to the plan you've established. Keep in mind, though, that 529 plans are considered to be owned not by the child, but by the person who establishes the account. (And it's the owner who determines which child in the family is to be the beneficiary.) Therefore, relatives might prefer to create their own 529 accounts, even though doing so duplicates the set-up fees (which vary by state but are all fairly low).

- Any withdrawals not used for qualifying college expenses are subject to taxes plus a 10% penalty. Think that's a problem? It actually might be an opportunity. Consider: If you die, your assets could be hit with an estate tax that's as high as 48% (see chapter 64). But if you transfer assets into a 529 plan — even knowing the money won't be used for college — the combined federal/state tax rate would be — at worst — 45%. And in many cases, the tax could be a lot less. This is why many grandparents need to consider 529 plans as an estate planning tool rather than a college savings device.

Without question, this is the most friendly, consumer-oriented college savings program ever created, and it's remarkably similar to my retirement planning tool for children (see page 624), except that this is for college, not retirement.

In fact, the program is so good I have one big concern: that parents will overfund it. By placing so much money into the plan — which is easy to do, given all the tax incentives — you might underfund your own financial needs, such as cash reserves and retirement planning. For this reason, we limit our clients' contributions to only 50% to 60% of the estimated present value of future college costs. (For a fuller discussion on that, see Chapter 3 of *Discover the Wealth Within You*.)

Dealing with College Costs Realistically

Every book on college planning I've read focuses on the incredible cost of a college education, admonishing parents that they need to sacrifice for 20 years to be able to meet this huge expense.

I don't agree, and that's why you're not reading much on college saving strategies in this book. The truth is that almost everyone is dealing with college costs the wrong way. That's because they're dealing with college *the old way*. But remember, **The Rules of Money Have Changed**, and you cannot approach the costs of college in a traditional fashion.

There are two reasons for this: First, you probably don't have the two decades you need to save for college. Second, you've ignored what is perhaps the primary problem with this entire subject: your kid's attitude (and maybe yours, too).

Let's face it: Going to college today is far different than it was a generation ago. We graduated either debt-free or with a small debt that was both tax-deductible and easily manageable.

That's not the case today. The best example I can give you is Bertha, the daughter of Lois and Jim. Bertha wanted to attend a private college that cost $26,000 per year. Dad obliged, mortgaging his house to pay for it.

Bertha planned to be a physical therapist. Late in her junior year, Bertha discovered she needed a master's degree to practice in her field, and she selected a Florida university. Dad, who by now had sent three kids to college, had exhausted his savings, so his ability to assist Bertha was sharply reduced.

Determined, Bertha borrowed as much as possible from her family, qualified for financial aid, and obtained credit cards and other personal loans. It all paid off: Today, Bertha is a successful physical therapist working in a major sports medicine facility, earning $42,000 per year.

She is also $45,000 in debt.

Between her student and personal loans and credit cards, Bertha's minimum debt payment is $1,100 per month, and she'll be saddled with that debt until she's 36 years old. And because she chose a career with no upward salary potential, her income is unlikely to improve. (She has contemplated becoming an administrator to make more money, but that would require going back to school for an MBA in hospital administration.)

Bertha can't change careers because she can't afford to go back to school. She can't quit her job because of her debt load, and she can't ever imagine being able to buy a house. And Dad, meanwhile, nearly lost his house in the process.

Then there's David, who called my TV show to ask how he could reduce his college loan bills. He explained that he owes $140,000, his monthly payment is $1,109 — and he's a schoolteacher who's also working part-time at his church.

Jason and Andrea had a similar story. Soon to graduate from law school, Jason will owe $90,000 in student loans and Andrea $72,000. They hope to work for big law firms — the only ones who will pay the $80,000 starting salaries Jason and Andrea are counting on to enable them to pay off their debts.

Still, as huge as Jason and Andrea's debts are, they actually are somewhat better off than Bertha and David. At least Jason and Andrea's salaries can grow as they build their careers. Bertha's can't, for when she becomes too expensive for her employer, they'll just dump her and hire some other kid fresh from grad school. And David is working in a career that's known for its lack of economic rewards.

Why didn't their parents or the schools warn these kids what they are facing? They have discovered their plight only after entering the workforce, rather than anticipating it before spending all that money.

Too many careers are like Bertha's: There is no relationship between the cost of obtaining the degree and the economic reward for having done so.

It is my contention that because of today's costs of college, we must approach the concept of going to college the same way we approach all other investments. Because today more than ever, a college degree is an investment. If you don't believe me, just ask your kids.

According to the University of California-Los Angeles' survey of incoming freshmen (Class of 1998), 75% said a "very important reason" in deciding to go to college was "to make more money." Their "essential or very important" objective was "to be very well off financially." These numbers are in stark contrast to students of 20 years ago: In 1971, only 40% of UCLA's freshmen felt the same way.

> And don't fret if the only thing your kids want from college is a wife or hus-band. According to Census Bureau data, the average married couple who both have degrees earns three times more than the average married couple who are both high school dropouts, and twice as much as couples who are high school graduates.

Thus, in the majority of cases, today's kids regard college as a means to improve their financial future, whereas those who went to college in 1950s and 1960s more often than not wanted to make the world a better place.

So while today's high school seniors think of college in terms of economic reward, their parents don't. This is how the disaster begins: The kids are making what they consider to be a practical investment, but their parents (who fail to see college in that light) don't equate the cost with the result.

In yet another example of how **The Rules of Money Have Changed**, parents need to change how they look at college.

Can I Have a Car?

How would you reply if your 18-year-old son came to you and said, "I have been looking at this hot, red Porsche Turbo. I've got to have it! It's only $88,000! Can I have it?"

You would refuse, of course, and none too quietly.

Yet when your son approaches and says, "I have been looking at this great school. I've got to go there! It's only $22,000 a year! Will you pay for it?"

Too often, Mom and Dad not only say yes, they will do whatever it takes to pay for it: They'll spend all their savings, they'll cash out the equity in their home, they'll borrow from their life insurance policies, they'll pull money from their company retirement plans, they'll get second jobs, they'll even ask relatives for assistance — all because it never occurs to them that they don't have to say yes.

But Mom and Dad think they do have to say yes. "After all, we're talking about my child's future! If I don't say yes, I will be responsible for destroying the one chance my child has for success! Money is not a concern here! If my child needs to spend $88,000 to go to college, then I'll do whatever it takes to make it happen!"

Years later, the parents are financially destroyed and/or the children are horribly in debt, both beyond their worst nightmares.

All because Mom and Dad took the financial advice of an 18-year-old. The kid said, "Have I got an investment for you!" and the parents bought it.

Four Ways to Survive the Cost of College

It's time we started challenging our nation's system of higher education, forcing colleges and universities to associate the cost of a degree with the economic reward one will receive when earning it. Demanding that families and young adults mortgage their futures is madness, and it's got to stop.

But until the system changes, you've got to change how you work with the system. To survive the costs of college, follow these four rules:

Rule #1: Tie Benefits to the Cost

Recognize that most high school seniors — and your kids probably are included in this group — can avoid expensive schools without any adverse affect on their careers. There's nothing wrong with having your son or daughter become, say, a teacher. Teaching is a fine profession. But let's face it: Teachers don't get paid a huge sum of money. Therefore, instead of spending $150,000 on a teaching degree, consider a school that costs $40,000 instead. Chances are the less expensive school will not adversely affect the child's ability to succeed.

In fact, a study from the National Bureau of Economic Research found that people who succeed in life do so because of who they are, not because of what college they attended. Indeed, the study found that graduating from top schools provided no difference in career or economic success. A top student who attends an average school will fare better in life than an average student who attends a top school.

Think about it:

- Most employers don't care where you went to school. Did your boss ask where you went to college? Probably not; the fact that you had a degree was enough. Employers are usually more concerned that you've got the experience and ability to do the job. If you don't believe me, ask the personnel office where you work about what they look for in a new hire.

- Many college graduates eventually settle in careers completely unrelated to their degree. Think about what your old college classmates are doing now. Ask around at work to see how many of your colleagues have a degree related to their current occupation.

- Many college graduates never get a job in their field, or quit within a few years to raise a family. Many of these never return to the work force — or they do so only after 10 or 20 years (which forces them to return to school to update their knowledge and skills anyway).

> Of course, many in today's workforce do owe their success to their alma mater, such as doctors, lawyers, engineers, scientists, and other professionals. But it's a small percentage of the total number of people who go to college.

> It's one thing to be working in a field unrelated to your college major — but it's quite another to be working in a field that doesn't require a college degree at all. In Washington, D.C., one-third of the drivers for the local Dominos Pizza franchise have college degrees. While most took the job because they couldn't find work elsewhere, many stayed because of the money: They often earn more than $50,000 a year. Reports one driver, a lawyer by training who now hopes one day to manage a store, "Imagine how far ahead I'd be if I hadn't wasted all that time and money on college and law school."

Rule #2:   Factor in the Cost of Going to Graduate School

If your child is planning to enter a field that requires an advanced degree, you'd better keep costs down at the undergraduate level.

Rule #3: Choose to Involve — or Exclude — Your Child

Either *completely include* your child in the process of deciding which school to attend, or *completely exclude* him. Too often, the child starts the conversation by announcing to the parents, "I am applying to Penn State, Brandeis, and Cornell!" Leaving the parents to figure out how to pay for it. That's the wrong way to approach it.

There are two right ways (take your pick):

1. Determine on your own how much you can afford to spend on your child's college education, just as you would when planning to buy a car, and then present this figure to your child. Tell her she must select a school that costs no more than this figure.

    Prohibit — rather than allow — your son or daughter from selecting a more expensive school and being responsible for the difference. Although some parents do this to instill financial responsibility in their children, it's a lesson too expensive for them to learn: All you'll do is saddle your kids with huge student loan debts that will haunt them for 10 years after they earn their degree. Besides, why would you let your child go into such debt if you're unwilling to let yourself do it? There are easier, better ways to teach a child financial responsibility (including the next point).

Or

2. Require that your child present you not only with the names and costs of the schools he wants to attend, but also a financial plan for paying for it. Provide him with all the information he needs to make these calculations, including your income, assets, and expenses. Join him in this effort, and teach him the economic realities of life. As you look for ways to reduce or manage the cost, let him be the first to suggest a less expensive school. If he doesn't, feel free to suggest it yourself. And always use your experience to guide him as he suggests impractical or unwise ideas, such as carrying huge debt loads or having you buy a house near the college to avoid the cost of a dorm.

> **If you're reluctant to ask your child to undergo this effort, or if you resist revealing the intimate details about your finances, remember that going to college is about becoming an adult. Besides, he'll learn all about your finances when you complete the financial aid form, anyway. So get over it.**

Rule #4: Consider Alternative Ways to Attend College

Nobody said you must attend college full-time over four years. Instead, consider:

- *Living at Home.* As much as 60% of the cost of college is room and board, not tuition. Living at home can cut the bill in half (but with a commensurate cut in the college experience).

- *Community Colleges.* Funny thing about a degree: It names only the school from which you graduated, not the school where you first enrolled. By attending a community college for the first two years and then transferring to a major university for the junior and senior years, you can save tens of thousands of dollars. And there's no huge sacrifice to the quality of the education, either, since freshman classes are just introductory, anyway. The best part: Employers will never know, since your resume only need show the school that granted your degree.

- *Home-State Colleges.* Attending a home-state school is far cheaper than an out-of-state or private college, and the quality of the education is often just as good — or better. One client who allowed his daughter to go to college across the country failed to anticipate the travel costs. It's a lot more expensive to fly cross country than to drive a couple of hours.

I once had a client ask us to help him figure out how to pay the costs of sending his daughter to Penn State. Since she did not live in Pennsylvania, the cost would have been about $80,000, and my client, though ill-equipped to handle it, was determined to send her there. When I asked why, he replied, "Because she's in the top 3% of her high school class." Then, bragging about her (as parents do), he added, "She's so talented, she even got a full scholarship to the University of Virginia."

I found it amazing that he was willing to pay $80,000 (that he didn't have) so "daddy's girl" could go to the school of her choice, even though she could have gone to a fine institution for free.

Such is the control that "a college education for my kids" has over parents.

- *Accelerated Programs.* Where is it written that it takes four years to get a degree? It often can be done in three. That would save 25% of the cost of room and board and enable your child to start earning a salary one year sooner than other students.

- *Time Off.* Where is it written that it takes four consecutive years to get a degree? Your child can work for a year or two to save for school, and then go to college for a year. Repeat until done. Many employers prefer graduates who have solid work experience to complement their degree. Many schools have cooperative education (co-op) programs. Check them out.

- *Employer Assistance.* Many employers provide tuition-reimbursement programs. So instead of shopping for colleges, maybe your child ought to shop for a job with a company that will pay for school.

- *Military Service.* The ultimate employer assistance program. Consider it.

Is College Right for Your Child?

Before you spend the tens of thousands of dollars it costs to get a degree, talk with your child to make sure college is the right choice. Today's economy is increasingly service-oriented, and with automotive diagnosticians (read: auto mechanics) earning up to $100,000, many fine careers are available that don't require a college degree. Others demand advanced degrees, even PhDs, so make sure your son or daughter is enthusiastic and committed (or as committed as an 18-year-old can be) before you agree to incur — or agree to let them incur — the massive financial expense that their decisions require.

Also keep in mind that, according to studies by the University of Iowa and the College Board, 33% of all college students drop out during their freshman year, and only 48% graduate after five years.

Remember: Refusing to be held hostage by college costs does not mean you are a bad parent. To the contrary, in the long run, you'll be a hero.

Chapter 54 - Does It Pay for Both Parents to Work While Raising Young Children?

If you're married, it's likely that both you and your spouse work outside the home. DINKs — dual income, no kids — are the norm. But what happens when DINKs start having children? Does it really make sense for both parents to work while raising young children?

There are two conflicting answers. The first answer says the costs of raising and supporting a family are so high that, to survive financially, both parents must work. The other contends that the other costs of having both parents work — emotional and stress-related — are so high that it's better for one parent to stay home.

Why Both Should Not Work

Let's examine what it costs to raise children. As we saw in Chapter 1, the federal government pegs first-year costs at $6,490 to $13,430. Unreimbursed medical bills for the obstetrician and hospital alone will be $1,200; maternity clothes, nursery furniture, baby-related equipment, clothes, diapers, formula, food, pediatrician, and other expenses constitute the rest.

But that excludes day care. If both parents work, add $10,000 to the bill. Thus, you're looking at perhaps $20,000 in first-year baby costs. At that price, many couples are convinced both parents must produce an income, and if one parent wasn't working before, the pressure to start is very high.

But is this the right conclusion?

Let's assume our new parents each earn $30,000 a year, for a combined income of $60,000. To maintain their ability to support the family, especially considering the new expenses that come with their baby, they feel both must keep working. But is this second income really necessary for financial survival?

A $30,000 annual income is $2,500 a month. From that, most people spend about $250 a month in commuting costs; this covers either the cost of an automobile and parking fees, or public transportation — your choice.

Also, you'll spend an average of $125 per month on work clothes. (On-the-job wardrobes extend beyond those who wear uniforms. Office workers buy suits and ties or silk blouses and pantyhose. It all adds up to about the same expense.) You'll spend an additional $120 per month on lunch, office gifts, and obligatory donations. And don't forget day care at about $800 per month. In total, you'll spend $1,300 per month in work-related expenses — about half of one spouse's total income. "That's no problem," you say. "I still net $1,200."

Oh, really?

Don't forget taxes. If you gross $2,500, you will lose about $1,000 in taxes. Therefore, your net after-tax, after-expense take-home pay is about $200 a month. That's less than $50 a week. If you work 40 hours a week and devote one hour daily dressing for work and commuting, you're going through all this for about $1.25 an hour. And that's on a $30,000 gross income!

It gets worse. Not only are you netting way below minimum wage, think about all the time you're not spending with your child and the additional stress added to the family by the fact that both the husband and the wife are working. Who stays home when the baby is sick? Who leaves that important meeting to race to the day care center before it closes? Will it be you or your spouse who takes vacation or sick leave because the plumber is scheduled to stop by? Considering all the non-economic issues affecting the family, does it really make sense for both parents to work?

Five Reasons Why Both Should Work

From this analysis, I may have led you to conclude "no." But it's not that simple. Thus far I have presented only half the issue, so let me come to the defense of women who have young children and who work outside the home. There are five reasons why it can make a lot of sense for both Mom and Dad to work:

Reason #1: Protect Your Career

If the wife gives up her job,[25] she could do irreparable damage to her career, because her colleagues (competitors?) who don't take five years off continue to climb the corporate ladder.

Reason #2:   The Lower-Earning Spouse Might Have The Health Insurance Benefits

That's a very good reason to keep working.

Reason #3: Don't Forget Retirement Benefits

Women in the U.S. typically retire with lower Social Security benefits than men, because women tend to work fewer years. Ditto for company pension plans; if you quit work for five years, you'll pay the price later in the form of a sharply lower retirement income. So forget about the small loss today — staying home with the kids can pose a huge economic loss later. For more on this subject, turn to Part X.

Reason #4: The Parent's Mental Health

Some people just are not well-suited to stay home with their kids full-time. They need adult interaction. One of my clients, a working mom, had a job whose income was so low she actually spent $35 a week more, net of child-care expenses, than she earned. When I mentioned this to her, she replied, "Well, it's cheaper than therapy!"

Reason #5: Improve your Child's Development

A friend who has a little boy once told me, "If my wife were to quit her job and stay home with Billy, he would have a total social circle of one person — his mommy. But in day care, he's learning social skills by being around 20 other kids." Point well taken: The value of interpersonal communication skills for a child shouldn't be dismissed.

---

[25]Let's admit it: The wife is the one most commonly affected here. Please note, however, that deciding who stays home should not be based on gender but on economics and individual preferences. In most cases, the spouse with the lower income is the more likely candidate to stay home.

So, should you work or stay home? Clearly, it's not an easy choice. Yet, more and more employers are offering flexibility that might help make it easier than before for both parents to work. Job sharing, flexible work schedules, and working from home are some of the options available in today's workplace that you should explore as you try to resolve this issue.

My point is that you have a choice. Too many parents do not realize that options exist. Too often, parents assume they must work without considering the alternative. To be a success with your financial planning, you always must examine your options. And proper planning is perhaps nowhere more important than when it comes to raising your children.

Chapter 55 - How to Protect Your Identity

Identity theft is a growing problem. Once stolen, thieves obtain money, services, products, and even jobs in your name.

Thieves sift through garbage to find sensitive information. They steal wallets and mail. They overhear your conversations in public places, or they trick you into giving them information over the phone or though the mail.

Much of your personal data is already publicly available, thanks to voter registration records, real estate transactions, and divorce proceedings. Increasingly, identity thieves have access to your information via the Internet.

If your identity is stolen, it can take years to clear your name. Your credit history might be ruined, and you might lose substantial sums of money. It is impossible to completely protect your information, but here are steps you may wish to take to reduce your risk.

1. Don't toss; shred instead. Buy a personal shredder for home use, and shred any documents that contain personal information. This includes credit card numbers, account numbers, Social Security numbers, birth dates, previous and current addresses, passwords, phone numbers, and driver's license numbers.

2. Shred all financial junk mail, such as subscription or donation requests, credit card offers, and "convenience" checks. Thieves search trash to find these forms, complete them, then steal the cards when they arrive in your mailbox. They start using credit cards you don't even know you have.

3. Shred utility bills, bank statements, and credit card receipts you plan to throw away. Store in a secure location those you retain. Carry only those identification cards you use. Secure or shred the rest.

4. Review your credit report at least annually. Make sure the data is accurate, and close any accounts you no longer use. If you find errors, contact the credit reporting agency, not the creditor that filed the information.

5. Having your mail delivered to your unlocked mail box allows easy access. Better: Use a locked mail box. Best: Have all mail delivered to a rented post office box. If a street address is required, rent a box at a commercial firm. Never

allow your financial institutions to mail statements, checks, or credit/debit cards to your home. Use your P.O. box address on all financial accounts. If you suddenly don't receive mail, contact the local post office immediately. Thieves are known to submit change of address forms that route your mail to them.

6. Get a new "non-published" telephone number from the phone company. It's not perfect, but it'll reduce access to your phone number and address. Expect to pay a fee for keeping your new number out of the telephone directory.

7. Photocopy all documents you carry in your wallet or purse. On that copy, write the telephone number and e-mail address for each source. Also carry with you the following information:

    TransUnion: 1-800-888-4213; fraud division: 1-800-680-7289
    Equifax: 1-800-685-1111; fraud division: 1-800-525-6285
    Experian: 1-888-397-3742; fraud division: 1-888-397-3742

    Also keep with you the telephone number for your state's department of motor vehicles.

    Keep this information with you, but stored away from your wallet or purse. This way, if your wallet or purse is lost or stolen, you can immediately issue notifications.

8. Your Social Security Number is the most important number to guard. With it, thieves can open bank and credit card accounts in your name. Unfortunately, your Social Security Number is easy to get once a thief has your name and address. Therefore, make it hard for the thief to get your address and telephone number.

    To learn more about how professionals use the Internet to get Social Security numbers illegally, go to www.backgroundcheckgateway.com or www.accurint.com. Also:

    Avoid using your Social Security Number as an ID number. If your state uses it as your driver's license number, request an alternative number from the state department of motor vehicles.

    If your SSN is on your checks, shred them and get new ones that omit the number.

If you use your SSN as an ID or password number, change your ID or password.

Never use any part of your SSN as a PIN, especially on the Internet or with bank accounts.

Never carry your SS card with you. Store it in a fireproof safe along with other important documents. If you have not done so already, memorize your SSN. Never carry any document bearing your Social Security Number.

Any time you are asked for your SSN, such as at the doctor's office, ask to use a different number. In most cases, your SSN is not required and is used by vendors unnecessarily. Try to avoid giving your SSN over the phone or on the Internet.

9. Limit the information you have printed on your checks — the less the better. Instead of using your first name, consider using your first initial. Avoid your middle name or initial. Do not include your driver's license number, Social Security Number, or telephone number. Never write a credit card or Social Security Number on a check.

10. Use checks only when paying bills through the mail; in stores, use charge or debit cards. Never add information to a charge card slip (such as your phone number or address). It is illegal to ask you to do so in most states. Always take your card receipts with you; check them against your monthly statement before shredding.

11. Do not use any part of your address or birth date as a PIN. Never write your PIN anywhere.

12. Ready to mail your bill payments? Don't leave them in the open. Thieves will grab them off your desk, use cleaning solvent to remove the payee's name, and replace it with another name that enables them to get the money. And once thieves have your checks or your checking account number, they can use computers to print checks with your name on them.

13. Never put any information about yourself on a post card or on the outside of an envelope other than a return address.

14. Stop giving people your mother's maiden name. It helps crooks access private information about you.

15. When a new credit card arrives, sign the back immediately using permanent ink. Never carry more than two credit cards. Don't give your credit card number over the phone unless you initiated the call, and never do so in a public place, including at work. Never give your credit card number when using a portable or cell phone. If a credit card you've ordered does not arrive promptly, call the card issuer.

16. When you buy an item, keep the warranty information, but don't mail the warranty reply card, especially if it is a post card. (Doing so offers you no protection you don't already have.)

17. Avoid entering contests that require you to provide your name, address, or other personal or financial information.

18. To restrict access to your personal data, remove your name from as many data bases as possible. For example, contact the Direct Marketing Association at www.the-dma.org. You can reach all three credit reporting agencies (Equifax, Transunion, and Experian) by dialing 888-567-8688 or 800-353-0809.

19. Keep important papers in a bank safe deposit box or in a home safe that is fire and burglar resistant. These documents include your Social Security Card; marriage license; pay stubs; credit cards; military papers and bank; investment; tax, and real estate records.

20. If your computer is connected to the Internet, set your computer to erase daily the sites you visit by completing the following steps. Click on "Start" and select "Settings." Click on "Control Panel" and select "Internet Options." When that page appears, go to "History." And set "Days to Keep" to zero. Also, install a "firewall" to keep thieves from accessing your electronic files via cyberspace. Remember that anything you say or attach in an e-mail could end up anywhere. Never include personal information in an e-mail. When you use a credit card to make a purchase on-line, look for a padlock that identifies it as a secure web site.

21. Remember that identity thieves are not always strangers. They could be co-workers, friends, relatives, roommates, and others physically or emotionally close to you. Thieves often steal from people they know, sometimes because

they know you are unlikely to suspect them, and sometimes because they know you are unlikely to punish them.

22. Learn more about protecting your identity at www.identitytheft.org.

What to Do If You Are a Victim of Identity Theft

Thieves who assume your identity work quickly to drain your bank and investment accounts and borrow money in your name. By the time you discover the theft — which can take months or even years — you might have lost hundreds, even thousands of dollars, and you may spend months or years untangling the web of mischief the thieves created. Until you clean up the mess, your credit report is likely to be in tatters; cashiers may treat you like a thief, and you will make dozens of phone calls in an attempt to straighten things out.

In spite of your best efforts, you may still become a victim. Therefore, prevention is not enough. You must also vigilantly monitor the following:

1. **Bank and credit card accounts.** By the time you learn that you've bounced a check, or are informed that your credit card limit has been exceeded, the damage is already done. Unfortunately, most financial institutions use U.S. mail to notify you; few phone or e-mail you. This delay can make the problem worse. To protect yourself, minimize the number of bank and credit card accounts you hold, and check the balances regularly. Most allow you to do this through automated telephone menus or the Internet.

2. **Mail service.** Know your billing and statement cycles. Bank, investment, and credit card statements that fail to arrive on time might have been stolen. Thieves could have raided your mailbox, found an old statement in your trash, or gleaned information from your check or credit card number when you used it in a store or restaurant. However they got it, they sometimes use the data to submit a fraudulent change of address form with the institution. They might create fake checks on their computers, or they might shop with a fake card that carries your number. So, if your mail is late, investigate.

3. **Your credit report.** Ideally, you'd look at it weekly to see if any accounts have been opened in your name without your knowledge, or if any of your legitimate accounts show unauthorized activity. Weekly is ideal because someone who

steals your identity will cause extensive damage during the first week to ten days. But let's get real — nobody looks at their credit report often due to the time and effort involved. So, examine yours at least annually. And if you see old accounts listed that you no longer use, close them.

Someone Has Stolen Your Identity — Now What?

If someone has forged a check on your account, laws in most states hold banks responsible for any loss. However, you must notify financial institutions about the problem in a timely manner. If someone illegally uses your credit card, your maximum liability for each account is $50. Debit cards are another matter: Your liability is $50, but only for the first two days after the card is lost or stolen. Your liability increases to $500 for the next 58 days, and after 60 days, your liability is unlimited. Thus, if you have a line of credit attached to your checking or savings account, you could lose thousands of dollars.

Obviously, as soon as you discover or suspect a problem, notify the institution that handles the account. Do the following:

1. Phone the institution. Each maintains a fraud division, so make sure you're talking to people able to take action. Maintain a log showing the telephone number, date, time of the call, and name and title of the person with whom you spoke. Add notes describing what was discussed and actions agreed to.

2. Send a certified letter, return receipt requested, to the person you spoke with, confirming the call and summarizing the conversation. If you send an e-mail instead, require that they confirm receipt.

3. Keep your original logs, notes, and documents. Upon request, send copies; never give originals to anyone.

4. Keep all records for at least seven years after you have resolved the last problem.

5. Close all credit card, investment, and bank accounts. Open new ones. This is a major hassle, but the alternative might be to lose all the money in those accounts. Ask each institution to place on each account the statement, "Account closed at customer's request."

Be careful when applying for a mortgage on-line.

The basic rule when applying for a mortgage: Know with whom you are dealing. Traditionally, home buyers obtained mortgages at their local banks. But during the last dozen years, partly thanks to the Internet, mortgage lenders located thousands of miles away now can compete with local lenders. The good news is that mortgage financing has become very competitive. This translates to a greater variety of loan programs, lower interest rates, smaller fees, and better service for consumers. To get a sense of how much competition is out there, just type "mortgage loans" into an Internet search engine: You'll get a list of thousands of web sites.

So...should you apply for a mortgage on-line? Well, as president of Edelman Mortgage Services Inc., I'm hardly objective on the subject. Suffice it to say this: If you're going to use an Internet mortgage firm, make sure the firm is legitimate. I say that because of many recent reports of on-line fraud.

Here's how the most common scam works: You search the web for the lowest mortgage rates you can find. You find what appears to be a low rate, offered by a firm whose name you've never heard. To apply for the loan, you complete a form on-line, providing all the information requested by every mortgage lender: your Social Security Number, name and account numbers of bank and investment accounts, credit card information, date of birth, employment and tax information, and so forth. You enter all the data and hit "send" — and off goes the information.

Within an hour, you get an email telling you that your loan is approved. But when you check on your loan at a later date, you discover that the web site no longer exists. Guess what? No web site — no loan. In addition to delaying or losing the chance to refinance, or buy the new home, you've also lost whatever money you paid to the mortgage lender. But if you think those upfront fees are the point of the scam, you're mistaken.

You realize this when you next use your credit card, only to discover that it and all your other cards have been maxed out. When you contact the credit reporting agencies, you learn that dozens of new credit cards have been issued in your name. You also discover that your brokerage and bank account balances have been transferred to untraceable offshore accounts.

You are the victim of identity theft.

Indeed, the crooks are not after a few thousand bucks in fake loan fees. They want YOU — your name, your assets, and your identity. With that data, they can seize tens of thousands of dollars, even hundreds of thousands, before being detected. And you made it easy for them by sending to them every piece of personal financial data about you. It's as though you walked into an alley at 2am,

approached a scruffy-looking guy, and said, "Quick, reach into my back pocket and grab my wallet! I won't notice for at least an hour!"

Fortunately, fraud remains uncommon, but it is increasing, and law enforcement efforts to curtail it — or obtain restitution for victims — are proving elusive. That's because the Internet is anonymous, and many crooks are operating overseas, outside U.S. jurisdiction.

This is not to suggest that you should not use the Internet for obtaining a mortgage, or any other product or service, for that matter. We offer on-line services ourselves, so obviously, the Internet is not the problem. No, the problem is in doing business with people you don't know. There are many fine mortgage and financial service firms operating on the Internet, so there is no reason for you to work with a firm you've never heard of — whether they are a click away or around the corner.

6. Issue "stop payment" requests on all missing or outstanding checks. Ask each bank and credit card company for a copy of its "fraud dispute form." Fill it out promptly and return by certified mail, return receipt requested.

7. Notify the following check verification companies that your checks have been stolen:

   International Check Service: 1-800-366-5010

   TeleCheck: 1-800-710-9898

   Certegy Check Services: 1-800-437-5120

8. If a financial institution is not supporting your efforts, call the Federal Financial Institution Examination Council at 202-872-7500. Carefully explain your problem and include a description of the financial institution that is not assisting you. You will be referred to the appro priate federal agency responsible for regulating that institution.

9. Phone all three national credit reporting agencies and ask each to place a fraud alert on your account. Ask also to have a victim's statement placed on your account requesting that no new accounts be opened without first contacting you personally. Find out how long the fraud alert and the victim's statement will remain on your account, and renew as needed. (Note: The agencies are not required to offer these services.)
   Transunion: 1-800-680-7289
   Equifax: 1-800-525-6285
   Experian: 1-888-397-3742

10. File a police report immediately in the jurisdiction where your problem occurred (for example, in the city where your wallet was stolen); many banks, credit card companies, and credit reporting agencies will request a copy. Keep in

mind that this type of crime, unless it occurred just minutes ago ("Hey! He just stole my wallet!"), is often a low priority for law enforcement. The more evidence and information you can provide the police, the more cooperative and helpful they'll be. Still, expect few results — and be downright astonished if they catch the culprit.

11. If there is any chance that the thief might use your Social Security Number, contact Social Security at: www.ssa.gov/oig/guidelin.htm click on "SS Number Misuse/Identity theft".

12. If you think the thief might be using your driver's license, contact your state's department of motor vehicles and ask to have a fraud report attached to your record.

13. Report your problems to the Federal Trade Commission at 202-452-3693. The FTC will investigate only if there is a pattern of identity theft in your area.

14. Never pay for any forged check, credit card purchase, or other fraudulent transaction for which a merchant may try to hold you liable. If presented with an invoice or demand for payment, explain the situation with the vendor. Be polite, friendly, professional, and communicative, but do not pay a debt that is not yours. If you pay a false bill in error, it is highly unlikely you will get your money back.

For more information on identity theft, go to the Federal Trade Commission's web site at: www.ftc.gov/bcp/conline/pubs/credit/idtheft.htm.

ric's money quiz

Here's a chance to see how well you learned the information contained in Part VII – The Best Financial Strategies. Don't worry if you get stumped — just re-read this part until it sinks in.
Remember, your financial future depends on it.

The answers are at the end of the quiz. No peeking!

---

1. **Which of the following can lead to debt?**

   O a. committing money today that you haven't yet earned
   O b. failing to alter your spending habits when your circumstances change
   O c. both of the above
   O d. neither of the above

2. **When paying off credit cards, you should first pay off the card with the:**

   O a. lowest interest rate
   O b. highest balance
   O c. lowest balance
   O d. highest interest rate

3. **Nationally, less than _____ of college students receive financial aid.**

   O a. one-half
   O b. one-fifth
   O c. one-third
   O d. one-fourth

4. **Which of the following strategies *will not* help you get out of credit card debt?**

   O a. get an American Express Card and pay off the balance each month
   O b. when you charge, immediately write a check to the credit card company
   O c. transfer balances to a credit card with a lower interest rate
   O d. pay the minimum balance due on your cards each month

5. **Which of the following is an example of an unexpected expense?**

   O a. washing machine repairs
   O b. mortgage payments
   O c. auto insurance bill
   O d. birthday presents

6. Gap insurance for a leased car:

   O a. pays the difference between the car's residual value and the car's actual value
   O b. pays for any damage to the car during the lease
   O c. pays any missed payments during the lease
   O d. both b and c

7. Leasing a car works best for people who:

   I.   drive less than 15,000 miles per year
   II. drive more than 15,000 miles per year
   III. keep their cars for four years or less
   IV. keep their cars for more than four years

   O a. I and III
   O b. I and IV
   O c. II and III
   O d. II and IV

8. Saving money in a child's name:

   O a. may hurt the child's ability to qualify for financial aid
   O b. offers a great tax benefit under current tax law
   O c. ensures that the child won't have control of the money later
   O d. none of the above

9. To pay for your child's college education, you should:

   O a. take out a home equity loan
   O b. take out student loans
   O c. invest in a college tuition prepayment plan
   O d. invest in mutual funds

10. After paying for child-rearing and work-related costs, how much might a spouse take home in net after-tax income, assuming a gross salary of $30,000

   O a. $20,000 per year
   O b. $1250 per month
   O c. $275 per week
   O d. $1.25 per hour

Answers: 1-c (pg.291)   3-c (pg.326)   5-a (pg.310)   7-a (pg.323)   9-d (pg.335)
           2-d (pg.296)   4-d (pg.297)   6-a (pg.321)   8-a (pg.331)   10-d (pg.347)

Part VIII
The Best Strategies for Buying, Selling and Owning Homes

There's a quiz at the end of this part!

To see how much you already know, skip to the
end of this part and take the quiz now. Then, read
the part and take the quiz again. You'll discover
how much you've learned!

Part VIII – The Best Strategies for Buying, Selling and Owning Homes

Overview - The American Dream

In this part, you will learn:

- How to buy your first home

- How to sell your home and buy your next home

- How to lower your taxes when selling your home

- How to handle your mortgage

- How to work with real estate agents

- All about the settlement process

Chapter 56 - Incorporating Home Ownership into Your Financial Plan

Too often, people buy homes in a vacuum — without considering how that purchase is going to affect other aspects of their lives. This can be a big mistake, and therefore you must recognize that owning a home holds very important implications for the rest of your financial plan. Although a fine goal, owning a home is not the ultimate financial planning goal, and in fact how you handle the issue of home ownership may well determine whether you achieve financial success.

Therefore, let's consider home ownership within the context of your financial plan. First, is the real estate industry best serving your interests, and second, can only two-income families buy homes?

Ignore What the Real Estate Industry Says You Can Afford

There is a big difference between what the real estate industry says you can afford and what financial planners say you can afford. As you'll learn on the following pages, lenders permit you to spend 40% and more of your gross income on debt — meaning mortgage payments and other debts — yet 30 years ago, that limit was 30%. The mortgage industry has slowly increased this limit because housing prices have grown more rapidly than incomes, and if they didn't increase the limit, today too many Americans wouldn't qualify for a mortgage. That, in turn, would mean bankers wouldn't sell loans and builders wouldn't build houses. That's not in their best interests.

Unfortunately, their best interests can conflict with yours, and if you buy a home by pushing this lending limit to its extreme, or by using some of the no- or low-money down loan programs that are available today (because you have to, not because you choose to), you face the very real risk of becoming "house-poor."

If you want to reduce that risk, keep your total debt payments (including your mortgage) to 28% of gross income, not 40% as the real estate industry allows. This way, you'll have a much-needed cushion to help you deal with the other financial aspects of your life, such as saving for college and retirement. But there is a problem with this self-imposed limit: It forces you to (a) increase your down payment, or (b) buy a less expensive home. You may have difficulty accepting either limitation, but I urge you to do so, because if you don't, you'll find yourself back at the 40% level, with all of the impending problems that brings.

What Happens if You Exceed a 28% Debt Limit

It's important that you don't exceed this 28% figure, for several reasons. Take the example of Marvin and Beth. In their 30s, each earns $35,000, so they bought a house based on their combined $70,000 income. Sometime later they had their first child, and Beth decided she'd like to stay home with the baby for a few years.

Unfortunately, Beth can't quit her job, because without her income the family can't afford the mortgage payments. Thus, Marv and Beth discover that when they bought the house, they relied on incorrect assumptions — the key being that they would continue to have a household income of $70,000 or more. Now, in order to keep the house, Beth must keep working.

It's hard to have sympathy for Marv and Beth, because their crisis is of their own doing: Beth changed her attitude about having a job. But what if this dilemma was forced upon them? It easily could happen: One might get laid off, become injured or ill and unable to work, or die. Since their ability to keep the house is dependent on both incomes, Marv and Beth would be in serious financial jeopardy if one income was lost (and therefore, proper planning is needed to guard against such possibilities).

Marv and Beth can reduce the risk of such a crisis — or avoid it entirely — simply by obtaining a mortgage that does not require a $70,000 income. And that, in turn, means they should set their limits at 28% (or lower) instead of 40%.

Indeed, not only did Marv and Beth assume their income would remain intact, they made a similar miscalculation regarding their expenses. If you had asked if they ever planned to have children, they'd likely have answered, "Sure, someday" — yet they completely ignored the financial considerations of actually having children.

This is a real trap, because as we saw in Chapter 1, the federal government says you're going to spend $337,690 raising each child to age 17 — $27,000 in the first two years alone! And when the kid reaches 18, she'll be off to college, which will cost another $180,000 to $300,000.

So if you plan to buy a house with the attitude that all you have to do is get your income and expenses into the 40% ratio, you're setting yourself up for serious financial troubles later.

Friends of mine live in a $350,000 home. They had no children when they bought the house; today they have three. Visit their home, and you'll see aging cars and furniture from their college days. The youngest child will be wearing clothes discarded from the eldest, and a nice dinner out was years ago — let alone their last vacation. Yet this couple is supposed to be living the "American Dream."

To avoid this trap, you must put things in perspective: Never make a financial decision that you'll live with for 30 years based solely on today's financial circumstances. Instead, take into consideration what your future lifestyle, income, and expenses are likely to be. For most young couples, one of those changes will be children, so if you haven't already read Chapter 54, do so now before continuing.

Chapter 57 - How to Buy Your First Home

Are You Ready for Home Ownership?

Answer these 10 questions to learn if you are ready to buy a home.

1. Are you sure you want to buy a home? Yes = 1 point.

2. Do you anticipate any large expenses in the next two years, such as buying a car or having kids? No = 1 point.

3. Do you expect to stay in your current job for the next two to three years? Yes = 1 point.

4. Do you expect your job to stay in the same location for the next three to five years? Yes = 1 point. (Is your employer thinking of relocating? How do you know until you ask?)

5. Do you know how much you can realistically afford to pay for housing? Yes = 1 point.

6. Do you have a favorable credit record? Yes = 1 point.

7. Do you have enough money for the down payment and closing costs?

    Yes = 1 point.

8. Have you been pre-qualified for a mortgage so you know how much you can borrow? Yes = 1 point.

9. Will your existing debt reduce your ability to qualify for a mortgage? No = 1 point.

10. Is the amount you can borrow sufficient to enable you to buy a home you can truly enjoy? Yes = 1 point. (Don't settle for something you don't love, for you could well live in your home a very long time.)

If you scored 8 points or more, you're ready to buy a home.

As I've said many times, **The Rules of Money Have Changed,** and this is perhaps more true in the area of home ownership than in any other aspect of personal finance. Therefore, be careful when seeking advice about buying a home, for asking the wrong people can cost you a ton of money.

For example, do not ask your parents for an opinion if the last time they bought a home was decades ago. The reason: The rules of yesterday do not apply today, meaning their advice could be 30 years out of date!

One thing, though, hasn't changed: Buying a home is difficult — perhaps even more so than ever before — and if you're not careful, your dream of owning a home can become a nightmare. Indeed, it is very easy to become house-rich and cash-poor.

The biggest difference between owning a home generations ago and owning one today is that homes no longer are the key to financial success. Owning a home was once the fulfillment of the American dream: If you had a home, a pension, and Social Security, you were set for life. But that's not true today. Still, owning a home does offer important benefits. To understand them, let's consider the alternative, which is to rent.

Compared to renting, owning a home has many advantages, including:

- the homeowner's monthly payment does not change, while renters face annual rent increases;

- a large portion of the homeowner's monthly payment is tax-deductible, but rent payments are not;

- the homeowner's monthly payments eventually stop (when the loan is paid off); renters pay rent as long as they live;

- homeowners keep a piece of each monthly payment, while renters never get back any of their rent payments;

- any increase in the home's value belongs to the homeowner; renters keep none of that profit; and

- homeowners can design and decorate their homes virtually any way they want, while renters suffer major restrictions.

For all these reasons, owning a home is an appropriate goal for most Americans. Let's show you how to do it right.

Do You Have Enough to Pay Cash for Your House?

Of course not.

With homes costing a national average of $147,800, according to the Statistical Abstract of the United States, it's clear that you don't have enough cash to buy a home. That means you'll have to borrow some money. This loan is called a mortgage, and it is the source of much confusion, frustration, and anguish for homebuyers.

Using a Mortgage to Help You Buy Your Home

Did you know that last year, Wal-Mart sold tens of thousands of drills to people who didn't want them? Scandalous!

Well, not really. These folks wanted a hole. To get it, they first had to buy a drill.

Indeed, sometimes we must work with a thing we *don't* want in order to get another thing we *do* want. So it is with real estate. In order to buy a home, you must have a mortgage. To get one, mortgage companies require you to work with septic and termite inspectors, appraisers, credit bureaus, settlement attorneys, title insurers, and others. Not that you want to deal with any of these folks, mind you, but you must deal with them if you want a mortgage. Not that you want a mortgage, of course, but you must get a mortgage if you want to buy a home. And you *do* want that. Thus begins what is for many a very frustrating, annoying, and time-consuming process — much of which seems completely unrelated to your goal of buying a home.

Part of the reason home buyers find the mortgage process so frustrating is that they don't understand it — nor do they want to. After all, they want a home, not a mortgage, so the mortgage is a mere detail — and an annoying one at that. But if you understand the process, you can make it work better for you, with less cost, inconvenience, and delay.

The Biggest Misconception in Real Estate

Many people believe a mortgage is a loan against the house. It's not. The truth is that a mortgage is a loan against your income.

As someone who owns a mortgage company, I can assure you that without sufficient income, you will not qualify for a loan. The reason lenders are willing to loan you money is because you have an income. (The reason they are willing to set the loan at such low rates of interest is because you post the house as collateral. Thus, if you fail to repay the loan, they can take your house and sell it to get back their money.)

Because your home's value is expected to remain intact (or even rise), bankers consider mortgages to be very low-risk investments. Therefore, they don't demand a high profit, and hence, the interest rate they charge you is very low compared to other interest rates in the marketplace.

> **Car loans, too, are offered at low interest rates, because the car collateralizes the loan. Interest rates for car loans are higher than for mortgage loans because cars decline in value, which places bankers at a higher risk if they must repossess and sell your car in the future. (Cars are also portable, meaning bankers have to find the car before they can repossess it. No such worry with houses.)**
>
> **Credit cards have the highest interest rates because they are unsecured loans: If you default, the bank has no collateral to seize, and thus, they cannot recover their losses. This higher risk for bankers translates into higher interest rates for you — and higher returns for them, to compensate them for lending money to you at such a high risk.**

Just because the bank accepts your home as collateral, don't think banks want you to default on your mortgage. Trust me: They don't want the house back. Banks are in the banking business, not the real estate business, and they want the interest you're supposed to pay, not your house. Witness the Savings and Loan crisis of the '80s: When people defaulted on their loans, S&Ls took back all the real estate. With no buyers at hand, the S&Ls went broke, too.

So, as I said, bankers don't want your house. They want you to repay the loan. And they know the only way you can do that is if you have a good income. That's why mortgages are loans against your income, not your house.

The Four Steps to Determining How Large a Mortgage You Can Get

The formula for buying a home is:

> This is why it is difficult for retirees to get a mortgage. Consider people who bought a house in 1957, paid it off in 1987, and retired in 1990. Now living on a small pension and Social Security, they want a loan, but the bank says, "How are you going to repay it?" With little income and no savings, they can't, so the bank refuses to give them a loan. This is why you should obtain home loans before you retire.

$$\text{Available Cash} + \text{Maximum Amount You Can Borrow} = \text{Maximum Purchase Price}$$

As you can see, how expensive a home you can buy is directly related to how much money you can borrow, and how much you can borrow is determined by four factors: your assets, your income, your debts, and your mortgage's interest rate.

FRANK & ERNEST   BOB THAVES

Frank and Ernest is copyright by Thaves. Used here with permission. All rights reserved.

Step #1: Determine How Much Cash You Have — or Can Raise

Start by listing all your assets: checking and savings accounts, mutual funds, stocks, bonds, and any other assets. Include amounts you expect to receive as gifts from family and friends. This grand total represents how much cash you can apply to the purchase price. *Let's say you have $35,000 that you can apply to the purchase of a home.*

Step #2: Determine Your Income

Add up all your income (if you are married, or if a second person is going to buy the house with you, such as a parent or unmarried partner, add income from both people) and be sure to include:

*   your gross pay, including overtime, part-time and seasonal pay, commissions, bonuses, and tips;
*   dividends from investments;
*   business income;
*   pension or Social Security income;
*   veterans benefits;
*   alimony; and
*   child support.

Let's say your total income is $60,000.

Step #3: Tally Your Debts

Include your partner's, if any, for such items as:

*   car payments (whether you own or lease personally);
*   alimony or child support payments;
*   student loans;
*   minimum monthly credit card payments (not the balance owed); and
*   any other debts that will exist for 10 months or more (for example, you can ignore car payments if the car will be paid off in less than 10 months).

Let's say your total monthly debts are $800.

Step #4. Determine Current Interest Rates

Let's say you talk with a mortgage broker who tells you that the following loans are available:

- 6% Fixed. This loan lasts 30 years, and the rate will never change.

- 4% 1-year Adjustable Rate Mortgage. This loan also lasts for 30 years. The interest rate is 4% for the first year, but will change every year, increasing or decreasing with current interest rates. The loan can rise no more than 2% in any one year and no more than 6% over the life of the loan. Thus, the highest rate this loan can charge is 10%, and it can't get that high before the fourth year.

The Two Mortgage Limits

Lending Limit #1

Now that you have all four pieces of information, let's determine how much you can borrow.
Lending Limit #1 states that your monthly mortgage payment (including taxes and insurance) must not exceed 33% of your income. *Since your income is $60,000 (or $5,000 per month), the maximum you can spend on a mortgage payment is $16,800 per year ($1,400 per month).*

> For more details about specific mortgage loan programs and how to work with a mortgage company, see Chapter 58.

To translate a monthly loan payment into a loan balance, look at Figure 8-1. It shows how much money you can borrow based on different interest rates. As you can see, the higher the interest rate, the less money you can borrow. *If you choose the 6% fixed-rate loan, the maximum amount you can borrow is $233,508, while you can borrow up to $293,245 if you choose the 4% ARM.*

So, by adding your loan amount to the $35,000 cash you have, you can buy a home that costs up to $268,508 (if you choose the 6% fixed rate) or $328,245 (if you choose the 4% ARM).

HOW LENDING LIMIT #1 AFFECTS A PERSON EARNING $60,000

If the rate is...	...you can borrow up to:	If the rate is...	...you can borrow up to:
4.00%	$293,245	7.50%	$200,225
4.25%	$284,588	7.75%	$195,418
4.50%	$276,306	8.00%	$190,797
4.75%	$268,381	8.25%	$186,352
5.00%	$260,794	8.50%	$182,075
5.25%	$253,530	8.75%	$177,958
5.50%	$246,570	9.00%	$173,995
5.75%	$239,901	9.25%	$170,176
6.00%	$233,508	9.50%	$166,497
6.25%	$227,377	9.75%	$162,951
6.50%	$221,495	10.00%	$159,531
6.75%	$215,850	10.25%	$156,232
7.00%	$210,431	10.50%	$153,049
7.25%	$205,226	10.75%	$149,976

FIGURE 8-1

Lending Limit #2

But we're not done yet, because **Lending Limit #2 states that your mortgage payment plus other monthly debt payments must not exceed 40% of gross income.** *Since your income is $60,000, your limit for both a mortgage and other debts is $1,800 per month. This presents you with a problem, because your total monthly debt payments are $2,200 ($800 in current monthly debts plus your new $1,400 mortgage payment).*

Therefore, you must either reduce the size of your mortgage (meaning you borrow less money, which forces you to buy a lower-priced house), or you must pay off some of your debts.

Let's say you choose to lower the size of your mortgage. That means your monthly payment cannot exceed $1,000 (because $1,000 plus your current debt payments total $1,800 — which is the maximum that Lending Limit #2 allows). Based on a $1,000 monthly payment, then, the most you can borrow under the fixed-rate 6% loan is $166,791, or $209,462 under the ARM loan. Combined with your $35,000 in cash, that means you can buy a house worth as much as either $201,791 or $244,462.

Now you begin to see why ARM loans are so popular: Their lower initial rates allow you to qualify for bigger loans, which in turn allows you to buy a more expensive home. The danger with ARM loans, of course, is that the first year's low rate could vanish in the second year. If interest rates rise in the economy, what could happen to your ARM over the next four years:

Year	Interest Rate	Monthly Payment
1	4%	$1,000
2	6%	$1,256
3	8%	$1,537
4	10%	$1,838

Thus, ARM buyers are gambling that interest rates won't rise, or that their incomes will rise fast enough to let them afford the higher payments. Those are mighty big bets, for if you're wrong, you could be unable to make the payments and you'll lose your home.

This is exactly why lenders have these two lending limits. Left unchecked, buyers would borrow beyond their ability to pay. And while it might seem that you're able to carry a larger payment than the $1,000 determined by our calculations above, lenders know better: They know that your mortgage does not represent the total cost of home ownership.

Indeed, you will incur many additional costs that renters avoid — including taxes, insurance, utilities, maintenance and repairs, improvements, and decorating.

You need to set money aside for these expenses, and that means you should not buy as expensive a home as you think you can afford.

> Guess what buyers of new homes discover the day they move in? There are no curtains or drapes on the windows! Jean refused to walk into the bathroom of our new house until I tacked sheets over the windows, and curtains became the top item on our shopping list!

Six Ways to Qualify for a Bigger Mortgage

All too often, home buyers discover they can't afford the house they want. Here are some ideas for increasing the amount you can borrow:

1. **Reduce your long-term debt.** Paying off credit cards, for example, can improve your ratios, allowing you to qualify for a bigger mortgage.

2. **Wait until you get more income**.

3. **Have another person join you in obtaining the mortgage**. By signing the loan application, their income is included (so are their debts) and they become legally obligated to fulfill the terms of the mortgage along with you. (So choose a co-signer carefully and make sure the co-signer understands the implication of this action).

4. **Use financing options that require lower down payments**.

5. **Use financing options that allow you to make lower monthly payments**.

6. **Wait for interest rates to drop**, for the lower the rate, the more you can borrow. If you can't (or don't want to) wait, you can lower the rate yourself. How? Read on!

How to Get a Lower Interest Rate

If you can't afford the home you want because interest rates are too high, you can "buy" a lower interest rate. *Say you want to borrow $150,000, and your lender offers you a fixed-rate loan at 6%. Unfortunately, that requires a bigger monthly payment than you can afford. What you need is a rate of 5% .*

You can get the lower rate you want by paying something called "points." *By paying three points, your lender will give you a 5% rate.*

One point equals 1% of your loan. Note: One point does not equal one thousand dollars (a common misconception). *Since you seek to borrow $150,000, one point equals $1,500 (1% of $150,000). Three points, then, is $4,500. Thus, for a one–time payment of $4,500 in this example, you can "buy" your rate down to 5% from 6%.*

Does it Make Sense to Pay Points?

The answer is: It depends[26] — in this case on:

- the spread between the no-point rate and the rate with points;

- how long you plan to keep the loan;

- whether you're dealing with a fixed-rate or adjustable-rate loan; and

- whether you have the cash to pay the points.

Which is better: the 6% loan with no points or the 5% loan with three points? A 6% loan would have cost you $899 per month vs. $805 for the 5% loan. Thus, paying three points lowers your mortgage payment by $94 per month. Since the points cost you $4,500, it will take you four years to recover that cost — not to mention the fact that by spending $4,500 on those points, you gave up the ability to earn interest on that money. That aside, if you keep your home (and your loan) for at least four years, you'll break even.

This is why you should not seek advice from someone who last bought a house 30 years ago. Then, all loans were 30-year fixed-rate loans requiring 10% down, unless you were a veteran buying a house through the G.I. Bill.

Today, you can choose from adjustable-rate loans, COFI loans, balloons, 5/25 and 7/23 programs, 10-year, 15-year and 30-year terms, 3% money down programs, no-documentation programs, and more. The advice of people whose last experience was 30 years ago is likely to be way out of date. Dozens of programs are available today that didn't exist until recently, and new ones are offered constantly. To learn about them, talk with a mortgage broker or lender.

Clearly, the longer you plan to stay in your home, the more sense it makes to pay the points in exchange for a lower interest rate. If you're planning to sell your home in just a few years, it would be foolish to pay points. However, every situation is dif-

---

[26]What a surprise.

ferent, and because interest rate programs constantly change, there is no simple answer or "rule
of thumb." A good financial advisor or loan officer can help you determine whether paying
points is best for your situation.

> **Please ignore "rules of thumb." They are silly attempts to simplify complex issues and they rarely work. For proof, just look at your own hands: By that standard, rules of thumb can be expected to apply only 20% of the time.**

Other Costs of Owning Homes

Points and other loan fees are not the only costs
you'll incur when buying a house. You must
obtain an appraisal, termite inspection, home inspection, credit report, and more.
Together, these "settlement costs" will be roughly 1% to 3.5% of the purchase price
of the home. This figure is in addition to any points you choose to pay.

The Three Kinds of Insurance That Protect Real Estate

There are three different types of insurance that apply to homes, and many people
get them confused, so let's cover them one at a time.

Protection #1: Private Mortgage Insurance

This type of insurance protects your lender, not you.

First-time home buyers, typically strapped for cash, want to buy their homes with
as little cash as possible. But the lender knows through experience that the less you
put down, the more likely you are to default. (Think about it: If you put down
$100,000 to buy a $300,000 house, walking away means you lose your $100,000.
But if you had put no money down, walking away costs you nothing. Thus, the
more money you put down, the less likely you are to default.)

Therefore, if you put down less than 20% of the purchase price, your lender will
require you to buy mortgage insurance. Known as PMI, Private Mortgage
Insurance protects the lender in case you default. The cost, which is included in
your monthly payment, is 0.65% or more of your original loan balance. Thus, if you
borrow $100,000, you'll pay $54.17 per month ($650 annually). That's why it may
make sense to make a down payment of 20%: Doing so will allow you to avoid
this expense, which adds up to many thousands of dollars over the life of your loan.

How to Beat PMI Without Putting 20% Down

Some lenders now let home buyers avoid PMI with as little as 5% down in exchange for a slight increase in the interest rate. Although this will translate into a somewhat higher mortgage payment, the payment will still be lower than if you were paying PMI. Also, remember that PMI payments are not tax deductible, but the extra interest you'd be paying is — further reducing the net cost of this alternative.

The recent introduction of these new loan programs serves as evidence of the continuing evolution of the mortgage industry, and why you need to seek counsel from those who monitor the latest developments.

Protection #2: Homeowner's Insurance

Homeowner's insurance protects you, not your lender.

If the home is damaged or destroyed, this coverage provides you the money you need to rebuild the home and replace its contents. Only a fool would own a home without such insurance, and indeed, your lender will require proof that you have it. You buy it from a property/casualty insurance agent (as opposed to a life/health agent). Some financial planners offer it as well.

Protection #3: Title Insurance

Title insurance comes in two parts, one to protect the lender and one to protect you. You must buy the part that protects the lender; it's your choice whether to buy the part that protects you.

Are you still paying for PMI on the home you bought years ago?

Most homeowners pay for mortgage insurance because they were not able to put down 20% when they bought their home.

But guess what? You could easily have 20% in your home now.

Say you bought a $150,000 house 10 years ago, with 10% down. You borrowed $135,000 and your monthly payment thus includes the cost of PMI (about $73 per month). Today, though, your current mortgage balance is only $117,000 (because you've made 10 years' worth of payments) and the value of your home has grown to $225,000. Thus, you have more than $100,000 in equity in your home — which is well above the 20% needed to avoid mortgage insurance!

If you're still paying for mortgage insurance, you need to write a letter to your mortgage company to tell them to eliminate that charge. You'll save hundreds of dollars every year!

Your property may have changed hands dozens of times over the past 400 years, especially if it's on the East Coast. Who's to say the person selling you the property really owns it? It is quite possible that the deed (or title) is defective. If that's true, you might not own the property you think you bought.

Title insurance protects you from the catastrophe of losing your home because someone challenges the validity of the title in court. This is why lenders require that you buy a policy to protect them, and why I strongly recommend that you buy a second policy to protect yourself.

You order a title policy for the lender during the mortgage application process, and if you order a second policy for yourself at the same time, the additional cost is quite low. Unlike other kinds of insurance, you pay for title insurance only once — at settlement — and it protects you for as long as you own the property.

The Settlement Process

Settlement is the formal process that transfers title (legal ownership) of the real estate from the seller to the buyer. The settlement also gives the buyer's lender (if any) a lien against the property. (A lien grants a financial interest in the property to the lender until the loan is repaid.)

The settlement process is governed by the Real Estate Settlement Procedures Act of 1974. RESPA requires that your lender give you a booklet which describes the settlement process in detail and advises you of your legal rights.

Pre-Settlement

Once your loan application is approved, somebody (chosen by either the buyer or the seller) will be designated to conduct the settlement. The settlement agent will order a survey of the property and a report on the status of the property's title. When these steps are completed, the settlement agent will prepare a Commitment for Title Insurance (sometimes called a Binder) and deliver it to your lender. The commitment informs your lender that, subject to

> **When refinancing, the title is not transferred but many of the same events occur because the owner's old loan must be repaid and the new loan obtained. The new loan also must be secured by a new lien on the real estate.**

certain approved exceptions, a title insurance policy will be issued for the lender at settlement to protect the lender's interests. All this preparation must be completed by the settlement date.

The Settlement

At settlement, the settlement agent will review the loan documents with you. The settlement agent's job is to:

- make sure all documents are properly signed and notarized.

- collect all funds required to pay settlement costs.

- pay-off any pre-existing mortgages on the real estate.

When everything is done and all the papers are signed, the seller gives to the buyer the keys to the house.

Post-Settlement

Following settlement, the settlement agent will record with the court all required documents, pay off any pre-existing mortgages, and make all disbursements required to complete the transaction. When all recording has been completed, the settlement agent will issue a Title Insurance Policy to your lender and, if you ordered it, one to you.

About Settlement Costs

Costs will vary depending on many factors, including:

- **Location of the Property.** Recordation and transfer taxes are payable to the state and local governments where the property is located. Each jurisdiction sets its own tax rates.

- **Purchase Price and Amount of Financing.** The purchase price and amount of financing will affect the recordation and transfer taxes and the title insurance premium.

- **Loan Fees.** Fees vary according to the lender you select and general economic conditions at the time you obtain your loan.

Within three days of applying for your loan, your lender is required by RESPA to give you a Good Faith Estimate of the settlement costs you are likely to encounter.

Who Gets the Drapes?

Imagine you find your dream home. It's 10 years old and listed for $200,000. You offer to pay $185,000 and the owners accept your offer.

Who gets the drapes?

All too often, questions like this go unanswered until you reach the settlement table. If the contract is silent about the drapes and other items, arguments are sure to arise between the buyers and sellers. Disputes easily can be avoided if the buyers, sellers, and their real estate agents prepare a well-thought-out contract.

When buying or selling a home, remember that no transaction has occurred until you reach settlement, which is where the property transfer actually takes place.

For the settlement company, the contract is King: If the contract doesn't specifically state that an item is to convey (go to the buyers), then, it doesn't — period. So if the contract doesn't say the curtains stay, then the sellers can take them. Likewise for the washer/dryer, refrigerator, and even the landscaping. (Sellers have been known to dig up the rose bushes!) Generally, any item that is bolted to or made a part of the home will convey unless otherwise specified.

Also, if the contract doesn't say the seller pays the points, the buyers better not expect them to do so. You can imagine the fights at settlement when verbal commitments are not reflected in the contract.

To make the process go well, be sure the contract covers everything. You should do this when the contract is first written and signed, but amendments later are okay, too — provided both parties sign the amendment.

Use as much detail as possible in the contract. Standard contracts convey many items, but the choices are not always all-inclusive and an item the buyers clearly want may be overlooked. To avoid this, buyers must make sure that everything they want conveyed is included in the contract and that the sellers acknowledge it in writing.

Remember: The settlement table is a poor place to try to renegotiate a contract. If all the terms are in writing, you'll avoid confusion. Be sure to write into the contract such stipulations as whether certain repairs are to be made before the final walk-through, or if the basement freezer comes with the house. Make no assumptions and don't let the other party's agent fool you into thinking that if it wasn't mentioned, it will be yours. Although the settlement company can help resolve differences, it can only enforce what is written in the contract.

Ask your real estate agent to tell you what conveys and what doesn't. Speak up if you suspect an item is not mentioned, for even the best real estate agents may miss what you see.

Above all, put it in writing. A properly written contract can help you avoid surprises on closing day.

Hire a Real Estate Agent to Help You Buy Your Home

Shopping for a new home is fun, and most first-time buyers enjoy their search for a new home. Regardless of whether you plan to buy a newly built home or a resale, a real estate agent can prove very worthwhile.

Before you start looking, create your "wish list" of everything you want in your new home. Decide what you want in the way of:

- **price range;**

- **location:** either for a particular part of town or proximity to work, schools, shopping, recreation, medical/rescue facilities, or family and friends;

- **structure:** condo, townhouse, single-family, or farm;

- **style:** ranch, Cape Cod, Tudor, Colonial, split-level, traditional, or contemporary;

- **features:** number of bedrooms, baths, first-floor master bedroom, washer/dryer, and other layout specifications; and

- **amenities:** circular driveway, side-load garage, deck, fireplace, security system, and other items.

> **Most agents can arrange for you to see 6–10 homes in a day (more than that and you'll forget what you saw).**

Once you develop your wish list, you have a choice: You can spend months visiting every home listed in the newspaper classifieds, or you can let a real estate agent do all the legwork for you. The vast majority of home sellers work with agents, and consequently, their homes are listed in the Multiple Listing Service, an electronic showplace of every home for sale in your area. Through the MLS, your agent can quickly identify homes that meet your criteria and arrange convenient times with the sellers for you to visit and inspect the properties.

In addition to identifying specific homes, real estate agents are a great source of information on the community and comparable prices. But the most important service they provide, once you find a home you want to buy, is presenting your offer to the seller.

> **Do not make an offer to the seller yourself, because you're not good at it. An offer is the first part of what often is the protracted, detailed negotiation of a legal contract, and you don't know how to play that game as well as real estate agents.**

As you'll soon discover, home buyers find themselves involved with a great many people, including lawyers, appraisers, mortgage companies, settlement companies, termite inspectors, home inspectors, and others, and your agent can refer you to qualified individuals and companies to help you through the entire process.

Who Does the Real Estate Agent Represent?

When working with a real estate agent to help you buy a home, be aware of one critical point: By law, the agent you hire works for the seller and anything you say to the real estate agent will be communicated to the seller. This is true even if you found the real estate agent, even if the agent shows you dozens of houses, gives you lots of advice, and spends lots of time with you — even if the agent has never met the seller before. **Real estate agents always legally represent the seller, and saying something to the real estate agent is the same as saying it to the seller.**

Most home buyers do not realize real estate agents legally represent sellers, and consequently, hundreds of thousands of home buyers pay more than they should for their homes because they lack representation in the negotiation process. In fact, not only do they lack representation, the person they think is on their side actually is a spy for the other team!

> Say the seller is asking $200,000, and you say to your real estate agent, "We love this house. Let's offer $180,000, but we're willing to spend the $200,000." Guess what? You just paid $200,000.

Think about it: You find and retain a real estate agent, as does the home's seller. Once negotiations begin, your real estate agent and the seller's real estate agent start negotiating. You think your real estate agent is negotiating with your best interests in mind, but the truth is your real estate agent doesn't work for you — he or she works for the seller! So, both real estate agents are teaming up against you, trying to figure out how much they can get you to pay for the benefit of their mutual client, the seller!

Too often, buyers fail to understand this legal relationship.

Working with a Buyer-Broker

You can avoid this problem by hiring a "buyer-broker." Under this arrangement, you and your real estate agent sign an agreement stating that your real estate agent legally represents you, the buyer. Many agents will agree to such an arrangement, and I strongly recommend it when you are on the buy-side of the transaction.

Some agents, depending on who their client is, sometimes will represent the buyer, and at other times, the seller. Working with such agents is fine provided you know what team each player is on at the time.

Who Pays the Real Estate Agent?

Whether you work with a traditional agent or a buyer-broker, real estate commissions — typically 6% of the sales price — are paid by the seller.

I mean, buyer.

Uh, let's try that again.

While it's true that the seller pays the agent's commission, let's face it: The seller would pay nothing to the agent if there's no buyer. Further, the amount of the commission is directly related to the sales price of the home: The higher the sales price, the higher the agent's commission. Since sellers know they are going to pay 6% to the selling agent (who will share it with the buying agent), sellers simply inflate their asking price by 6% to cover this cost. Thus, while agents get their commissions from sellers, it's really the buyers who pay for it.

> When you're trying to buy a house, only work with one agent. Remember: Agents get paid only when a transaction occurs. If several real estate agents show you the same house, who is entitled to the commission?

In fact, "avoiding the commission" is the only reason people cite for wanting to avoid real estate agents. By skipping the agent, people think a given house will cost 6% less. Indeed, on a $200,000 house, that's $12,000 — a lot of money!

But it's unlikely you'll ever see the savings. Why? Because the seller already has an agent and their agreement entitles the agent to a 6% commission. If as a buyer you fail to retain your own agent, the selling agent's commission isn't cut to 3% — they just keep the entire 6% for themselves! So don't think you (the buyer) will save money by not hiring an agent. The commission is built into the price of the home whether you have an agent or not.

And I'll bet hiring a real estate agent — a good one — actually will save you money. They'll apply all their years of experience, salesmanship, and negotiating skills to convince the seller to lower the sales price, perhaps even more than the 6% you were trying to save on your own. A good real estate agent, for example, even may be able to convince the seller to pay some of the points and settlement costs for you.

If you are serious about buying a house, don't worry about wasting an agent's time. Most buyers inspect 20 to 30 homes before they buy, but can see only 6-10 in a day. That means you're going to spend at least two or three days with your real estate agent. Don't worry about all the time you're taking, for that's why agents get paid.

By the same token, if you're not serious about buying a house, please be considerate of the agent's time; if he's spending Saturday with you, he's not spending it with someone else — and time is money. Spend as much of the agent's time as you need to find the place you want, but only if you're serious.

Should You Buy a New Home Instead of a Resale?

Many first-time home buyers buy townhouses with the intention of moving up to single-family homes later. Given the choice of buying a newly built townhouse vs. a resale, many prefer to buy new — where they get to choose floor plans, options, and even colors for carpeting, paint, and bathroom tile. But make sure you fully understand the economic implications of buying a new home vs. a resale.

First, the future value of your house will be determined by your builder. If you buy a brand-new townhouse in a new development, the builder likely will continue to build homes in your neighborhood for several years. That means your future selling price will be based on whatever he is then selling his homes for — and in fact, yours probably would sell for less than his. After all, why should prospective buyers choose your "old" townhouse when they can get a new one — giving themselves the same opportunity to buy state-of-the-art construction and appliances along with the same choice of designs and colors as you enjoyed?

Of course, if the builder raises his prices, your home's value will rise, too. But either way, you will compete against the builder for as long as he's building in your neighborhood.

Another concern is that since the homes are all being completed in roughly the same period of time, most buyers move in during the same period and many move out at the same time, too. The result is often a saturated market which keeps resale prices down.

Remember: When buying your home, think like a seller, for you will be one someday. To that end, don't wallpaper a newly built house for at least one year. The house will settle and the wallpaper will tear. (It's okay to paint.) Design and decorate your home so it will be appealing to potential buyers. If you paint your dining room purple, as my wife and I did (don't ask), be prepared to repaint it before you sell (as we did), because just as you don't always like the decorating you find in other people's homes, buyers will not share your taste, either (as we learned).

Chapter 58 - All About Mortgages

Which Loan Program Is Right for You?

As you explore financing options, be wary. Some programs offer low down payments, low interest rates, low closing costs — or a combination of all three — and they can be enticing. Remember, though, that mortgage bankers make money by selling you a loan, not by servicing the loan throughout its 30-year life. (Bankers actually sell their loans to loan servicing companies. If you later default on your loan, the bank which sold you the loan has no risk — nor does the real estate agent who sold you the house.)

Therefore, bankers create many programs simply because they know they can sell them, but that doesn't mean you should buy them.

Fixed-Rate Mortgages

A fixed-rate loan is the most common. With this loan, which normally is for a term of 15 or 30 years, your interest rate never changes, and your mortgage payments stay the same. Fixed-rate loans are considered "safe" because the rate never changes. Thus, you need not worry about your rate rising in the future. *If you choose a 6% 30-year fixed rate, you will pay 6% per year for the life of the loan. The rate will never change.*

Adjustable-Rate Mortgages

ARMs offer lower initial interest rates than fixed-rate loans, and many people who choose them do so because they are unable to qualify for loans at current fixed rates. Thus, many people must either choose the ARM or forget about buying a house. But if (when?) interest rates later rise, the buyers could find themselves unable to afford the new higher payments. The result: They lose the house anyway. So when choosing a loan program, make sure you can handle the loan under its *worst-case* scenario, not its *initial terms.*

As discussed in Chapter 57, ARM rates start low but can rise up to 2% per year, not to exceed 6% over the life of the loan. *Thus, if your 1-year ARM starts at 5%, your rate could rise to 7% in year two, 9% in year three, and 11% in year four. The rate could never exceed 11% over the life of the loan.*

A 1-year ARM changes its rate after the first year, and again every year after that. A 3-year ARM maintains a fixed rate for the first three years, then changes annually thereafter, although some 3-year ARMs change their rates only every three years.

The 5/25 Mortgages

In this 30-year loan program, the initial rate is lower than the fixed rate but higher than the ARM, and the rate will remain in place for the first five years. At the end of the 5th year, the rate will be reset to current fixed rates. Unlike ARMs, there is no upper limit to this loan. *Current fixed rates are 6%, but you obtain a 5/25 loan with an initial rate of 5.25%. After five years, current fixed rates are 9%, so your loan's rate changes to 9% and will remain at this high level for the next 25 years.*

The 5/25 is uncertain. Therefore, the only home buyers who are suitable for this loan are those who are <u>sure</u> that they will sell the house within five years. If you know you're moving within five years, the 5/25 is a great program, because you essentially receive a fixed-rate loan for the five years you'll own your home, but at a rate lower than true fixed-loan rates. But woe to you if your plans change and rates jump: You could find yourself paying an astronomical rate, and you may even lose your house.

A similar program is the 7/23, which fixes the rate for the first seven years instead of five. Other variations exist as well.

The COFI ARM: Use With Care or It May Burn You

Which would you choose: a loan with a high rate of interest that cannot change or a loan with a low initial rate that might rise later? This is the ongoing debate between fixed-rate loans and ARMs. Maybe an ARM will be cheaper in the long run, maybe not.

Which would you choose?

The COFI ARM may be your answer. Its rate is based on an average that banks in the Western states pay their depositors (the rate that banks pay is their cost of attracting deposits), and this "cost of funds index" gives COFI its name. Most

COFI ARMs are based on the Federal Home Loan Bank's 11th District, whose rates move more slowly than interest rates in other indexes. Because ordinary ARMs rely on the T-bill and similar guides, homeowners who have an ordinary ARM are much more likely to see a big rise in their rate than those who have a COFI ARM.

While COFI rates are lower than ordinary ARMs, that's usually true only for the first three months. After that, the COFI rate will change monthly or annually for the next 30 to 40 years. ARMs, by contrast, lock in their rates for one-year or three-year periods.

COFIs Offer Three Payment Choices

You choose a COFI loan with an initial interest rate of 5.15%.

You will receive in the mail a monthly invoice instead of an annual coupon book, and this invoice will give you three payment choices.

Let's further say that the index later rises to 7%.

Payment Choice #1: The Fully Indexed Payment

This is the payment you need to make in order to pay off the mortgage in 30 years. This payment will change whenever the 11th District's rate changes. That's why the 11th District is so popular: Its changes are smaller and less frequent than other indexes, reducing the risk that next month's invoice will be a big jump over this month's invoice.

Under Choice #1, you'd make a full principal and interest payment based on the current 7% rate.

Payment Choice #2: Accrued Interest Only

This is a payment of interest only, no principal, and therefore the payment is less than that required by Choice #1. This is great if money is tight one month or if the index jumps suddenly, but the downside, of course, is that your loan's balance doesn't go down. Next month, you'll still owe as much as you owed this month.

To prevent you from having a "perpetual mortgage," homeowners who consistently choose this option will find their loans recast every five years. In other words, if you make interest-only payments every month, your loan is recalculated after the fifth year so it is paid off in the remaining 25 years. This way, the loan won't exceed 30 years.

Under Choice #2, you'd pay only the interest, but still based on the current rate of 7%.

Payment Choice #3: The Minimum Payment

This amount is the same as the payment that was in effect at the loan's inception, and therefore this payment will be lower than the other two choices. That's the good news. The bad news, of course, is that this option can create negative amortization.

Under Choice #3, your payment would be based on the old 5.15% rate — and since that's less than the current rate, the shortfall would be added to your principal balance, meaning you now owe more than you did last month.

The effect is similar to that of paying the minimum payment on a credit card: Even though you are making a payment each month, you're not paying enough. Therefore, the debt not only doesn't go away, it continues to grow, making it even more expensive and difficult to pay off.

I don't like to recommend Choice #3 for obvious reasons, and there is concern that some consumers may not realize the impact of selecting Choice #3. If so, they could find themselves burned by this very hot COFI.

Figure 8-2 compares the monthly payment of a COFI loan vs. a 1-year ARM at current rates. As you can see, COFI rates are usually lower than 1-year ARM rates, but not always: in early 2003, the reverse was true.

A COFI ARM can be attractive because it uses a more stable index, your payment options are flexible, and you get the ability to buy a home you otherwise might not be able to afford. You should consider a COFI ARM, though, only if you are comfortable with it; a person who will lie awake at night worrying about rate changes probably should avoid this loan — and all ARMs, for that matter.

COFI vs. ARM

Principal and interest payment for $150,000 loan assuming no increases in base indexes

| Year | Month | COFI | | | | 1-Year ARM | |
		Rate	Option-1	Option-2	Option-3	Rate	Payment
	1	3.45%	$669	n/a	n/a	4.25%	$738
	2	3.45%	$669	n/a	n/a	4.25%	$738
	3	3.45%	$669	n/a	n/a	4.25%	$738
	4	5.15%	$818	$649	$584	4.25%	$738
	5	5.15%	$818	$649	$584	4.25%	$738
	6	5.15%	$818	$649	$584	4.25%	$738
1	7	5.15%	$818	$649	$584	4.25%	$738
	8	5.15%	$818	$649	$584	4.25%	$738
	9	5.15%	$818	$649	$584	4.25%	$738
	10	5.15%	$818	$649	$584	4.25%	$738
	11	5.15%	$818	$649	$584	4.25%	$738
	12	5.15%	$818	$649	$584	4.25%	$738
2	1-12	5.15%	$818	$649	$584	5.25%	$826
3	1-12	5.15%	$818	$649	$584	6.25%	$916

(Rates as of 1/2003)

FIGURE 8-2

Dozens of other programs are available, too, and more are added all the time. That's why you need to sit down with a financial professional who can suggest the program that is best for you.

How to Choose a Mortgage Company

Ask people what they look for in a mortgage, and they'll tell you, "The rate." But seeking a good rate is a poor way to choose a mortgage company — simply because all lenders get their money from the same place. Therefore, everybody has the same cost of doing business and the same loan programs with virtually the same interest rates.

Thus, it's rare that you'll find a "great deal" offered by one firm that another can't match. Our experience with my own mortgage company has convinced me of this. But there is one area where one firm can set itself apart from another: service.

"A banker: The person who lends you his umbrella when the sun is shining and wants it back the minute it rains."

—Mark Twain

As every home buyer has learned, the mortgage process is an ugly one. You are asked to submit a zillion documents (they ask for them one at a time), and then they want you to reverify what you already told them. Then all the third parties get involved: the appraiser, credit bureau, termite inspector, well and septic people, title company — and nobody ever seems to talk with each other, leaving you to do all the work, worrying about whether it will get done in time for settlement!

Therefore, after you verify that rates are competitive, you'll be much happier if you choose a mortgage broker or banker who has an excellent reputation for providing high-quality service.

When to See the Mortgage Company

When preparing to buy a house, most people start with a real estate agent. That seems to be the correct first step — after all, it's a house you want to buy — but it's not. A house may be something you want, but you're not going to get it without a mortgage. Therefore, you should talk first with a mortgage broker, not a real estate broker!

Three Advantages of Getting Pre-Approved

Why bother looking for a house if you don't know whether you can get a mortgage, or how much of a loan you can get? After all, your mortgage will determine how expensive a house you can buy. Many real estate agents, in fact, will not work with a client until after they've been approved by a lender.

Advantage #1: You Avoid Disappointment

There's nothing worse than finding the home of your dreams, only to discover later that you can't afford it. By going to the lender first, you'll determine how much house you can buy before you start visiting homes beyond your price range.

Advantage #2: You Save Significant Amounts of Time

While you're searching for a home, the mortgage application process can be underway. Too often, people start this process only after they spend three months finding the home they want. This forces them to spend another three months waiting for their loan's approval. Starting the loan process now will save you a lot of time.

Advantage #3: Pre-Approval Can Be a Major Negotiating Weapon

With a pre-qualification letter in hand, you can complete the purchase of a home in as little as two weeks, instead of the usual three months. Many sellers are in a hurry to sell and will accept a lower offer in exchange for a quicker settlement. If two people bid on the same house, the person whose loan is pre-approved will win the contract.

So choose your mortgage company first, get pre-qualified, and *then* hire a real estate agent.

Mortgage Bankers vs. Mortgage Brokers

Most banks offer loans, and going to them is like shopping at a Ford dealer: You won't get a Chevy, no matter how good the Chevy might be. Therefore, you need to compare offers from several banks. Or you can work with a mortgage broker.

Brokers represent dozens of banks. Although the broker serves as middle-man, his or her services will not cost you anything extra. That's because brokers get loans at wholesale rates, and pass them along to their clients at retail prices, just like any business. The difference between wholesale and retail is how brokers make money. Therefore, you get the same rate from a broker as if you went directly to the lender yourself. In fact, because of their volume, many brokers are able to offer their clients better deals than you can get by talking to banks on your own.

The choice is yours.

Does Your Mortgage Company's Appraiser Know How to Count?

We've talked about how the mortgage process can be confusing. Often, that's a good description for the appraisal process, too. All lenders require an appraisal to confirm that the property is worth what they're planning to lend. Your mortgage company will hire an independent appraiser (the cost usually is $300 — at your expense, of course), and you have to accept whatever they say.

That's fine, except that they don't always say what you want them to say. Based on the description that follows, can you tell me...

How Many Bathrooms Are In This House?

John and Kathy want to buy a four-bedroom colonial. The main bedroom features a master bathroom, and the other bedrooms off the upper level share a full bathroom. A powder room is in the hallway on the main level. The finished basement has paneling and carpeting throughout, recessed lights, and a wet bar. It also has a fifth bedroom and full bath. To obtain a mortgage, John and Kathy need to have the house appraised. According to the appraisal, *how many bathrooms are in this house?*

Before you read the answer below, please don't go nuts. Because you're wrong. You counted three and a half. Sorry, you're wrong.

The correct answer is two and a half.

When reviewing a property, appraisers include only those features which exist above-grade. The basement is below-grade, and thus neither the bedroom nor the bathroom built there are included in the normal count.

But don't worry. The appraisal form does provide for a separate section on basements, which is where you'll find information about those improvements.

The moral to this story is that the mortgage banking industry doesn't see the world as you might expect. What begins as a simple effort can become very complex, so as you move through the mortgage process, don't be surprised by the unexpected. If you see or hear something that doesn't look right, call your loan officer. Chances are, a simple explanation will alleviate your concerns.

And should you discover a mistake, bringing it to your mortgage company's attention will enable them to fix it for you.

And above all, don't go nuts.

Chapter 59 - How to Buy Your Next Home

Just because you bought a house once doesn't make you an expert. The truth is that buying your *next* home offers many important differences — not the least of which is the fact that for the first time, you have a house to sell. So let's look closely at how to handle these two important financial transactions simultaneously.

Disposing of your current home could take eight to 10 months (if all goes well). The first step is to hire a real estate agent to sell your home. Do this at least one month before you plan to put the house on the market. Your agent will tell you how to prepare the house for sale (this is the first of many ways the agent will prove his or her worth to you). The goal is to make the house as presentable as possible. Depending on how much work your home requires, it could take a month or more to get your house in selling condition. Depending on how active the real estate market is at the time you sell and the marketability of your home, it could take from several weeks to many months to find a buyer, so the sooner you get a real estate agent involved, the sooner you'll sell the house. Once you find a buyer and sign a contract, you must wait for settlement, which generally takes 60 to 90 days. The result: eight to 10 months to sell your home.

Your real estate agent likely will suggest, among other things:

- **Clean and clean up! First impressions are vital;**

- **Repair major items such as windows, plumbing, and appliances;**

- **Repair little things, too, such as loose doorknobs or sticking doors;**

- **Repaint and recarpet as needed. Spending some money here will help you sell for a higher price;**

- **Get your lawn and driveway/walkway in good condition;**

- **Too much furniture makes a room look small. Remove some pieces to let the house show better;**

- **Too little furniture makes a house look barren. Add some pieces from another room;**

- **Make closets look bigger by keeping them organized; and**

- **Get the bathrooms and kitchen looking their best.**

Remember: Good real estate agents sell dozens of homes every year, and they know what motivates buyers. If your real estate agent makes a suggestion, act on it.

Should You Hire a Real Estate Agent to Help You Sell Your House?

I know a great real estate agent you should hire. He's very enthusiastic and well-intentioned. He's also completely honest and trustworthy, and he really wants to do a great job for you.

"A good architect can improve the looks of an old house merely by discussing the cost of a new one."
—**Anonymous**

On the other hand, he has never sold a house before. He has never taken a real estate course, does not hold a real estate license, and knows nothing about real estate law. He has no background in sales or marketing and doesn't know anyone in the real estate business. He does not know how to find prospective buyers (although he's confident that won't be a problem) and he admits to being completely unfamiliar with the elements of negotiating a real estate contract — in fact, he's never even drafted a real estate contract. He does not have access to the Multiple Listing Service (he's not even sure what that is or what it offers) and he knows nobody in the mortgage, title settlement, or related fields, nor does he know anything about those businesses.

But like I said, this guy is honest, motivated, and wants to do a great job for you. Oh, and best of all, *he's free*.

Would you hire him?

No, of course not. It's obvious why such a person is willing to work for free: Nobody would ever think of paying him! Yet, if you're planning to sell your home on your own, without the benefits of a real estate agent, this is exactly who you are hiring: You're hiring yourself.

No other person would hire you to sell their home, so why are you hiring yourself to sell yours? Admit it: The only reason is because you want to save the 6% commission that real estate agents charge. Yet, as we discussed in Chapter 57, it's really the buyer who pays the commission, because sellers simply increase their sales price to cover this expense. So get over it. Hire the real estate agent and move on.

> Do you think you'll be able to inflate your price by 6%, skip the real estate agent, and pocket the difference? Nice try, but there isn't a buyer in the world — especially one who's using an agent, as most are — who will let you get away with that stunt.

Even if you were paying the commission (rather than the buyer), I can give you three reasons that make the cost worthwhile:

• A real estate agent is likely to get a higher price for your home than you will on your own because the sales price is determined by negotiation, and real estate agents are experts at contract negotiation;

• Buyers will say things to a real estate agent that they won't say to the seller, and the agent can use this information to your advantage; and

• The buyer is likely to be represented by a real estate agent. Do you want to negotiate alone?

Buyers are Liars, and Sellers are Tellers

Buyer was inspecting Seller's house.

Buyer casually mentions, "I was hoping the master suite was on the main level."

Seller, asked why he's moving, says, "I've got to be in Dallas next week for a new job."

When they start negotiating, Seller is at a disadvantage. He thinks Buyer is lukewarm about the house, because Buyer expressed disappointment about the location of the bedroom, yet Buyer knows that Seller is in a hurry to sell.

Buyers pretend that things are important to them which aren't, while sellers say things to buyers they should not say because it weakens their negotiating position. Either way, careless sellers hurt themselves by interacting with potential buyers.

The only way to make sure you don't hurt yourself *is to not have any conversation with a potential buyer*. That means someone else has to do the talking for you, and that someone should be your real estate agent.

Four Tips for Working Successfully with a Real Estate Agent When Selling a House

You need to hire a real estate agent and then follow these tips:

Tip #1: Leave the House When the Agent Shows it to a Potential Buyer

Sometimes, agents give you little notice. "I've got someone who'd like to see the house. Can we come over in 15 minutes?" You need to (a) say yes, (b) clean up, and (c) get out of the house.

Don't be in the house when it is being shown, for two reasons. First, you might say something stupid, like, "You can't see that water stain on the wall, can you?" Second, buyers feel uncomfortable walking around someone else's home if the owners are there. Your presence will intimidate buyers, and they will not spend a lot of time in your house. The less time they spend in the house, the less likely they will buy it. Get out of the house.

Tip #2: Take Your Pets With You

Some people hate animals. At best, a pet is a reminder that the house will be filled with stains, odors, or other problems. At worst, your pet could literally chase them out of the house. I know you love Muffy, but she will not help you close the sale.

Tip #3: Turn off the TV and Radios

Let them focus on the house, not Oprah.

Tip #4: Keep All Lights On, and Open the Curtains to Let the Sun Shine In

Make sure all the rooms of the house are inviting.

If you let agents do their job, you'll sell your home quicker, for more money, and with less hassle than if you try to do it yourself.

Should You Rent Your Current House?

Ask people where they plan to get the cash to buy a new home and most will answer, "From the equity in my old house." But by selling your old house, you give away any future growth in that property's value. Realizing this, many homeowners debate whether they should sell their old home or keep it as a rental. Here's how to decide which course of action is best for you.

Do you have any equity in your current home?

In other words, can you sell your house today for more than you owe on it? Remember to consider the costs you'll incur to sell the place, including the agent's commission.

If you *do not* have equity in your house, it's an ideal candidate for renting.

If you *do* have equity in the home, ask yourself the following question:

Do you need to use that equity as a down payment on the new home?

If you do, you must sell your home. If you don't, you can rent or sell it.

Renting can be enticing, for it offers these benefits:

- It lets you avoid selling your house now. This is especially valuable if selling now would produce a loss. By waiting, maybe you can get a higher price later.

- When you eventually sell the property, you might get a tax deduction if you sell it for a loss.

- Provided your annual adjusted gross income is less than $100,000, you may enjoy annual tax savings through "depreciation," which lets you slowly deduct from your taxable income the cost of the building (not the land under it).

- You might be able to rent the property for more than what it costs you to maintain it.

But don't think renting is an easy road to riches. There are major drawbacks, including:

- If you don't sell now, your property's future value might be even lower later.

- You are likely to incur a "negative cash flow," meaning your rental income will not be enough to cover your monthly expenses.

- It is likely your property will be vacant at least occasionally, such as when a tenant leaves but a new one hasn't yet moved in. When predicting rental income, mortgage lenders assume rentals are vacant 25% of the time.

- Each time a tenant moves out, you'll incur cleaning and fix-up costs — from carpet cleaning and painting to major repairs.

- Depreciation, that oft-cited benefit of real estate investors, is not a gift from Congress — it's a loan! Every dollar depreciation saves you in taxes lowers your cost basis, which means that when you sell the house, you pay a larger capital gains tax. Thus, depreciation lowers your taxes today but increases your taxes later.

- It's difficult to refinance a rental property should interest rates drop. And most important,

- The Hassle Factor (see Chapter 18).

The Shared Equity Deal

What if you don't want to rent your house but can't sell it? Here's the answer, in the example of Tom and Karen. They bought their original house for $200,000, putting 10% down and financing the $180,000 balance; their monthly payment is $1,200. They now want to move to a bigger place, but due to a soft real estate market, their house would sell for only $180,000.

They don't want to sell their house because they don't want to lose the $20,000 they had put down, but they don't want to become landlords, either. Because they don't need the equity from the old house to get into the new house, they are ideal candidates for a shared equity deal.

Along come Ed and Trish. Newly married with a baby, they make good incomes and easily can afford a $1,200 mortgage payment, but they haven't been able to save the $20,000 or so it takes to buy a house. Like most young couples, they want to own, not rent, but buying a home seems out of reach. Like Tom and Karen, Ed and Trish also are ideal candidates for a shared equity deal.

Karen places an ad in the local paper saying, "Own your home with no money down," and Trish responds. Here's how the deal works: Tom and Karen, the two sellers of their home, agree to sell their home to four buyers: Tom, Karen, Ed, and Trish. Thus, Tom and Karen, who once owned 100% of the property, now own 50%; Ed and Trish own the other 50%. Thus, they are sharing the ownership, or equity, of the property.

In a separate legal agreement signed by all four parties, it is agreed that Tom and Karen contribute the down payment — the $20,000 they already have in the property. Ed and Trish agree to be responsible

A client called me one day rather discouraged. He'd been trying to sell his house for six months, without success. He originally listed the property at $410,000 (which he knew was too high), then dropped the price to $389,000 (in the range of other sales in his neighborhood). Still, no offers.

"My Realtor wants me to cut the price to 374,000," he told me. "But I want to see if anyone will accept $389,000 first. "

"How long do you figure it will take to get an offer at $389,000?" I asked him.

"Four or five months," he replied.

"How quickly do you think the house will sell if you price it at $374,000?" I asked.

"Right away!" he gushed. "It's already on the low side compared to recent sales on my street, and I've got a finished basement. At $374,000, it's a heckuva deal."

I had one last question for him. "What are your monthly carrying costs for the property?"

"Well," he answered, "between the mortgage payment, utilities, maintenance and such, I'd say about $4,000 a month."

I told him to price the house at $374,000 immediately, as his Realtor had suggested, and I hope you can see why. If it takes him four months to sell at $389,000, he'll spend $16,000 carrying the property until then — leaving him with $373,000. Thus, he'd actually make more money selling for $374,000 now than by selling for $389,000 in four months (assuming he's able to sell for that price at all! — More likely, he'll end up cutting the price to $374,000 eventually, anyway, and he'll merely have wasted four months and $16,000.

Remember, as I showed you in Chapter 2, don't focus on how much you earn. It's how much you keep that counts.

for all mortgage payments, repairs, maintenance, and decorating expenses. The four also agree to share any required repair expense of $1,000 or more.

They further agree to sell the property in five years. The proceeds of the sale will be disbursed in the following order:

1. the mortgage will be paid off;

2. all selling expenses will be paid, including the real estate agent's commission;

3. Tom and Karen will receive back their original down payment of $20,000; and then

4. any remaining proceeds will be split equally among all four parties.

Let's assume the property grows 6% per year over the five years. If so, the house would be worth about $243,000. They owe the bank $170,000 and the real estate agents $14,500. Then Tom and Karen get their $20,000 back. The remaining cash — $23,500 — is evenly divided, giving $19,250 to each couple.

This is a great deal for everybody. From Tom and Karen's $20,000 down payment, they get back $39,250. That's a total return of 96%, or an average annual return of 19%!

And Ed and Trish, who got into the house with no cash outlay, now get $19,250 to use as a down payment on their next house, which they'll own all by themselves. And because they made the mortgage payments during the five years, they enjoyed big tax deductions while the shared equity deal was in effect.

If Ed and Trish don't want to move at the end of the term, they simply use their share of the equity to buy out Tom and Karen. In fact, that's the most common way people end a shared equity deal.

This strategy is used most often within families, where the kids — young, newly married — have good incomes but no cash, while Mom and Dad have assets and lots of their own home equity. The kids don't want to ask Mom and Dad for a loan, and the parents don't really want to give them one...
...so they strike a business deal: They all buy the house together, with Mom and Dad owning half and the kids owning half. The parents make the down payment and the kids cover everything else. Three or five or seven years later (the parties

decide), the parents get a great return on their investment and (assuming the house's price has increased) the kids get their own house.

If you're a would-be seller, you'll find that shared equity deals often offer you lower risk than if you treated your home as a rental, because your tenants regard themselves as owners and they treat the house accordingly. They don't trash it, they don't call at 3 am to have something fixed, and most important, they won't miss any mortgage payments because doing so voids their share of the deal.

What's the downside? By offering a shared equity deal, you are giving away half the future growth of the property. And if home prices go down or stay level, your share will not grow. But considering the alternatives, this might be a price worth paying.

The Chicken or the Egg

So which should you do first — buy the new or sell the old? Most second-time buyers buy the new one first, so it ought to be no surprise that this is wrong. The reason: Since most buyers cannot afford to carry two homes, they offer the seller a "contingency contract," which says that their purchase of the new home is contingent on the sale of their old house.

For anyone who is buying a home while already owning one, contingency contracts make perfect sense, and if your circumstances require you to buy a new home before selling your old one, then I agree you should offer a contingency contract. But ideally, do not buy a new home until you have already sold the old one.

Why? Because everyone else is offering contingent contracts, too, and sellers hate them. Think a moment like the seller: You want to sell your house and along comes a buyer. "I want to buy your house, and I'll pay your asking price — but my house has not sold yet, and I will not buy yours unless and until it does." Do you have a deal? There's no way to tell. But accepting that offer forces you to take your home off the market anyway, for as much as 90 days. If the buyer fails to sell his home, your deal falls through. That's why sellers hate contingency contracts.

It's also easy to see why your real estate agent will be able to strike a better deal for you if you are able to buy a home without worrying about selling another. Again, think like the seller: Say you hold an open house and you receive two offers. The first agrees to pay your asking price of $200,000, on a contingency basis, while the other offers you only $192,000 and offers to go to settlement in two weeks with no contingency. Which will you take?

Most sellers will accept the lower offer, and with good reason: The contingency contract might not reach settlement for 90 or 120 days, and in the interim you must continue to make your mortgage payments. At $1,300 per month, that's an additional $4,000 or $5,000 — and then you've still got to hope the buyer sells their home. But by taking the lower offer, you know you've got a deal. And because of all the mortgage costs you'll save over the next few months, it's really just as good a deal as the higher offer. Your real estate agent knows how to make this a strong negotiating point — especially if you took my advice in Chapter 57 and got pre-qualified for your mortgage loan.

"Look, Mr. Seller, I know my client's offer is not as much as you wanted, but it's *not contingent*. If you take a contingent offer that's $10,000 more than what my client is offering, you've got to wait months for that guy to sell his house, and then another 90 days to close the deal. My clients are asking for no contingency, and they've been pre-approved for their mortgage: You could go to settlement and be out of here in just two weeks!"

That's a powerful pitch. So if you want to save money and increase the likelihood that the buyer will accept your offer, buy your next home *with no contingency*.

Of course, that means you need to sell your current home first. If you do, you could be homeless for a time — because you sold one before buying the other. If that worries you, here's the solution: Place a contingency on the home you're *selling* instead of the one you're *buying*. Tell the buyer of your old house that you need a 10-day or 30-day contingency to find a place to live. Most buyers won't object (since they're fumbling with their own mortgage application process anyway), and it'll give you the time you need to make an offer on a new home.

Remember: It is always easier to buy your next home than to sell your existing one.

What Is Your Home Worth?

The client I described in the sidebar earlier had bought his house in 1988 for $325,000. He finished the basement, added a deck, landscaping, and other improvements. He figures he spent some $60,000 on all these extras. So, what is his home worth?

Whatever someone is willing to pay him for it. What my client paid for his house is irrelevant. How much he spent on improvements and upgrades is irrelevant. His current mortgage balance is irrelevant. And, most shocking to some, what he thinks the home is worth also is irrelevant.

The only number that matters is the one offered to him by a buyer.

If You're Building a New Home

Very often, home buyers and sellers (and you're both!) are working with tight timetables often with deadlines imposed by others. If you are building a new home, have plans in place in case the builder does not finish on time.

And if you are working with a small builder, what would you do if your builder failed to complete construction? This happened to a client of ours: His builder was killed in a small plane crash, and the house was only two-thirds finished. I suggest that if you are working with a small builder, buy an insurance policy on the builder to protect yourself in case the builder dies or becomes disabled. The cost is low because you're buying the insurance only for a short time, yet you'll be protected in case the builder becomes unable to finish the house.

How to Handle the Mortgage on Your Next Home

As I've said, buying your next home is different from buying your first, and nowhere is that more true than when it comes to your mortgage.

The price you paid for your first home was determined by your mortgage company. They told you how much money you could borrow and how much cash you needed in order to complete the deal. You had no choice but to agree, so in the weeks and months before you bought the home, you scrimped and saved, you stopped eating out, you sold assets, you received gifts and loans from family and friends, and in the end, you became cash-rich. Then, on settlement day, you wrote the largest check you had ever written and in an instant you went from cash-rich to house-poor. You were never happier, more excited — or more scared.

The reason you wrote that large check is because the mortgage company said you had to, and as big as that check was, it was the least amount required in order for you to qualify for the loan. So you wrote a check for $20,000 or $30,000 or whatever — not because you wanted to, but because they required you to. By brute strength, through sheer force of will, you came up with whatever cash was necessary to get yourself into that house.

Well, now you're in the house. Next, you sell it, and after commissions and other selling expenses, you have $50,000 in equity. You plan to buy a new home that costs $300,000.

Most buyers buy their second homes the same way they bought their first home: By writing a check for 100% of their assets. There are two reasons people do this: (1) because they did it before, and (2) because the price of their new home is frightening.

When you bought your first home, you did whatever it took to raise the money your lender required. Since you emptied your bank account last time, it seems natural to do it again. And you've got another reason to make a big down payment: The bigger the down payment, the lower your monthly payment.

But while it made sense for you to devote all your financial assets to a down payment when you bought your first house, it does not make sense to do it when buying your next house.

Last time, you bought your house on brute strength alone. This time you can do it with finesse. You see, you must recognize that there's a big difference between *what the lender requires* and *what you can afford*. The first time you bought a house, there was no difference. Then, what your lender required *was* what you could afford (barely!), so the two numbers were the same. Your lender required that you put down a certain amount, so you scraped the money together and wrote a check.

But this time, it's different.

This time you're buying a $300,000 house, and the lender is requiring just 10% down. That's $30,000. Yet you've got $50,000 from the sale of your first house. So this time, what they require is not the same as what you can afford. This time, you can afford to put down *even more* than what is required.

Don't do it.

Don't give lenders more than they require. Instead, give lenders only the minimum they want and take out as big a mortgage as they will give you.

Five Great Reasons to Carry a Big, Long Mortgage

If you're concerned that reducing your down payment will increase your monthly payment, relax: That's a good thing. In fact, I want you to carry as big a mortgage as possible. Why? Here are five great reasons:

Reason #1: Mortgages Don't Affect Home Values

The value of your home will rise or fall regardless of the size of your mortgage. Its ability to grow in value has nothing to do with the amount of equity you hold in it. Therefore, having lots of money in home equity is like having money in a mattress: It's not earning any interest. You would never keep $100,000 under your bed, yet lots of people have a quarter million in their walls. In other words, *keep the money out of the house.*

Reason #2: Your Mortgage Is the Cheapest Money You'll Ever Buy

Most people have debt — credit cards, auto loans, student loans, personal loans — but the lowest-cost loans without question are mortgage loans. And unlike most other loans, you get a tax deduction when paying mortgage interest. If you are in the 33% combined federal/state income tax bracket, the government subsidizes a third of your mortgage interest. That means a 6% home loan costs you only 4%. Compare that to an 18% credit card, where none of the interest is deductible. Result: Your home loan is a fraction of the cost of a credit card. So get a big mortgage, enabling you to use your cash to pay off other debts. In other words, *keep the money out of the house.*

Reason #3: You Might Need the Cash

Can a financial, medical, family, or marital problem ever arise? Sure it can. Job loss, illness or injury, college — the list of troubles that may descend upon us is endless. Any of these problems could require massive amounts of cash — and it'll be small consolation if you have a home that's fully paid for. True, in the event of a job loss, it's nice to know there's no mortgage to pay. But having your home paid for doesn't mean you can buy food, either.

Consider the example of a retired couple with little savings, but who own their home outright. Suddenly, one suffers a catastrophic illness, resulting in long-term care costs that average $5,000 a month. Living on a fixed income, the other spouse can't pay these new bills. But the house is worth six figures, so the spouse seeks a bank loan, offering to post the home as collateral.

This sounds good, but banks do not like to lend money to a retiree, as discussed in Chapter 57. With no income, there's no way to repay the loan, and the bank doesn't want the house — it's in the banking business, not the real estate business. So the only way to get the cash out of the house is to sell it. Result: The couple loses their home of 40 years.

> To avoid mortgage insurance, it's okay to put down as much as 20%, but not more.

The solution to problems like this is prevention: Take the cash out of the house now — before you think you need it. Invest that equity and use the investment income to help you make the new mortgage payments. At today's mortgage rates, your investments should be able to generate enough to do this, and even if the investment earnings are a little less, it's worth it for the benefit of having access to that money, should it ever be needed. By taking the money out of your house now, you'll be better able to handle a crisis when it strikes. My point: When you have cash, you have choices. When the cash is tied up in a house, you have few options. In other words, *get the cash out of the house.*

Reason #4: Tax Law Encourages You to Have a Mortgage

Our nation's tax code favors owners — owners of businesses, owners of assets, and owners of homes. If you own a home without a mortgage, you're missing out on many of these wonderful advantages, and you're costing yourself money.

Say you get a new, big mortgage. That means you have a new monthly payment to make, and you're spending interest you weren't spending before.

But you also now have a large sum of money available to you that you didn't have before — and you can invest that money to earn interest, dividends, and capital gains. And here's the best part: For most Americans, the interest you pay on your mortgage is deductible at your ordinary tax rate, while the dividends and capital gains you earn on your investments are taxed at much lower rates.

For example, say you get a 6% mortgage and you invest the proceeds, earning the same 6% return on your investments. Thanks to the mortgage interest deduction, that loan only costs you 4% (assuming a combined 33% federal and state income tax bracket). And, thanks to a 15% tax rate on dividends and long-term capital gains, your after-tax return on your investments is 5.1%. And that's assuming your investments earn only as much as the loan costs — which is a very conservative assumption indeed (if you don't believe me, read Part IV).

In other words, *get the cash out of the house.*

Reason #5:   If You Don't Borrow it When You Buy, You Can't Deduct it Later

Under tax law, mortgage interest is deductible only for acquisition debt, or in some cases, acquisition debt plus $100,000, subject to limitations. Say you sell your $300,000 home and buy a new one for the same price. If you pay cash for the new home (which you can afford to do with the proceeds from the sale of your old home), you will lose the tax break and liquidity discussed earlier. But worse, if you later decide to take out a home equity loan, only the first $100,000 will be tax deductible. On the other hand, if you took out a 90% mortgage ($270,000) when you bought the home, the entire amount would be deductible. In other words, *keep the cash out of the house.*

A 30-year Mortgage Is Better than 15

On a $150,000 loan at 6%, a 30-year mortgage would cost $900 per month, but mortgage bankers will tell you that for only $365 more per month, you can get a 15-year mortgage instead. Thus, they say, you'll own your home in half the time and save $95,915 in interest charges. Sound great?

Well, try this: Choose the 30-year mortgage and invest the extra $365 you were willing to give the bank. Assuming you earn 10%, at the end of 15 years you'll have saved $110,435 after taxes — virtually the same as your mortgage's outstanding balance of $106,572. So, you can pay off your mortgage if you want, giving you the equivalent of a 15-year note.

Why do this if the numbers are the same? For all these great reasons:

- Because your cash remains available to you if you need it for other purposes;
- Because cash tends to be tight after buying a new home, so the lower payment will prove very helpful;
- Because that extra $365 mortgage payment goes toward principal, not interest, so there's no tax break by making it;
- Because you lose your tax deduction quicker on the 15-year note than on the 30-year; and
- Because your mortgage payment stays fixed but your income grows with inflation, meaning you get to pay off today's fixed loan with cheaper, future dollars.

In other words, keep the cash out of the house.

There is one caveat to this strategy: You must religiously set aside the $365 each month. If you don't, you'll have nothing in 15 years but 15 years left on your mortgage. A good planner or advisor can show you how to set up a systematic investment program so you'll be sure to save that $365.

At first thought, a big 30-year mortgage may seem risky. But if you really think about it, it's the only way to go.

I've been saying this for the last 15 years, and the rest of the financial planning community is finally agreeing with me. The April 1998 issue of *The Journal of Financial Planning*, published by the Institute of Certified Financial Planners, contains the first academic study undertaken on the question of 15-year vs. 30-year mortgages. Their conclusion? The 30-year loan is best. Like I've been saying all along.

ric's money quiz

Here's a chance to see how well you learned the information contained in Part VIII – The Best Strategies for Buying Selling and Owning Homes. Don't worry if you get stumped — just re-read this part until it sinks in. Remember, your financial future depends on it.

The answers are at the end of the quiz. No peeking!

1. To succeed financially, your total debt payments (including your mortgage) should not exceed _____ of your income.

    ○ a. 20%
    ○ b. 28%
    ○ c. 16%
    ○ d. 44%

2. A mortgage is a loan based on:

    ○ a. the current value of the house
    ○ b. the future value of the house
    ○ c. your income
    ○ d. your car payment

3. A "point" equals:

    ○ a. 1% of the loan amount
    ○ b. 1% of your loan balance after your down payment
    ○ c. .1% of your loan balance after your down payment
    ○ d. $1,000

4. Real estate agents legally represent:

    ○ a. the buyer
    ○ b. the seller
    ○ c. the mortgage company
    ○ d. none of the above

5. Which type of mortgage loan is considered the "safest?"

    ○ a. adjustable-rate
    ○ b. fixed-rate
    ○ c. 5/25
    ○ d. none of the above

6. You choose to pay the accrued interest on a COFI ARM. This means:

    ○ a. your payment will consist of both principal and interest
    ○ b. your loan's balance won't go down
    ○ c. you will owe less next month than you did this month
    ○ d. a and c

7. **A shared equity deal might be good if you:**

   ○ a. are buying a house and have little or no money for a down payment
   ○ b. are having difficulty selling your house but do not want to rent it
   ○ c. want to help your children purchase a home but don't want to give them a loan
   ○ d. all of the above

9. **You plan to move. Which should you do first?**

   ○ a. buy a new home before you sell your current house
   ○ b. turn your current house into a rental
   ○ c. sell your current house before you buy your new home
   ○ d. it doesn't matter which you do first

8. **Which of the following is *not* a reason to carry a big, long mortgage?**

   ○ a. mortgages affect home values
   ○ b. if you don't borrow when you buy, you can't deduct it later
   ○ c. a 30-year mortgage is better than a 15-year mortgage
   ○ d. you get a tax deduction for the interest you pay

10. **You should hire a real estate agent:**

    ○ a. when buying a home
    ○ b. when selling a home
    ○ c. both
    ○ d. neither

Answers: 1-b (pg.372)   3-a (pg.376)   5-b (pg.387)   7-d (pg.401)   9-c (pg.404)
          2-c (pg.369)   4-b (pg.383)   6-b (pg.389)   8-a (pg.408)   10-c (pg.384, pg.397)

Part IX
Taxes, Taxes, Taxes

There's a quiz at the end of this part!

To see how much you already know, skip to the
end of this part and take the quiz now. Then, read
the part and take the quiz again. You'll discover
how much you've learned!

Part IX – Taxes, Taxes, Taxes

The bad news is that you've been paying taxes your entire adult life. The good news, though, is that today's tax rates are the lowest you've ever seen. This Part will show you how taxes work and how you can avoid paying more than necessary.

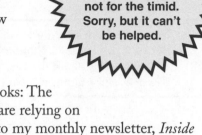

Warning! This part deals with complex tax issues and is not for the timid. Sorry, but it can't be helped.

The information that follows is current as of December 31, 2003. That's the problem with books: The data can be outdated quickly. To make sure you are relying on more current information, consider subscribing to my monthly newsletter, *Inside Personal Finance.*

Chapter 60 - How Investments Are Taxed

As you learned in Part II, people buy investments because they expect them to produce income, grow in value, or both. Which type of profit will your investments produce? The answer is important, because the tax implications are very different. Let's look at them one at a time.

Interest and Dividends

Sometimes, investments produce income. This is called either *interest* or *dividends*. As Chapter 5 told you, bank accounts and bonds produce interest and stocks produce dividends.

That distinction is important, because interest is taxed at your ordinary income tax bracket, but most dividends are taxed at a maximum rate of just 15%.

You must pay the tax on interest and dividends in the year in which it is paid, even if you reinvest them. For example, say you earn interest from your bank savings account. Whether you receive that interest in cash or leave it in your account, you must pay taxes on it when you file your tax return.

Capital Gains and Losses

If your investment rises in value, the profit is called a capital gain; if it falls in value, the loss is a capital loss.

> **You may have heard people refer to "paper" losses. They're referring to "unrealized" losses, meaning losses on investments they haven't yet sold. Until you sell paper losses, your loss isn't real — at least, in the opinion of the IRS. But your spouse's opinion is a different story.**

Surprisingly, the IRS does not want to know about your unrealized capital gains and losses. Instead, the IRS only wants you to report your realized gains and losses. Here's the difference: Your gains and losses are "realized" only when you sell an asset. Until then, the gains and losses are "unrealized" — and the IRS doesn't want to know about them until you sell.

Keep in mind these three pieces of good news when dealing with gains and losses:

- If you have capital losses, you can use them to reduce any capital gains you might have. The result is that you pay less in capital gains taxes.

- If your losses exceed your gains you can use up to $3,000 of these "net losses" to reduce this year's overall income tax. If you have net losses in excess of $3,000, you can use the excess in future years (or you can file amended returns for the past three years to get refunds for those years).

- If you have a "net gain," the tax rate is no more, and probably less than, the rate you pay on interest.

I say "probably" because the rate you pay on capital gains depends on your income tax bracket, the asset you are selling, and how long you owned it.

One important point: Capital gains and losses do not occur until you actually sell an asset. Say you own a stock that pays $300 in dividends and grows in value by $500. Although you must pay taxes on the $300 dividend this year, you do not pay taxes on the $500 gain until you sell the stock.

Most taxpayers pay 15% in capital gains taxes. But there are exceptions to this:

- If you are in one of the lowest two income tax brackets, you pay only 5% (until the amount of your gains pushes you into a higher bracket; at that point, you pay the normal 15% capital gains rate).

- If you sell an asset within one year of buying it (called a "Short-Term Gain"), you don't get to use the "Long-Term Gains" rate of 15% or 5%. Instead, you must use the Short-Term Gains rate, which is the same as your ordinary income tax rate. That's a lot higher than 15% — as much as 35%. Thus, from a tax perspective at least, you should hold all assets for at least one year and a day before selling, for selling within one year will force you to pay a lot more in taxes.

- If you sell a collectible, the gain (as if you're ever going to report it) is taxed at your ordinary income tax bracket, but not higher than 28%. (However, certain coins and bullion qualify for the lower capital gains rates.)

- If your gain is the result of depreciation from the sale of investment real estate, the tax rate is your ordinary income tax bracket, but not more than 25%. (If you don't know what depreciation is, you probably don't need to worry about this.)

- Gains from the sale of certain types of small business stock (which you probably don't own) are taxed at 14%. I don't know why.

How to Mix-and-Match Gains and Losses From Different Holding Periods

Each year, you report your realized gains and losses on your tax return, using Schedule D. (Plan on spending a lot of time with this form.)

Specifically, the IRS wants to know what you sold, the quantity, dates of purchase and sale, the cost, and profit or loss. You must list separately Short-Term and Long-Term investments. After everything is separated, first examine the Short-Term category. Use any losses within this group to offset any gains within the group.

If You Have a Net Short-Term Loss

If you have a net Short-Term loss, you may use this loss to reduce any net gain in the Long-Term group, applying the Short-Term loss first to short-term gains. If you still have a net loss at this point, it means you've had a really lousy year and you may apply your net loss against any net gain in the Long-Term group.

If, after doing all this, your net result is a loss, you generally can reduce your taxable income by the amount of the net loss (up to $3,000; losses beyond this amount can be used in future years or applied retroactively to any of the past three years' tax returns).

If your result is a profit, this capital gain will be taxed at capital gains rates.

> **Remember: It's the trade date that determines the holding period, not the settlement date. And naturally, there's an exception to the use of the trade date: For most installment sales, you can use the dates you receive each installment, instead of the actual trade date, thus entitling you to the lower capital gains rate.**

If You Have a Net Short-Term Gain

If you have a net gain in the Short-Term group, you may use this gain to reduce any net loss in the Long-Term group. If the result is a gain, it is taxed at your ordinary tax rates and if the result is a loss, it reduces your ordinary income by up to $3,000, with losses beyond this amount used in future years (or applied retroactively to any of the past three years' tax returns).

Are you getting all this?

Obviously, anyone who's bothered to read this far realizes that the rules are quite complex, and your individual circumstances will determine your actual tax liability or refund. And if all this wasn't complicated enough, those who reinvest mutual fund dividends have an even more difficult time with Schedule D, because each dividend reinvestment is considered to be a new purchase of fund shares; and each sale must appear separately on Schedule D, under Short-Term or Long-Term as appropriate. (Below, you'll learn more about mutual fund taxation. I bet you can't wait!)

Furthermore, you are allowed to include your expenses of buying and selling. For example, when buying stock, your cost basis is the stock's cost plus commissions.

When selling, your gross proceeds are the stock's value minus commissions. This reduces gains and increases losses, thus lowering your taxes.

As you can see, Schedule D is complex and requires extensive record-keeping. I suggest you ignore the preceding couple of pages and instead hire an accountant.

How Mutual Funds Are Taxed

There are many advantages offered by mutual funds (explained in Part V), but taxation of mutual funds is not one of them. In fact, it can get downright tricky — as if the last few pages weren't bad enough.

Recall that mutual funds are not investments, but rather pools of money that buy investments. Say you own a stock fund and the fund manager buys a stock. Further say the stock pays a dividend and grows in value, and the fund manager then sells the stock. You will receive a dividend distribution, which is taxable as all dividends are taxed, and you also will receive a capital gains distribution, taxable at capital gains rates.

> *"The language in which the act is couched is involved and [its] rhetoric, bewildering. It contains sentences hundreds of words in length in which clauses are added to clauses and provisos heaped upon provisos."*
> —Taxpayer A.C. Rearick, complaining in 1914 about the income tax law adopted the year before

Thus, even if you might have owned the fund for just a month or two, and even though you have not yet sold the shares of your fund that you originally bought, it's quite possible that you could receive a long-term capital gain distribution. This would occur because the fund sold an asset that it had held for the requisite period of time (more than 12 months), even though you have only held the fund for a short period and haven't sold any shares yet.

You Are Overpaying Taxes on Your Mutual Funds

All this leads to a surprisingly common mistake among mutual fund investors: they pay taxes twice on their mutual fund profits. I'll bet this is true even for those who automatically reinvest their distributions.

The IRS contends that when your fund declares a dividend or capital gain, it is your choice to reinvest this distribution or not. Since most investors choose to reinvest, *millions of mutual fund investors* **overpay** *the taxes due on their mutual funds.*

Here's how it happens: Let's say Casey invests $10,000 into a bond fund that pays a 6% annual dividend, or $600. Casey automatically reinvests this $600 and the fund gives him more shares. At tax time, Casey must pay taxes on the $600 he earned that year.

If Casey were to do this for five years, he would earn a total of $3,000 in dividends (I'm ignoring compounding to keep this example simple), and he'd pay taxes each year along the way. At the end of the five years, his fund would be worth $13,000 (his original investment of $10,000 plus the $3,000 in dividend reinvestments). Thus, if Casey were to sell his fund, he would receive a check for $13,000. Therefore, he would owe nothing in taxes because he had already paid them.

But many fund investors blow it. They forget they've paid taxes each year on the dividends; when they sell their fund and get their check for $13,000, they also get from the fund an IRS Form 1099 stating that amount (it's called *gross proceeds*). They dutifully give the 1099 to their tax preparer who asks, in an effort to determine the profit they earned (and thus the tax owed), "How much did you invest in this, anyway?"

And they say, "Ten grand," and the tax preparer records that they made a profit of $3,000, includes it on their Schedule D, and they end up paying taxes on that profit all over again! This sounds preposterous, but I can assure you it is perhaps the most common tax mistake made by mutual fund investors.

Do you see the trap? Most investors think the "amount invested" is the amount of money they sent to the fund. But the IRS says all reinvested dividend and capital gain distributions count as "investments," too. Therefore, when Casey's accountant asked how much Casey invested, Casey's answer should have been $13,000 — not $10,000!

> *"Collecting more taxes than is absolutely necessary is legalized robbery."*
> —**Calvin Coolidge**

You can avoid this problem simply by following these steps:

- saving all your mutual fund statements, and

- when your tax preparer asks you a question, *don't answer*.

Instead, give your preparer the statements you collected.

(Casey's reply should have been, "How much did I invest? I don't know. That's what I hired you for! Here — take my statements and figure it out yourself!")

If you prepare your own taxes, be aware of this trap.

Chapter 61 - How Your Home and Other Real Estate Is Taxed

The Taxpayer Relief Act of 1997 dramatically changed the tax rules regarding the sale of real estate. Now, you must separate all real estate into two categories: your personal residence and everything else.

"Everything else" — meaning real estate other than your home — is taxed like all other assets: profits and losses are subject to the capital gains rates described in Chapter 60.

Your home also is taxed under these rules — but with two important differences:

> If you converted rental property to a principal residence, or vice versa, you can't use this exclusion on gain attributable to depreciation taken after May 6, 1997.
>
> If you don't know what depreciation is, then you don't own rental property, so don't worry about it.

Important Difference #1: Your Home's First Half-Million in Profits Are Tax-Free

Every time you sell your home, the first $500,000 of gain (for married couples, that is — it's $250,000 for singles) is excluded from the capital gains tax. You get to enjoy this tax break regardless of your age, even if only one spouse owns the property, and even if you are not living in the home when you sell it. This is provided you owned the home and you occupied it as your primary residence for at least two of the five years prior to the date of sale.

Important Difference #2: You Get No Deduction for Selling at a Loss

If your home is worth less than you paid for it, you get no tax break when you sell your home.

So, while Congress has chosen to allow profits to be tax-free, it has done so by denying tax deductions to those who have losses.

Chapter 62 - How Family Loans Are Taxed

It might seem strange to see this chapter included in a part focusing on taxes, because everyone knows that loans to friends and family members are not taxed. That's true — provided you handle the transaction correctly. Otherwise, you're in for a nasty surprise.

A Loan Is a Legal Affair, Not a Family Affair

Like most people, you'd do just about anything for family members or close friends. But what if they want to borrow money from you? Should you lend it to them?

No — unless you are prepared to sue them.

Lending money to a friend or family member is one of the quickest and surest ways to damage your relationship. If the person can't or won't repay the loan, you'll begin to resent him or her. If the person is a member of your side of the family, your spouse may begin to resent *you*. If you start to pressure the person for the money, he or she may start to avoid you. Other friends or family members can become unwittingly caught in the middle, and before you know it, family gatherings and social gatherings become rife with tension.

And if the emotional implications aren't enough, consider this: The only reason the person is asking you for money is because banks and credit cards — as well as other friends and family members — have already turned him down. If no one else will lend him money, why should you?

Get it in Writing

If you are going to lend the money, make sure you do it properly. You must handle the transaction at "arm's length" — meaning as you would with a stranger. You must draft a loan agreement that will be signed by both parties. If the borrower is offended, or claims that your desire to put it in writing demonstrates that you don't trust him, do not loan him the money. Any honest and reasonable borrower would be happy to sign a loan agreement. If they plan to pay you back, they will be happy to say so in writing. By the same token, anyone who is insulted over a request to commit to the transaction in writing never intends to pay you back.

Five Elements to Include in Your Loan Agreement:

Element #1: The amount of money that is being loaned.

State this in numbers and letters, to avoid claims of miscommunication. Don't just write "$5,000." Print "five thousand dollars and no cents" on the document as well.

Element #2: The date the money is to be loaned and returned.

Be specific. "Sometime next year" or "after college graduation" doesn't work. What if he never graduates?

Element #3: The interest rate you are charging for the loan.

Yes, you must charge interest on the loan. Family members are allowed to charge rates below current market rates, but the IRS requires you to charge *some* rate of interest — and it must be reasonable. If you loan the money at no interest, the agency will consider the loan to be a gift — making you (the lender) liable for gift taxes.

This is particularly important if you lend money to your kids or other relatives to help them buy a home. I've seen situations where Dad lends the kids $50,000 for this purpose, establishes a formal loan agreement but does not charge interest. That's a bad move, for three reasons:

- Dad is liable for taxes on the interest he didn't earn;

- Dad is unable to seize the house if the kids default on their primary loan. By not listing the house as collateral against the loan, Dad will watch his money vanish if the first mortgage lender forecloses; and

- Because the loan was not formally secured by the house, the kids get no mortgage interest tax deduction for any interest repayments they make to Dad. (Note: The loan does not need to be recorded to qualify for the mortgage interest deduction. Recording the loan serves to preserve Dad's place in line with other creditors in case of default.)

I can see Dad's face when an IRS auditor says, "You should have charged your son 6% interest when you lent him money to buy that house, so we're going to tax you as though you did." On a $50,000 loan, that'd be $3,000 in interest Dad should have earned per year. Over several years, that'd be a lot of income, and that means Dad could be hit with a big tax bill on this "phantom income," not to mention the IRS interest and penalties for not reporting it.

> **And, Dad, don't try to claim that you made a gift to the kids, or they'll nail you with a gift tax of as much as 55%. Or charge it against your lifetime exclusion for estate taxes (keep reading this chapter to learn about gift and estate taxes).**

And don't charge a token interest rate, either, because if you do, the IRS could decide that the difference between what you charged and what the market bears constitutes a gift, again triggering a gift tax against Dad. The IRS, which publishes a table showing current rates, does permit loans to family members at below-market rates, but make sure you've got a bona fide agreement and make sure the kids make regular payments.

Element #4: The payment schedule that the borrower must follow.

State whether you will require periodic payments or a balloon payment, or some combination. Here are four types of payments you might require the borrower to make:

Sample Payment #1: Monthly payment of principal and interest

This is called an amortized loan, and works like your auto loan or home mortgage. In the early months, most of the payment is interest, with the bulk of the principal being repaid in the final months. Defaulting during the term of the loan means the borrower still owes most of the money he borrowed.

Sample Payment #2: No monthly payments

The full loan and all interest are to be repaid at the maturity date. This is a good choice when borrowers currently have little money or income, but it's a higher risk for the lender, since it requires the borrower to come up with a substantial amount of money at a later time.

<u>Sample Payment #3</u>: Monthly payments of interest only

Known as a "balloon" loan, this is a hybrid of the above two. The monthly payments are smaller than the first example, but the final payment is smaller than the second example.

<u>Sample Payment #4</u>: Any other combination of the above

Just make sure the arrangement is clearly explained in the loan document.

Element #5: Penalties for not meeting the above terms

You must state what the penalties are for missed payments and bounced checks. State the grace period, and make sure you assess the penalty if it applies. Failure to abide by the rules you establish could cause the IRS to conclude that it is not a true loan agreement.

A Silver Lining if the Loan Is Not Repaid

If the borrower doesn't pay you back, you are entitled to take a deduction on your tax return for this "bad debt." But to win this deduction, the IRS wants to know that you've tried everything to get the money back — which may include taking the borrower to court.

Are you prepared to sue a close friend or family member? If not, then you may not be able to take this deduction.

Clearly, lending money to family members can be treacherous. If you are willing to do it when approached, the first thing to say is this:

"If we are to proceed, this must be handled as an arm's-length transaction, as though I were a bank and you were the customer. I'm going to charge you interest and demand timely repayment — and everything will be in writing. Are you willing to accept these terms?"

If the borrower balks, let him go elsewhere for the loan.

Chapter 63 - How Gifts and Inheritances Are Taxed

Aunt Edna just sent her favorite niece a check for $15,000. Does the niece owe taxes on this money?

No, but Aunt Edna does.

Welcome to the wacky world of gift and inheritance taxes. To determine whether taxes are due, what kind of taxes are due, and who owes them, you must examine the item given (or bequeathed) and the relationship between the donor and the recipient (or heir). The following seven scenarios cover just about every situation you might encounter.

> What's the difference between a gift and an inheritance? Simple: An inheritance is a gift from a person who has died. This is important — to the IRS as well to the donor (especially if it's you, because you'd rather give a gift than an inheritance, I'm sure.)

Scenario #1: Gifts of Cash and Cash Equivalents

Let's get back to Aunt Edna and her niece. The niece pays no tax of any kind; all she needs to do is cash the check and party.[27]

But Aunt Edna has a problem. Tax law says you can give away only $11,000 to any one person in any one year; gifts above this amount are subject to the gift tax. Since Edna gave her niece $15,000, Edna could be required to pay gift taxes on $4,000. How much is the gift tax? The same as the estate tax: It starts at 45% and climbs to 48%. (You'll read more about estate taxes in the next chapter.)

> We're focusing on gifts first. We'll get to inheritances later.

Now you see why the donor pays the gift tax and not the recipient: It prevents people from giving away all their assets during their lifetimes in order to avoid estate taxes upon their deaths. Thus, whether the donor gives it away now or bequeaths it later, the same tax rate will apply.

> For definitions of cash and cash equivalents, see Chapter 6.

---

[27] Er, ah, I mean invest it prudently.

As onerous as the $11,000 per-person per-year limit might seem, it's not as restrictive as it first appears.

Take a married couple with three married children and five grandchildren. Grandma can give $11,000 to each of her three children ($33,000), to each of her children's spouses (another $33,000) and to each grandchild ($55,000). That's $121,000. And Granddad can do the same thing, for total annual gifts of $242,000 — all without incurring any gift taxes. On January 1, they can do it again. Thus, this family can transfer $484,000 to the kids in a remarkably short period of time. This in turn can be a big help if your goal is to reduce the value of your estate for estate tax purposes (which is the most common reason people make large repetitive gifts to family members).

Of course, making gifts to all these people might not be a good idea. If a divorce occurs, for example, the grandparents could discover that they've given perhaps $110,000 to an ex-in-law and children they may never see again. Think carefully before using this strategy.

These rules do not apply to gifts made to charities; you can give virtually unlimited amounts to charities, and to be entitled to a tax deduction for doing so, the date that appears on the check is the date that the gift is considered to be made.

The "cash it by Dec. 31" requirement does not apply to cashier's checks.

If you make a gift by writing a check during the holiday season, make sure the recipient cashes that check by December 31. The reason: The IRS considers gifts to be made in the year the check is cashed, not the year in which you write the check.

This could have a huge impact on you. Say you give your grandson $11,000 for Christmas 2004, but he doesn't cash the check until January 2005. If you give him more money in 2005, you'll be subject to the gift tax — because he was slow in getting to the bank! If you're trying to reduce your estate (see sidebar), make sure recipients of your checks cash or deposit them promptly.

Scenario #2: Gifts of Non-Cash Items

Would things be different if Edna gave her niece a car instead of cash?

No! If the value of the item is greater than $11,000, you're creating a gift tax problem.

Scenario #3: Gifts of Capital Assets

Would things be different if Aunt Edna gave her niece stock worth $15,000?

Yes! Not only would the gift tax issue remain, a new tax also would be under consideration: the capital gains tax. As you learned in Chapter 15, Aunt Edna will pay a capital gains tax (or declare a capital loss) when she sells her stock. She avoids this tax if she instead gives the stock to her niece. Which is a very nice tax break for her.

But not for her niece. For when you give away stock that has grown in value, the recipient of your stock receives your cost basis, too — meaning the niece, in this example, will pay the capital gains tax when she sells the stock.

This obviously closes another tax loophole. There's no way to avoid the tax merely by giving the stock away: Either Edna sells the stock and pays the capital gains tax, or she gives the stock to the niece, who sells it and pays the tax. Either way, someone is going to pay the tax, and the IRS doesn't really care who it is.

The only way to completely avoid the capital gains tax is to die (admittedly, a little extreme) or give the stock to a charity. To learn how Edna, her niece, and the charity all can profit from such a gift, read chapter 65.

If Edna's capital gains tax bracket is higher than her niece's, it would make sense for her to give the stock to the niece and let the niece pay the tax. If the niece is in a higher bracket, the opposite would be true: Let Edna sell the stock, pay the tax and give the net proceeds to her niece. Clearly, open conversation is needed before the gift or sale of stock is made.

Scenario #4: Inheritances of Cash and Cash Equivalents

If Edna dies and bequeaths money to her niece, the niece pays no federal inheritance tax (as there is no such thing). If there's any tax owed, it's paid by Edna's estate before the distributions to her heirs are made. You'll learn more about the estate tax in the next chapter.

Scenario #5: Inheritances of Capital Assets

Tax-wise, it's much better for Aunt Edna to bequeath stock to her niece than to give it to her. That's because people who inherit capital assets such as stocks inherit them at their current value, rather than at the donor's original cost. This is called a "step-up in basis" and, as explained in Chapter 15, it means the niece will not have to pay any capital gains tax when she sells the asset.

> Remember, bequests are made by a person who's died; gifts are made by people who are alive. Thus, while from a tax perspective, it's better to make bequests. I'm sure Edna would rather make a gift!

> When determining the cost basis, the executor can choose the date of Edna's death, or the date six months later.

For example, say Edna bought a stock many years ago for $5,000. On the day she died, the stock was worth $17,000, and the niece inherits it. Here's what happens:

- If the niece sells the stock for more than $17,000, she will owe capital gains taxes only on the amount she gets above $17,000.

- If she sells the stock for less than $17,000 (which would occur if the stock has fallen in value since Edna died), the niece will incur a capital loss and therefore be entitled to a tax deduction.

- If the niece decides to keep the asset, she will receive, from that point forward, whatever interest or dividends the asset produces, and she'll be liable for the taxes on that income.

- If she eventually sells the asset, she'll incur a capital gain or loss as described above.

- If she later gives the asset to another person during her lifetime, the recipient will receive the asset at the niece's

$17,000 cost basis. (As described earlier, there is no step-up in basis for gifts you make during your lifetime.)

- If she later bequeaths the asset to another person, her heir will inherit it along with a new step-up in basis, as described above. Thus, capital gains taxes are never paid on family heirlooms that are passed from generation to generation.

Scenario #6: Inheritances of Retirement Account Assets

If you are the beneficiary of someone's retirement plan, be it a 401(k) plan, IRA or any other retirement plan (see Part X), you may or may not incur a tax liability. It depends on your relationship to that person and whether he or she had begun to receive mandatory minimum distributions from the account in accordance with IRS rules.

While Part X deals with mandatory minimum distributions from IRAs and other retirement accounts, this section will examine the issue of inheriting such an account.

If You Are the Spouse of the Decedent

If the decedent had not yet begun mandatory distributions

You may do one of three things: Leave the account in your spouse's name (even though he or she is now deceased), roll over the money to your own IRA account, or take the money and run.

If you leave the money in your spouse's IRA

You must begin to make distributions on or before the later of :

- December 31 of the year following your spouse's death, or

- December 31 of the year in which your spouse would have turned 70½. In this case, you'll base the distributions on your life expectancy (for more on life expectancy charts, see Part I).

If you rollover the money to your own IRA

You will not incur any income tax. When you begin to make IRA withdrawals in the future, you will pay income taxes at that time.

If you do not leave the money in an IRA

You can spend the money as you wish, but you will be liable for income taxes on the amount you withdraw.

If the decedent had already begun mandatory distributions

You may continue to receive annual distributions from the account equal to what your spouse had been receiving, or you may rollover the money into your own IRA account.

If you want to continue receiving the same distribution from the account as your spouse had been receiving

You may do so, provided that your spouse had begun mandatory (rather than *voluntary*) minimum distributions. Mandatory minimum distributions are based on life expectancy tables and other data (see Part I), and if your spouse had begun to receive these distributions, you may continue them for the remainder of your lifetime.

However, some people withdraw money from their IRAs prior to age 70½, which while allowable, is not subject to the mandatory minimum distribution rules. Therefore, if your spouse was taking voluntary distributions, you cannot base your distributions on the amount he or she had been receiving. Instead, you must handle the account as though distributions had not yet begun, and this scenario is explained next.

If you want to rollover the account to your own IRA

You may do this, and if you do, you will not have to pay income taxes (nor will you be able to spend the money) until you make withdrawals from your account.

If You Are Not the Spouse of the Decedent

You are prohibited from rolling the money into your IRA. Therefore, income taxes must be paid on the money you receive. How this is done depends on whether or not the decedent had begun making mandatory minimum distributions.

If the decedent had not yet begun mandatory distributions

There are three ways to pay the income tax:

Tax Payment Option #1: Pay the Tax Right Away

If you choose to receive the entire account right away, you will receive a check for the proceeds, and you will owe taxes on the entire amount this year, payable at your ordinary income tax bracket.

If it's a large amount of money, this distribution easily could push you into the highest tax bracket, forcing you to lose nearly half of the money to federal and state income taxes. To avoid this problem, consider the next two options.

Tax Payment Option #2: Pay the Tax Within Five Years

Instead of paying the tax all at once, you can pay it five years later. By delaying the tax for five years, you avoid being pushed into a higher tax bracket this year. Of course, there are two problems with this idea: You'll be pushed into that top bracket in the fifth year, and you won't receive your inheritance until then, either.[28]

A better solution might be to take a portion of the money each year over five years. By spreading out the income, you might be able to avoid getting pushed into the top tax bracket. Of course, this will still force you to delay receipt of some of your inheritance, but if you were merely going to reinvest the money anyway, leaving it invested in the decedent's IRA might be just as good.

---

[28]You didn't think you could receive the money without paying the tax, did you?

Tax Payment Option #3: Pay Over Your Life Expectancy

You may choose to withdraw the money from the decedent's account over the course of your life expectancy. By doing so, you receive only a small portion of the account each year, and this will help you avoid being pushed into a higher tax bracket. The downside is that you will not receive the entire proceeds from the account right away. In fact, you'll never receive a lump sum, but instead merely a monthly or annual income stream. These distributions must begin by December 31 of the year following the owner's death. Most people who do this roll it over to a "Decedent IRA." If you don't need the money now, this might be the best option, because with it, you can invest as you wish, let the money continue to grow tax-deferred, and withdraw it only at the rate required based on your life expectancy.

If the decedent had already begun mandatory distributions

If you wish, you can liquidate the entire IRA immediately. If you do, you'll owe income taxes on the entire balance.

If you prefer, you can elect to continue receiving annual distributions from the account instead. This will spread out the tax liability over many years (as well as your receipt of the money).

You'll find further information on the tax implications of IRA Accounts in Chapter 67.

Scenario #7: Inheritances of Life Insurance Proceeds

Life insurance proceeds are tax-free to the heir.

It is possible that the estate is liable for estate taxes on the life insurance, however. To learn how to avoid this problem, see the next chapter.

Chapter 64 - How Estates Are Taxed

People get so confused about this subject because estate taxes operate exactly opposite from how all other taxes operate. Here's what I mean:

- If you **do not** earn income, you **do not** pay income taxes.

- If you **do not** purchase goods, you **do not** pay sales taxes.

- If you **do not** smoke cigarettes, you **do not** pay cigarette taxes.

- If you **do not** drive a car, you **do not** pay gasoline taxes.

- If you **do not** earn a profit on your investments, you **do not** pay capital gains taxes.

But...

- If you **do not** plan your estate, you **<u>do</u>** pay estate taxes.

Thus, in all other areas of your life, you avoid taxes simply by *doing nothing*. But doing nothing when it comes to estate planning is exactly how you will pay taxes. Indeed, estate taxes are optional: You pay them only if you fail to take the proper steps to avoid the tax. This chapter is designed to show you the proper steps.

The Magic Number

When a person dies (the *decedent*), his estate is distributed to his heirs.[29]

Before heirs receive anything, the IRS has first dibs. The *estate tax* is assessed against the estate's *net worth*, which is simply what the decedent *owned* (the assets) minus what the decedent *owes* (the liabilities).

---

[29]For the purposes of this discussion, we're using "he" as the one who dies and "she" as the survivor, because that's what happens to married couples 80% of the time. And while we're at it, let's offer one "G-d forbid" to cover the rest of the book.

And in case you're keeping score, only 3% of the U.S. population has a net worth in excess of a half million dollars.

If your net worth is less than $1,500,000, your estate is not subject to estate taxes. But every dollar above that figure will be subject to tax — and the tax rate starts at 45%!

Two Mistakes in Your Arithmetic

If you think you're not worth $1,500,000, don't make the mistake of thinking you have nothing to worry about, for two reasons.

Math Mistake #1: You Did Not List All Your Assets

In addition to your ordinary assets, such as your home, cars, bank accounts, investments, IRAs and personal possessions, you also need to include:

- **the face amount of your life insurance policies.** You'll read about Steve in Chapter 74. He bought $250,000 worth of life insurance.? For tax purposes, that $250,000 — the death benefit — is included in his estate. (That's right: the death benefit, not the cash surrender value.)

- **the present value of future pension benefits.** If you were to die, will your surviving children be entitled to your pension? If so, you must include in your estate the current value of the pension income that your kids are to receive during their lifetimes. In other words, your estate will pay taxes on money it doesn't yet have![30]

Math Mistake #2: You Think You Are Worth Less Than $1,500,000

Keep one point in mind: *You're not dead!* (I know, because if you were, you wouldn't be reading this book.) By the time you are dead, you almost certainly will be worth $1,500,000 — *and more!*

---

[30]This is not a concern if your pension income will be paid to a surviving spouse.

WHAT WILL YOUR ESTATE BE WORTH?

If your net worth doubles every decade
(7.2% annual growth rate)

Age	Assets	Tax Rate
45	$200,000	0%
55	$400,000	0%
65	$800,000	0%
75	$1.6 million	45%
85	$3.2 million	48%

FIGURE 9-1

Let's look at Beth, age 45, whose net worth is $200,000. Assuming her assets double every 10 years (which would happen with a 7% annual growth rate), Beth will be worth $400,000 at age 55 and $800,000 by 65 — thus presenting her with a tax problem. And she's still not dead! By 75, she'll be worth $1.6 million and $3.2 million by age 85. Her tax liability by then would be well over $1 million. Now that's a problem!

How to Reduce Your Estate Tax

To solve this problem, you need solid planning. Let's see the difference we can make. Each of the following examples are based on Mike and Sue, who have a net worth of $4 million. For simplicity, we'll assume their assets are split equally between them, although in real life it's rarely that simple. We'll also assume Mike dies first and that Sue dies shortly afterward, before the estate increases in value.

Simple Wills

Our first example, shown in Figure 9-2, assumes that Mike and Sue leave every-thing to each other, then to their kids after the surviving spouse dies. As explained in Chapter 78, this is called a *simple will*.

Mike dies, leaving everything to his wife Sue. When she dies, she leaves everything to their children.

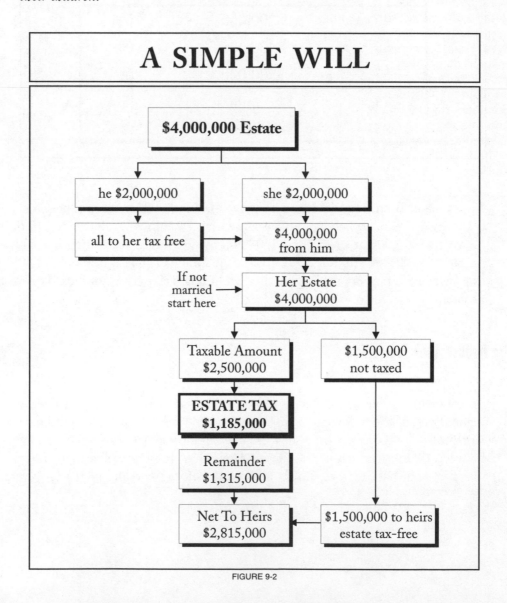

A SIMPLE WILL

$4,000,000 Estate

he $2,000,000

she $2,000,000

all to her tax free

$4,000,000 from him

If not married start here

Her Estate $4,000,000

Taxable Amount $2,500,000

$1,500,000 not taxed

ESTATE TAX $1,185,000

Remainder $1,315,000

Net To Heirs $2,815,000

$1,500,000 to heirs estate tax-free

FIGURE 9-2

Chapter 78 shows the administrative problems posed by simple wills. Here we see that simple wills create huge tax liabilities as well. But interestingly, the tax problems occur not at Mike's death, but at Sue's. This is because you are permitted to leave an unlimited amount of money to your spouse without incurring any estate tax. Thus, Mike can leave his entire $2 million to Sue (making her worth $4 million) and no tax is due. This often lulls people into falsely believing that they need not worry about estate taxes.

> As mentioned in Chapter 71, 85% of all women in the U.S. die unmarried, divorced, or widowed. Thus, women cannot assume that a man always will be around to handle the finances. If you find this comment degrading, mention this to your mother or grandmother. She will react with fear or denial, not indignation.

The kids expect to inherit Sue's assets tax-free when she dies. After all, there was no tax when Dad died, so it follows that there will be no tax when Mom dies, too. Right?

Wrong. When Sue dies leaving $4 million to the kids, only(!) the first $1,500,000 passes tax-free. The rest — $2,500,000 — is subject to taxes at a rate of 48%. Sue's estate thus will pay $1,185,000 in taxes, and her children will inherit only $2,815,000 million, instead of the $4 million Sue expected.

It doesn't have to be this way. Through proper planning, we can dramatically cut that tax bill, safely and securely, simply by following the rules provided by Congress.

Estate Taxes Are Optional

Congress made estate taxes *optional*: You pay only if you fail to take the steps needed to avoid the tax.

The first step, shown in Figure 9-3, is to use a *Bypass Trust* (so named because it allows a portion of your estate to "bypass" the tax; It's also known as an A/B trust, a unified credit trust and a credit shelter trust). *Mike leaves Sue only $500,000, placing the remaining $1,500,000 in the Bypass Trust.*

Since Sue receives only $500,000, her estate is worth $2,500,000 (her 2 million plus Mike's $500,000). Therefore, the estate tax at her death is only $465,000, a savings of $720,000.

But, Sue wonders, what about the $1,500,000 that Mike placed into the Bypass Trust?

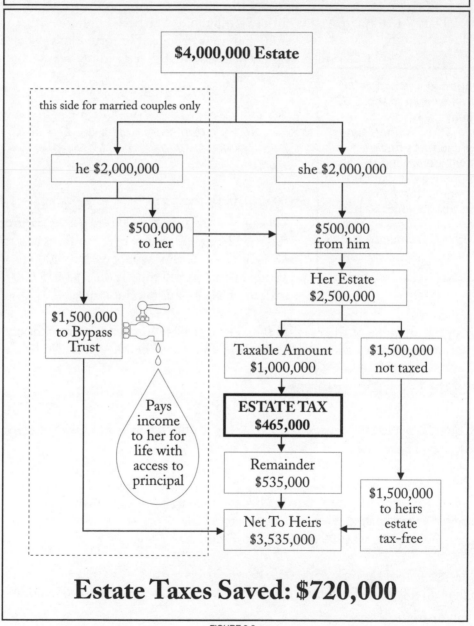

WILL WITH A BYPASS TRUST

$4,000,000 Estate

this side for married couples only

he $2,000,000

she $2,000,000

$500,000 to her

$500,000 from him

Her Estate $2,500,000

$1,500,000 to Bypass Trust

Pays income to her for life with access to principal

Taxable Amount $1,000,000

$1,500,000 not taxed

ESTATE TAX $465,000

Remainder $535,000

$1,500,000 to heirs estate tax-free

Net To Heirs $3,535,000

Estate Taxes Saved: $720,000

FIGURE 9-3

It goes to the kids tax-free.

That's great, but what about me? Have I lost $1,500,000?

Not at all. Think of a trust as a bucket. As the *donor*, Mike:

- places money (or other assets) into the bucket;

- sets rules regarding the management and distribution of the money (within IRS limitations);

- names one or more people to serve as trustee, whose job is to follow the rules Mike established; and

- names one or more people as beneficiaries.

When Mike creates his Bypass Trust, he names his wife Sue as both trustee *and* primary beneficiary; the kids are secondary beneficiaries.[31] Mike further states that Sue, as beneficiary, is entitled to receive both income and principal from the trust throughout her lifetime, provided that the trustee agrees that the distribution is needed for her *maintenance, education, support, and health* (known in estate planning circles by the acronym MESH). Any assets remaining in the trust at Sue's death then pass to the children, who are the secondary beneficiaries.[32]

Thus, has Sue lost the $1,500,000 that Mike gave to the trust? Not at all. To get the money, she simply needs permission from the trustee — who is herself!

But since Mike placed the $1,500,000 into the trust, it is excluded from the estate tax calculation, which in turn saves $720,000 in estate taxes.

> **Figure 9-3 actually shows only half of the actual estate plan. The second half, a mirror image of the first, is for Sue, and her will also contains a Bypass Trust. We need both halves because we don't know who will die first.**

"I'm proud to be paying taxes to the U.S. The only thing is — I could be just as proud for half the money."
—**Arthur Godfrey**

---

[31]Unless they are minors. If so, see Chapter 79.
[32]Since this subject involves lawyers, fine print abounds. Talk with a legal advisor for more details.

The kids, therefore, inherit $3,535,000 — $2,035,000 from Sue and $1,500,000 from Mike's Bypass Trust.

Bypass Trusts Are Limited to $1,500,000

If the Bypass Trust is such a great deal, why is Mike placing only $1,500,000 there? Why not his entire $2 million?

Because it won't do him any good. Remember that Congress allows you to leave an unlimited amount to your spouse, but only $1,500,000 to a non-spouse. Therefore, if Mike had left more than $1,500,000 to the trust, everything above that amount would have been taxed, defeating the purpose. This reveals the secret to the Bypass Trust: It preserves Mike's ability to pass $1,500,000 to his kids tax-free, an ability he would have lost if he had first left everything to his wife. Since Sue also is able to pass $1,500,000 tax-free to the kids at her death, Bypass Trusts allow married couples to shelter up to $3,000,000 from estate taxes.

"The art of taxation consists in so plucking the goose as to obtain the largest possible amount of feathers with the smallest possible amount of hissing."
—John Baptiste Colbert

Bypass Trusts are not needed when the estate is less than $1,500,000, since there is no tax on estates valued up to that amount. But for married couples whose estates are between $1,500,000 and $3,000,000, the Bypass Trust will completely avoid all estate taxes.

The $1.5 Million Figure Increases Every Year, but...

The amount of money you can leave to heirs without incurring the estate tax is $1.5 million for 2004, and this figure rises to $3.5 million by 2009. In 2010, it gets even better: In that year, you can leave heirs an unlimited amount of money. That's right: the estate tax disappears completely in 2010.

But the tax comes back in 2011! And it returns with a vengeance: Starting in 2011, you'll be able to leave heirs only $1 million tax-free.

...The Bypass Trust Works Only for Married Couples...

It's an example of how the tax code discriminates against those who are not married — and why, if you are married, you *must* establish these trusts while you both are alive. When one spouse dies, it's too late.

...And Only for U.S. Citizens...

Bypass Trusts work only when both spouses are U.S. citizens. If you are worth more than $1,500,000 and married to a non-citizen, you need to see an estate attorney to learn about a Qualified Domestic Trust. This trust was designed to reduce the estate taxes for Americans who marry non-citizens.

Insurance Trusts

Although the Bypass Trust protects $3 million of Mike and Sue's money, we still have work to do, for they still would lose $465,000 to estate taxes. The solution can be found in Figure 9-4, which uses an Irrevocable Life Insurance Trust in addition to a Bypass Trust.

While both are alive, Mike and Sue establish and give money to an Irrevocable Life Insurance Trust. They name the children as both trustees and beneficiaries. The trustees (read: children) use the money in the trust to buy a special type of life insurance policy, called a "survivorship life" policy.

> "It isn't what you earn as much as what you save that counts in the long run."
>
> —Anonymous

This type of policy, also called *second-to-die,* (a) insures the lives of both Mike and Sue, (b) is owned by the trust, and (c) names the trust as beneficiary.

Although Mike and Sue are *both* insured, this policy does not pay a claim at the first death. There's no need because there's no tax liability at that time. Rather, the death benefit is paid at the second death (hence, the policy's name), and it insures both Mike and Sue because we don't know who will die first. (We could buy two policies instead — one on Mike and one on Sue - but that's more expensive. Besides, we don't need coverage on both of them — just on the one who dies second. This is why the insurance industry created this type of policy.)

WILL WITH A BYPASS TRUST AND AN INSURANCE TRUST

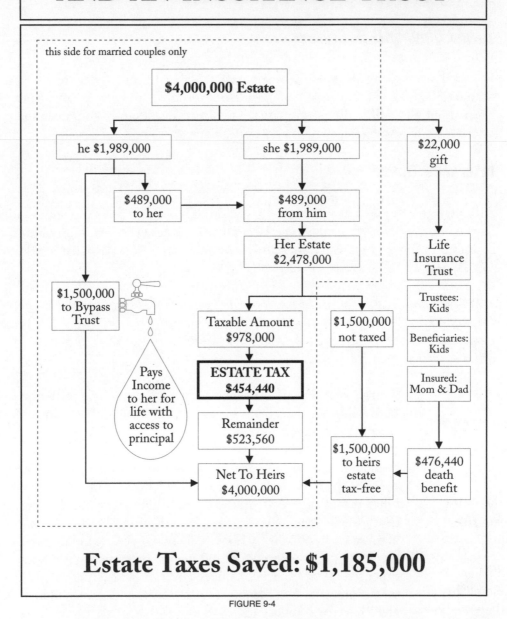

this side for married couples only

$4,000,000 Estate

he $1,989,000

she $1,989,000

$22,000 gift

$489,000 to her

$489,000 from him

Her Estate $2,478,000

Life Insurance Trust

Trustees: Kids

Beneficiaries: Kids

Insured: Mom & Dad

$1,500,000 to Bypass Trust

Pays Income to her for life with access to principal

Taxable Amount $978,000

$1,500,000 not taxed

ESTATE TAX $454,440

Remainder $523,560

$1,500,000 to heirs estate tax-free

$476,440 death benefit

Net To Heirs $4,000,000

Estate Taxes Saved: $1,185,000

FIGURE 9-4

At the second death, the insurance policy pays the death benefit to the trust, which in turn distributes the money to the children.

How much money? If you set it up correctly, the amount of insurance paid to the trust will equal the amount owed in estate taxes. Thus, instead of estate taxes being paid out of the estate, the taxes are paid by the proceeds of the insurance policy. Sure, Mike and Sue pay the policy's premium, but that's a tiny amount compared to the actual estate tax itself. In fact, you can pay 90% of your estate taxes or more this way.

> *"The difference between a taxidermist and a tax collector? The taxidermist takes only your skin."*
> —Mark Twain

Second-to-die life insurance also makes it possible to obtain insurance even if one spouse is uninsurable. Since the carrier doesn't pay until the second death, it is largely unconcerned about a spouse who might be in poor health, provided the other spouse's health is better.

Not Just a Clever Way to Sell Insurance

This strategy is not simply a back-handed way to get you to buy life insurance. The alternative is to pay the taxes out of your assets, which would be far more expensive.

Besides, if you already own insurance, you might not need to buy a new policy. You may be able to transfer existing policies to the insurance trust. This provides two benefits: It removes the insurance from your estate (which lowers your estate tax liability) while providing the money that the kids need to pay the tax.

I once met with a new client whose net worth was $10 million. His estate tax would have been roughly $5 million, or half his estate. To avoid that problem, he bought a $5 million insurance policy. When I asked him if he had established a life insurance trust, he replied that, no, he had bought the policy in his own

> Another reason for not owning your own life insurance is Medicaid. Before Medicaid will pay for your long-term care expenses, it can force you to cancel your insurance policies, using the cash value that has accumulated to pay for your long-term care costs. But if your trust owns the policies, Medicaid cannot make this demand. For more on long-term care, see Chapter 73.

name. His insurance agent never mentioned anything about a trust. But by owning the policy himself, the death benefit was now part of his estate. Thus, he no longer was worth $10 million, but rather $15 million — and the estate tax was now $7.5 million instead of $5 million! His agent didn't solve the problem — he made it worse!

This is why you need an insurance trust: If Mike and Sue tried to solve their estate tax problem by buying insurance on their own, instead of through a trust, they would have increased the estate tax instead of reducing it!

Thus, if you are 65 or older and are worth more than $1,500,000, you should not own your own life insurance policies, for the death benefits would merely increase the size of your estate, which increases the tax your estate will owe.

A Warning When Transferring Policies to an ILIT

When you transfer a policy you own to an insurance trust, make sure you don't die for three years. If you do, the IRS will deem that you made the transfer "in contemplation of death," and your estate will be required to pay taxes on the value of the death benefit as though the transfer had never occurred.

Chapter 65 - How to Make Money by Giving it Away

That might sound a little crazy. But you can do it, through the little-known Charitable Remainder Trust.

In fact, with the CRT, you can lower your current income taxes, avoid capital gains taxes, maintain or even increase your income for life, donate large sums to charity, and still leave everything to your kids and grandkids.

Sound good? Read on.

You establish a trust with some of your assets, such as stocks, bonds, or real estate. You then name a favorite charity as beneficiary. You get an immediate income tax deduction because the gift is irrevocable, although the charity must wait for the death of you and your spouse before receiving your gift.

Next, the trust converts these assets into income-producing ones (if they aren't already). If you donated land, for example, you might have the trust sell the property and buy bonds.

Don't worry about capital gains taxes, either, because a charitable trust doesn't pay any taxes. (If the asset had appreciated, you would have lost a third of the value to taxes if you had sold them yourself. But the trust can sell the assets for you — tax free.)

This trust annually must pay out at least five percent of its initial market value.[33] You decide who gets the income, how much they get, and for how long — and you can name yourself if you want.

> *"Many people who are not charitably inclined sure are patriotic."*
> —**Anonymous**

Assuming you take the income for as long as you or your spouse live, the charity will receive whatever's left at the second death. But what about your kids? After all, their inheritance is going to charity.

To replace that inheritance, the trust buys an insurance policy on you and your spouse equal to the size of your gift, naming your children (or whomever) as beneficiaries.

---

[33]Based on the date the asset was transferred to the trust.

Premiums are paid from the income produced by the trust's assets and, upon the last death, they'll receive the policy's death benefit — which is as much as they would have gotten had you left the original assets to them in the first place.

And here's another advantage: Because your heirs receive their inheritance from insurance, not your estate, the cash passes to the kids free of income taxes, estate taxes, and probate.

These trusts once made sense only when giving away millions of dollars. But today, you can set up a CRT at little cost or effort for gifts as small as $20,000.

So take a close look at these trusts. You could help yourself, your family, and a charity.

Some fine print: You can name more than one person or organization to receive income, but at least one must be a non-charity. You must specify whether the pay-outs are to be in dollars, or percentages. Your tax deduction is based on a complex formula involving the value of the trust's assets, the annual income you're to receive, and how long you're to receive it. The IRS publishes tables determining these figures. Also, there are limits on tax deductions for charitable gifts and the Alternative Minimum Tax could apply if your gift involves appreciated property.

Use Your IRA for Bequests to the CRT

Another good idea if you want to make bequests to a CRT is to donate your IRA (or a portion of it) instead of your cash or other assets. Why? Because when you make a donation from your IRA, you avoid both the estate tax *and* the income tax on that money. That reduces your taxes and increases the amount you leave for your family — or the charity itself.

"Having lots of money doesn't change anything. It just amplifies it. Jerks become bigger jerks, and nice guys become nicer."

—Ben Narasin

ric's money quiz

Here's a chance to see how well you learned the information contained in Part IX – Taxes, Taxes, Taxes. Don't worry if you get stumped — just re-read this part until it sinks in. Remember, your financial future depends on it.

The answers are at the end of the quiz. No peeking!

1. When calculating the value of your assets for estate tax purposes, which of the following would *not* be included?

   - O a. a $1 million life insurance policy
   - O b. a newly built home
   - O c. lines of credit on credit cards
   - O d. the face amount of your life insurance policies

2. If Dad gives money to his son:

   - O a. Dad is subject to the gift tax on all the money he gives his son
   - O b. the son pays income tax on all the money Dad gives to him
   - O c. Dad is subject to the gift tax, but only on amounts above $11,000
   - O d. the son pays income tax, but only on amounts he receives that are above $11,000

3. Bypass Trusts are best suited for:

   - O a. widows trying to avoid probate
   - O b. married couples with a net worth of more than $1,500,000
   - O c. beneficiaries wishing to bypass their inheritance
   - O d. everyone needs a Bypass Trust

4. You own a life insurance policy with a death benefit of $100,000. The policy has a cash surrender value of $15,000. Your daughter is the beneficiary. When you die your estate might have to:

   - O a. pay an estate tax on $15,000
   - O b. pay an estate tax on $115,000
   - O c. pay an estate tax on $100,000
   - O d. your estate will not have to pay estate taxes on this policy

5. When selling your primary residence, the first $500,000 of gain for married couples ($250,000 for singles) is excluded from the capital gains tax if you are what age?

    ○ a. at least 70½
    ○ b. at least 59½
    ○ c. over 55
    ○ d. age doesn't matter. It matters only that you have lived in your home for two of the last five years.

6. If you were unmarried and died in 2004 and your estate was worth $2 million, how much was subject to estate taxes?

    ○ a. $500,000
    ○ b. $1,375,000
    ○ c. $1 million
    ○ d. $1.4 million

7. How much can you leave to a Bypass Trust without incurring a tax problem?

    ○ a. as much as you want
    ○ b. up to your exemption amount
    ○ c. $1,500,000
    ○ d. twice your exemption amount

8. Each year you report your realized gains and losses on your tax return using:

    ○ a. IRS Schedule A
    ○ b. IRS Schedule B
    ○ c. IRS Schedule C
    ○ d. IRS Schedule D

9. By establishing a Charitable Remainder Trust, you can:

    ○ a. lower your income taxes
    ○ b. avoid capital gains taxes
    ○ c. make a gift to charities of your choice
    ○ d. all of the above

10. When a mutual fund pays a dividend or capital gain distribution, what is the tax effect?

    ○ a. you pay *income tax* on the dividend and *capital gains tax* on the capital gains distribution
    ○ b. you pay *capital gains tax* on the dividend and *income tax* on the capital gains distribution decrease
    ○ c. you pay *capital gains tax* on both
    ○ d. you pay *income tax* on both

Answers: 1-c (pg.438)   3-b (pg.445)   5-d (pg.424)   7-b (pg.444)   9-d (pg.449)
               2-c (pg.429)   4-c (pg.448)   6-a (pg.441)   8-d (pg.422)   10-a (pg.417)

Part X
Retirement Planning

There's a quiz at the end of this part!

To see how much you already know, skip to the
end of this part and take the quiz now. Then, read
the part and take the quiz again. You'll discover
how much you've learned!

Part X – Retirement Planning

Retirees have three primary sources of income: pensions, savings they've accumulated in their company retirement plans, and Social Security. (Yes, there is a difference between pension plans and retirement plans, and we'll cover both in this part.)

Chapter 66 - Pensions

Pensions are technically called *defined benefit plans*. Through them, your employer promises to give you a specific monthly income (or in some cases, a *lump-sum* check in lieu of a monthly income) starting at retirement. The amount you receive is calculated by a formula that considers your salary, the number of years you've worked for the company, and other factors. The formula is different at every company, so check with your employer to learn how much you can expect to receive at age 60, 62, or 65, based on your employer's calculations.

Most workers entitled to a pension at retirement are offered several options regarding how to collect the benefit. The two most common options are *single life annuity* (which gives you a monthly income for life, but which stops upon your death) and *joint and survivor annuity* (which provides you with a smaller monthly income but which continues as long as either you or your spouse is alive).

Figure 10-1 shows the options faced by one of my clients who recently retired. The single life option would provide Tim with $3,500 every month for as long as he is alive, but following his death, his wife Marcia would receive nothing.

The joint and survivor option gives him $2,650 a month ($850 less), but should he die prior to Marcia, she would continue to receive the same $2,650 he had been receiving for as long as she lives.

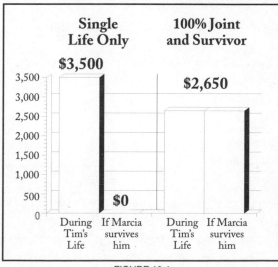

FIGURE 10-1

You can see Tim's dilemma: Should he choose a higher income, which stops at his death, or accept a smaller income which also protects his wife?

Which would you choose?

The overwhelming majority of workers choose the joint and survivor option. In fact, federal law requires that Marcia provide written consent if Tim chooses anything else, because after all, it's Marcia who is at risk here.

Single Life or Joint and Survivor Benefits?

When Tim chooses joint and survivor benefits, he's leaving Marcia a benefit payable upon his death. Quite simply, he's buying a life insurance policy! The cost of the policy in his case is $850 per month (the difference between the income provided by the single life option and the joint and survivor option), and the death benefit is $2,650 a month. But note these restrictions:

- Marcia is not entitled to a lump-sum check. She gets only a monthly check.

- Tim is stuck with the lower income for his entire lifetime, even if Marcia dies first. He can never return to the higher income offered by the single life option.

- Tim cannot change the beneficiary from Marcia to other heirs.

- Tim cannot name contingent beneficiaries in case Marcia dies first; and

- Assuming Marcia outlives Tim, all benefits stop when she dies. There is no residual value or inheritance for heirs, and there is no compensation to Tim's family in the event she dies shortly after him.

An Alternative to the Joint and Survivor Option

For all these reasons, Tim chooses the single life option, and uses the extra $850/month to buy his own life insurance policy. This strategy is called *pension maximization* or *pension enhancement*. By cutting out the middleman (his employer), Tim got a better deal for these reasons:

If they both live:

- The policy can become fully paid for, meaning they can stop paying premiums but the policy will continue to provide benefits; and

- This strategy can cost less, letting Tim and Marcia enjoy the money they save every month.

If Tim dies first, Marcia can:

- Take the entire lump-sum at any time if she needs it; and

- Pass any assets she didn't use during her lifetime to children or other heirs upon her death.

If Marcia dies first, Tim can:

- Cancel the policy and (depending on when she dies) get a refund of most or all of the premiums he had paid; and

- Name additional or replacement beneficiaries, such as children.

In Tim's case, we calculated how much Marcia would need as a lump sum if he died first. This money, when invested, would provide her with a monthly income of $2,650, equal to the joint and survivor benefit, which she won't get because he chose the single life option.

This policy cost Tim $657 a month, meaning our strategy saved him $143 a month — every month for the rest of his life! On top of that, he and Marcia enjoyed all the benefits noted above.

COMPARING YOUR OPTIONS

	Pension Max	100% Joint and Survivor
Provide income for my survivor upon my death	yes	yes
Monthly premiums required	yes	yes
Premium payments are flexible	yes	no
Premiums cease if my survivor pre-deceases me	yes	no
Benefits payable if my survivor pre-deceases me	yes	no
Benefits payable if my beneficiary and I die at the same time	yes	no
I can cancel at any time	yes	no
If I decide to cancel, I can get some or all of my money back	yes	no
The benefit increases	yes	no
My survivor can elect a lump-sum payment	yes	no
My survivor has multiple options for income upon my death	yes	no
My survivor can designate a beneficiary to receive benefits after my survivor dies	yes	no
I can leave benefits to a favorite charity	yes	no
I have control of this plan from day one	yes	no

FIGURE 10-2

Eight Problems with Pension Max

When this idea works, it's wonderful. Unfortunately, it doesn't always work. Watch out for these problems:

Problem #1: Health Risk

You must be healthy enough to qualify for the insurance. *Solution:* Obtain the coverage before you choose an option because your decision almost always is irrevocable. If you choose the single life option and then discover you can't buy insurance, your spouse will be in serious financial jeopardy if you die first.[34]

Problem #2: Age Risk

The cost of insurance increases as you get older. Thus, if you wait until retirement to implement this strategy, the cost of insurance might be too high to make the strategy effective. *Solution:* Buy the insurance 10 years *before* retirement. By obtaining coverage at age 50 or 55, the cost is significantly lower, and you can even arrange it so that your premium payments stop by the time you retire, if you choose.

Problem #3: Income Risk

If you lose income from other sources, you won't be able to pay the premium. No premium, no policy. No policy, no benefit. *Solution:* Use a vanishing premium policy and be fully committed to funding it.

Problem #4: Inflation Risk

Pension max doesn't normally provide for increases in income, but your pension might. *Solution:* Alter the strategy to match your pension's benefits.

---

[34]And you probably will die first because your spouse, so angry at what you've done, will kill you.

Problem #5: Interest Rate Risk

If interest rates drop, the cost of your life insurance policy could increase, altering the economics of your strategy. *Solution:* Use a whole life or universal life policy with very low interest rate assumptions (see Chapter 74).

Problem #6: Marital Risk

If the marriage goes bad, the retiree might cancel the policy or change the beneficiary to someone other than the spouse. *Solution:* Have the spouse own the policy. By owning it, the spouse controls it.

Problem #7: Management Risk

The spouse may not know how to manage the lump sum proceeds provided by the insurance policy, yet his or her lifetime income is dependent on doing so successfully. *Solution:* Establish a plan now for handling the assets, or have handy the name of a trusted advisor to whom the spouse can turn for guidance.

Problem #8: Health Insurance Risk

A spouse who doesn't receive survivor benefits from the company might lose the company's health benefits as well. *Solution:* Find out in advance and, if this is so, include in the pension max strategy the cost of replacement health coverage. (And of course, make sure you and your spouse can qualify for health insurance coverage, too!)

Pension Max generally doesn't work for federal or military employees. For these workers, the joint and survivor option is known as the Survivor Benefit Plan, which states that upon the spouse's death, the worker can cancel the SBP deduction, thereby returning the worker's pension benefit to the full amount of the single life option. Also, federal pension incomes rise with inflation and spousal medical benefits are tied to participation in the SBP. Most private employers don't offer these features.

So before you choose the single life option, be sure you carefully consider all the risks.

Should You Choose Monthly Income or One Lump Sum?

When you leave your company, you may be offered the choice of a monthly income or one single check, known as a *lump-sum distribution*. If you take a lump sum, you must provide for your own monthly income — for the rest of your life. That frightens many people, for what if you lose the money?

It's so frightening, in fact, that many people refuse to take the lump sum. Instead, they choose the monthly income. That's the wrong move, for these reasons:

- You are not in control of how your former employer handles your money.

- Your monthly income is almost certain to be less than if you were to invest the money yourself. Employer-provided annuities are rarely competitive in the marketplace.

- The cost of living will rise, but your monthly check will not. This will hurt as you get older.

- In most cases, you won't ever have the chance to take that lump sum again or leave it to your heirs.

For all these reasons, you're much better off investing your own money. So when your employer offers you that check, take the money and run.

When you do, you can put the distribution into an IRA to defer taxes, or you can keep the money and pay taxes.

"Before you decide to retire, take a week off and watch daytime television."
—Dr. Laurence J. Peter

Using Income Averaging to Lower Your Taxes

If you reached age 50 by 1986, you can reduce or avoid that penalty by taking advantage of "income averaging," a special IRS formula that lets you pay taxes at below-normal rates.

To be eligible, you must (a) retire, (b) receive a total distribution from the qualified plan in one taxable year, (c) be at least 59½ years old or age 50 by 1986, and (d) have been in the plan at least five years. Averaging is complicated, so let a tax advisor do the calculations for you.

Rolling over your distribution into an IRA is the simpler choice. This postpones payment of all the taxes until you actually use the money. Whenever we have compared the results, 5- or 10-year averaging has never worked better than a rollover.

Where to Invest Your Lump Sum

Whether you income-average or use an IRA, your most important decision is where to invest the money, and it is here that competent investment advice is of the most value.

As we explored in Part I, don't make the mistake of focusing only on current income needs, or inflation will destroy your lifestyle. Instead, be sure to allocate at least part of your money for growth. Remember: If you and your spouse both live to age 65, odds are one of you will live to age 90. Make sure you don't outlive your money!

CLOSE TO HOME   JOHN MCPHERSON

5-5   © 1994 John McPherson/Dist. by Universal Press Syndicate   Mc PHERSON

© John McPherson. Reprinted with permission of Universal Press Syndicate. All rights reserved.

"Here's your allowance. You're free to do with it as you please, but I strongly recommend that you put 25 percent of it away for retirement."

Chapter 67 - IRA Accounts

An IRA is the most common type of retirement plan. These are maintained individually rather than in groups (we'll talk about company retirement plans in the next chapter). With any retirement plan, you know how much money is being placed into the plan, but you have no idea how much the plan will be worth when you retire. Thus, retirement plans are technically known as *defined contribution plans*, and they are the exact opposite of defined benefit plans (see prior chapter), where the result is known but the amount that needs to be contributed is not.

There are three kinds of IRA accounts, and we'll cover them each in detail:

- Deductible IRA

- Non-Deductible IRA

- Roth IRA

Before we examine the differences between the various IRAs and determine which is best for you, let's make sure you understand how they really work. To find out how much you know about IRAs, take my IRA quiz:

Ric's IRA Quiz

Question #1
IRA stands for Individual Retirement Account. *True or false?*

Question #2
An IRA is an investment. *True or false?*

Question #3
Banks sell IRAs. *True or false?*

> *"Retirement: The first day of the rest of your life savings."*
> —Anonymous

The answer to all three questions is *false*.

IRA stands for Individual Retirement *Arrangement*, not Individual Retirement Account. An IRA is a provision of the tax code — Section 408 of the Internal Revenue Code, to be exact — under which you *arrange individually* (as opposed to through a group) *for your retirement*. An IRA, therefore, is not an investment, but simply money the tax code treats differently from other money.

Therefore, banks do not sell IRAs. What do banks sell? CDs. That means you can have a CD with or without an IRA. Is the CD in an IRA any different from one outside it? Not at all. Sure, the tax treatment is different, but the CD itself is the same.

If you open an IRA at a bank, you'll get a CD. In fact, banks have done such a good marketing job, many people think IRAs are investment products and that banks are the only place to get them. It's so pervasive that my firm gets calls from people asking, "What are your IRAs paying these days?" This is a silly question: Since IRAs are not investments, they don't "pay" anything.

Rather, think of an IRA as a bucket. The IRS says if you put $3,000 (the annual maximum allowed by law; increases to $4,000 in 2005, and those 50 and older can contribute an extra $500) into the bucket, you can use that money to buy and sell investments as you wish and, provided the money stays inside the bucket for the required length of time (which varies with each IRA; details will follow), you won't have to pay taxes that year on the profits you earn.

As we explained in Chapter 28, tax-deferred growth is a very important benefit because a dollar that is not taxed grows more quickly than a dollar that is.

It's important to emphasize that you can buy almost any investment you want with that $3,000: You can buy CDs, savings accounts, money markets, Treasury bills, and more. In fact, you can choose from virtually everything we have covered in this book, including stocks, bonds, U.S. Government Securities, mutual funds, variable annuities, fixed annuities, limited partnerships, gold, international securities, foreign currencies, real estate — almost anything, provided that any asset you buy stays in the bucket. You also may sell at any time any investment you previously bought, and replace it with something else, provided all the transactions occur — and the proceeds stay — in the bucket. You will pay no taxes until you withdraw money from the bucket. That's all there is to it.

Thus, if you get an IRA at the bank, you're going to get a CD; if you go to an insurance agent, you're going to get an annuity; and if you go to a stockbroker, well, who knows what you'll get!

Question #4

Tom, 35, has $6,000 to invest and has decided to place half the money into a high-risk growth stock and half into a U.S. Treasury Bond. Which of the two should Tom place into his IRA? *For this question, which is designed to show you the proper way to handle your IRA, assume you have an "either-or" choice between these two individual securities; ignore the notion of mutual funds.*

What do you think is the correct answer? If you answered, "The stock!" I'm willing to bet you thought, "Tom is not going to touch the money until he retires in 25 years, so he can tolerate a higher level of risk." That's what you said, isn't it? Well, you're wrong.

If you answered, "The bond!" I'm willing to bet you thought, "Tom is depending on this money for his retirement, so he can't play games. He needs to be conservative with his IRA." If that's what you said, you're wrong, too.

There is a correct answer, which I'll give you in a moment, but first I want you to understand why both of the above answers are wrong. Both imply that the determining factor is *risk*. One answer favors high risk; the other low risk. Both are wrong. After all, Tom is going to buy both investments. If the stock goes broke, is he going to feel any better because that investment was or was not inside the IRA?

"Yes, Tom, you went broke — but don't worry: Your money was/wasn't inside your IRA!"

That sounds silly, doesn't it? And that's why both of the above answers are wrong. Since IRAs are not investments, the subject of risk is not relevant.

The correct answer is the *government bond*, and by now you should know why: because of tax law.

Remember that an IRA has a special tax advantage: The money grows tax-deferred. Chapter 15 showed you that the profit from high risk growth stocks comes from growth in value. Also remember from Chapter 15 that one of the advantages of owning stock is that you pay no taxes on the gain until you sell. In other words, your stock is *already* tax-deferred. But, as you'll recall from Chapter 5, bonds generate interest, and that interest is subject to tax every year.

So put it all together: By placing the bond in the IRA, its interest is sheltered from taxes until you withdraw the money at retirement. And if you keep the stock until retirement, it too grows tax-deferred, even though it is not in an IRA.

Remember: The whole idea of an IRA is to shelter from taxes money that ordinarily is not sheltered. That's why you need to place the bond inside the IRA. Putting the growth stock inside the IRA serves no useful purpose.

And I can give you two more reasons to choose the bond instead of the stock for Tom's IRA:

• By keeping the stock outside the IRA, its profits upon sale will be taxed at capital gains tax rates. If the stock was placed inside the IRA, its earnings would be taxed upon withdrawal at ordinary income tax rates, which can be higher than capital gains rates; and

• By keeping the stock out of the IRA, any losses in value are tax deductible. This would not be the case if the losses occur inside an IRA.

Thus both profits and losses enjoy tax-favored treatment outside IRAs. Clearly, tax law is telling us to place bonds inside IRAs and keep stocks outside.[35]

Question #5
It does not matter when you contribute to your IRA, provided you do so by April 15. *True or false?*

The answer is *false*.[36]

As with all savings efforts, you should contribute to your IRA as soon as possible, but most taxpayers don't because they treat their IRA contributions as a debt, not

---

[35]Again, please note that this discussion is limited to individual stocks and bonds. Mutual funds, regardless of what kind, always are ideally suited for use both inside and outside IRAs. This is because all mutual funds are required to pay capital gains distributions annually (when they have gains to distribute, that is!). Thus, all mutual funds generate an annual tax liability, unlike individual stocks. (Mutual funds once enjoyed the same tax deferral as stocks, but the Tax Reform Act of 1986 eliminated that advantage.)

[36]Frustrated yet?

an investment. "My goodness, taxes are due April 15th — I've got to get money into my IRA by then!" is the common attitude.

I actually have seen people borrow from their credit cards in order to make their $3,000 IRA contributions. They think buying an IRA is the same as buying a sweater!

With an IRA, of course, you're not *spending* money, you're saving it. That's why you need to contribute as soon as possible. Over 30 years, assuming you earn 10% per year, you will have $72,137 *more* by opening your account on January 1 instead of April 15 of the following year. Think about it: *15 months is worth $72,137.*

Okay, now that you understand the basics of IRAs, let's look at each type one-by-one.

IRA #1: The Deductible IRA

Deductible IRAs offer two major benefits:

• You do not pay taxes on the money you contribute until you make a withdrawal; and

• any interest, dividends, or capital gains that accumulate in the plan also are tax-deferred until withdrawal.

Thus, by contributing to a Deductible IRA, you get a tax break this year. Plus, the profits grow tax-deferred, and you'll pay taxes on the account in the future.

IRA #2: The Non-Deductible IRA

Many Americans are not eligible to contribute to a Deductible IRA. For many of these people, an option is the Non-Deductible IRA. As the name suggests, contributions do not entitle you to a tax deduction.

Occasionally, I come across someone who says Form 8606 is not a problem. "I do my own taxes, and I know how to do this," they say. But that's not the point! You've got to keep track of the form for the rest of your life, which could be 40 or 50 years from now, and I'm willing to bet that sooner or later (a) you're going to forget to file the form; (b) between now and retirement you're going to lose the forms you previously filed; or (c) you're going to become ill, and your spouse will take over the chore of filing the tax return — and your spouse won't know what you know.

Keep in mind that IRA rules are less than 20 years old, and the vast majority of people who have contributed to IRA accounts are still employed. Thus, all the attention has been focused on how to get money into IRAs, not out. Stockbrokers, for example, receive heavy training on how to establish IRAs, and they are well versed on the contribution rules, procedures, and limitations. But few brokers, and fewer investors, are familiar with the withdrawal provisions. It's a time bomb waiting to explode, and it's set to go off when today's generation enters retirement.

All this raises a question: If you are not permitted to contribute to the Deductible IRA, should you contribute to the Non-Deductible IRA, assuming that you're eligible?

No.

If you cannot deduct your contribution yet make one anyway, you must file IRS Form 8606, *Nondeductible IRAs (Contributions, Distributions, and Basis)*, every year you add to or make a withdrawal from an IRA. This form tells the IRS that you already paid taxes on a portion of the money that you had contributed to the IRA.

What happens if you don't file the form, or if you file but fail to keep a record of it for the rest of your life? There is a $50 penalty for failing to file, and if you don't keep your records in order, you'll have to pay taxes when you withdraw the money — even though you already paid taxes when you contributed to the IRA years earlier. Indeed, you'll pay taxes twice on the same money!

Have You Made Non-Deductible IRA Contributions?

When IRAs were created, anyone with earned income was eligible. But the Tax Reform Act of 1986 placed limits on eligibility.

Consequently, many people who opened a deductible IRA in the early '80s continued adding to their accounts in the late '80s and into the '90s, but on a Non-Deductible basis.

Have you done this? Have you commingled Deductible and Non-Deductible IRA contributions into one account? It's a common mistake, and if you've done this, you've got a big problem: Unless you keep very good records, including IRS Form 8606 each yeaaar, you're going to be taxed on the entire account balance when you make withdrawals, even though only part of the money ought to be taxed.

The best solution is to establish two IRA accounts, one for the non-deductible contributions and one for the deductible ones. Label each account accordingly. For example, one account would read, "The IRA Account of Shirley Mason," while the other would read, "The non-deductible IRA Account of Shirley Mason." This way, it'll be easy to remember where the Non-Deductible monies are and how much you contributed on that basis. Simply place into the non-deductible account an amount equaling your total Non-Deductible contributions; leave all interest and profits in the regular IRA account. Contact your bank, broker, or financial planner handling your account for help correcting this problem.

Two Great Alternatives to the Non-Deductible IRA

Since you should not make a Non-Deductible IRA contribution, where does this leave you? Do you lose your only chance to let money grow tax-deferred?

Not at all! There are two excellent solutions to consider. To learn about the first, the Roth IRA, keep reading. As for the other, just return to our discussion on variable annuities (Chapter 28). With annuities, there's no tax deduction, but the money grows tax-deferred until withdrawal — just like a Non-Deductible IRA!

And the annuity gives you three major advantages over the Non-Deductible IRA:

- There's no limit on the amount of money you can contribute each year, unlike the IRA, which limits you to $3,000;

- you can delay withdrawals until age 90, unlike the IRA, which requires that you begin withdrawals at age 70½; and

- you don't have to deal with IRS Form 8606.

So, instead of using a Non-Deductible IRA, you should be using a Roth IRA and/or a variable annuity, where you'll have all the benefits of the Non-Deductible IRA without its hassles.

IRA #3: The Roth IRA

This is the newest IRA created by Congress, named for William Roth, then U.S. senator from Delaware who sponsored the legislation.

Like the Non-Deductible IRA, you don't get a current tax deduction when making contributions, but unlike the Deductible and Non-Deductible IRAs, withdrawals from the Roth IRA will be completely *tax-free*, provided:

> **Some people think Form 8606 is worth the hassle because they can withdraw their non-deductible contributions tax-free at retirement, but it's not true.**
>
> **Say you have $12,000 in IRA accounts, of which $2,000 was contributed on a non-deductible basis using Form 8606. If you think that at retirement you'll be able to withdraw the non-deductible money first, tax-free, you're wrong: IRS rules state that each withdrawal from an IRA must be a *pro-rata* distribution of deductible and non-deductible dollars. Thus, since $1/6^{th}$ of your IRA (2,000/12,000) is non-deductible, only $1/6^{th}$ of each withdrawal is tax-exempt. Clearly, Non-Deductible IRAs are not worth the hassle.**

- You leave the money in the account for at least five years after making the first contribution and

- You reach age 59½ (with exceptions for death or disability).

Also, unlike Deductible and Non-Deductible IRAs, both of which require you to begin making withdrawals by age 70½ and prevent further contributions after that age, the Roth IRA has neither restriction.

Congress also established a provision enabling you to convert your Deductible and Non-Deductible IRAs to a Roth IRA, provided your adjusted gross income is below $100,000. I am not covering this information here for two reasons:

- I covered this topic in great detail in my book, *The New Rules of Money*; and

- I hate this idea. Don't do it.[37]

---

[37]To learn why, go read my other book. Hint. Hint. Cough. Wheeze.

Please do not confuse my disdain for Roth Conversions with my attitude regarding the Roth IRA. Many people have misquoted my position on this, so I want to make sure this point is made: I like the Roth IRA for new contributions, and I often recommend it to my firm's clients. But I don't like the idea of converting old IRAs to the Roth. They are two very different issues, as I explain fully in *The New Rules of Money*, and there is absolutely no conflict in this advice.

One more note: Although Non-Deductible IRAs still are permitted, there's no reason to contribute to them, since the Roth IRA is basically the same thing, only better, assuming you are eligible to contribute to a Roth IRA (since withdrawals from the Roth will be tax-free while withdrawals from Non-Deductible IRAs will be taxable).

I don't know if you've been keeping score, but it seems we've got three IRAs from which to choose for your current year contributions. Which is the right one?

You'll find the answer in the special pull-out IRA chart included with this book. As you can see, the current IRA rules are enormously complex.

Let me summarize here what you'll discover in the special pull-out IRA chart:

The first place to save is in your company retirement plan — even before you consider any form of IRA. That's because most company retirement plans are far superior to IRAs, as you'll learn later in this Part. So, here's the deal:

If you *are* eligible to participate in a company retirement plan:

Do so to the maximum extent you are permitted — but only to the extent that such contributions are tax-deductible. (Do not place after-tax contributions into your company retirement plan.) Then place $3,000 into the Roth IRA (if eligible — see fold-out chart). After that, continue investing for your retirement with a variable annuity.

If you are not eligible to participate in a company retirement plan:

Invest $3,000 into a Deductible IRA. After that, continue investing for your retirement with a variable annuity.

So, as you can see, each (except, of course, the Non-Deductible IRA) has its place in the retirement planning spectrum. To summarize, here they are, presented in the order you should contribute to them:

1. your company retirement plan, provided the contributions are tax-deductible

2. a Deductible IRA

3. a Roth IRA

4. a variable annuity (covered in Chapter 28).

Two Methods You Can Use to Move Your IRAs

If you have an IRA in a bank, credit union, or S&L, I'll bet you're itching to move it by now — especially if you're like the many folks who have the bulk of their savings in IRAs.

You can move money from one IRA account to another in two ways: The first is fast but hard, the other is slow but easy.

Method #1: IRA Rollovers

The fast/hard method is a *rollover*. This occurs when you tell your IRA *custodian* (i.e., your bank, broker, or whomever is handling the account for you presently) to liquidate your account and give you a check for the proceeds. It is very important that you tell your custodian the following: "I intend to roll these funds over to another IRA account. Therefore, <u>DO NOT</u> withhold taxes." If you fail to state this (they might want you to sign a form containing this language), the custodian could withhold 20% of your account for taxes. Watch out for this trap.

When you liquidate an IRA at a bank, S&L, or credit union, be prepared for an argument, but they'll eventually comply — especially if you raise your voice in their lobby. My experience has shown that personnel at these institutions often claim that taxes must be withheld, to which you should loudly and defiantly yell, "Why won't you give me my money!?" The louder you say it, the quicker they'll cave in.[38]

When you get the money, simply deposit it into your regular checking account. You then have 60 days to "roll the money over" (hence, *rollover*) to your next IRA. If you do so within this time period, there is no tax implication of any kind.

Make sure you follow the rules perfectly. You are permitted to rollover each IRA only once every 12 calendar months (not once a year, mind you, but once every 12 months). Thus, if you have two IRA accounts, the 12-month clock on the first account does not affect the 12-month clock on the second account.

However, the 12-month clock does pertain to *all the money inside* that given IRA account. Say you have $10,000 in an IRA account and you rollover $2,000 from it to another IRA account. The remaining $8,000 cannot be rolled over for 12 months.

Don't blow this like Jeremy did. He had $150,000 in an IRA account, and via a rollover, he moved $25,000 of it to a new IRA account. Two months later, he moved the remaining $125,000 to the new account.

Bad move, said the IRS. Because only one rollover is permitted every 12 months within each IRA account, the second rollover is void. Therefore, the $125,000 was considered to be a premature distribution, and Jeremy had to pay taxes on the money.

And that's not all. Because Jeremy had rolled over the $125,000 into his new IRA — which he wasn't allowed to do — this contribution was subject to a 6% excess contributions penalty. That penalty is assessed for every year the money was in the IRA. Since it took Jeremy three years to learn all this, that penalty cost him an additional 18%. Thus, of the $125,000 he started with, Jeremy lost 49% — $61,250 — to taxes. *Yeouch!*

Thus, rollovers are *fast*, because you can do them in a day, but they're hard, because you've got to tolerate a shouting match with your bank, and you must follow the rules to avoid nasty surprises.

---

[38]Make sure the bank is filled with customers when you do this.

Method #2: IRA Transfers

The other way to move your IRA — and the one that would have enabled Jeremy to avoid his problem — is called a *transfer*. Through a transfer, you instruct your *current* IRA custodian to send your money directly to the *new* IRA custodian. You do not personally receive the money as an interim step, as you do with a rollover. Thus, there is no 12-month rule regarding transfers; you are permitted to execute them without limitation. Transfers, therefore, are very easy. You simply sign a form (given to you by your new IRA custodian) and the new custodian will do the rest. But transfers are *slow*. They often take four to six weeks to complete.

> **People often get confused between rollovers and transfers because the IRS uses the same words for different reasons.**
>
> **When you open an IRA, it is considered a *contributory* account. If you move that money to another IRA account, the new account is called a *rollover* account — and it's called a rollover account whether you move the money there via a rollover or a transfer.**
>
> **Thus, you can roll over money to a rollover account, and you can *transfer* money to a rollover account.**

The delay should not surprise you. After all, what do you think your current IRA custodian does when it receives the transfer request? Loses it, of course! In my experience, the new custodian often has to send a second request to the old custodian before the transfer occurs. So be patient when doing transfers.

Combining Contributory IRAs and Rollover IRAs

Many custodians don't like to combine contributory IRA accounts with rollover IRA accounts because regulations require custodians to track the source of all the money in the account. But from a consumer's perspective, there's no difference between the two.

Well, okay, one difference: If you move money from an employer's retirement plan to an IRA, you are permitted to move that money back to another employer's plan later — but only if the money was held in a separate rollover IRA account in the interim. If you commingle the retirement plan money with other IRA money, you lose this option. (As you'll see later in this chapter, I am unimpressed with this feature; thus, my advice is to go ahead and combine your IRAs. It'll cut your paperwork.)

Beware the Tax Trap When Moving Money from an Employer's Plan to an IRA

It's the most Orwellian law I have ever seen, and it affects every company retirement plan in the nation. Under this law, which became effective January 1, 1993, the government can force your employer to give the IRS 20% of the money in your company retirement account and then, because you didn't receive the money, make you pay taxes on it plus a 10% penalty.

The law affects you if you leave your job and are eligible to receive distributions from your company's retirement plan, such as a 401(k), 403(b), or Profit Sharing Plan (all of which we'll discuss in the next chapter).

Before this law took effect, you were allowed to request that your employer send you a check for the full value of your company's retirement account, and you had 60 days to roll the money over to an IRA account. Provided you met the 60-day rule, you would not be required to pay taxes on the distribution and the money would continue to grow tax-deferred until you made a withdrawal at retirement.

But this law changed all that. Employers now are required to withhold 20% of any rollover distribution paid directly to you, sending the 20% to the IRS.

Since 20% of your money will be withheld at the source, you have no opportunity to roll it over — and separate IRS rules say that any retirement funds you don't roll over are subject to both taxes and a 10% penalty. So, on the one hand, Congress says you can't have the money, and on the other hand, the IRS says you're going to pay taxes and penalties because you didn't roll over the money — even though the reason you didn't roll it over is because Congress wouldn't let you have it!

Here's how the law could hit you: Assume you have been with your employer for 15 years and are now separating from service (because of retirement, termination, lay-off, office relocation, etc. — the reason doesn't matter), and further assume that you have accumulated $100,000 in your employer's 401(k) plan.

If your employer sends you a check, under rules in effect since 1993, you will receive only $80,000. The rest — $20,000 — will be withheld for taxes. Since you can't rollover what you don't have, you must pay taxes on that $20,000, which is about $6,600 (assuming a 33% combined federal/state income tax bracket). Then, the IRS will penalize you another 10% — $2,000 — if you are under age 59½, for a total of $8,600!

Two Ways to Avoid the Tax

Here are two ways to solve the problem:

Solution #1: Use Other Savings

Take $20,000 from other savings, add it to the $80,000 your employer gave you, and roll over the full $100,000 into an IRA. Then, when you file your tax return in April, acknowledge the fact that your employer withheld $20,000 from your distribution, and you'll get it back as a tax refund.

There are three problems with this solution: First, most folks don't have $20,000 lying around to replace what the employer withheld. Second, you've got to wait until next April to get your money back (depending on what month you leave work, you could wait nearly a year). And three, most folks don't know they can do this.

Solution #2: Do a Transfer

Transfers, rather than *rollovers*, are not subject to withholding requirements. Thus, instead of having your employer send the money to you, withholding 20%, instruct your employer to send the money directly to your IRA account. The IRS also allows you to receive the check from your former employer provided the check is made payable to your IRA custodian. Either method will avoid the 20% withholding requirement.

If you are changing jobs, the law also lets you demand that your old employer send your money directly to your new employer for deposit into the new employer's retirement plan. Unfortunately, the law does not require that your new employer accept the money.[39]

---

[39]Don't ask.

MOVING MONEY FROM AN EMPLOYER PLAN TO AN IRA

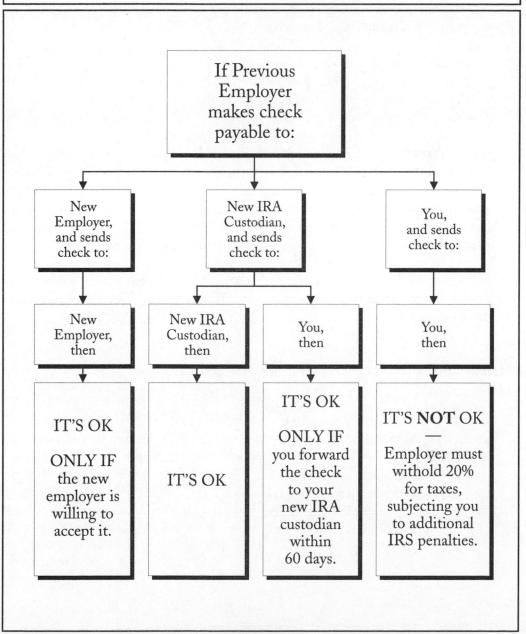

FIGURE 10-3

Although it might seem that the transfer rules effectively avoid the new withholding requirement, this law nonetheless is creating havoc on millions of Americans for these reasons:

- The law has received little publicity. Most workers are unfamiliar with the rules and therefore do not know they should do transfers instead of rollovers. And since the request usually must be made prior to leaving the company, and is irrevocable, many find out too late.

- Leaving your job is traumatic, especially during a forced layoff. If you are losing your job, how you handle your rollover seems like a trivial detail. After all, many displaced workers worry more about how they are going to eat rather than how they are going to invest.

For both these reasons, many workers lose significant amounts of money to this forced tax — meaning that this law is hurting most the group who can afford it least: the newly unemployed. The biggest irony is that for all its mandated withholding, the law does not raise any new revenue. It merely accelerates the receipt of taxes that the IRS would have collected in the future anyway from workers who received but did not roll over their company retirement plan assets.

This situation demonstrates Congress' penchant for solving today's problems at the expense of tomorrow and is all too fine an example of how **The Rules of Money Have Changed**.

Give Yourself a Short-Term Loan from Your IRA — Tax-Free

You can liquidate money from your IRA account and use it without tax consequences provided you put the money back into an IRA account within 60 days. I don't recommend this, but the strategy might come in handy if you have a temporary cash flow problem and you need to get your hands on some money for a short time. This is why the IRS lets you do this only once every 12 months. Remember also that even though there are no fees from the IRS, liquidating the investment might cause you to incur other costs.

Withdrawing Money from Your IRA

A few years ago, my wife Jean excitedly ran into the house and shouted, "There's a mouse in my car!"

That's ridiculous, I thought. After all, she never actually saw the mouse. But she had hard evidence (if you know what I mean) that it was there. My first question, to no one in particular: How on earth does a mouse get into your car?

As I soon discovered, that was the wrong question. What I should have asked was: How on earth do you get a mouse *out* of your car?

This concept also applies to IRAs. Everyone in my industry focuses on getting consumers to invest in IRAs. All the brokerage firms and banks, all the mutual fund companies, all the financial magazines, and talk shows — they all do the same thing: They show you how wonderful IRAs are, and encourage you to send in your money.

What they don't typically tell you is how to get the money *out*.

And that is certainly something you're eventually going to want to do. Therefore, we need to talk about IRA withdrawals, because if you thought there were a lot of rules regarding contributions, wait until you get to *distribution*. You ain't seen nothin' yet.

To start, let's visit Goldilocks.

The Goldilocks Rules

If you want to make a withdrawal from your IRA, you've got to be very careful. In fact, like Goldilocks, you must do it *just right*.

Goldilocks, you'll recall, was unhappy until she found a bowl of porridge that was *just right* — not too hot or too cold — and a bed that was *just right* — not too hard or too soft — and you, too, must make sure you handle your IRA distributions *just right*. Specifically, you must avoid withdrawing money too early, too late, or too little.

Goldilocks Penalty #1: Too Early

If you withdraw money prior to age 59½, you'll be subject to a "premature distributions" penalty of 10%. That's in addition to the regular income tax (both federal and state).

If you withdraw money from the Roth IRA prior to age 59½ (or before five years have elapsed since your first contribution, whichever is longer), the penalty issue is extremely complex, and not worth covering here. Make sure you see a tax expert if you plan to withdraw money from a Roth IRA prematurely ('nuf said).

How to Beat the 10% Penalty on Early Withdrawals

While you can't avoid owing the income tax when you make a withdrawal from your Deductible or Non-Deductible IRA, you can avoid the 10% penalty — if you receive the proceeds in the form of *Substantially Equal Periodic Payments*.

Under SEPP rules, withdrawals must be made at regular intervals over a period of not less than five years or until you reach 59½, whichever is later. For example, someone starting SEPP withdrawals at age 40 must continue to do so until age 59½, while a 57-year-old must do so until age 62.

While SEPP won't help much if you need all the money right away, it could help if you simply need a steady income stream.

Goldilocks Penalty #2: Too Late

For all IRAs except the Roth, you must begin to withdraw money by April 1 of the year following the year in which you turn 70½.

For example, say you reach age 70 on July 10, 2004. That means you are 70½ on January 10, 2005, so you must make a withdrawal from your IRA by April 1, 2006, and by each December 31 thereafter.[40]

---

[40]If you wait until April 1, 2006 to make the distribution that was required for 2005, you'll have to make two distributions in 2006 — one for 2005 (due April 1, 2006) and one for 2006 (due December 31, 2006).

If you fail to make the withdrawal, you will pay a 50% penalty (yes, 50%!) on the amount you were supposed to withdraw but didn't. And that's in addition to the regular tax.

One Hapless Family

If you're trying to imagine what might happen if you fall victim to these rules, consider the plight of Dr. Gabler's family.

Dr. Gabler practiced medicine for 47 years, and like many physicians he was able to accumulate substantial amounts of money in his retirement accounts. At his death early in 2003 at age 82, his IRAs and other retirement accounts[41] were worth $3 million. He also owned two homes and other assets of sizable wealth, which he left to his children, but he chose to name as beneficiary his 12 grandchildren for their future college educations.

It was a few months after Dr. Gabler died that one of his daughters, Judith, came to see me. She had just seen the accountant handling the estate tax return, and she wasn't happy.

You see, Dr. Gabler's IRA is considered part of his estate, making it subject to a 48% federal estate tax (see Chapter 64). Cost:($810,000)

Dr. Gabler also made the unfortunate decision of leaving his IRA directly to his grandchildren. Therefore, his estate must pay a 48% Generation Skipping Tax. There is, however, a deduction for the estate taxes already paid. Cost: $331,200.

And, of course, money distributed from an IRA is taxable at both the federal and state levels as ordinary income. Although there are some adjustments for the above deductions, the tax nonetheless is at the 43% combined marginal federal/state bracket. Cost: $741,234.

---

[41]The Goldilocks rules pertain to the total value of all your retirement accounts, not just IRAs.

The result is shown below.

Gross Value of IRA:	**$3,000,000**
Less Estate Tax	(810,000)
Less Generation Skipping Tax	(331,200)
Less Income Taxes	(741,234)
Net After-Tax Value to Heirs	**$1,117,556**
Split Among 12 Grandchildren	**$93,130**

I think you see why Judith was so unhappy.

The Perils of Bad Tax Advice

And I didn't improve her mood. Because her father had already died, virtually nothing could be done to avoid the huge taxes his estate was incurring. As we'll learn in Part XII, proper estate planning could have avoided almost all of this cost, but planning must be done before death occurs. Once a person dies, it's almost always too late, as it was in this case.

The irony is that Dr. Gabler's tax preparer probably made the situation worse. People who hire accountants tend to give them one mission — lower my taxes! — and Dr. Gabler was probably no different. So, when he turned 71 and his accountant said he needed to start making withdrawals from his IRA, Dr. Gabler withdrew only the minimum. After all, he had plenty of money from other sources, and he didn't need income from the money in his IRA. And since any money he withdrew from it would be taxed, it made sense to him to keep those withdrawals to a minimum.

And since the accountant knew he needed to keep Dr. Gabler's taxes low or face his client's wrath — and maybe even lose the client's business — he didn't make a fuss when Dr. Gabler insisted on withdrawing only the minimum.

Unfortunately, by withdrawing only the minimum each year, the IRA continued to grow in value — so much so, that by the time Dr. Gabler died, the account was worth $2 million, resulting in the problem you saw above.

Thus, because he wanted to keep his income taxes low each year, Dr. Gabler's estate eventually had to pay a federal estate tax and a generation skipping tax — on top of the income taxes he so desperately wanted to avoid. Remember: When it comes to taxes, you can defer and delay, rarely avoid.

Indeed, Dr. Gabler was penny-wise and pound-foolish. By keeping his current taxes low, he allowed his future taxes to soar. And because many tax preparers have tunnel vision — seeing only this year's tax return instead of their client's complete, long-term tax picture — they often fail to provide the guidance and counsel their clients need. Avoid this trap. Be careful when making financial decisions, for good short-term moves often can be very bad in the long term.

Goldilocks Penalty #3: Too Little

This is directly related to Goldilocks Penalty #2. Whereas #2 forces you to begin making withdrawals by age 70½, #3 applies if you fail to withdraw *enough*.

I'm talking about something called *required minimum distributions*. To determine this figure, the IRS offers a formula.

The distributions are intended to last your entire lifetime. However, you can base them on your life expectancy, or the combined life expectancies of you and your beneficiary (typically your spouse).

To help you determine how long you and your beneficiary are supposed to live, use the IRS' Uniform Distribution Table (or the Joint and Last Survivor Table when your spouse is your sole beneficiary and is more than ten years younger than you).

Once you know your life expectancy, figuring out how much money to take from your bucket seems simple enough. For example, if you have $198,000 in your IRA and your life expectancy is 22 years, simply divide the $198,000 by 22, and withdraw $9,000 the first year. But this ignores the fact that your IRA is continuing to grow in value, and if you don't take this into consideration, you might find that you have failed to withdraw enough money.

One year from now, your life expectancy will be less than it is right now. Therefore, you must recalculate the amount that you withdraw each year, based on each year's current life expectancy plus the value of your account as of December 31st. Assume that it is one year later and on the previous December 31st, your account is worth $212,000. Your new life expectancy is 21.2, so you must withdraw $10,000 next year.

Chapter 68 - Company Retirement Plans

As we discussed at the beginning of the last chapter, all retirement plans — whether individual or company-sponsored — offer two major benefits:

- You do not pay taxes on any of the money that is contributed to the plan until you begin withdrawals, and

- Any interest, dividends, or capital gains that accumulate in the plan are tax-deferred until withdrawal.

We've examined individual retirement arrangements. Now let's look at the different kinds of plans offered by companies for their employees.

Retirement Plans for the Self-employed

Do you have any self-employment income? If not, skip this section. But if you are in business for yourself — even if only part-time — keep reading.

If you have any self-employment income, from baby-sitting to shooting wedding videos, you may be able to set aside some of your income into a tax-deductible retirement plan. Here are the choices available to you:

The Simplified Employee Pension Plan

Known as a SEP-IRA, this is as easy to use as IRAs (and almost identical as well). But SEPs offer one major advantage over IRAs: Instead of being limited to a $3,000 annual deductible contribution, you can put away 25% of your self-employment income, up to $40,000. You are permitted to do this even if you or your spouse participates in another pension or retirement plan.

SEPs involve minimal disclosure and reporting requirements. You can contribute different amounts from year to year, and you can wait until April 15 to contribute for the previous year (or later if you file an extension). Other plans must be established by December 31.

Some companies offer a retirement plan called a *Money Purchase Plan*. It works like the Employer's Basic Contribution to a 401(k): Deposits come from the employer, must be the same every year, and employees are not permitted to add money from their own paychecks.

Other companies offer a *Profit-Sharing Plan*, which is the same as the 401(k)'s Profit-Sharing contribution. The money comes from the employer, but the amount of the contribution can vary year to year. Again, employees are not permitted to contribute themselves.

Still other employers offer what's known as the paired-plan system, which is a combination of the two.

When 25% Equals 20%

Although the law says you can place up to 25% of your net taxable income into a SEP-IRA, the correct figure is really 20%. Here's why:

Say your net self-employment income (that's your profit minus expenses) is $10,000. Twenty-five percent would be $2,500, which you'd place into a SEP-IRA. But that would reduce your net taxable income to $7,500[42] — and $2,500 of $7,500 is 33% — meaning you've contributed too much to the SEP, leading to major headaches with the IRS.

Thus, the correct amount you would be permitted to place into your SEP would be $2,000, which is only 20% of $10,000.

Clear as mud, huh?

Consider a SIMPLE Plan (though it's not so simple)

The SIMPLE (Savings Incentive Match Plans for Employees) works if you don't have another qualified retirement plan. The maximum contribution for 2004 is $9,000; if you are 50 or older, you can contribute an additional $1,500.

If you have employees, you are required to contribute 2% of each employee's compensation if they don't participate. If they do contribute, you must match dollar-for-dollar, up to 3% of each employee's compensation.

---

[42]Contributions to a SEP reduce your net taxable income because SEP contributions are considered to be a normal business expense, and like all normal expenses, are deductible from your business's gross revenue.

The Sole-owner 401(k) Plan

This is the newest retirement planning idea to come from Congress, and it's designed for you and your spouse, whether your business is a sole proprietorship or a corporation. As an employee of your business, you can contribute up to $13,000 in 2004 ($16,000 if you are 50 or over). And as the employer, you can boost that figure to 25% of compensation, not to exceed $40,000.

Since you are both employee and employer, and since these contributions limits change yearly, you should seek the help of a tax advisor to help you determine the maximum contribution you can make to a solo 401(k) plan.

401(k) Plans — The Grandest of All Retirement Plans

The 401(k) plan — so-named by the tax code section that created it — is offered by more companies than any other type of retirement plan, so if your company offers a plan, it's likely to be this one. If so, you need to understand how it works.

The Four Contribution Methods of 401(k) Plans

Method #1: The Employer's Basic Contribution

This contribution usually is a percentage of payroll.

Ken, 45, makes $40,000 a year and his company contributes 1% of his pay to the 401(k) plan every year. Although the money is Ken's, he is not taxed on it, and the money grows tax-deferred inside the plan.

Method #2: The Employee's Voluntary Contribution

Depending on where you work, you may be permitted to contribute up to $13,000 in 2004 ($16,000 if you are 50 or older).

Ken is allowed to invest up to 5% of his paycheck into the 401(k) plan. He gets a tax deduction for the amount he contributes, and like the employer's contribution above, this money grows tax-deferred.

Method #3: The Employer's Matching Contributions

Through this method, the company contributes a percentage of what the employee contributes.

Ken's company adds 25 cents to the plan for every dollar that Ken puts in himself. This increases Ken's stake by 25%, yet he is not taxed on this money, and it too grows tax-deferred until he retires.

Method #4: The Employer's Profit-sharing Contribution

This is an additional contribution that the company voluntarily makes each year based on the firm's profits.

Ken's company typically gives Ken a bonus equal to 3% of his pay, which is deposited into the plan on Ken's behalf. Like the other contributions, this one too is not taxed and it grows tax-deferred.

Thus, of the four ways money goes into a 401(k), only one comes from the employee — making these plans a great deal for workers!

All told, Ken contributes $2,000 of his own pay to the 401(k), a contribution that costs him only $1,340 because the contribution entitles Ken to a tax deduction that saves him $660 in taxes. On top of that, Ken's employer adds another $2,100 — $400 in basic, $500 in matching, and $1,200 in profit-sharing contributions — and all of it is in pre-tax dollars, which grow tax-deferred. Thus, for every dollar Ken contributes to his 401(k), his employer contributes $1.05. Put another way, for a $1,340 investment, Ken's account is worth $4,100 — and that's before his account earns a penny from interest, dividends, or capital gains!

Without question, the 401(k) plan is indeed the grandest of all retirement plans!

Where to Invest Your 401(k) Money

In most 401(k) plans, each employee must decide where to invest his or her money, and employees usually can choose from four or five options. The most common choices are:

•   a fixed account (equivalent to a CD or money market account)

- a bond mutual fund

- a balanced mutual fund

- a U.S. stock mutual fund

- shares of the employer's stock

Given these choices, which of the following is the best way to invest your 401(k)?

a) Invest 100% in the fixed account.

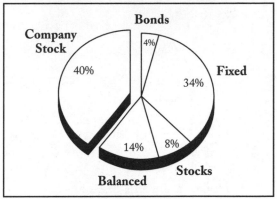

HOW EMPLOYEES INVEST THEIR 401(k)

FIGURE 10-4

b) Invest 100% of your contri-bution in the fixed account and 100% of *your employer's* contributions in the stock fund.

c) Invest 100% in the stock fund.

d) Invest 100% in shares of the employer's stock.

e) Invest 20% in each of the five choices (or 100% in the balanced fund) so that you are highly diversified.

Which answer did you choose?

The worst choice is (a), yet 34% of all the money in 401(k) plans nationwide is invested there. People choose fixed accounts because, not understanding how money works, they have an excessive fear of losing money. But you know better (having read Part VI).

Likewise, (b) and (e) are the wrong choices, too, for they both involve fixed assets. If this seems to contradict my earlier discussion on diversification, you're right: It does. That's because *you must handle your company retirement plan differently from the way you handle all your other money.*

To understand why, answer these questions:

1. How often are you paid? (*At regular intervals, right?*)

2. Does that ever change? (*Nah.*)

3. Is the amount of your paycheck the same each time?
    (*For most workers, yes.*)

4. Is the amount deducted from your paycheck for the 401(k)
    the same each time? (*Yes.*)

Have you figured it out yet? Your paycheck comes at regular intervals and, at each interval, you contribute the same amount of money. What does this sound like?

Dollar cost averaging, of course.

And as we learned in Chapter 46, dollar cost averaging works best with stock mutual funds. Therefore, the correct answer is (c): You should place 100% of your 401(k) contributions into the most volatile stock fund available in your plan.[43]

Two More Reasons Why (c) Is the Best Choice

If dollar cost averaging is not enough to convince you, here are two more reasons to choose (c):

Reason #1: Most of Your 401(k) is Free Money, So Treat it That Way

If your employer contributes to your 401(k) on your behalf, as Ken's does, you've got a profit even before your money is invested! In Ken's case, the stock market could drop by 56%, and the amount he contributed — $2,000 — still would be intact. So shed your fears about "losing money." It's not "yours" you lose.

Reason #2:   Even a Total Loss Wouldn't be So Bad

Say Ken allocates 100% to the stock fund and, two days after payday, the stock market crashes. So what?

---

[43]Hah! I bet you thought the answer would be "it depends." Not this time. But for the one exception and two cautions that you'll soon discover, everyone should always place 100% of their retirement plan allocations into the stock fund all the time. This strategy is as smart as it is shocking.

Think about it: Ken, age 45, is paid twice a month, or 24 times per year. Assuming he retires at 65, he'll get 480 paychecks over the rest of his career. If the market crashes this week, destroying the value of this week's contribution, so what? Ken's got 479 contributions to go. And all of them will be made *after* the market drop has occurred, giving Ken the chance to buy at new low prices. This is dollar cost averaging at its best!

One Exception and Two Cautions About Selecting (c)

They say exceptions prove every rule. So be it. Here are three pieces of fine print to consider before you implement this strategy:

The Exception: If You Plan to Withdraw the Money Within the Next Few Years

Dollar cost averaging needs time to be successful. If you're planning to withdraw the funds within four or five years, this strategy is not appropriate. Choice (e) would be a smarter idea.

Caution #1: Do Not Transfer into the Stock Fund all the Money Currently in Your Plan's Account

That's not dollar cost averaging — that's lump-sum investing. And the proper way to invest lump sums, as we discussed in Chapter 44, is to diversify. So, *existing assets* should be invested according to choice (e), and 100% of all *future contributions* should be invested according to choice (c).

Caution #2: Make Sure You Choose the Diversified Stock Fund

Do not choose (d): Do not invest in shares of your employer's stock, regardless of how successful your company is or how successful you expect it to be.

The reason is this: If you suddenly were in need of money, you might have to turn to the money in your retirement plan. But the reason you might need money is because you lost your job. And maybe you've lost your job because the company went broke. The experiences of workers at Enron and WorldCom, among others, should convince you of the dangers of buying company stock. As many employees at these companies discovered, your retirement plan could be worthless — at the very time you need it most.

Therefore, I always advise employees to sell company stock. It's not because I don't like your company; it's simply a matter of diversification. Remember, in your efforts to achieve financial success, you have only two weapons: Your money and your time. Don't invest both in the same place.

> **If your employer lets you buy company stock at a 15% discount — many do — buy as much as it will allow and sell it all the very next day. You'll have a 15% profit literally overnight. Not bad for a day on Wall Street. If you could do that every day, your annual rate of return would be 5,475%!**

Retirement Plans for Employees of Non-Profit Organizations

If you work for a hospital, school, or other non-profit organization, you may be eligible to participate in a 403(b) plan, also known as a *Tax-Sheltered Annuity* or *Tax-Deferred Annuity*.

403(b) plans are the non-profit version of 401(k) plans and, therefore, the strategy for a 403(b) is the same as for a 401(k). But there are a few differences between the plans themselves:

* 403(b) plan contributions may be placed only into mutual funds or annuities;

* Profit-sharing is not permitted, since you work for a non-profit organization;

SALLY FORTH   HOWARD & MACINTOSH

Reprinted with special permission of King Features Syndicate.

- You can participate in a 403(b) plan even if other employees do not (unlike 401(k)s, which require participation by a majority of employees); and

- Contributions made into 403(b) plans prior to 1987 do not have to be withdrawn beginning at age 70½. Only contributions and earnings that occur after 1986 are subject to the age 70½ minimum withdrawal rules, and any money you withdraw in excess of the minimum requirements permanently reduce the pre-'87 account balance.

The Cost of Not Participating in Your Retirement Plan

If you are 30 years old, and

- You contribute $3,000 per year to your retirement plan for the next 35 years, and

- Your account earns 8% per year,

Then, at age 65, your account will be worth $516,950.

But if you delay your participation just one year, beginning instead at age 31, your account will be worth only $475,880 — a loss of $41,070!

If your employer matches as little as 25 cents on the dollar, your total loss would be $51,338!

And if you earn 10% and if your employer matches 50 cents on the dollar, your loss would be $114,965!

Yet despite the power of early and consistent savings, only 75% of eligible employees in the U.S. participate in their company retirement plans.

You need to participate in your retirement plan as soon as your employer permits and to the maximum extent you're allowed. It's the best place to save for the future. And you might as well participate: Depending on your income and marital status, being *eligible* to participate in a company retirement plan (whether or not you do participate) makes you unable to deduct a contribution to your IRA. So you might as well join your employer plan. For many workers, it's that or nothing.

Chapter 69 - Social Security

Will Social Security exist when you retire?

When I ask that question in my seminars, those over age 45 say yes and those under 45 say no. As a planner, I believe Social Security will continue in some form, if only due to political pressure, but I make no predictions about what the benefit levels will be or how old you'll have to be to receive them.

Under current law, the maximum Social Security retirement benefit for a worker and spouse who retired in 2003 was $31,338 per year. Therefore, even if Social Security continues as is, it alone is not likely to provide you with a comfortable retirement.

The current age to be eligible for full Social Security benefits is shown in Figure 10-5, those born after 1959 are not eligible for full Social Security benefits until age 67. (They can start receiving benefits at 62, but they will get 30% less than if they wait until 67.

SOCIAL SECURITY

The Age You're Eligible for Full Social Security Benefits

Year of Birth	Years	Months
before 1938	65	0
1938	65	2
1939	65	4
1940	65	6
1941	65	8
1942	65	10
1943-1954	66	0
1955	66	2
1956	66	4
1957	66	6
1958	66	8
1959	66	10
1960 and after	67	0

FIGURE 10-5

Social Security at 62 or 65?

If you're a near-retiree, you can start receiving Social Security at age 62, although you will receive throughout your lifetime less than 80% of what you would have received had you waited until your full retirement age. So, which is the right choice: Start at 62 with 80% of benefits, or wait in order to receive 100%?

The answer: It depends[44] — on whether you will stop working at 62. If you are

[44]Here we go again.

planning to cease receiving *earned income* (as opposed to investment income), go ahead and start collecting Social Security at 62 — for as Figure 10-6 shows, you'll be better off for the next 14 years. If you live beyond age 75, you'll wish you had waited until after your 65th birthday to begin receiving benefits, but we don't know if you'll live that long! So, since you're here now, take the money and run.

> *"The rich get richer and the poor get jobs."*
> —Anonymous

But maybe you're 62 and you don't need the money. So you figure you might as well delay collecting Social Security benefits, to get the higher income at a later time.

Wrong move.

If you start taking benefits at 62 and invest that monthly check, the interest you'll earn on that money over the next three years will more than off-set the fact that you're receiving a smaller amount by not having waited. In fact, the interest can be so worthwhile that the person who delays collecting Social Security may never catch up. So, when you turn 62, take the money and run.

If, however, you plan to continue working, wait until you stop working, or until you reach full retirement age, before you begin receiving Social Security. The reason: Retirees who have not reached full retirement age lose one dollar in Social Security benefits for every two they earn over $11,520 in 2003.

> **You get *earned income* from a job or business. *Investment income* comes from interest and dividends.**

SALLY FORTH HOWARD & MACINTOSH

Reprinted with special permission of King Features Syndicate.

TAKING SOCIAL SECURITY AT 62 IS BETTER THAN WAITING UNTIL 66

Starting at 62

Age	Amount	Amount Received
62	$9,600	$9,600
63	$9,984	$19,584
64	$10,383	$29,967
65	$10,799	$40,766
66	$11,231	$51,997
67	$11,680	$63,677
68	$12,147	$75,824
69	$12,633	$88,457
70	$13,138	$101,595
71	$13,664	$115,259
72	$14,210	$129,469
73	$14,779	$144,248
74	$15,370	**$159,618**

Starting at 66

Age	Amount	Amount Received
62	$0	$0
63	$0	$0
64	$0	$0
65	$0	$0
66	$13,500	$13,500
67	$14,040	$27,540
68	$14,602	$42,142
69	$15,186	$57,328
70	$15,793	$73,121
71	$16,425	$89,546
72	$17,082	$106,628
73	$17,765	$124,393
74	$18,476	$142,869
75	$19,215	**$162,084**

It takes 14 years to catch up! Will you live that long?

FIGURE 10-6

Chapter 70 - Why Retirement Plans Are Not Enough

As outstanding as pensions and retirement plans are, they are not enough to satisfy your retirement income needs. Yet many workers who are covered by these programs often have terrible personal savings records. Many are in for a shock when they discover at retirement that their retirement income is a fraction of their pre-retirement pay.

For example, workers earning $50,000 a year, who plan to retire with nothing but a pension and Social Security, can expect their income to drop 36% the day they retire. That's right: They'll get pensions worth only 44% of pre-retirement pay and Social Security will provide only another 20%.

Could you afford a 36% pay cut right now? If you can't, what makes you think you'll be able to afford such a large cut at retirement? Remember "43,800" from page 11!

It's even worse for higher paid workers. If your final pay is $150,000, pensions and Social Security together will replace only 36% of your income. You'll lose a whopping 61% of your income when you retire!

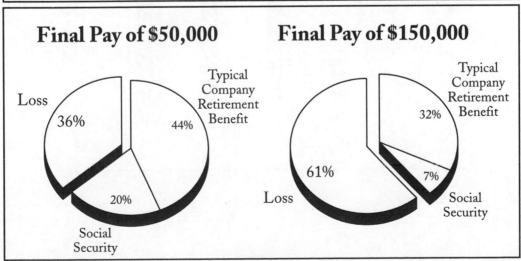

HOW MUCH INCOME WILL YOU LOSE AT RETIREMENT?

FIGURE 10-7

If you're thinking that's not a problem for you because you don't earn anywhere near $100,000, think again: If you and your spouse jointly earn $50,000 today, a mere 4% annual pay increase over the next 20 years will place your income above $100,000. So, as important as it is that you participate in your company retirement plan, you need to save even more.

YOU WILL CONTINUE TO EARN MORE AND MORE MONEY

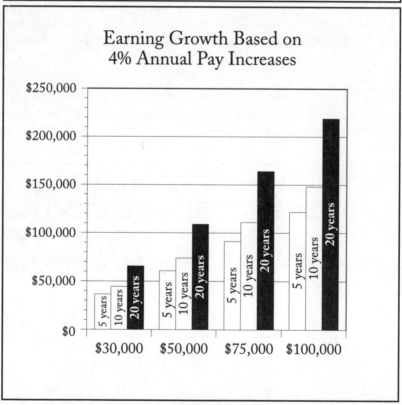

FIGURE 10-8

Chapter 71 - Women and Retirement

Retirement planning is a critical issue for many women. Although the majority of adult women are married, 85% die alone — unmarried, widowed, or divorced. Also, older women generally have worked fewer years and earned less money than men.

The result, according to the Social Security Administration, is that only 37% of women over 62 receive Social Security benefits based solely on their own work records, and these women receive on average only 76% as much as men. In fact, 63% of all women over 62 qualify for higher Social Security benefits as the *wife* of a worker rather than as a worker themselves. Indeed, the Older Women's League reports that the total median annual income for women 65 and older is 43% less than the median income for men of similar ages.

While this trend may change over the next 40 years as women in today's younger generation achieve more economic parity with men, it is undeniable that many older female Americans face a difficult situation. In fact, in 1988, Social Security accounted for more than 90% of the total income for one third of older unmarried women.

The problem extends beyond Social Security, too: Since women tend to spend more years outside the workforce (raising families and maintaining the household), and since they tend to earn less when they do work, according to the U.S. Census Bureau, they qualify for pensions only half as often as men do.

Similar statistics are found in their rates of personal savings: Retirement-age women have half the amount of personal savings as men their age.

Perhaps the most telling statistic is cited by the American Association for Retired Persons: Although only 12% of all elderly people live in poverty, 74% of them are women.

Clearly, women who ignore retirement planning do so at their own peril, so if you're a woman and you didn't pay much attention to this page, read it again. And if you're a man, you need to share this page with your mother, your wife, and your daughters.

ric's money quiz

Here's a chance to see how well you learned the information contained in Part X – Retirement Planning. Don't worry if you get stumped — just re-read this part until it sinks in. Remember, your financial future depends on it.

The answers are at the end of the quiz. No peeking!

1. **IRA stands for:**

   - ○ a. Individual Retirement Account
   - ○ b. Individual Retirement Arrangement
   - ○ c. Individual Retirement Assistance
   - ○ d. Individual Retirement Assets

2. **When contributing to a company retirement plan, ____ of your money should be invested in the stock mutual fund.**

   - ○ a. 100%
   - ○ b. 75%
   - ○ c. 50%
   - ○ d. 25%

3. **The maximum annual income a worker and spouse who retired in 2003 can receive from Social Security is about:**

   - ○ a. $24,000
   - ○ b. $31,000
   - ○ c. $44,000
   - ○ d. $54,000

4. **Which of the following is *not* true about annuities:**

   - ○ a. the money grows tax-deferred until you withdraw it
   - ○ b. there's no limit to the amount you can contribute each year
   - ○ c. you can delay withdrawals until age 90
   - ○ d. you must file IRS form 8606

5. **Regarding withdrawals from your IRA account, there are penalties if you:**

   I. withdraw money at too young an age
   II. don't begin making withdrawals by a certain age
   III. withdraw too little in a given year
   IV. withdraw too much in a given year

   - ○ a. I only
   - ○ b. I and II
   - ○ c. I, II, and III
   - ○ d. I, II, III, and IV

6. If you liquidate an IRA, you have _____ to roll the money over to another IRA without incurring a tax liability.

   ○ a. 30 days
   ○ b. 60 days
   ○ c. 90 days
   ○ d. 6 months

7. If you fail to make a withdrawal from your IRA after you turn age 70½, you must pay a _____ penalty on the amount you were supposed to withdraw, in addition to regular income taxes.

   ○ a. 10%
   ○ b. 15%
   ○ c. 25%
   ○ d. 50%

8. Whether or not you can deduct a $3,000 IRA contribution is based on:

   ○ a. your marital status
   ○ b. your income
   ○ c. whether or not you or your spouse are eligible to participate in a retirement plan at work
   ○ d. all of the above

9. If a 30-year-old contributes $2,000 per year to his retirement plan for 35 years, and the account earns just 8% per year, his account will be worth $344,633 by age 65. If he delays his participation just one year, however, how much *less* will his account be worth at retirement?

   ○ a. $2,160
   ○ b. $3,475
   ○ c. $15,643
   ○ d. $27,380

10. A person who earns $50,000 and is retiring this year, who plans to rely on the typical company pension plus Social Security, can expect to see his income cut by:

   ○ a. 5%
   ○ b. 15%
   ○ c. 25%
   ○ d. 36%

Answers: 1-b (pg.464)   3-b (pg.494)   5-c (pg.480)   7-d (pg.481)   9-d (pg.493)
          2-a (pg.490)   4-d (pg.468)   6-b (pg.473)   8-d (foldout) 10-d (pg.497)
                                                        IRA chart)

Part XI
Insurance

There's a quiz at the end of this part!

To see how much you already know, skip to the
end of this part and take the quiz now. Then, read
the part and take the quiz again. You'll discover
how much you've learned!

Part XI – Insurance

Overview - How to Manage Risk

Forget what you know, or what you think you know, about insurance. Ignore what you've heard from insurance agents and put aside your biases. In this part, I'm going to tell you the truth about insurance and its proper role in a financial plan.

No matter what you've been told, no matter what you think, there is one purpose — and only one purpose — for insurance: To protect against a financial loss. The key word is *financial*, for we are not protecting against *losses* themselves.

As a financial planner, I can't protect you from suffering a loss, but I can prevent you from suffering *financially* as a result of incurring a loss. For example, I can't prevent you from getting in a car accident, but I can prevent you from losing money as a result of it.

Thus, insurance protects us from the adverse economic impact caused by a loss. If there is no financial loss, there is no need to protect against it financially.

Have You Insured Your Shoes?

I'll bet not, because if you lose them, you'll just buy another pair. You don't need to insure your shoes because losing them would not present a significant financial loss.

But your house is another matter. Losing *that* certainly would constitute a major financial loss. That means we've got to figure out a way to manage the risk that you might lose your house. Financial professionals often refer to insurance, therefore, as *risk management*.

> **Indeed, anybody who offers to conduct a "risk management analysis" for you is often nothing more than an insurance salesperson.**

Four Ways to Manage Risk

Financial losses can occur if you die; are injured; become sick; if your property is damaged, destroyed, or stolen; or if you get sued. We must protect ourselves financially in case any of these events occurs. In other words, we must manage these risks, and there are four ways to do so.

To illustrate, say you need to get a package across town, but you fear the dangers of highway traffic. You could:

1) **Avoid risk.** Refuse to drive. But then the package does not get delivered.

2) **Accept risk.** Driving a car is dangerous, but you accept the risk in order to deliver your package.

3) **Reduce risk.** Drive carefully and wear a seatbelt.

4) **Transfer risk.** Have someone else deliver the package for you.

To apply these four management techniques against, say, the financial consequences of having your house burn down, you can:

1) Refuse to buy a house in the first place (*risk avoidance*).

2) Buy the house and ignore the problem or hope it never happens (*risk acceptance*).

3) Install smoke detectors and fire extinguishers throughout the home to help you to discover and extinguish the flames before major damage occurs (risk reduction).

4) Force someone else to pay for the loss if the fire occurs (*risk transference*).

The last strategy is what insurance is all about.

Chapter 72 - Protecting Your Largest Financial Asset

Your largest asset is not your house, your health, or your company pension.

For almost everyone who is still working, your largest asset is *your ability to produce an income.* Thus, the most important type of insurance is *disability income insurance* (DI). You need it more than any other kind of insurance — more than life, health, homeowners, or auto insurance. In fact, in my firm's planning practice, we typically are far more concerned that our clients own disability coverage than life coverage.

Although everybody who earns a living needs disability insurance, according to a survey by the Consumer Federation of America, 82% of American workers don't have long-term disability coverage or believe that what they have is inadequate.

There are two reasons why:

Reason #1: "It won't happen to me"

I bet you think "bad stuff" only happens to the other guy. Well, to the other guy, you're the other guy. Consider this: 48% of all mortgage foreclosures in this country are caused by disability. When somebody gets injured or ill, they can't work. They then lose their job and thus their income. With no income, they can't make their mortgage payment and the bank forecloses. If you thought people lose their homes because they're deadbeats, alcohol or drug abusers, criminals, or compulsive gamblers, think again. They're good, honest people who merely suffer a disability.

Although only 18% of workers believe they have adequate DI coverage, virtually all home-owners have insurance on their homes. I'll bet you do, too. Yet has any house on your street ever burned down? Unlikely, because the odds of that happening are only one in 1,200.

Yet your odds of suffering a disability before age 65, one that lasts 90 days or more, is an incredible 1 in 8. So if you think it won't happen to you, maybe — just maybe — it might.

In fact, as Figure 11-1 shows, actuaries can predict with remarkable accuracy the probability that a disability will occur. For example, someone who is age 45,

ODDS OF DISABILITY

Death vs. Disability
Prior to Age 65

Age	Death	Disability
25	24.1%	34.8%
30	23.5%	33.1%
35	22.8%	31.3%
40	21.8%	29.1%
45	20.4%	26.3%
50	18.3%	22.6%
55	14.9%	17.6%
60	9.3%	10.6%

FIGURE 11-1

THE AIR BAG PHENOMENON

Chance of Occurrences
Among Men and Women
Ages 45–65

Condition	Resulting in Death	Resulting in Disability
Hypertension	-73%	+70%
Heart Disease	-29%	+44%
Cerebrovascular	-48%	+36%
Diabetes	-27%	+36%
All Four	-32%	+55%

FIGURE 11-2

statistically, is 26% certain to suffer a long-term disability prior to age 65. Those are pretty awesome odds, and I certainly would not want to bet against them — yet that's exactly what you're doing if you do not have disability insurance.

The Air Bag Phenomenon

Interestingly, the reason you are so *likely* to suffer a disability is exactly because you are so *unlikely* to die. Since 1960, the frequency of death from the four leading causes have sharply *decreased*, while the frequency of disability has sharply *increased*. I call this the Air Bag Phenomenon.

If you live in a major metropolitan area, you'd agree that there are 10 rush hours every week, one each weekday morning and evening.[45] How often do you hear of a traffic accident in those rush hours?

Every time, of course.

But in how many do you hear that a driver was killed in a rush hour accident? That's much less common. Since fatalities are unusual, most of us don't give those accidents a second thought, other than to complain that someone made us late. But the truth is that

---

[45]In many cities, people will argue that there's just one rush-hour per week: It starts Monday morning and ends Friday evening.

someone is getting hurt in those accidents. After all, you're not likely to avoid injury after sustaining a collision at 55 mph.

And that's my point: Due to the advent of airbags, many people now survive auto accidents, who 10 years ago would have been killed. But this does not mean accident victims just walk away from the scene. Rather, it simply means they go to the emergency room instead of the morgue.

Indeed, a study by the University of Pittsburgh showed that people protected by an air bag who are involved in a high-speed, head-on collision often suffer a variety of injuries caused not by the collision, but by the airbag itself — including burns to the chest and face, loss of hearing and vision, and broken forearms. Airbags also fail to prevent legs from being broken. And research from the University of Florida revealed that many drivers whose lives were saved by airbags suffer injuries that are not readily apparent to rescue workers, such as lacerations to the liver. Thus, airbags do not assure that you will survive injury-free if you are in an accident.

So while airbags have been very good news for the life insurance industry (as the number of highway fatalities has dropped), it has been bad news for the health and auto insurance industries (which pay the medical expenses of accident survivors).

Indeed, medical advances can be felt far beyond the highway. A generation or two ago, a worker who suffered a heart attack on the factory floor would have died. Today, paramedics and emergency medical technicians arrive in minutes, ready to stabilize and transport the patient to the hospital — by helicopter, if necessary. Throughout much of the country, EMTs are able to install pacemakers *right at the scene*.

And there's more. Has your liver gone bad? No problem. We'll give you a new one. Clogged arteries? We'll predict the stroke before it occurs, give you a quadruple bypass, and you'll be back on the tennis court in six weeks. Failed kidneys? We'll hook you up to a machine that will take over the job.

Modern medicine can do many things. Above all else, it can *keep you alive*. But that doesn't mean you'll never miss a day of work.

Quite the contrary. In a study of more than 2,000 severely ill patients from five medical centers around the country, the *Journal of the American Medical Association* reported that nearly a third of the families lost most of their life savings as a result of the patient's illness. The study found that although 96% of patients had some form of medical insurance, 31% still lost their savings.

"Home care and disability costs may now be more devastating to patients and their families than the costs incurred in the hospital," said the study. These expenses include the unreimbursed costs of home care, health aides, special transportation, and related medical costs. In addition, 29% of the families studied lost a major source of income, either because the patient no longer could work, or because another family member had to quit a job in order to care for the patient.

So if you think a disability won't happen to you, or if you think it won't result in a financial burden, think again.

Reason #2: "It's Too Expensive"

Without question, DI coverage is expensive. Annual premiums can be 1% to 3% of your annual salary. And that's why many people ultimately reject DI insurance. "I can't afford it," they say.

Turn this argument around. The reason you need to buy disability insurance is exactly why you don't want to buy it.

Have you ever seen one of those insurance commercials on late-night TV? "For just two dollars a week... you cannot be turned down... veterans only..." and other nonsense. These policies are only two bucks a week because the insurance companies know they're not going to pay a claim!

If you look at the fine print, you'll see that the benefits for the first several years often are limited to a return of the premiums you've paid, minus administrative costs. Since most buyers of this awful coverage are a gizzillion years old, the carriers know the buyers will die before they qualify for a claim. Thus, the carriers collect $2 a month, for which they do nothing in return. That's why coverage is so cheap. For the carrier, that $2 premium is virtually pure profit!

This is the main thesis of the insurance world. A policy is cheap when the insurance company knows it is unlikely to pay a claim. But policies are expensive when there is higher probability that you will file a claim. Therefore, the more expensive the policy, the more you need the protection.

Think Like the Seller

It might help if you examine the situation from the insurance company's point of view. If only one house in 1,200 is likely to burn down and each house is valued at $250,000, then how much does an insurer need to charge each of the 1,200 homeowners to be able to pay the claim for the one house that burns down? The answer is:

$$\frac{1 \text{ Claim of } \$250,000}{1,200 \text{ Homes}} = \$208/\text{Per Home}$$

Toss in administrative expenses, profits, and payouts for other forms of damage, such as lightning, theft, and flood, and the typical homeowner's insurance bill is about $350. Thus, from the insurer's perspective, the cost of a policy is directly related to the likelihood and cost of a claim. This explains why homeowner's insurance is cheap, and why DI coverage is expensive.

The Cost of Disability vs. The Cost of Death

Look at Figure 11-3. Mike, a 35-year-old male nonsmoker in good health, buys a $250,000 life insurance policy. If Mike were to die, the insurance company would owe his survivors $250,000.

On the other hand, if Mike bought a $2,000 disability income policy and suffered a disability, the insurance company would owe him $2,000

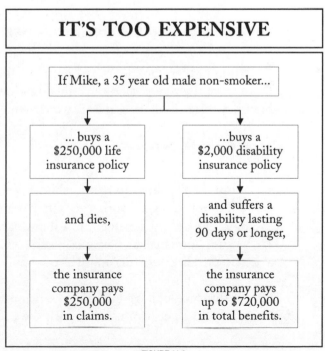

IT'S TOO EXPENSIVE

If Mike, a 35 year old male non-smoker...

... buys a $250,000 life insurance policy

...buys a $2,000 disability insurance policy

and dies,

and suffers a disability lasting 90 days or longer,

the insurance company pays $250,000 in claims.

the insurance company pays up to $720,000 in total benefits.

FIGURE 11-3

per month — for as many as 30 years. That would be as much as $720,000 in claims!

That's why disability insurance is expensive — and why you need it.

The Problems with Group DI Coverage

Of those who have DI coverage, most have it only because it is provided by their employer. But group coverage has several problems:

- the group policy's definition of disability is far too restrictive;

- your employer can cancel the coverage at any time;

- the insurance company can cancel the benefit at any time;

- if you leave your employer, you lose the benefit; and

- the cost of the coverage can increase.

Two Groups of Workers Who Really Need Their Own DI Policy

In addition to these problems, red flags rise for two groups of workers: those who plan to leave their jobs, such as women who want to stop working for a few years while they raise children, and any worker who intends to become self-employed.

Group One: Moms-to-Be

One of my clients, about to have a child, planned to quit her law practice with the intention of returning to work after a few years. By leaving her firm, she would lose her employer-paid DI coverage, and she would not be able to obtain a policy on her own because homemakers have no income. (*Income* is the primary criterion used by carriers in deciding whether to give you a policy. No income, no policy.)

To solve this problem, we told her to buy a non-cancellable DI policy *before* she left the firm. Buying her own policy meant she could keep it even after she left the firm. If she later returns to the work force, regardless of her new occupation, the coverage moves with her.

If you're wondering why she needs DI coverage after she becomes a homemaker with no income, you're confusing *no income* with *no work*. As any mother can tell you, she'll be working plenty — and she'll be the only person in the world crazy enough to do her job for free. (Okay, maybe Dad or another relative also would be willing. Maybe.) If she gets hurt or falls ill, she'll have to pay someone else to take over, such as a nanny or housekeeper. Without DI coverage, from where would the money come?

Group Two: Budding Entrepreneurs

Similar problems occur for those preparing to become self-employed. Another client of ours, working for a defense contractor, planned to become a self-employed consultant in the same field.

Like the lawyer, he would be unable to obtain disability income insurance after he began his consulting practice because the insurance company would want to know the amount of his income over the past two years *from his current occupation*. Since his consulting business would be brand new, his income would be zero, and he would not be eligible for coverage for two years. Therefore, you must buy your own non-cancellable DI policy *before* you become self-employed.

You Have Only Two-Thirds as Much Coverage as You Think You Have

If your DI coverage is provided to you as an employee benefit, you have only two-thirds the coverage you need. This is because your disability benefit probably equals 60% of your pay, a widely-followed industry guideline. It is based on the fact that insurance payments are tax-free under federal law. Thus, earning 60% of your pay tax-free is the same as earning 100% of your pay and then paying taxes on it.

But — and this is a big BUT — if your employer pays the premium for you, the disability income becomes taxable, yet the amount you receive *is still only 60% of your pay*. Since you'll lose about a third (20%) to taxes, you'll have only 40% left. That's a problem.

Therefore, if your employer pays for your coverage, you need to consider buying a supplemental policy on your own. The good news is that you probably need to buy only enough to replace the 20% you lose to taxes, and since that's not much insurance, it's not very expensive (often only a few hundred dollars a year).

Eight Reasons Never to Buy a Policy Based on Price

When shopping for a disability policy, don't buy based on cost, for the cheaper the policy, the less likely your claim will be covered — or if it is, the less money you will receive. In fact, there are several factors affecting the cost of a policy. Let's take a look at them.

Cost Factor #1: Who Says You're Disabled?

Disability insurance is not as simple as life insurance. With life insurance, there is no debate regarding the legitimacy of the claim: If you die, they pay. But what about a disability? What exactly does *disabled* mean? And who decides you've met the definition — your doctor or the insurance company's doctor?

This is perhaps the most important factor affecting the value — and cost — of a disability contract, and why you cannot buy a policy merely based on price. Cheap policies have a definition so strict that it is unlikely you will ever qualify to receive payments, while more expensive policies have more favorable definitions.

For example, is a surgeon who loses a finger disabled? Don't be too quick to say yes. After all, a surgeon certainly can teach or consult, and her income might not suffer in the least — despite the fact that she no longer can perform surgery.

Thus, standard disability income policies would not consider her to be disabled. Standard contracts say you must be unable to perform the duties of *any occupation* for which you are prepared by training or experience. In other words, if you can sell magazine subscriptions over the phone, you might not be considered disabled. This is why the Social Security Administration, which uses a "totally disabled" definition, denies more than 90% of the claims filed.

If you are a white-collar worker, therefore, or one who works in a specialized field, you need a policy that will pay benefits if you are unable to perform the duties of *your own occupation*. With an "own-occ" policy, our surgeon would be considered disabled and entitled to benefits even if she continued to earn a living as a professor of medicine.

Cost Factor #2: Your Occupation

The more dangerous your job, the more likely you'll be hurt, and thus the more expensive the policy. Workers in high risk occupations find that DI coverage is either unusually expensive, with benefits payable only for five years or less, or not available at all. By contrast, general office workers can get coverage at a lower cost with full benefits payable to age 65.

Occupational classes are very specific, with several classifications for many occupations. For example, nurses who work in an emergency room might be classified differently from nurses who work in an administrative capacity. Each classification would be charged a different premium — all based on the risk of injury. In addition to your job's specific duties, insurers consider your age, sex, even leisure activities (insurers frown on scuba-diving, hang gliding, motorcycle riding, car racing, and piloting airplanes, for such activities often lead to serious injury), and then they price your policy accordingly.

> **A freelance writer, working out of his home, cannot qualify for disability insurance. Why?**
>
> **It's not because many accidents occur in the home. Ask yourself this: If you became disabled, where would you go? Home, of course! Well, if you work at home, how will they know when you're better? Thus, insurers often don't like to provide benefits for people who work in their home.**
>
> **This example shows that the insurance industry looks at DI in strange and unusual ways.**

Cost Factor #3: The Waiting Period

You can set your waiting period (i.e., the amount of time that must elapse before you will receive benefits) at 0, 30, 60, 90, 180 or 365 days. The shorter your waiting period, the more expensive the policy. A 90-day waiting period generally is the most cost-effective because most disabilities do not last 90 days. Insurance companies know this and, therefore, you'll save a lot of money by choosing a 90-day wait over a 60-day wait, but the relative savings are not as much by choosing a 180-day wait over a 90-day wait. Keep in mind, though, that "self-insuring" for the first 90 days could cost you $10,000 or more in out-of-pocket expenses. So make sure you maintain sufficient cash reserves (see Chapter 6).

Cost Factor #4: Inflation Protection

Buying a policy based on today's income is fine for now, but inflation will cut the value of your policy. Therefore, better policies either guarantee to automatically increase your benefits each year or give you a guaranteed option to increase your coverage along with increases in the Consumer Price Index.

Cost Factor #5: Does Protection Increase as Your Income Grows?

Since your income will grow over time, you need a policy that will let you increase your coverage to keep pace with it. Because your health may change, it's important that the benefit be guaranteed without you having to repeat the application process — which could prohibit you from obtaining additional coverage in the future.

Cost Factor #6: How Long are Benefits Payable?

Lots of policies pay benefits for only five years. That doesn't do you a lot of good unless you're close to retirement. Therefore, get a policy that pays benefits to age 65. But be forewarned: This is not always possible. Workers in high-risk occupations or those with pre-existing conditions often cannot get full-career coverage.

Cost Factor #7: Will the Policy Pay a Partial Benefit if You're Partially Disabled?

Say you suffer a back injury and your doctor wants you to work only four hours a day. Some policies would pay nothing because you're not totally disabled, but better (and more expensive) policies pay partial benefits to make up for the hours you can't work, or the money you can't earn (provided you show a loss of income of at least 20%).

Cost Factor #8: Is Your Policy Both Guaranteed and Non-Cancellable?

Guaranteed means the policy's cost can't rise. Non-cancellable means you are covered as long as you pay your premiums — even if you change jobs or quit working.

"Everything is funny as long as it is happening to someone else."

—**Will Rogers**

One Dumb Feature You Need to Avoid

To overcome the objection that DI coverage costs too much — and to help agents make the sale — many insurers offer an option called the Return of Premium Rider. This rider (so-called because it's an addendum to the insurance contract) says if you do not suffer a disability, you are entitled to a partial refund (usually 50%) of the premiums you paid.

This is a popular option, but it's really quite dumb. After all, buying the policy is in direct conflict with the rider. You buy the policy in case you become disabled, but you buy the rider in case you don't. It doesn't make sense!

It makes even less sense when you realize the cost. Buying the rider increases the cost of the policy by 20% to 40% for the privilege of getting half your money back. It's a wonderful example of the smoke and mirrors that are so pervasive in the insurance industry. Avoid this trap.

Why You Should Not Deduct Premiums as a Business Expense

If you own a business, you can deduct the cost of your DI policy as a normal business expense. If you do, you'll give yourself a tax deduction, which in turn lowers your cost of buying the policy.

Don't do it.

If you do, the disability income, should you ever receive it, would become taxable. Therefore, you should pay your premiums personally, with no tax write-off, so that any disability income payments you receive will be tax-free.

Chapter 73 - Long-Term Care

Long-Term Care insurance is an excellent example of how **The Rules of Money Have Changed**. Many people have not dealt with this subject for the simple reason that, until now, nobody ever had the need.

In ancient Greece, for example, life expectancy at birth was 20. When the Declaration of Independence was signed, life expectancy was still just 23; the median age was 16. Even as recently as 1900, most Americans died by age 47.

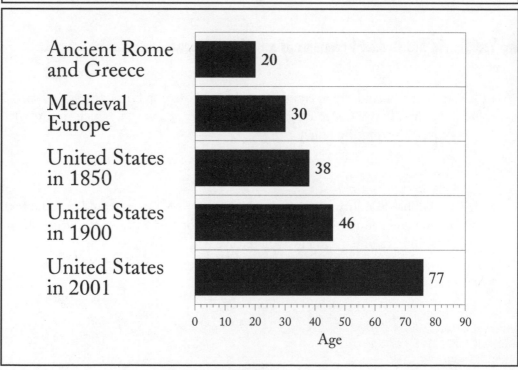

FIGURE 11-4

If you're under the age of 40, you probably think the subject of long-term care doesn't apply to you. But it does — not only because you will one day be old enough to worry about it — but because you will be faced with the problem as your *parents* get older.

Indeed, the Marriott Corporation found that although the median age of its employees is 35, some 15% say they have elder-care responsibilities. And in a study of workers at several major corporations, the consulting firm Cobley & Hunt found that, of caregiving employees:

- 1% were forced to quit their jobs in order to provide care for an elder;

- 11% take off an average of six days per year to provide routine elder-care;

- 100% incur workday interruptions to provide routine elder support; and

- 20% incur excessive use of physical, mental health, and Employee Assistance Plan Services.

Face it: Long-term care is an issue you will face at some point in your life — and probably much sooner than you think.

These figures are confirmed by the percentage of Americans who reach age 65. In 1870, only 2.5% of all Americans made it. By 1990, that percentage had increased five-fold to 12.7%. Today, 35 million people are over 65 — and the figures continue to grow.

We can thank advances in medicine and public health for our newly extended lifelines In 1900, communicable diseases were the leading causes of death, but today, most deaths result from heredity, lifestyle and the environment. That's why people in the 1940s and 1950s rarely died of heart disease: They were more far more likely to die from a contagious disease long before they reached what we would now consider "old age."

LEADING CAUSES OF DEATH

1900	2003
1. Pneumonia	1. Accidents
2. Tuberculosis	2. Cancer
3. Diarrhea	3. Heart Disease
4. Nephritis	4. Suicide/Homocide
5. Diphtheria	5. HIV

FIGURE 11-5

Just how long are people living today? Consider:

- Life expectancy at birth is now age 77;

- people in the fastest growing age group in this country are those over 85;

- if you and your spouse both reach age 65, one of you can be expected to live to age 90;

- 90% of all the people in world history who ever reached age 90 are alive today; and

- Willard Scott won't wish you a happy birthday unless you are least 100.

Old cars break down more often than new ones, and the same is true for people. As our bodies wear out, we find ourselves requiring assistance with daily life. Called the Activities of Daily Living, insurance companies typically define these as eating, dressing, bathing, toileting, transferring (getting from bed to chair), and maintaining continence. The need for assistance with ADLs is so common, and the cost so large, that:

- more than half the women and about one-third of the men who reach age 65 will spend some time in a nursing home;

- seven out of 10 couples can expect at least one partner to use a nursing home after age 65;

- the average cost of a nursing home is about $66,000 per year;

- half of all older Americans who live alone will spend themselves into poverty after only 13 weeks in a nursing home;

- 56% of couples spend their income down to the poverty level after one spouse has spent six months in a nursing home; and

- two out of five people 65 and over will need long-term care. Half will stay in a facility six months or less, while the other half will stay an average of two and a half years.

These statistics come as a shock to most of us. Indeed, as a nursing home admissions officer once told me, the most common remark she hears when admitting a new patient is, "I never thought I'd live this long."

The Three Levels of Long-Term Care

We'll talk more about the cost of care and how to pay for it. But first, it is important that you become familiar with the three types of care.

Level #1: Skilled Care

Defined as *continuously medically necessary*, these cases represent the horror stories about growing old: of people tied to their beds, connected to tubes, suffering from some chronic ailment. But in reality, only one-half of one percent of Americans require this level of care, so unless you have a medical or family history that predisposes you to it, it's statistically unlikely that this will happen to you.

Level #2: Intermediate Care

This is care provided under a doctor's supervision. Only 4.5% of the nursing home population falls in this category.

Level #3: Custodial Care

All other long-term care patients — 95% — receive custodial care, which is little more than room and board. It is based on the mere premise that you're finding it difficult to maintain one or more of the Activities of Daily Living. Often, Mom is in a retirement facility because she cannot live alone at home anymore, and the kids are unable to care for her.

The result: Mom enters a retirement home. She will find her meals prepared, her room cleaned, and someone to remind her to take her medication.

> **And, almost always, it is Mom. Wives survive their husbands 80% of the time, and 72% of nursing home residents are women. More than 85% of all women in this country die single — unmarried, widowed, or divorced. (See Chapter 71.)**

How to Pay for Long-Term Care

This is why neither private medical insurance nor Medicare pays for long-term care. It's simply not a medical need. So who pays? *You do*, until you can no longer afford it. Thus, we can group all Americans into three broad groups: the wealthy, the middle class, and the poor.

If you are wealthy and can afford the $66,000+ annual cost, long-term care may not be a financial concern for you.

If you are middle class, you must pay for the cost of long-term care from your income and assets until you run out of money.

If you are poor (which is where many in the middle class eventually find themselves) and cannot afford to pay for the care you need, you will be covered by Medicaid.

Supposedly, therefore, everybody in the U.S. who needs care will receive it, even if they can't afford it. But if you're going to rely on Medicaid, you are assuming:

- Medicaid still exists when you need it;

- a Medicaid bed will be available in your community when and where you need one; and

- you will be admitted by that facility.

Even assuming that the patient requiring institutionalized care is able to find it, a problem remains for his or her spouse. If all of the family's income and assets are devoted to paying for the care of the institutional spouse, where does that leave the still-at-home spouse (also known as the community spouse)?

> **Do not confuse Medicaid with Medicare.**
>
> **Medicaid is the federal welfare program for the poor. Medicare is the federal medical insurance program for those over 65. Although virtually all American retirees qualify for Medicare benefits, Medicare does not pay for long-term care expenses. Medicaid does, but only the poor qualify to receive its benefits.**

A Crisis for the Middle Class

This is why long-term care is a crisis for the middle class. The wealthy, after all, can afford the cost without sacrificing the lifestyle of their spouse or family members. And the poor enjoy a similar advantage, not because they can afford it, but because they are not required to.

Thus, it's the middle class which suffers the most, economically-speaking.[46] Unfortunately, those in the middle class also have the most misconceptions about who pays for long-term care. As already mentioned, health insurance does not cover this cost. And according to the U.S. Health Care Financing Administration, only under special circumstances does Medicare pay part of the costs of long-term care. Here's why:

- Medicare pays only if the patient has been hospitalized for three consecutive days within the 30 days prior to entering a nursing home (60% of patients fail this test).

- The facility must be Medicare-approved (only 20% of the nation's 20,000 nursing homes qualify); and

- Even if the above two criteria are met, Medicare pays only for the first 21 days in full. Medicare requires a patient co-payment in excess of $100 per day for the next 80 days, and Medicare pays nothing after the 100th day. Medicare also stops paying as soon as your health care provider determines that your condition is chronic and is not going to improve — even if the 100 days are not yet up.

"No problem," you say to yourself. "I'll just become poor and get Medicaid to pay." Before you try that, make sure you know the truth about Medicaid. If you decide to spend down your assets — or if you're forced to — you need to know how Medicaid operates (again, assuming it still exists).

The Medicaid Asset Test

As the rules stand at this writing, Medicaid places your assets into three categories: non-countable, countable, and inaccessible.

---

[46]What else is new?

- **Non-countable assets** include your house (but only if you have a spouse who lives there), car, jewelry, household goods, personal effects, prepaid funeral, and $2,000 in cash.

- **Countable assets** include second homes and any additional cars, plus all savings and investments, including CDs, stocks, bonds, mutual funds, annuities, IRAs, and retirement plans — even the cash value of your life insurance policies.

- **Inaccessible assets** include gifts and anything placed into irrevocable trusts. These assets will be deemed by Medicaid to be exempt transfers (meaning gifts or transfers into trusts will be allowed) or non-exempt transfers (meaning the gifts or transfers are disallowed). If the transfers are deemed non-exempt, Medicaid will deny benefits for a period of time based on when the non-exempt transfers occurred.

Under Medicaid rules, the community spouse may keep non-countable assets, but is forced to liquidate countable assets. Furthermore, in most states, the community spouse is allowed a monthly income of less than $2,000; the institutional spouse is allowed $30 to $40 per month. Medicaid takes all income above those amounts, including Social Security income, pensions, interest income, annuity income, and alimony payments.

Although Medicaid will not take your house if a spouse lives there, you will lose your home when your spouse dies or goes to a nursing home. When your house eventually is sold, Medicaid will recover the sale proceeds — even if it has to wait until after you've died to do so. So you can forget about leaving your house to the kids.

The solution? Actually, there are three of them. Let's look closely at each:

Solution #1: Qualify for Medicaid By Transferring Assets

Clearly, Medicaid will pay only if you have few assets. Logically, then, make sure you don't have assets. Therefore, *transfer your assets to your children now.* This will make you poor, and by being poor, you'll qualify for Medicaid.

If you don't transfer your assets to your children, you'll just spend everything you own on long-term care costs until you have nothing left anyway. Either way, you'll be broke. So wouldn't you rather give your assets to your kids instead of to a nursing home?

Four Problems with Transferring Assets

If you think this sounds reasonable, watch out for these four big problems:

Problem #1: Yeah, Right

You'll find it very hard to give everything you own to your (spoiled rotten!) kids just as you've reached that time in your life when you can start enjoying yourself. In other words, this recommendation, um, usually doesn't go over very well.

Try convincing your parents to give you all their money.

"No, really, Dad, you need to give me everything you own right now. It's for your own good!" Yeah, right.

Problem #2: Medicaid Is Aware of This Trick

If you made gifts during the 36 months prior to filing your claim for benefits, Medicaid will deny the claim — 60 months for gifts you make to a trust. This rule is specifically intended to prevent people from asset-shifting. And please note an important change in Medicaid rules: If you file a claim at any time during the 36-month waiting period, Medicaid will restart the clock. Therefore if you plan to use this strategy, assets must be transferred well in advance of the need for long-term care, and be sure you don't file a claim until you're sure the 36-month waiting period has expired. Also, be aware that transferring assets to a spouse does not shield the assets from Medicaid.

Have you brought assets into your marriage?

Many people who marry later in life bring assets into the marriage, like Ruth. Her husband died when she was 47, leaving her his 401(k), their home, plus life insurance proceeds. Five years later, Ruth remarried. She kept all her assets in her name and filed a separate tax return. When her second husband needed long-term care, he quickly spent down all *his* assets. But Medicaid permitted Ruth to keep only $2,000 per month; all *her* other income had to be spent on her husband's care before Medicaid would pay benefits. Thus, over the next several years, Ruth was forced to spend down to the poverty level, too.

> Regardless of whose money it was or where it came from — inheritances, savings, retirement plans, or insurance proceeds — Medicaid will deny claims until both spouses spend virtually all their money on long-term care. The fact that the money originally belonged to the community spouse does not matter.

Problem #3: Attempts to Asset-Shift Are Stymied by the IRS

Under gift tax rules (see Chapter 63), you may give to any one person only $11,000 per year (you may give unlimited amounts to your spouse, but as shown above, doing so has no effect). So, even if you try to give your money away, the IRS will restrict the speed with which you may proceed.

Problem #4: This Strategy Is Unethical ...

Please remember that Medicaid is funded by taxpayers to help the truly needy of our society— not as a middle-class tax-dodge to protect your assets.

Problem #5: ... and Illegal, Too!

Congress knows that few consumers have the imagination or knowledge to effectively execute an asset-shifting strategy. So, to discourage professional advisors from sharing this information, Congress passed a law that made it a felony for advisors to counsel or assist consumers in their efforts to shift assets. Therefore, don't bother asking your lawyer, accountant, or financial advisor for help; the smart ones won't provide it.

Solution #2: Divorce Yourself from Medicaid

For all five reasons noted above, transferring assets is not as simple or as easy as it first appears. This is why some elder-care attorneys suggest strategy number two: *Divorce*. The institutional spouse leaves all assets under a divorce decree to the community spouse; Medicaid cannot claim assets transferred in such a manner.

Three Problems with Divorce

This isn't necessarily a great idea, either, because:

- The same ethical problem exists as noted above;

- If you thought it was tough for Mom and Dad to handle the thought of giving everything to their kids, just try to get them to file for divorce after 45 years of marriage simply because one of them is declining in health. Not only is it unlikely they'll do it — it's one heck of a commentary that our laws even encourage such an action; and

- Medicaid is aware that many couples are divorcing for economic rather than marital reasons, and the agency is starting to challenge this strategy. Where claimants have recently divorced and decreed all their assets to their ex-spouses, Medicaid has gone to court, arguing that under the divorce decree, the institutionalized spouse did not get his or her fair share of the marital assets. Why argue that position? Because if Medicaid wins, as much as half the marital assets return to the institutional spouse, which Medicaid then can seize.

Solution #3: Long-Term Care Insurance

This is the least-evil solution.

Although buying insurance is never fun, given the alternatives of transferring assets or getting a divorce, it is the least evil choice. For that reason, clients who are not independently wealthy should consider buying a policy — even as early as age 40 or 50.

Here's why: The cost of coverage is related directly to your age at the time you buy the policy (rates are unisex; there is no cost difference between men and women — not yet, anyway)[47]. Since a person age 50 is not likely to file a claim for 20 years or more, the carrier has many years to collect premiums. Thus the cost for that 50-year-old is quite low — about $150 per month in many cases. That's extremely affordable, especially considering that the cost of policies skyrockets with

> Many wealthy Americans buy long-term care insurance even though they don't need to. Why? Because they'd rather spend several hundred dollars on a policy instead of many thousands on the care itself, preserving their assets for their children.
>
> Indeed, for many people, long-term care insurance is not just a smart way to protect you, it's a smart way to protect your assets, too.

---

[47] While the cost of most policies will remain unchanged once they are purchased, your policy's cost could increase if you select an inflation protection option. Also, while insurers can't increase the cost of a single policy, they are permitted to seek state approval to change the cost of their contracts for all policyholders.

age. If you don't buy a policy until age 65, the cost could exceed $3,500 per year, or $7,500 by age 75.

Many feel that buying a policy in their fifties is unnecessary, since it is likely to be years — even decades — before they'll need the coverage. (But it's more likely than you might think: 11% of nursing home residents are under age 60. Most of them are accident victims, which can occur at any age.)

Two Reasons to Buy Long Term Care Insurance at Young Ages

Although it's true that a 50-year-old is unlikely to need the coverage for many years, it nonetheless makes sense to buy it young. Why? Consider Figure 11-6, which compares the cost of a typical long-term care policy for different ages:

LONG-TERM CARE INSURANCE

Age	Annual Cost		Total Cost to Age 85	
	Married*	Single	Married*	Single
Age 50	$1,462	$1,827	$51,166	$63,958
Age 55	$1,746	$2,183	$52,384	$65,480
Age 60	$2,315	$2,893	$57,867	$72,333
Age 65	$3,167	$3,960	$63,348	$79,186
Age 70	$4,751	$5,939	$71,267	$89,084
Age 75	$7,269	$9,086	$72,688	$90,860

Based on $180/day coverage   *price for each spouse

FIGURE 11-6

Reason #1: It's Cheaper When You're Younger

Thus, the 50-year-old pays 30% less in total payments over his lifetime than the 75-year-old and is protected for 35 years instead of just 10. The insurance industry is sending you a clear message: Buy this policy when you're young, because you'll save a lot of money in the long run.

Reason #2: You're More Able to Qualify

And you're more likely to qualify for it, too — and that's the second reason you need to protect yourself at younger ages. On the application form, you'll be presented with a list of medical conditions. If you have any of them, you will be declined or asked to pay a higher premium. But at age 50, when you're unlikely to have symptoms, you are better able to get the coverage.

Thus, you need to buy a policy when you're young enough to afford it and healthy enough to qualify.

Seven Features to Look for in a Long-Term Care Policy

Here's a list of some "uninsurable conditions" that would cause an insurance carrier to deny long-term care coverage:

- **Reliance on another person or assistance devices to perform two or more of the Activities of Daily Living**
- **AIDS, AIDS-related Complex**
- **Alzheimer's Disease, Dementia, Memory loss**
- **Amputation or Blindness due to disease**
- **Cirrhosis**
- **Cystic Fibrosis**
- **Kidney Failure — Dialysis**
- **Lou Gehrig's Disease**
- **Multiple Sclerosis**
- **Diabetes with insulin use**
- **Pancreatitis**
- **Paralysis**
- **Parkinson's Disease**
- **Schizophrenia**
- **Sickle Cell Anemia**
- **Spinal Cord Injury/Myelitis**
- **Stroke**

There are a lot more exclusions, but you get the point. People in their 50s and 60s often do not display any of these conditions, but many in their 70s and 80s do. If you wait too long to obtain your policy, you might be no longer insurable. Make sure you obtain your policy before you need it.

#1: $180 Per Day in Coverage

This figure approximates the current cost of nursing homes. You can obtain more or less coverage, with corresponding changes in cost. Remember: Many people do not need a policy covering 100% of the cost of care because of other income sources. Depending on your situation, you might be fine choosing reduced benefits in exchange for a more affordable premium.

Feature #2: At Least Three Years of Coverage

Five or six years of coverage is better, and you should also consider lifetime benefits. After all, more and more people are entering assisted living facilities, and many others receive care in their own homes. So even though less than 2% of residents stay in a nursing home more than five years, you need to think beyond nursing homes, for long-term care is much more than just that.

Feature #3: A 90-Day Waiting Period

Delaying the start of benefits is an excellent way to reduce the premium, but this means you "self-insure" for the first 90 days, which could cost you about $18,000. Make sure you have enough in cash reserves to afford this outlay (see Chapter 6).

Feature #4: Inflation Protection

Because the cost of care will increase over time, you need to make sure that the benefit amount you buy today maintains its purchasing power in the future. Inflation protection is a must for those under 70, and still suggested for those over 70.

Feature #5: Gatekeeper

Who certifies that you are not able to perform two of the Activities of Daily Living that qualify you to begin receiving payments from your policy? Ideally, it will be your doctor who makes that determination, not someone from the insurance company.

Likewise, how disabled must you be in order to receive benefits? Some policies say you must need "substantial" assistance, while others say you need "hands-on" assistance. You want a policy that offers the most liberal definition, or you could find your claims delayed or even denied.

Feature #6: Waiver of Premium Included

This feature allows you to stop paying premiums once you've received benefits for 90 days.

Feature #7: Home Health Care

When it comes to nursing homes, people wait as long as possible to go, and they return home as quickly as they can. This crucial feature, which is found in almost all policies these days, pays for adult day care or for home visits by a nurse or home health aide to assist you with medication, dressing, bathing, preparing meals, eating and toileting.

But make sure the home health care benefit is the same as for care in a facility. Some policies pay only 50% to 75% of the regular benefit for home care. Also try to find a policy that pays for housekeeping chores, meal preparation, and clothes washing, in addition to medical and ADL services. Especially good are policies that pay for home modification (to install wheelchair ramps, grab bars in bathtubs, and the like) as well as respite care and care advisory services.

> We find that many adult children buy these policies for their parents, because the kids would rather spend $4,000 a year on a policy now than $50,000 a year on mom's care later. That's smart planning.

As with disability insurance, never buy LTC coverage based on cost, because the cheaper the policy, the less likely it will meet your needs.

You'll find more information on Long-Term Care in *Discover the Wealth Within You*.

Chapter 74 - Life Insurance

When it comes to the subject of life insurance, I'm willing to bet that

...you don't *understand it*...

...you don't *like it*...

...but you *bought it anyway*.

That doesn't make sense, does it? Can you imagine any other product that millions of people buy but which so few understand?

It is also noteworthy that the only source of information for most consumers is the agent who sells you the policy. That's hardly the proper environment for a proper education. Therefore, this chapter is devoted to ending your confusion about life insurance. Hold your applause, because it's not that complex a subject — it's just that the insurance industry wants you to think it is.

Consider, for example, the following list:

- Mortgage Insurance
- Credit Life Insurance
- Accidental Death Insurance
- Stock Redemption Policies
- Key Person Coverage
- Second-to-Die Coverage
- First-to-Die Insurance
- Cross-Purchase Policies
- Split-Dollar Policies
- Reverse Split-Dollar Policies

These policies do not represent different types of insurance, but rather different uses of plain ol' life insurance. But in many cases, you could be hard pressed to realize it.

The Basic Elements of a Life Insurance Policy

Actually, life insurance is quite simple. Like all insurance policies, life insurance is a contract between you and the insurance company. You promise to pay a certain amount of money over a certain period of time and, provided you do so, the insurance company promises to pay a death claim.

Steve, a non-smoking male age 35 in good health, buys a $250,000 policy to make sure his young son will be able to afford college even if Steve dies before he has a chance to save enough money.

In this example:

- The *owner* of the policy is Steve, and as owner he is responsible for paying for it. The money Steve pays is called the *premium*.

- Steve is the insured, too, meaning that when he dies, the insurance company has to pay...

- ...the *death benefit* (also called the *face amount*) which in this case is $250,000, and the insurer must pay this money to...

- ...the *beneficiary* of the policy, whom Steve (as the policy owncr) chooses.

Despite all the marketing glitz, there are only two kinds of life insurance contracts: temporary and permanent. Let's examine them one at a time.

Term Insurance

Temporary insurance, more commonly known as term, has two main features: the amount of the death benefit and the price of the policy. The contract is quite simple: When you die, the insurance company pays.

Term insurance gets its name from the fact that it covers you for a specific term, or *period of time*.

> *"Whoever created the term 'life insurance' had to be the sales genius of all time."*
> —Robert Half

Auto insurance is another type of term insurance: When you buy auto insurance, you're betting you're going to have a car accident within one year. Term life insurance works the same way: You're betting you're going to die, and the insurer is betting you won't. If you don't die, you must buy the insurance again — and you must do this every year until ... well, until you win the bet!

The Three Kinds of Term Insurance

You can choose from three kinds of term insurance:

- **Annual renewable term (ART)**. The cost goes up each year because, as you get older, you become more likely to die. This type of policy costs little when you're young and is very expensive when you're old.

- **Level term** locks in the cost for a period of 5 to 30 years. At the end of each period, the cost increases dramatically. Over the long run, level term is less expensive than ART.

- **Decreasing term** is the opposite of ART: Instead of increasing the cost each year to adjust for the increased likelihood that you'll die, decreasing term keeps the cost the same but does so by lowering the death benefit.

BABY BLUES   KIRKMAN & SCOTT

© Baby Blues Partnership. Reprinted with Special Permission of King Features Syndicate.

One of the Biggest Rip-offs in the Insurance Industry

The most common form of decreasing term sold today is so-called "mortgage life" and it's one of the biggest rip-offs in the industry. Mortgage life is sold primarily to new homeowners. The pitch goes like this: Kevin and Harriet are thrilled with their new home, and they really stretched to buy it. Since Harriet stays home with the kids, the family depends on Kevin's income. If Kevin dies, Harriet and the kids could lose the house.

Mortgage insurance to the rescue! (Or so claims a pesky insurance salesman.) For one low annual premium that will never increase, Kevin can buy a policy *with a death benefit equal to the outstanding mortgage balance on his house.* Thus, if Kevin dies, Harriet will own the home outright.

That's a nice idea, but it's completely smoke and mirrors, because there's no such thing as "mortgage" insurance. After all, Kevin's not insuring his *mortgage*; he's insuring his *life.* But by calling it "mortgage" insurance, companies fool you into thinking the policy is something other than what it is, and they slap a huge price on it — as much as 300% or 400% more than what they would have charged if they just called it what it really is: life insurance.

If that weren't bad enough, mortgage policies have two other problems:

•   As Kevin pays off the mortgage, the mortgage balance goes down, and with it the amount of insurance, even though the cost of living goes up.

•   If Kevin dies, the insurance company writes a check directly to the mortgage lender. Harriet will never see the money, even though she might need it for other, more pressing reasons (such as paying for college — or just buying food). Who says she'll want to pay off the mortgage, anyway, just because Kevin dies? (See Chapter 59.)

If you're worried that your spouse might lose the house if you die, a better idea is to buy life insurance sold as life insurance. The policy will be much less expensive and, since the death benefit will be paid directly to Harriet, she'll be able to choose for herself how the money should be used.

Permanent Insurance

The other type of insurance is permanent, and there are three variations, just as there are three variations of term life. The original type of permanent insurance is known as *whole life* because it covers you for your "whole life."[48] There are also *universal life* and *variable life* policies, and we'll discuss them all in detail for you.

First, let's return to Steve to see how permanent life insurance works.

Steve thinks about buying a term policy for a cost of about $300 a year.

Term life is cheap, because Steve's age and health suggest that he's unlikely to die within the next year. As he gets older, of course, his chances of dying increase, and the policy's cost increases as well. By the time Steve is 70 years old, the policy could cost $5,000 or more per year.

> **That's the problem with term insurance: 50% of all life policies sold in the U.S. are term policies, yet less than 5% ever pay a claim. Why? Because young people buy them — and relatively few people die when they're young. Thus, young people pay until they can't afford it anymore. Then they cancel the policy just as they reach an age when they are most likely to need it.**
>
> **This is why the insurance industry loves to sell term life insurance. They know the premiums they collect are almost entirely free money, since policyholders will cancel the policies before they die — meaning the insurer will never have to pay a claim.**

This problem was solved by the introduction of whole life insurance.

"Instead of insuring you for one year," the industry tells Steve, "How about if we insure you for your whole life — for the fixed price of $3,000 per year, guaranteed never to rise."

The insurance company is willing to give Steve a policy for his whole life (instead of just one year) but they want him to pay $3,000 per year for the policy. Why are they charging Steve $3,000 for the policy when the term cost is only $300? Because

---

[48]Real creative, these insurance people, huh? Like I said, this stuff isn't very complicated.

THE COST OF COVERAGE

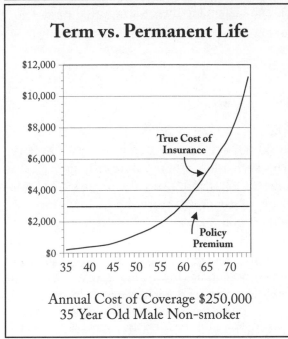

Term vs. Permanent Life

True Cost of Insurance

Policy Premium

Annual Cost of Coverage $250,000
35 Year Old Male Non-smoker

FIGURE 11-7

they know that in future years, $1,300 won't be enough. Thus, like the squirrel storing acorns for the coming winter, they place the excess ($2,700 in the first year alone), into a side fund (called the *accumulation account*) where it will earn interest.

As Figure 11-7 shows, Steve's premium payments are higher than the actual cost for about 22 years, after which they become too little. At that time, the insurance company takes money out of the accumulation account to make up the shortfall between Steve's payment and the policy's actual cost.

Therefore, a whole life policy has three features: the same two as term (the death benefit and the cost of coverage) plus the *cash value build-up* of the accumulation account. This third feature is critical, for the more your accumulation account is supposed to grow, the less you must pay in premiums. Indeed, the cash value is responsible for all the smoke and mirrors found in life insurance policies. Here's the story of how it all began.

Whole Life

In permanent life's original form, called "whole life," *everything* is guaranteed: the cost of the policy, the death benefit, the future cash value, *and* the interest rate that the policy earns in order to achieve that cash value.

If you were the insurance company, would you make these guarantees conservative or aggressive? Conservative, of course, because you must deliver what you promise. And so it is with whole life: You can be confident that a whole life policy will do what the agent tells you it will do.

The problem, though, is that this conservative structure produces an expensive product. Since the carrier must guarantee the rate of return on the policy, it must set a low rate (and whole life policies do just that: The guaranteed rate is usually 4% to 5%). Meanwhile, other players in the financial world, such as mutual funds, can generate much higher returns because they're not making their customers any promises.

Buy Term and Invest the Rest?

This led to the "buy term and invest the rest" school of financial planning. This strategy holds that Steve is nuts to pay $3,000 for a policy that costs $300, because the carrier credits the $2,700 excess with such a low rate of interest. Therefore, it is argued, Steve should buy term insurance for $300 and invest the other $2,700 into mutual funds. In future years, he'd be able to use profits from the mutual fund to pay for the increased premiums of the term policy.

This is all very logical (assuming you have the discipline to fully execute the strategy), and it has caused thousands of people to cancel their whole life polices — to the joy of the mutual fund industry and the consternation of the insurance industry.

To counter the competition, insurers responded in 1977 with the second form of permanent insurance: *universal life*.

Universal Life

Universal life offers Steve a guaranteed interest rate similar to that of a whole life policy, but if the carrier earns more interest, it will credit Steve with the higher rate. Thus, if the carrier earns 9%, Steve will get 9%, but if the carrier earns 2% or even loses money, Steve is still guaranteed to get 4% (the policy minimum).

What's the point of all this? Well, by assuming that they'll earn a higher return than the 4% guarantee — say, 7.5% — the carrier can assume its future cash value will be much higher, too. Since the carrier would be amassing more money in the accumulation account, it would need to collect less from Steve. Therefore, the carrier charges Steve much less than $3,000 — $1,700 in fact — and this makes the policy much more competitive in the marketplace.

One Problem with Universal Life

Universal life has proved to be a very popular product. However, you need to be aware of one significant potential problem: The interest rate assumption used by the carrier might be wrong and, if so, the policy will not perform as planned. If the carrier fails to earn that return, Steve will find that his premiums will increase. Worse, he could be unable to pay the higher cost. If that were to happen, the policy would be canceled.

This is exactly what happened to thousands of people who bought universal life policies in the late 1970s and early 1980s. Back then, interest rates were 15%. Thus, carriers assumed they would earn 15% for the next 40 years. Of course, rates since then have been much lower, and carriers are no longer earning anywhere near those high levels.

As a result, insurance companies have cut their rates like everyone else. As a result, the assumptions they once used have become invalid — meaning that since the carriers are not earning 15%, their policies are not accumulating as much cash as projected. That means policyholders must make up the difference — in the form of higher premiums. Thus, many policyholders are being told that their premiums are increasing — even though they bought "permanent" insurance to avoid that problem. And they have little choice, for if they don't pay the higher premiums, they'll lose their coverage.

This can be a big problem, but you can avoid it. How? Simply by knowing what you're buying. If you understand universal life and recognize the possibility that future premiums might increase, there's no problem. After all, your alternative is to buy whole life and pay those higher premiums today. So, many people conclude that it's better to choose universal life (and acknowledge the possibility that premiums might rise) instead of paying those higher costs now as whole life would demand. Others argue that whole life is better because you enjoy the confidence of knowing that your premiums never will increase.

So which is best? It depends.[49]

If you want to be certain that your premium will never rise, choose whole life.

---

[49]This is getting tiresome.

If you want to pay less now, choose universal life, and be aware that you may have to pay a higher amount later if current assumptions about future interest rates prove to be wrong.

Variable Life

The third type of permanent policy is *variable life*. This type of policy allows you to invest your excess premiums into mutual funds. The good news is that your accumulation account may grow more quickly than in either whole life or universal life. The bad news is that it might not grow at all, for in a variable life policy, *there are no guarantees*. If the mutual fund goes down in value, so does your accumulation account. In fact, if you choose a stock fund and the stock market crashes, your policy might be canceled for lack of funds.

For this reason, I am not a fan of variable life policies, but I must emphasize this is a personal bias. Put me in a room with other qualified advisors and we'll argue all day. In my opinion, the increased profit potential is not enough of a reason to buy it. After all, the policy's primary purpose is to protect against a financial loss, not to generate profits. If you seek profits, why not buy a mutual fund or variable annuity and skip the insurance altogether? It's a question no variable life proponent has ever answered to my satisfaction.

How to Comparison Shop for Permanent Life Insurance

As mentioned, each of the permanent life policies has three variables: the death benefit, the premium, and the assumed interest rate. Thus, when comparing one permanent life proposal to another, make sure two of the three variables are the same. This allows you to solve for the third: Whichever has the best buy (i.e., the highest death benefit, the lowest premium, or the most cash value as projected in the 20th, 30th, or 40th year) is the best buy.

There is a fourth variable, but neither you nor your agent can manipulate it. It's the policy's efficiency, which determines how much of your premium will earn interest. (All premiums first pay the mortality charges, underwriting expenses, and other costs of the policy; what's left then earns interest in the cash value account.)

For example, say carrier ABC credits the cash value with 5% interest and carrier DEF credits 6%. You'd think DEF would produce a higher cash value in 20 years, but that's not necessarily true. If DEF's expenses are higher than ABC's, DEF's cash value in the 20th year could be lower than ABC's — even though DEF offered the higher rate.

This often happens, and is another example of the smoke and mirrors used by the insurance industry.

An agent can use any figure he or she chooses in order to make the policy look as good as they want.

By jacking up the assumed interest rate, a clever (deceptive) agent can knock hundreds of dollars off the annual cost shown on a policy proposal. An unethical agent once gave a client of mine a proposal featuring a 14% interest rate assumption — even though the carrier was then paying 6%. Not only would the carrier be unable to sustain a 14% annual rate over 20 years, it wasn't even doing it at the time!

Remember: To help them close the sale, agents can change the variables to make an insurance proposal look any way they want. In fact, this is one of the causes of the insurance industry's bad reputation.

For Which Variable Should You Search?

It depends[50] — on whichever one is most important to you. Some people want the most death benefit they can afford. Others want to keep their premiums within a certain budget, while still others want to build up a certain amount of cash value by a certain date in the future.

Regardless of which variable you shop for, it is vital that the assumed interest rates in each proposal be identical — and realistic. If one carrier currently is paying 5% and another 5.5%, have both produce proposals showing identical interest rates. And make sure the rate they use is reasonable. The rate should be similar to current CD rates.

---

[50]Aaaarrrrrrrgh. See footnote 7.

When 7.5% is not 7.5%

Figure 11-8 shows a $250,000 universal life insurance proposal for Steve. The cost is $1,698 per year.

SAMPLE PERMANENT LIFE PROPOSAL

End of Year	Age	Annual Premium	Total Paid	Cash-In Value	Death Benefit
1	36	$1,698	$1,698	$0	$250,000
2	37	$1,698	$3,396	$0	$250,000
3	38	$1,698	$5,094	$45	$250,000
4	39	$1,698	$6,792	$1,680	$250,000
5	40	$1,698	$8,490	$3,404	$250,000
6	41	$1,698	$10,188	$5,236	$250,000
7	42	$1,698	$11,886	$7,164	$250,000
8	43	$1,698	$13,584	$9,191	$250,000
9	44	$1,698	$15,282	$12,681	$250,000
10	45	$1,698	$16,980	$18,638	$250,000
11	46	$1,698	$18,678	$21,014	$250,000
12	47	$1,698	$20,376	$23,506	$250,000
13	48	$1,698	$22,074	$26,124	$250,000
14	49	$1,698	$23,772	$28,871	$250,000
15	50	$1,698	$25,470	$35,116	$250,000
16	51	$1,698	$27,168	$38,427	$250,000
17	52	$1,698	$28,866	$41,900	$250,000
18	53	$1,698	$30,564	$45,537	$250,000
19	54	$1,698	$32,262	$49,355	$250,000
20	55	$1,698	$33,960	$58,812	$250,000
21	56	$1,698	$35,658	$63,453	$250,000
22	57	$1,698	$37,356	$67,394	$250,000
23	58	$1,698	$39,054	$73,651	$250,000
24	59	$1,698	$40,752	$79,306	$250,000
25	60	$1,698	$42,450	$92,438	$250,000

FIGURE 11-8

In 25 years, according to this proposal, Steve will have paid a total of $42,450 in premiums, yet the cash value will be $92,438! Thus, an insurance agent would say that if Steve is alive in 25 years, he could cancel the policy and get back twice as much as he paid. Steve can double his money — and have free insurance for 25 years!

Wow! This is great! (Or, at least, that's how the agent wants you to feel.) There's only one problem: The agent has lied. To produce this proposal, the agent told Steve the policy's assumed rate of return on the cash value is 7.5%. That's not a problem *per se*. After all, that was comparable to long-term U.S. Treasury rates in effect at the time the proposal was produced, so it would be fair to assume the carrier could earn such a return.

No, the problem is much more insidious than that.

> *"What if everything is an illusion and nothing exists? In that case, I definitely overpaid for my carpet."*
> —Woody Allen

If you invested $1,698 per year (the annual cost of the policy) for 25 years at an average annual return of 7.5%, you would have $124,131. But the proposal says the cash value would be worth only $92,438. What happened to the other $31,693?

Obviously, the policy is not really paying 7.5% (compounded monthly) on your premium payment of $1,698. You see, the insurance company first subtracts commissions, then mortality charges, administrative expenses, policy fees, underwriting costs, and so on, and what's left then earns 7.5%. The effective return, in fact, is really just 5.95%.

Don't be too hard on Steve's agent. I am an approved continuing education instructor for insurance, and I can tell you that many agents are unaware that the assumed rate shown on their company's proposals does not reflect the true effective rate paid by the policy.

Insurance Is for Insurance's Sake (Duh!)

This is why you must never buy insurance for *investment* purposes. Buy insurance for *insurance* purposes.

Never buy insurance with the goal of creating a gain. Buy it only to protect against a loss. In fact, it is illegal to make a profit from insurance, and those who try to do so are guilty of insurance fraud.

If that's true, you might be wondering how Steve can buy a $250,000 life policy. Won't his family "profit" from his death?

Not at all. That $250,000 death benefit merely compensates the family for lost wages if Steve dies. If Steve wanted his family to truly profit, he'd buy a $10 million policy. Yet, no carrier would let him because there is no "insurable need," meaning Steve's death would not produce a loss to anyone of $10 million.

So why doesn't Steve just buy ten $1 million policies from ten different carriers? He can't do that, either, because each carrier would ask how much coverage he has in force or applied for with other carriers. If he lies in order to get the coverage, well, that's insurance fraud.

This is not necessarily intended to imply that you should buy term and invest the rest, nor that you should buy whole life instead of variable life.

I am simply saying that when buying a permanent policy (of whatever flavor), pay only enough in premiums to allow the cash value to grow to an amount *sufficient to keep the policy in force*. Do not try to accumulate huge sums of cash value for the simple reason that *you're never going to see the money*.

The reason? Either you die, or you don't.

- **Say Steve were to die in the 25th year.** If so, the death benefit to his heirs would be $250,000 — not $250,000 + $92,438 = $342,438. The fact that the policy shows $92,438 in cash value is meaningless to Steve's beneficiaries.

- **Say Steve doesn't die.** Instead, if he borrows from the $92,438 as his agent said he could, the annual cost of the loan (at 8% interest) would be more than $7,000 — and that's in addition to the cost of the policy premium. And guess how much the death benefit will be when Steve does die? It will be $157,562 — $250,000 minus the $92,438 Steve took. At that point, Steve will be required to pay interest on the money he "borrowed" from his policy.

In other words, Steve won't "earn" $92,438 — he'd just be stealing it from his heirs! Taking the money negates the very reason he bought the policy in the first place: to protect his family.

Heads, the insurance company wins. Tails, Steve loses. Do not play with a two-headed coin, and do not allow your insurance policy to build up a large cash value.

Which Type of Insurance Is Best?

Like so many other areas of personal finance, the type of insurance you should buy depends[51] on your circumstances. Each offers strengths and weaknesses, as Figure 11-9 shows.

COMPARING TYPES OF INSURANCE

	Term Insurance	Whole Life	Universal Life	Variable Universal Life
Low Initial Cost	✓			
Permanent Protection		✓	✓	✓
Guaranteed Premiums		✓		
Current Returns			✓	✓
Premium Flexibility			✓	✓
Choice of Investments				✓

FIGURE 11-9

---

[51] I'm gonna quit highlighting this.

Generally, the longer you plan to keep your policy, the better off you will be with a permanent policy. The cross-over point is between 8 and 12 years, depending[52] on your age and health. If you plan to keep the policy for eight years or less, term has the lowest overall cost, but if you keep the policy longer than 12 years, permanent will be cheaper in the long run. This is because you can cancel the policy and get a refund of the cash value that has accumulated, which ought to compensate you for the extra premiums you paid. Between eight and 12 years, which policy is best must be determined on a case-by-case basis.

For most of us, though, it's not a question of one or the other, for most people have more than one need for insurance. Steve, for example, needs to be sure his son can afford college, but he also must be sure his wife doesn't lose their home. One need will disappear soon, the other may not. Thus, some of Steve's insurance needs are temporary while others are more permanent. For this reason, many clients need two policies, one temporary and one permanent.

> **About half the time our firm advises clients to cancel the life insurance they already have because they don't need it anymore. If the kids are out of college, if the house is paid for, and if you're retired, your death may no longer present the financial loss to others as it once did. If so, you can cancel your policies, save yourself some money, and skip the rest of this chapter.**

The One Group of People Who Never Need Insurance

Nineteen percent of all life insurance policies sold in this country insure children under the age of 12. What an incredible waste of money.

We all love our children dearly and no loss could match the tragedy of the loss of a child. But, such a loss would not be *financial*, which of course is the reason for buying insurance. If you are concerned about funeral costs, add a $10,000 child rider to your own policy. The cost will be less than $25.

What bugs me are the mail and phone calls from agents that new parents start receiving within weeks of their baby's birth. Often, these pitches warn mommy and

---

[52]Seriously.

daddy that they need to start saving for the baby's future. Another pitch says parents need to buy insurance "while your child is healthy enough to qualify for the coverage."

One example has the parents buy a $75,000 policy for just $26 a month. The pitch says that when the child reaches age 21, the child can cash in the policy. Thus, you get $5,410 at age 21 — plus free insurance for 21 years!

Sounds great — until you realize that if you instead had invested that $26 per month over 21 years into a mutual fund earning 10% per year for 21 years, you would have $22,138 — far more than what the policy would have produced! If an agent tells you to buy a child policy, ask yourself whether the agent is thinking about the benefits to your child — *or his!*

Six Problems With the Life Insurance You Already Own

First, your coverage has been eroded by inflation. If you bought a policy 20 years ago, your death benefit is a fraction of what you need today. Maybe you need more.

Second, you have too much insurance. Although the policy you bought 20 years ago is not worth very much, it nonetheless could be too much because the reason you bought the policy may no longer exist.

Third, you have the wrong kind of coverage. If you have only group insurance, your coverage is dependent on your job. This lack of portability poses the same problems we discussed earlier regarding disability insurance (Chapter 72).

Fourth, you're paying too much for the coverage you do have. If you bought your policy before 1980, the insurer priced it as though you were going to die in your 60s, since that's what the actuarial tables back then said would happen. Today's mortality charts, of course, say you'll live well into your 80s and insurers have lowered the cost of coverage accordingly. So, swapping your current policies for new ones could save you lots of money, even though you're older now.

Fifth, your policy's assumptions are invalid. If you bought your policy in the '70s or early '80s, the interest rate assumptions may be wrong and, if so, your policy is not accumulating as much cash value as you think. At best, your premiums may rise. At worst, the policy may be canceled. Either would be unpleasant.

And sixth, you have too many policies. Buying one $200,000 policy costs less than two $100,000 policies. Why? Because every policy contains flat expenses, such as policy fees, that are unrelated to the amount of coverage. If you buy two policies instead of one, you pay these costs twice instead of once. Therefore, explore swapping your many policies for newer, fewer ones. You could save hundreds every year.

One Dumb Feature You Need to Avoid

In an effort to increase your premium — and therefore the commission — your agent might suggest you add a rider to your policy called an *accidental death benefit*, sometimes called "double indemnity."

Under this rider, your heirs receive additional money if your death is caused by an accident. This is absurd, because death is death: Dying from a bus accident instead of cancer is not going to change your family's need. Therefore, get the coverage you need and skip this rider. Ditto for "cancer life" and similar policies which pay only if you die from certain causes, such as cancer or an airplane crash. Remember: Life insurance should cover death itself, not merely certain causes of death.

A woman once told me that her husband's company provided five times his salary if he died in an air crash while on business travel. "If he dies of a heart attack," she joked, "I'm driving him to the airport!"

Chapter 75 - How to Protect Yourself From ~~Lawyers~~ Lawsuits

In a world where you can sue and win for being served coffee that is too hot, you need to protect your money.

And you can, with an umbrella liability insurance policy. These policies provide a minimum of $1 million in coverage for nearly anything that might happen. Merely having a homeowner's or auto policy isn't enough, for too many things can happen that are unrelated to your home or car. Besides, most homeowner's policies cover you for only $100,000 to $300,000, and auto liability insurance often provides just $50,000. Those figures are peanuts in a liability suit.

What if you bump into an elderly woman with your grocery cart, causing her to fall and break her hip, or if your foot slips off the brake causing you to hit the car in front of you, which causes that car to hit a pedestrian?

Remember: If a claim against you exceeds your insurance limit, you're on your own for the rest. Don't risk it. Get an umbrella liability insurance policy instead. They are very affordable, typically costing under $250 per year. But because insurers are providing a lot of coverage at little cost, getting a policy is not always easy. Your premium — and whether or not you qualify — is based on where you live, the cars you own, whether your household has drivers under age 26, your driving record, prior claims, and other factors.

Many carriers will sell you an umbrella policy only if you buy your homeowner's and auto coverage from them as well. A few carriers will provide a stand-alone umbrella policy, but only if you maintain "minimum" coverage on your primary policies. The best course is to talk with the agent who sold you a homeowner's policy.

Chapter 76 - Should You Buy from an Insurance Agent or Insurance Broker?

When buying any form of insurance, should you work with an insurance agent or broker? To understand the answer, first understand the difference.

Captive agents are employees of an insurance company. As such, they represent the carrier exclusively, just as a Ford dealer sells Fords exclusively: No matter how good a Chevy is, no Ford salesman will sell you one. Some of the biggest insurance companies are captive agencies.

Independent agents, or *brokers*, represent many carriers — often dozens. Thus, independent agents are free to shop with many carriers to find the one that offers the best policy at the best price for the client. Brokers, therefore, do the shopping for their clients, alleviating the need for their clients to shop on their own.

Therefore, you should either work with one broker, or with *several* agents, since agents will give you policies from only one carrier each.

I have seen agents claim to be brokers in an effort to dissuade their clients from talking to the competition. If you are unsure, ask your broker to name the carriers he or she works with, and if you doubt his or her veracity, ask to see their licenses. In most states, agents must have one license for each carrier they represent. Another good test is to ask for a business card. If it contains the name or logo of a specific insurance company, that's who they represent. Period.

Chapter 77 - How Safe Is Your Carrier?

Although consumers have always had questions about their policies, few ever questioned the stability of their insurance company.

Until some major providers went broke.

With the collapse of Baldwin United, Executive Life of California, Mutual Benefit of New Jersey and Confederation Life, among others, consumers rightfully are concerned that their insurer might go broke — taking much-needed insurance protection with them. An unfortunate example of how **The Rules of Money Have Changed**, consumers must be certain that their carrier is financially healthy, for it must be in business when you file a claim decades from now.

Five major ratings companies evaluate carriers, and their rating systems are shown in Figure 11-10.

The easiest way to learn the rating and strength of a carrier is to ask your agent (if she won't show you documentation, find another who will).

Keep in mind that high ratings do not guarantee that a company is in good health: Executive Life was top-rated only weeks before it went broke. Also, don't be worried if an agent recommends a carrier you've never heard of. There are 4,000 life insurance companies in the United States, and the vast majority don't sponsor golf tournaments or half-time shows on television.

RATING SERVICES

Description	A.M. Best	S&P/ D&P	Moody's	Weiss
Superior Negligible Risk	A++ A+	AAA	Aaa	A+
Excellent Small, Slightly Variable Risk	A A-	AA+ AA AA-	Aa1 Aa2 Aa3	A A- B+
Very Good	B++ B+			
Good High Claims-Paying Ability For Now	B B-	A+ A A-	A1 A2 A3	B B- C+
Adequate Less Protection Against Risk	C++ C+	BBB+ BBB BBB-	Baa1 Baa2 Baa3	C C- D+
Below Average Higher Risk Factor	C C-	BB+ BB BB-	Ba1 Ba2 Ba3	D D- E+
Financially Weak High Risk Factor	D	B+ B B-	B1 B2 B3	E E-
Not-Viable (or about to be)		CCC CC D	Caa Ca C	F
State Supervision	E			
Liquidation	F			

FIGURE 11-10

ric's money quiz

Here's a chance to see how well you learned the information contained in Part XI – Insurance. Don't worry if you get stumped — just re-read this part until it sinks in. Remember, your financial future depends on it.

The answers are at the end of the quiz. No peeking!

---

1. **Your largest financial asset is:**

   ○ a. your house
   ○ b. your health
   ○ c. your ability to produce an income
   ○ d. your company pension or retirement plan

2. **According to a study by the *Journal of the American Medical Association*, nearly _____ of 2,000 critically ill patients lost their life savings as a result of the illness.**

   ○ a. 5%
   ○ b. 12%
   ○ c. 16%
   ○ d. 31%

3. **_____ out of 10 couples can expect at least one partner to use a nursing home after age 65.**

   ○ a. one
   ○ b. three
   ○ c. five
   ○ d. seven

4. **Disability insurance benefits generally equal _____:**

   ○ a. 100% of your pay and are taxable if you pay for the policy but tax-free if your company pays for the policy
   ○ b. 60% of your pay and are tax-free if you pay for the policy but taxable if your company pays for the policy
   ○ c. 75% and are always tax-free
   ○ d. 80% and are always taxable

5. **If you have assets and need long-term care, the cost will be covered by:**

   ○ a. your medical insurance
   ○ b. Medicare
   ○ c. Medicaid
   ○ d. none of the above

6. Which of the following features should you look for in a long-term care policy?

   I.   inflation protection
   II. home care coverage
   III. at least $180 per day in coverage
   IV. prior hospitalization required

   ○ a. I, II, III
   ○ b. I, II
   ○ c. I, III, IV
   ○ d. II, III, IV

7. The type of life insurance which allows cash value to grow at competitive interest rates but which cannot lose money is known as:

   ○ a. term life
   ○ b. whole life
   ○ c. universal life
   ○ d. variable life

8. The one type of life insurance whose premiums are guaranteed never to rise is known as:

   ○ a. term life
   ○ b. whole life
   ○ c. universal life
   ○ d. variable life

9. The one group of people who never need their own life insurance policy is

   _____.

   ○ a. single mothers
   ○ b. children
   ○ c. widows
   ○ d. the unemployed

10. An "accidental death benefit" rider:

   ○ a. provides additional money if your death is caused by an accident
   ○ b. increases your premiums
   ○ c. is a waste of money
   ○ d. all of the above

Answers: 1-c (pg.507)   3-d (pg.520)   5-d (pg.522)   7-c (pg.538)   9-b (pg.546)
           2-d (pg.509)   4-b (pg.513)   6-a (pg.530)   8-b (pg.537)   10-d (pg.548)

Part XII
Estate Planning

There's a quiz at the end of this part!

To see how much you already know, skip to the
end of this part and take the quiz now. Then, read
the part and take the quiz again. You'll discover
how much you've learned!

Part XII – Estate Planning

Overview - Managing and Distributing Wealth

Thus far, you've learned how to protect, accumulate, and manage wealth. Now you're going to learn the final phase of money management: how to distribute wealth.

To preserve your wealth for your heirs, we're going to try to make you broke — because the more money you have when you die, the more the IRS will collect. If you're like most people, you're probably intimidated by the subject of estate planning. No doubt you've heard it's complex. But, like insurance, the basic concepts are quite simple.

To begin, please understand that everyone — including you — has to deal with estate planning for the simple reason that everybody has an estate, not just rich people. That often comes as a surprise: When I once asked a new client about the size of his estate, he replied, "I don't have an estate. I just have a house and some savings." He thought estates were the exclusive domain of the Kennedys and Rockefellers, but the truth is that everyone has an estate.

Your estate is simply the total value of everything you own minus debts. And the goal of estate planning simply is to transfer your assets to your heirs after your death, or for you to receive assets from a deceased relative. This part will show you how to do it.

Chapter 78 - Your Will

When a person dies, their assets are given to their heirs. This raises a question: Who gets what?

That's why you need a will. Through it, you leave instructions for the disposition of your assets. Typically, wills tell us:

- whether to pay off mortgages and auto loans;

- what debts are to be eliminated;

- what debts are not to be paid off;

- what assets are to be sold, such as real estate or businesses;

- to whom remaining assets are to be given, including family heirlooms and items of sentimental value, as well as financial assets;

- when assets are to be distributed (immediately, at some specified time in the future, or upon satisfaction of certain conditions);

- who is to be "legal guardian" and assume responsibility for raising minor children;

- who is to ensure that all these instructions are implemented correctly (called the "executor" or "personal representative"); and

- any other instructions you wish to leave.

Your Will or Theirs?

Do you have a will? If you answered, "No," think again, because the truth is that *everybody has a will.*

If you die without having written your own, your estate will use a standard one written by your state government. It's called *dying intestate* and, if you rely on it, you give up the opportunity to disburse your assets as you wish. Odds are, in fact, you won't like what the state will do with your assets. For example, in some states, if you have children from a prior marriage, dying intestate means your spouse gets only one-third of your assets, the kids get two-thirds. In other states, intestacy means assets might pass to parents, in-laws, brothers, sisters, even aunts, uncles, and cousins instead of the people you wish.

Furthermore, failing to write a will means you give up the right to name a guardian for your minor children. Do you really want a judge to make that decision for you?

Nine Questions to Help You Choose a Guardian for Your Kids

The most common excuse offered by parents of young children for putting off writing a will isn't the thought of dying. No, what brings the process to an immediate halt is trying to decide who will raise the children.

Because of this question, many parents do the worst thing: nothing. And that means the decision, if it becomes necessary, will be made by a judge in probate court. Don't let that happen to you. Don't let a stranger decide who will raise your kids.

If you're stuck on how to choose a guardian, the following will help you:

With pen and paper, answer the following questions, providing as much detail as possible. If you are deciding as a couple, answer these questions separately and then compare your answers. Many of these questions will take some thought, so you might not be able to answer right away. That's okay. Answer what you can in the first sitting and set a deadline to finish the rest.

> *"Money doesn't solve problems — it just creates new ones!"*
> — Ric Edelman

Question #1: Who Are All the Candidates?

Listen to your gut instinct and answer the remaining questions with these people in mind.

Question #2: Is it likely that the candidate(s) will live for many years?

Remember, you are planning for the event that your kids have just lost their parents... losing your replacements can be twice as devastating. A lot of people want to name grandparents, but are your parents too old?

Question #3: How is each candidate's health?

Are they physically and mentally able to accept the responsibility? Do they have the energy? This is another caveat for grandparents. They may be great as weekend baby-sitters, but having your kids permanently is a very different notion. Are they up to it?

Question #4: Do the candidates have kids of their own? If not, do they know how to raise children? If so, would adding yours to their household be too much for them to handle?

Raising a family is expensive and hectic, particularly for two-income families. Your proposed guardians already may have a full plate. Conversely, if they don't have kids, are you confident they know how to raise children?

Question #5: Do the candidates have time to raise your kids?

Are they a two-career family or does one parent stay home? Is one or the other particularly important to you?

Question #6: What are the candidate's views on education and religion?

Do you insist upon home-schooling or private education? Do they share your religious beliefs? Will the candidates raise your children with the same values and cultural traditions as you would have provided?

Question #7: Where do the candidates live?

Moving your kids to some far-away place after losing their parents can make a difficult transition even more difficult, for they will have lost not only their parents, but litcrally everything they are familiar with — school, friends, nearby relatives, favorite places and pastimes. You'll want to try to avoid this problem, but sometimes the best candidate doesn't live nearby. In such cases, perhaps the transition can be eased. For example, let them finish the school year where they are, if possible, or provide the money for them to visit friends for extended periods.

Question #8: Are the candidates a young married couple?

If so, you might want to consider adding a statement about who gets your kids if they divorce. And if one of them dies, would you feel comfortable letting the survivor raise your kids?

Question #9: Are the candidates financially secure?

While you shouldn't let wealth (or lack thereof) be the sole basis for choosing one candidate over another, you do want to know your kids will be in a financially stable and safe environment. While you probably want to leave all your money to your kids,[53] be realistic about the financial impact raising them will have on their guardians. Indeed, the guardians are sure to incur expenses associated with raising your kids, such as adding a room onto their house or buying a bigger car, let alone providing food each day, so you should make your asscts available to help them. Otherwise, the guardian (or the guardian's spouse or children) could become frustrated. Thus, you must carefully balance several issues: You want your money used for the benefit and welfare of your kids and to have the assets available to help the guardian as needed, but at the same time you want to protect against the squandering of the assets by the guardians or others (maybe even your own kids!). A good estate planning attorney can help you achieve these goals.

As you consider these questions, feel free to change your mind. You also may find that you preferred certain people for some questions but not others. That's okay, too. This process is all about identifying the strengths and weaknesses of potential guardians. Often, the most appropriate person is the one who scored generally well, as opposed to one who scored great in some areas but terrible in others.

If you are deciding as a couple, only after you each reach a decision should the two of you compare notes. By having written down the *reasons* for your preferences

---

[53]See the following section for important information about leaving money to minors.

beside each question (and not just the names), each of you can better understand the other, and perhaps his or her reasoning is more sound than yours.

Then: *Choose someone!* Pick a guardian you both can agree on, even if that means you each accept someone who is not necessarily your favorite — and please, after choosing, be sure to ask your choice to accept the nomination. Force him or her to sleep on it, and require that his or her partner (if any) consent.

> *"A man becomes a conservative at that moment in his life when he suddenly realizes he has something to conserve."*
> —Eric Jubler

Above all, remember: Failure to make a choice is itself a choice. Until you name someone, you are agreeing to let the probate court decide, where all the people you considered above (and possibly others) will fight it out with the judge acting as referee. It's a very difficult task for a judge, since he or she has never met you and will have no idea what you would want. That's why judges often select the first family member to show up at the courthouse!

If the thought of making a choice sends you into a panic, remember that you can always change your mind. Several of our clients change their minds every other year, as circumstances in their families change. If your parents seem the best option today, pick them. In a few years, when they've gotten older or become ill, you can change your selection. Or maybe today's choice marries someone you don't like, or suffers a setback of some kind. No problem. Just base your decision on the facts as they are today, and rest assured that as times change and people change, your mind can change as well.

How to Accept an Offer to be a Child's Guardian

Being asked to serve as guardian is the highest honor a parent can bestow on you. But the title is not an honorary designation. Rather, there are important legal, financial and family issues involved — and too often, all parties ignore the details.

Don't let that happen to you. If you are asked to serve as guardian, accept (assuming you are inclined to do so) only if the parents fulfill the following requirements:

1. They must have both their wills and/or trusts:

    a. name you (and your spouse, if you are married) as Guardian(s) for all the children. Think twice if you are asked to serve for only one or some of their kids.
    b. leave their assets to or in a trust or into Custodial accounts (formed under the Uniform Transfer to Minors Act) for the benefit of the children, naming a Trustee of the trust or Custodian of the UTMA accounts.

As the above implies, the law requires that parents name a guardian for the money as a separate act from naming a guardian for the children. It is often recommended that the financial trustee or custodian be different from the guardian of the children. By having a third party control the assets, there is additional oversight that can help insure that the assets are used for the benefit and welfare of the children.

Read Chapter 53, and further in this chapter, for additional information on this topic.

Finally, require that the parents provide you with current valid copies of both wills and all trust/custodial documents. They should:

2. Provide you with a letter, signed and dated, that affirms their desire for you to serve as Guardian. Ideally, you should receive a newly signed copy of this letter annually. There are two reasons for this:

    •   First, it will serve as a contemporary acknowledgment of your desire that could prove essential with family members and the court.
    •   Second, sentiments and circumstances often change with time, and this activity will help you reconfirm the parents' desire, giving them the opportunity to change their mind and select different guardians.

3. Inform all family members — including the children — of their decision. Everyone — parents, grandparents, siblings and cousins, on both sides of the family — must be told of their decision to name you guardian for the children. This will do much to reduce the risk of a legal challenge upon their deaths and help make the transition for the children less stressful than it will inevitably be.

4. Leave each child with at least $500,000. If the parents' current assets (home minus mortgage, investments and savings) comprise less than this amount, they

should obtain life insurance to make up the difference. A 15-year term policy on each (or solely on the primary breadwinner) is an inexpensive way to meet this need. The primary beneficiary should be the surviving spouse, and the secondary beneficiary should be the trust or custodial account(s) that they establish in #1b above.

5. Write several letters of personal wishes. One joint letter from both parents should be addressed to you, the guardians). It should state their wishes for the children and instructions regarding their upbringing. The letter should include their thoughts (in no particular order) on money, discipline, family, religion, marriage, education, career, politics, love and life, to help guide you in your new role. The parents should place this letter in a sealed envelope and give it to you now with instructions as to when you are to read it (now or upon their deaths). Then, the parents each should write additional letters to each of their children and give them to you for safekeeping with instructions regarding when to give them to each child.

By going beyond the notion of guardianship and handling the decision in a practical way, you will be demonstrating to the parents that they have made the right decision.

Why Not to Leave Big Bucks to Little Kids

The most common estate planning mistake parents make is to name children under 18 as direct beneficiaries of IRAs or life insurance policies (usually as the secondary beneficiaries). It seems to make sense to do so. After all, you bought the policy (or, your employer gave it to you) to protect your spouse and pay for your kids' future college costs, so it seems logical to name your spouse as the primary beneficiary and your kids as the secondary beneficiaries in the unlikely (and unthinkable) event that both of you die. Indeed, your life insurance agent (or benefits officer at work) didn't object, so what's the problem?

The problem is that your kids (if they're under 18) will not get the money, even though they are named in the policy as the secondary beneficiaries.

Instead, the money will go into the registry of the court, which will name a guardian of the money for the kids. Even if your will names a guardian for the kids, the *money* must get its own guardian.

Why isn't the money covered by your will? Because IRAs and life insurance proceeds go directly to beneficiaries named in the policy, bypassing any instructions contained in a will. Although your will names a guardian for the kids (it better, or the court will decide that, too! — see the prior section), the IRA account or insurance policy controls these assets.

Thus, by naming your minor children as beneficiaries, the IRA or insurance proceeds will be turned over to the court, which will appoint a financial guardian to manage the assets, and most distributions must be approved by the court. There is no assurance that the court will appoint as financial guardian the same person you named as the children's guardian in your will.

> *"Money isn't everything, but it sure keeps you in touch with your children."*
> —J. Paul Getty

Chances are, after a year and thousands of dollars in legal fees, the life insurance money will be placed into a custodial bank account for the kids (until they turn 18, which typically is the latest age that a court may place money beyond the reach of a child). But once they're 18, the kids get the money — and they just might choose a sports car over college, despite your intentions.

What's the solution?

In your will, establish a children's trust and name it as the secondary beneficiary. You can even set up the children's trust in your own living trust (more on that later). That will avoid probate as well as court guardianship proceedings — and you get to determine at what age your kids are entitled to receive the money. (You may decide to withhold the funds from them until well beyond age 18.)

A second, simpler option is to designate as the insurance beneficiary a custodian under a UTMA (Uniform Transfers to Minors Act) or UGMA (Uniform Gifts to Minors Act) account. The insurance money will go directly into the account, which will be managed for the benefit of your kids by the custodian you've named. This custodian can be the same person who's serving as the kids' guardian, and distributions can be made at any time for the kids' support and education.

If you name as your secondary beneficiary "my estate," that means the asset will be distributed in accordance with your will. That means, in turn, that you need to specifically address in your will how the IRA or insurance proceeds are to be handled. For example, you might state that the assets are to be held in trust until the children graduate from college.

Protecting your family through IRAs, company retirement accounts, and life insurance is a smart thing to do, but you need to make sure you handle them properly or your plans could be thwarted. So, don't name your minor kids as direct beneficiaries. That may be the easy thing to do, but it could prove very costly.

For more on IRAs and company retirement plans, see Chapters 67 and 68. For insurance, see Part XI. For trusts continue with this part and for UGMA/UTMA, turn to Chapter 53.

Even Single People Must Write a Will

With no spouse or children, many single people think they don't need a will, but this is wrong. Why? Because even single people have debts, assets, and family members, and instructions still are needed.

Do you want your parents to receive your assets or would you rather split your assets among your siblings? What if you want to leave money for nieces or nephews for their college education? Without a will, your family won't know your intentions and, hence, your wishes will not be enacted.

Do You Have a Non-Married Partner?

Take the example of Joe and Susan, who have been living together for five years. They've accumulated some joint assets (furniture, cash, and a car) and some joint debt (a line of credit and a car loan), and they're living in a townhouse Joe bought the year before he met Susan. Then Joe has a car accident.

What Happens if Your Partner Dies

Say Joe died in the crash, and like many young people, he had no will. Consequently, his assets — including his savings, the townhouse, and his half of the property he owned with Susan — all pass to his parents. Susan receives nothing. Not only that,

Susan is now homeless and dependent upon Joe's parents to help her pay off the loans and other bills she and Joe accumulated together.

Clearly, the law does not protect unmarried partners. Oral agreements and understandings are not recognized under state law: If you have an unmarried partner (whether you live together or not), the only way to protect each other is for you both to write wills naming the other as your heir so that when either one dies, the assets will pass to the surviving partner.

If you have no will, or if you do not specifically name your partner in your will, he or she likely will receive nothing upon your death. Assuming you have no children, whatever you own will go to your parents (if they are alive) or to your brothers and sisters (if your parents have pre-deceased you).

What Happens if Your Partner Lives

Let's assume Joe survives the accident, but is injured and hospitalized. What can Susan do to help manage his affairs, such as paying bills and authorizing medical treatment? Without two additional legal documents (a durable power of attorney and a health care power of attorney), not much. Susan does not have the rights of a spouse; she cannot access Joe's checking account or sign a release for surgery — even if she knows Joe's wishes. Joe's doctors won't discuss his condition with her, and Joe's family can even bar her from seeing him in the hospital! Her only alternative is to go to court to seek permission to act on his behalf, a time-consuming and costly proposition — and one likely to meet with opposition from Joe's family.

These problems can be avoided with durable powers. With a durable power of attorney, you name a person to act on your behalf should you become unable to manage your own financial affairs. The person you name as your "attorney-in-fact" can access your bank account to pay bills, sell securities to obtain cash for medical expenses, file your income tax return, and renew leases. A second durable power — the health care power of attorney — appoints someone (typically the person named in your durable power of attorney) to make health care decisions on your behalf, assuming you're unable to make them for yourself. The health care power of attorney also allows physicians to discuss your medical treatment with that person, even though they are not related or married to you.

If your partner is the person you most trust and to whom you would like your assets to go when you die, each of you needs to get wills and durable powers now to save each other problems in the future.

Being Married Is Much Simpler, Right?

Most married people write a "simple will," leaving everything to their spouse, or to their children if their spouse dies first. Yet this strategy, simple in concept, could lead to unexpected problems for the simple reason that life isn't so simple.

A Simple Will Might Not Protect Your Children

Richard and Ashley have two children. Richard dies, leaving everything to Ashley. Ashley then marries Tom, a widower with three children of his own. Then Ashley dies, leaving everything to Tom. When Tom dies, he leaves everything to his three kids. The result: Richard's money goes to Tom's kids; Richard's kids get nothing. Got that?

This is an excellent example of the problems created by a simple will. A better solution is for Richard to leave his assets to a trust, not to Ashley. Under the law, a trust is the same as a person. It can own assets, have debts and financial obligations, and so on. But a trust is a pretty dumb person, so it needs someone to tell it what it is supposed to do, and it needs someone to help it do these things.

For example, Richard can create a trust and give it all his assets upon his death. He can instruct the trust to give to Ashley all the money she needs, whenever she needs it. Or, he can place limits on how much or how often she is allowed to receive money. It's his trust, so he can set the rules any way he wants.[54] (Isn't America great?)

Since the trust doesn't get Richard's assets until he dies, someone other than Richard must be appointed to operate the trust (in conformance with Richard's rules). Who should Richard appoint as trustee?

In this case, his wife Ashley. After all, the money is for her benefit, so why force her to turn to a third person every time she needs money? The trust in this example is intended to protect Richard's kids in case Ashley dies, not to protect Ashley from herself, so naming Ashley as trustee is a fine idea.

> **If we were concerned about Ashley's ability to handle the money, we'd name someone else to serve as trustee or co-trustee. Richard could name another family member, a friend, even a lawyer, banker, or financial advisor.**

Thus, Ashley has access to the trust's assets during her lifetime — the same access, in fact, as though Richard had left it all to her directly. But Ashley doesn't "own" the assets, so in the event of her death, the money stays in the trust for the benefit of their kids; Ashley can't give the money to anyone else when she dies, and Tom can't make a claim on it. Thus, Richard has succeeded in protecting his kids without hurting Ashley. Since we don't know who will die first, Ashley would write a will with the same provisions in case she dies first and Richard remarries.

A Simple Will Might Not Protect Heirs Who Cannot Handle Money

Do you *really* want to leave all your money to your 18-year-old? Images of sports cars and weeks at the beach flash through my mind, and I don't see a textbook anywhere.

Do you *really* want to leave your money to your relative who has a drug or alcohol problem, who gambles, who can't hold a job, or who is abusive? Or to that relative who never seems to have any money, is always bouncing checks, living paycheck to paycheck, and is constantly borrowing money from family and friends?

Do you *really* want to leave your money to these people?

Of course you do, because you love them. But you also realize that giving money to someone who can't handle it is like giving a drink to a drunk — you're certainly not doing anybody any favors.

This is perhaps the most fatal flaw of a simple will: Named heirs will receive your assets without restriction. And often, restrictions are exactly what are needed.

In such situations, a better idea may be to leave your money to a trust. You can set rules stating:

> This is why I don't like those will-making software programs. Although they can produce simple wills, you now have lots of reasons why a simple will might not be best for you.
>
> And these programs might not reflect laws in your state. The bottom line: You don't know if the program is producing a document that gives you everything you need. You can't ask it questions, and you can't hold it liable for its errors.
>
> Forget the software. See a lawyer. A small amount of money spent here may save your family thousands or hundreds of thousands of dollars and a lot of grief.

- **How soon.** You can delay availability of money for a certain period of time or until heirs reach certain ages; even spread out distributions over time.

- **How much.** You can grant heirs access to interest only, to a certain percentage of the trust's principal, to both, or to any combination.

- **How often.** You can state whether money is to be distributed whenever the person requests it, or you can release assets on a schedule, like an allowance.

- **How so.** You can require that your money be made available only for certain purposes, such as paying for college, or only under certain conditions, such as a medical need.

As you can see, "simple" wills are not always best, because life is not always so simple. Talk with an attorney who specializes in wills and trusts before you write your will.

A Terrible Place to Keep Secrets

Do you know what your parents plan to leave you? Have you told your kids what you plan to leave them?

Many parents never plan ahead. Even those who do rarely discuss the subject with their kids. Take the quiz below and see how you score.

If you're the son or daughter:

- Do you know where your parents keep their wills?

- Do you know who their executor is?

- Do you know how they plan to divide their assets?

- Do you know who they want to receive certain items of sentimental value?

- Have you told them how you feel and what you think about the above questions?

If you answered "no" to any question above, you need to have a serious conversation with your parents.

If you're the mother or father:

- Have you told all your kids where you keep your will?

- Have you told all your kids who your executor is?

- Have you told all your kids how you plan to divide your assets?

- Have you told all your kids who you want to receive certain items of sentimental value?

- Have you asked all your kids how they feel and what they think about the above questions?

If you answered "no" to any question above, you need to have a serious conversation with all your children.

A will is a terrible place to keep secrets, yet that's exactly what most Americans have done. The reasons don't matter. What does matter are the consequences of keeping secrets. Maybe you have not experienced any problems yet, but chances are you will.

I say this because my colleagues and I have seen problems arise in dozens of our clients' families. If you haven't talked with your family, you are setting the stage for them to suffer the same problems. Here are some we've seen:

Family Problem #1: The Child's Plan Thwarts the Parent's Plan

Mom, a widow, has $400,000 in assets. She's concerned about her health and anticipates that she'll eventually live in a nursing home. She fears that spending all her money on long-term care[55] will mean leaving nothing for her only daughter and grandson.

---

[55]For a complete discussion of planning for Long-Term Care, see Chapter 73.

To avoid this problem, Mom hires an estate attorney and executes an elaborate estate plan designed to protect her assets from the costs of long-term care. Mom's plan effectively supports her desire to leave her assets to her daughter and, in turn, to her grandson.

Some years later, Mom, now 84, indeed enters a nursing home. Her assets have been protected: Her daughter now owns and controls all $400,000. Since Mom has no assets, her expenses are covered by Medicaid.

Next, the daughter, herself now 63, suffers a heart attack and dies. *She had not written a will of her own.*

Because the daughter dies intestate, the state orders that her son receive only one-quarter of her money. The rest is awarded to her surviving mother. Mom gets back $300,000 of the $400,000 she was trying to pass on. And because Mom now has the money, Medicaid claims it as reimbursement for the expenses it had paid on her behalf.

Thus, while Mom had created an estate plan to shelter her assets, her efforts were thwarted because her daughter did not create an estate plan of her own. If her daughter had written even a simple will — naming her son as sole heir — he would have gotten the entire $400,000. Instead, he got only a fraction.

When you write your will, make sure the people to whom you're giving your money understand what you're doing — and why. Make sure they understand what they have to do and make sure they do it. Otherwise, all your efforts might be for naught.

Family Problem #2: You Love Your Children Equally

Many parents are terrified of showing favoritism among their children.[56] To avoid that problem, many parents avoid writing a will at all. By saying nothing, you eliminate the risk of hurting your children. But as we've seen, this is a terrible solution.

---

[56]Not that parents don't favor one child over another, just that they don't want their children to find out about it.

The next most common tactic is to leave all your assets equally to all your children. You love them all equally (or, at least, you want them to think so), so let's just let them divide up everything equally. This is often the worst thing you can do.

When one of my clients died, she left everything to her son and daughter equally. Among her assets was a condo at the nearby shore, worth about $140,000. The son, who lived far away, wanted to sell it and split the money with his sister. The daughter, who lived an hour's drive from the condo, wanted to keep it, as her own family enjoyed using the condo on weekends each summer.

He wanted to sell. She didn't. He offered to buy her out. She refused. He is now suing her, and they haven't spoken to each other in three years. *Thanks, Mom.*

The correct strategy would have been for Mom to either (a) leave the condo to one child, and other (equivalent) assets to the other child, or (b) sell the condo and give equal amounts of the cash proceeds to each child for them to do with as they please.

Remember: The only asset that can be split evenly and easily is cash.

Family Problem #3: You Think Your Kids Love Each Other

My kids get along great, you say. They'd never fight with each other over something like an inheritance.

Oh, yeah?

I'll concede that your three children love each other and are great friends. But funny things happen over time. Such as marriage. Your three children will bring into the family three spouses. And just wait until in-law #1 finds out that, upon hearing news of the death, in-law #2 raced over to the house, rifled through the drawers, and is now in possession of Grandma's diamond ring or Granddad's coin collection.

"She always intended it for me!" someone all-too-often claims. If you don't expressly tell everyone your intent, you're setting the family up for a huge fight.

> **And I mean tell everyone — not just the person to whom you plan to give the item. If you make a private promise, no one else will believe them. Tell everyone, write it down in something called a "letter of intent," and attach it to your will.**

Rather than leaving property to everyone equally, have your will instruct that all your assets be liquidated, with the resulting proceeds divided equally. It's easy to split dollars, not so easy to split houses, televisions, cars, jewelry, and furniture.

This idea might be hard to accept because many people associate their sense of self with their possessions. Therefore, you might resist the idea of instructing that all your worldly goods be sold at auction. But if this attitude prevents you from establishing clear rules for the handling of your assets at death, you're setting the stage for a major fight among your heirs.

You're also being unrealistic. If you leave all your worldly possessions to your kids, guess what they're going to do with all your stuff? Sell it at auction, of course. Haven't you ever seen those signs along the highway? *"Estate Sale This Saturday."* That sign means someone died and their kids are having a big yard sale.

> **Also, if you totally omit a family member from your will, they can challenge the will in court. Talk with a lawyer before you disinherit someone.**

If you think your kids are going to keep all the stuff in your house, think again: Your kids already have a house of their own, and it's already full of their own stuff. So get over it and instruct that your assets be liquidated. That way, your kids won't have to fight about it.

Family Problem #4: You're Mistreating the Problem Child

If you're like most parents, you consider your children to be your pride and joy. Unless one of your kids is a lazy, no-good, rotten bum — the kind of person who would spend in a month whatever money you left him, no matter how much you leave.

You might be tempted to cut this person out of your will, leaving your money to the rest of the family. Be careful if you plan to do that, for the strategy might not be as effective as you think.

You see, as a loving parent, you're always there for this child. Others of your family, in fact, have had to go without as you've devoted additional effort and attention to the problem child. Now, in your will, you want to set things straight. You'd like to give money to the other family members. They could use it, they deserve it, it's their reward for their years of helping the problem child, too. Besides, if you give the money to the problem child, he'll just squander it in a short time.

So, you might think, you'll just cut the problem child out of the will.

I've come across several cases where this was done, and in each case, the result was the same: The other children feel remorse at the fact that the problem child was disinherited and, knowing this, the problem child takes advantage of their guilt and generosity. The result: Each of your pride and joy becomes a surrogate parent to the problem child.

By giving your money only to your pride and joy, you condemn those children to a lifetime of supporting the problem child. A better solution, although it might not seem so at first, is to give the problem child an equal share and let it be known throughout the family that *that's it*.[57] "Don't rely on your brothers and sisters like you relied on us. We took care of you because we're your parents, but they are not. They have their own kids to care for. *Leave them alone*."

If you do not give this instruction to the problem child — with the full knowledge of the pride and joy — your hopes will not be realized.

Family Problem #5: You're Mistreating Your Pride and Joy

One of my clients had four children. One became a surgeon, another a teacher, the third "wants to be an actor," and the fourth has three children and is happily married to a civil servant.

---

[57]Better still, put the problem child's money into a trust, having the trust pay an allowance over the child's expected lifetime. This is called a Spendthrift Trust. To learn more, talk with an estate attorney.

In their wills, my clients intended to leave their assets to three of their children, with only a token amount to the one who became a doctor. When I inquired as to why, they explained, "He's doing much better than his brother and sisters, so he doesn't need the money." They wanted to leave their money to the kids who needed it most.

Without realizing it, my clients had chosen to punish their son for achieving success. They had not told him of their plans, because it never occurred to them that he might not understand.

And he might not. "I should have become an actor instead of working my butt off for eight years in medical school!" he may say. Animosity between him and his siblings could ensue.

> **Or maybe he would understand — but his wife and kids may not.**

NON SEQUITUR   WILEY

If the son does not learn of his disinheritance until after his parents have died, his brother and sisters will be the recipients of his anger and frustration. And that's assuming he knows his parents' reasoning. An even worse case is that he doesn't know why they cut him out of the will — only that they did. He could become very hurt and confused. In the end, he could challenge the will in court, demanding his share.

His parents had not envisioned any of this. They could prevent all these problems merely by talking with him, explaining their thoughts and concerns and asking his opinion. He's going to offer his opinion sooner or later, and sooner is much better, while there is time to change it.

The One Asset You Must Pass On

If there's one thing you must leave your family, it's this: Peace. Don't set the stage for a family war, or Thanksgiving dinner will never be the same. Talk with your family about your plans and about theirs. Above all else, remember: A will is a terrible place to keep secrets.

Chapter 79 - Estate Administration

Estate administration deals with transferring assets from your parents to you after they've died, or from you to your heirs following your death. As we begin this chapter, it is important that you remember this point: *Estate administration has nothing to do with estate taxes.* That's because *estate administration* is based on laws set by individual states, while *estate taxes* are assessed by the federal government.

Since we're going to leave estate taxes behind and focus on estate administration, set aside for the moment everything we covered in the previous chapter.

How Assets Pass to Heirs

When a person dies, everything he or she owned is transferred to heirs in one of two ways: through operation of law or through probate court. *Operation of Law*, as the name implies, pertains to assets covered by specific laws. This includes:

- **Accounts which feature a named beneficiary,** such as a life insurance policy, an IRA or other retirement account. When the account owner dies, the beneficiary receives immediate ownership and control of the asset.

- **Joint accounts**, legally called either "Joint Tenancy With Rights of Survivorship" or "Tenants by the Entirety." When one joint owner dies, the asset immediately is owned by the other. A common example is when a husband and wife have a joint checking account.

All other assets — and I mean *all* — pass to heirs according to instructions in the will. (As Chapter 78 revealed, those who have not written a will use one provided by their state government.)

Just because Steve's will says his wife Sue is to receive everything doesn't mean she does: All wills first must be proved valid, even those provided by the state. And this is the job of the Probate Court.

The Three Dreads of Probate Court

Probate has several disadvantages, as anyone who has gone through the process can tell you, including:

Dread #1: Extensive Time Delays

In most states, probate lasts a minimum of one year and, due to backlogs, it can last several years. During this time, the assets are frozen and generally unavailable to heirs. This delay is intended to give creditors time to get paid and relatives time to challenge the will. The more challenges, the greater the delays — perhaps for decades.

Dread #2: High Legal Fees

Depending on where you live, lawyers can charge as much as 5% of the value of the estate. Therefore, you should try to avoid naming a lawyer or bank to serve as your will's executor (now called the personal representative). Instead, appoint a family member and give them the authority to hire a lawyer for assistance as needed. This will save your estate tens of thousands of dollars in legal fees.

Dread #3: No Privacy

Probate is a public process, meaning anyone curious enough to inquire can read your will and learn the value of your estate, and who you named as your heirs. Probate is not without its advantages, of course. It provides court oversight of the executor's actions and limits the time for someone to dispute the will.

The Longest Probated Will in History

This dubious honor belongs to Marilyn Monroe. When she died on August 5, 1962, she left equal shares of her estate to her psychoanalyst and her manager. The psychoanalyst, in turn, left his half to a mental health center, while the manager's portion went to his children.

The estate is still being probated. The manager's children feel they are entitled to the psychoanalyst's share, because he left the money to an institution instead of to a person, and the manager's children contend this was not Marilyn's intent. Why are they fighting 40+ years after her death? Because Marilyn's estate generates an income of more than $1 million a year. That's worth fighting over.

Two Ways to Avoid Probate

Avoiding probate is an appropriate goal. Unfortunately, as with everything else we've learned, there's a right way and a wrong way to do it. The wrong way could cost you thousands.

The Wrong Way

Avoiding probate is simple: Just title all your assets jointly with your spouse. This works fine, provided (a) you have a spouse, and (b) your combined estate is below $1,500,000. But if either (a) or (b) is not true, holding assets jointly with another person is a terrible solution, for while it avoids probate, it creates another — very expensive — problem. Let's see how this often happens:

Mom, a widow, owns one major asset, a house worth $180,000. She wants her only daughter Ann to inherit it.[58]

Ann and her mom know about probate all too well, having gone through it when Ann's father died a few years ago. Mom is getting up in years, and she wants Ann to avoid probate on Mom's estate.

Mom thinks Ann can avoid probate by having Ann become a joint owner of the home, along with Mom. Therefore, Mom retitles the house from her name only to joint owner-ship with Ann.

This indeed enables them to avoid probate. But as I've stressed, probate is an administrative matter, not a tax matter. So this is where it gets interesting.

Since Mom's estate is below $1,500,000, she knows no estate taxes will be due at her death.

---

[58]Although the case described here refers to real estate, you should be aware that it applies equally to any type of financial asset, including bank accounts, mutual funds, stocks, and other property.

She's right. But in one of the nastiest tricks of the tax code, Mom and Ann are fooled into thinking they do not have to worry about taxes at all, when in fact they merely do not have to worry about estate taxes. Since Mom's estate is below $1,500,000, they are right that Mom's estate will not incur an estate tax, but they have forgotten about the capital gains tax (see Chapter 15).

Mom bought the house 40 years ago for $30,000. It is now worth $180,000.

Tax law says that if you sell an asset for more than you paid for it, you must pay taxes on the profit (the *capital gain*), which in this case is $150,000. If Mom had remained sole owner, leaving the house to Ann via her will, Ann would have received the house as an heir via the (dreaded) probate court.

But that's not what they did. To avoid probate, they put Ann's name on the deed of the house along with her mother. Ann, no longer an *heir*, is now an *owner*. And tax law treats owners very differently than heirs.

If Mom remained sole owner, Ann would have inherited the house at its current value of $180,000 (the *stepped-up basis*), meaning she'd be able to sell it without incurring any capital gain and thus with no capital gains tax. But as an owner, she inherited the house with Mom's original cost basis of $30,000 intact. As a result, when Ann sells the house, the $150,000 profit will be subject to capital gains taxes. In other words, while Ann has avoided probate and does not incur any estate tax, she could have to pay federal capital gains taxes of as much as $22,500. That's a pretty stiff cost to avoid probate.[59]

Five More Reasons Not to Title Assets Between Generations

If Mom and Ann's story isn't enough to stop you from titling assets between generations — or, frankly, with anyone other than your spouse — following are more horror stories for you to consider. Remember: These pitfalls apply to all kinds of assets — mutual funds, stocks, bonds, and bank accounts — not just real estate.

---

[59]It's possible that the capital gains tax might be somewhat lower than this example suggests, because Mom herself enjoyed a stepped-up basis on Dad's half of the house, which she inherited when he died. You should rely on a good tax or financial advisor who can calculate the tax for your situation.

Reason #1: The Child Might Die First

Dad has a bank account containing $40,000. He adds his son's name to the account. Then, his son dies. The IRS, holding that the son was a 50% owner in the property, requires the son's estate to pay estate taxes on $20,000. Thus, Dad loses as much as $9,600. Dad can avoid this only if he can prove that the property was originally his, and not his son's — something that can be difficult to prove.

Reason #2: The Child Might Steal Your Property

Sometime after Dad adds his son's name to his bank account, the son makes a substantial withdrawal. The bank permits the son to do this without notifying the father, because the son — being a joint owner — now has legal access to the assets.

Reason #3: You Could Lose Your Assets if Your Child Is Sued

I'm sure you believe that your child would never steal your money. But is it possible that your son or daughter might get into a car accident? If your child loses a judgment, the court could order that half of any assets he holds jointly with you be given to the victor.

Reason #4: You Disinherit Other Children

Not realizing that operation of law takes priority over a will, Mom adds the name of her eldest daughter to all her bank and investments accounts for convenience. When Mom dies, her will — which instructs that all her assets be distributed equally among her four children — is moot, because all her money and investments passed directly to the one daughter listed as joint owner on Mom's accounts! If the daughter chooses, she can keep all the money, and there's little her brothers and sisters will be able to do about it. If she tries to fulfill Mom's wishes by redistributing the assets to her siblings, she'll discover that doing so constitutes making a gift from her to them, rather than an inheritance from Mom to her children. That means the IRS will subject the redistributed assets to a gift tax — at the same tax rates as those used to assess estate taxes.

Reason #5: The Parent Causes the Child to Lose Big Tax Breaks

In each of the above cases, it's the parent who suffers. But sometimes the child can be the one at risk. In a recent case, Dad helped his son buy a house, and to protect his father's financial interests, the son added his dad's name to the deed. The son then accepted a job transfer to another state and sold the house. He returned to his dad the money his father had put up. The son then deducted his moving expenses on his tax return. The IRS denied 50% of the deduction, arguing that the son owned only 50% of the property. It didn't matter that the father was on the deed merely to satisfy the lender's requirements. Nor did it matter that the father was a family member — the IRS held that the father didn't qualify as a "family member" because he was not a dependent. And the IRS even ignored the fact that the father's name was removed from the deed prior to settlement. The key issue, the IRS said, was that the father was an owner at the time the son agreed to take the new job.

> Too many lawyers who prepare living trusts never make sure that their clients actually retitle assets into the trust. Yet without retitling your assets, all that legal work is for naught. As soon as your lawyer completes your trust document, take it to your bank, broker, and other financial advisors. And make sure your attorney handles any real estate you own.

Such are the games that tax laws play. By solving one problem, you create another. How then, can you avoid both?

The Right Way

Enter the Revocable Living Trust.

In our example, Mom should establish a revocable living trust, naming herself as both trustee (to retain control over the assets she places in the trust) and beneficiary (during her lifetime), and naming Ann as the beneficiary upon her death. *Revocable* means Mom can put assets into the trust and take them out at any time. *Living* means this trust is in effect only during Mom's lifetime, and *Trust* means the assets are owned by the trust, not by Mom.

Because the house is owned by the trust, not by Mom, it does not go through probate when Mom dies, but passes directly to Ann (the beneficiary). Because the house is worth less than $1,500,000, there is no estate tax, and because Ann inherits the house at the stepped-up basis of $180,000, there will be no capital gains tax when she sells it for that amount, either.

Thus, the revocable living trust allows Ann to inherit the house without probate and without taxes.

This illustrates how the easy solution (in this case, joint ownership) often is the wrong solution, and why proper estate planning is critical.

Pros and Cons of Revocable Living Trusts

A revocable trust has many advantages. Through it:

- **Your estate avoids probate.**

- **You distribute your assets as you wish** (your instructions simply are in the trust agreement as well as in your will).

- **Your decisions are not public.** Nobody knows about John Wayne's estate because he used a living trust.

- **You make it harder for disgruntled heirs to complain.** In most states, a disinherited heir cannot challenge a trust as easily as they can a will.

- **You can direct how you want your assets to be managed during your lifetime should you become incompetent.** You can set the rules in the trust and appoint someone to manage your affairs for you.

> Notice that the first four bullets are irrelevant to the person setting up the trust, because they address things that occur after you die. But the final point addresses an area that should be of critical importance to you, for it could well determine your quality of life in your final years. That is reason enough to establish a living trust.

Like all legal matters, living trusts do have disadvantages:

- **The trust is of no value unless you move assets into it.** Remember, a trust is a bucket: Unless you place assets into the bucket, the bucket itself is of no value. Thus, after you establish the trust, you need to change the name of all your assets from "John Smith" to "The Revocable Living Trust of John Smith." Doing so does

"Put not your trust in money, but put your money in trust."

—Oliver Wendell Holmes

not change John's access or legal control of the account; it simply allows the asset to skip probate upon John's death.

- **Living trusts do not avoid taxes.** These trusts are revocable, meaning you can put assets into them and take assets out at any time. Since you have this control, the assets continue to be considered yours for tax purposes (for annual income taxes, capital gains taxes, and estate taxes). That's why a comprehensive estate plan consists of several trusts, some (such as Bypass Trusts) to avoid estate taxes and others (such as living trusts) for estate administration.

- **It's more expensive to set up a trust than simply to retitle an asset into joint names.** You've got to decide if you have sufficient probatable assets to make the effort worthwhile. If you are married and all you own is a house and some IRAs, a living trust could be of little benefit.

Chapter 80 - Other Estate Planning Tools

The law provides for many solutions to estate planning needs. Some of the basic ones that most people need include:

- **Living wills,** which you use to declare your preferences for medical treatment in the event you become terminally ill;

- **Durable powers of attorney for health care**, which allow another person to make medical decisions for you if you are unable to make them for yourself; and

> In many states, these two documents have been replaced by a Medical Directive.

- **Durable general powers of attorney,** which allow another person (usually a spouse) to sign legal documents for you. The key word here is durable, for ordinary powers become void if you become incapacitated. Be aware that you are granting the person you name in this document unlimited access and control of all your assets.

By executing these documents now, you avoid the risk that someone else might go to court to be named your guardian in the event you become incapacitated.

Chapter 81 - When to Revise Your Will

Like financial plans, estate plans require periodic review to make sure they remain current and viable. You should review your estate plan if:

- your marital status has changed,

- your state of residence has changed,

- your income or net worth has changed,

- your health has changed,

- family members have died or been born,

- five years have passed.

FRANK & ERNEST   BOB THAVES

Frank and Ernest is copyright by Thaves. Used here with permission. All rights reserved.

ric's money quiz

Here's a chance to see how well you learned the information contained in Part XII – Estate Planning. Don't worry if you get stumped — just re-read this part until it sinks in. Remember, your financial future depends on it.

The answers are at the end of the quiz. No peeking!

---

1. **What portion of Americans die without a will?**

   O a. 0%
   O b. 20%
   O c. 40%
   O d. 80%

2. **You should revise your will:**

   I.   when your marital status changes
   II. when you have a baby
   III. if you move to another state
   IV. if five years have passed

   O a. I, II
   O b. II, III
   O c. I, II, III
   O d. I, II, III, and IV

3. **Revocable living trusts do not:**

   O a. distribute assets
   O b. avoid probate
   O c. reduce estate taxes
   O d. protect privacy

4. **After a revocable living trust has been created for you, you need to:**

   O a. rewrite your will
   O b. name new beneficiaries
   O c. retitle assets into the trust
   O d. name a trustee

5. **IRA and life insurance proceeds:**

   O a. go directly to the named beneficiaries
   O b. go to whomever your will designates
   O c. automatically go to your next-of-kin
   O d. go to the guardian you appointed for your children

6. **Your estate is:**

   O a. the value of everything you own
   O b. the value of everything you and your spouse own
   O c. the value of everything you own minus debts
   O d. the value of everything you and your spouse own minus debts

7. Which of the following is an advantage of having assets go through probate court?

    ○ a. assets are passed to the heirs quickly

    ○ b. there are few costs

    ○ c. the value of your estate is kept private

    ○ d. none of the above

8. Mary's husband John dies. Which of John's assets must pass through probate court?

    ○ a. John's IRA account

    ○ b. the proceeds of John's life insurance policy

    ○ c. John's portion of the house he and Mary owned jointly

    ○ d. none of the above

9. With a revocable living trust:

    ○ a. the bulk of your assets go through probate

    ○ b. your decisions are public

    ○ c. you can direct how your assets are to be managed if you become incompetent

    ○ d. it is easier for disgruntled heirs to challenge your decisions

10. _____ accounts allow owners to name a beneficiary:

    ○ a. joint

    ○ b. retirement

    ○ c. mutual fund

    ○ d. bank

Answers: 1-a (pg.558)   3-c (pg.584)   5-a (pg.578)   7-d (pg.579)   9-c (pg.584)

               2-d (pg.585)   4-c (pg.584)   6-c (pg.557)   8-d (pg.578)   10-b (pg.578)

Part XIII
How to Choose a Financial Advisor

There's a quiz at the end of this part!

To see how much you already know, skip to the end of this part and take the quiz now. Then, read the part and take the quiz again. You'll discover how much you've learned!

Part XIII – How to Choose a Financial Advisor

Overview - The Most Important Financial Decision You Will Make

The world of personal finance was once simple.

In the old days, if you wanted a savings account or if you needed to borrow money, you went to a bank. If you wanted to invest, you went to a stockbroker. And if you needed insurance, you saw an insurance agent.

It's not so simple anymore. Today, there is an incredible array of new products, as we've discussed throughout this book. You want to buy a bond? That sounds easy enough. But which kind? There are municipal bonds, government bonds, and corporate bonds. You can buy convertible bonds, bonds with equity warrants, Dutch auction notes, and dual currency bonds. Then, of course, there are indexed bonds, junk bonds, option-related bonds, and pay-in-kind debentures. And don't forget zero-coupon bonds and flip-flop notes, not to mention zebras, bunny bonds, and LYONs and TIGRs and STRIPs (oh, my!).

And that's just bonds. I haven't even mentioned stocks and options. Or mutual funds. How about annuities, limited partnerships, real estate investment trusts, and guaranteed insurance contracts. Then there are oil & gas deals, foreign currency options, and collateralized mortgage obligations. But then again, I think maybe I don't want to mention them after all.

As if all these new products weren't enough, today there is a seemingly endless variety of people who will sell them to you. Today, everybody is moving in on everyone else's turf. Bankers are selling stocks and bonds, while stockbrokers will lend you money. Some insurance agents will sell you anything *but* an insurance policy. IBM offers its own mutual funds. AT&T has its own credit card. General Electric and General Motors each have bigger consumer loan programs than Bank America. And Circuit City actually makes more money charging interest on its credit card than selling merchandise in its stores.

So, today, you are faced not only with the dilemma of what products to buy, but who to buy them from. How do you go about it, to whom can you turn for help with all this?

Enter the financial planner.

Created in the past 30 years, the financial planning profession is a response to the increasing complexity of today's economic marketplace. Financial planners can be found in many different companies — banks, brokerage firms, accounting firms, insurance companies, and of course, in financial planning firms. They use different titles, and carry lots of different credentials. But once you boil it all down, you reach a common denominator. All planners work with one goal in mind: to help you make financial decisions.

No matter what they call themselves, whether it's account executive, investment advisor, financial consultant, or financial planner, their job is to help you analyze your finances and give you advice regarding investments, insurance, taxes, wills & trusts, and mortgages — in a way that helps you achieve your financial goals.

Working with a financial planner should be a fun, close, warm relationship. It should not be adversarial. You should like your planner as a person, and he/she should be someone with whom you want to spend time.

If you choose your planner well, your planner should become an important part of your life, and you should be together for a lifetime. After all, financial planning is a lifetime activity, and a good planner can help make the process both fun and profitable for you.

FRANK & ERNEST   BOB THAVES

Chapter 82 - Financial Planners vs. Money Managers

A financial planner creates custom-designed plans and investment programs for each client. A money manager, in contrast, invests each client's money identically.

If a manager decides to sell Ford stock, he or she will sell Ford out of every client's portfolio, and if he or she wants to buy Intel, every client will own it. Thus, every client's portfolio is identical and their results will be identical.

Mutual funds, for example, are run by money managers, and every investor in a given mutual fund has the same results as every other investor of the fund. The only differences are caused by the dates a given client might open or close an account. In many cases, financial planners refer their clients to money managers — often via mutual funds, annuities, or wrap accounts.

Private money managers — those not running mutual funds or annuities — are expensive. They typically charge annual asset management fees of up to 3% per year — in addition not only to your planner's fee, but to the trading expenses the manager incurs on your behalf as well.

Planners who work with private money managers say their clients receive personal attention. Others argue that private money managers really do nothing you can't get from ordinary mutual funds at far less cost. For more on the comparison between private money managers and those who operate mutual funds, see Chapter 26.

"The aim of all legitimate business is service, for profit, at a risk."
—Benjamin C. Leeming

Chapter 83 - Industry Designations vs. Federal and State Licensing

There is a big difference between federal licensing requirements and industry designations. The former is required; the latter are desired.

Unfortunately, "desire" can mean many things. Some practitioners want to demonstrate that they have a high level of knowledge. But others merely want people to think they have a high level of knowledge. As a result, over the past two decades dozens of organizations (some non-profit, others very for-profit) have surfaced, each offering one or more designations to planners willing to fork over the fees for them.

By holding one or more of the designations below, a planner would be suggesting that he has a certain amount of experience or knowledge. And although all the planners of my firm and I hold many designations, in the eyes of the government, all of them are meaningless.

- AAFMA Fellow   American Academy of Financial Management & Analysts Fellow
- AAMS   Accredited Asset Management Specialist
- ABA   Accredited Business Accountant
- ACEP   Accredited Continuing Education Provider
- AEP   Accredited Estate Planner
- AFC   Accredited Financial Counselor
- ATA   Accredited Tax Advisor
- ATP   Accredited Tax Preparer
- BCE   Board Certified in Estate Planning
- BCI   Board Certified in Insurance
- BCM   Board Certified In Mutual Funds
- BCS   Board Certified in Securities
- CAA   Certified Annuity Advisor
- CAIA   Chartered Alternative Investment Analyst
- CAM   Chartered Asset Manager
- CAP   Chartered Advisor in Philanthropy
- CAP   Chartered Annuity Professional
- CCPS   Certified College Planning Specialist
- CCRA   Certified Review Appraiser
- CCTS   Certified Corporate Trust Specialist

- CDP   Certified Divorce Planner
- CEA   Certified Estate Advisor
- CEBS   Certified Employee Benefit Specialist
- CEP   Certified Estate Planner
- CEPP   Certified Estate Planning Practitioner
- CEPS   Certified Elder Planning Specialist
- CFA   Chartered Financial Analyst
- CFC   Certified Financial Consultant
- CFG   Certified Financial Gerontologist
- CFLA   Certified Financial Management Analyst
- CFM   Certified in Financial Management
- CFMP   Certified Financial Marketing Professional
- CFP   Certified Financial Planner
- CFS   Certified Funds Specialist
- CFSSP   Certified Financial Services Security Professional
- ChFC   Chartered Financial Consultant
- CIC   Certified Insurance Consultant
- CIC   Certified Investment Counselor
- CIMA   Certified Investment Management Analyst
- CIMC   Certified Investment Management Consultant
- CISP   Certified IRA Services Professional
- CLBB   Certified Lender Business Banker
- CLF   Chartered Leadership Fellow
- CLTC   Certified in Long-Term Care
- CLU   Chartered Life Underwriter
- CMA   Certified Management Accountant.
- CMFC   Chartered Mutual Fund Counselor
- CPC   Certified Pension Consultant
- CPCU   Chartered Property Casualty Underwriter
- CPhD   Certified Philanthropic Development
- CPM   Certified Portfolio Manager
- CRA   Certified Retirement Administrator
- CRC   Certified Retirement Counselor
- CRCM   Certified Regulatory Compliance Manager
- CRP   Certified Retirement Planner
- CRPC   Chartered Retirement Planning Counselor
- CRPS   Chartered Retirement Plans Specialist
- CRSP   Certified Retirement Services Professional
- CSA   Certified Senior Advisor
- CSOP   Certified Securities Operations Professional

- CSS   Certified Senior Specialist
- CSTSA   Certified Specialist in Tax Sheltered Accounts
- CTEP   Chartered Trust and Estate Planner
- CTFA   Certified Trust and Financial Adviser
- CTFA   Certified Trust and Financial Advisor
- CWM   Chartered Wealth Manager
- EA   Enrolled Actuary
- ELS   Estate Law Specialist
- FIC   Fraternal Insurance Counselor
- FICF   Fraternal Insurance Counselor Fellow
- FLMI   Fellow Life Management Institute
- GFA   Global Financial Analyst
- LTCIS   Long Term Care Insurance Strategist
- LTCP   Long Term Care Professional
- LUTCF   Life Underwriter Training Council Fellow
- MCEP   Master Certified Estate Planner
- MFP   Master Financial Professional
- MS   Master of Science
- MSFS   Master of Science in Financial Services
- PFS   Personal Financial Specialist
- QFP   Qualified Financial Planner
- QPA   Qualified Pension Administrator
- REBC   Registered Employee Benefits Consultant
- RFA   Registered Financial Associate
- RFC   Registered Financial Consultant
- RFE   Registered Financial Engineer
- RFP   Registered Financial Planner
- RHU   Registered Health Underwriter
- RMU   Registered Mortgage Underwriter
- RPP   Registered Para Planner

Federal Securities Licenses

In order to sell securities, planners must hold a federal securities license. These licenses are offered by the National Association of Securities Dealers, a quasi-governmental agency empowered to license and regulate the industry. Although there are many NASD licenses, planners tend to hold one of two:

NASD Series 7 - General Securities

This is the license held by virtually all stockbrokers and the majority of financial planners. It permits advisors to offer and execute transactions pertaining to stocks, bonds, government securities, municipal bonds, mutual funds, unit investment trusts, closed-end funds, limited partnerships and options.

The only security not covered by the Series 7 is commodities trading (which requires the Series 3). If the advisor also holds a state life/health insurance license, the advisor also is permitted to offer variable annuities. The Series 7 examination is considered to be among the most difficult of any field, with a national pass rate of only 30%. Continuing education requirements also must be met.

NASD Series 6 - Mutual Funds

This allows an advisor to recommend only mutual funds, unit investment trusts and closed-end funds. Many insurance agents who seek securities licensing choose the Series 6 because, being much more limited, it is much easier to obtain than the Series 7. Continuing education requirements also must be met.

NASD Series 63 - Blue Sky Laws

Each of the states require that advisors demonstrate expertise with state securities laws as well, known as the "blue sky" laws. After passing the Series 6 or Series 7, an advisor must satisfy state regulators by pass-

> Although being a Registered Investment Advisor does not constitute financial planning expertise, you should never work with a planner who is not registered. Why? Because it's a federal crime not to register (do you want to work with an advisor who is not obeying the law?)
>
> Besides, the only advisors who are not registered are (a) crooks or (b) people who are so uninformed that if they don't even know about SEC registration rules; so you have to wonder what else they don't know.
>
> Actually, there is another group of advisors who are not registered. They are (c) those who don't have to register. This includes stockbrokers, insurance agents, attorneys, and accountants, because the SEC holds that such persons provide advisory services that are merely incidental to their other activities. Therefore, such professionals are exempt from SEC registration. So, don't be surprised if your broker, insurance agent, lawyer, or tax preparer is not registered — provided that the advisory service they provide is merely incidental to the other services they give you.

ing this examination. Until both the Series 6 or Series 7 and the Series 63 are passed, advisors are prohibited from offering recommendations to clients.

State Insurance Licenses

Advisors wishing to offer life insurance and annuities must pass state-administered insurance examinations. Most states require that applicants attend a 40-hour class, followed by a rigorous examination. There are substantial continuing education requirements as well.

Registered Investment Advisors

Any person who provides financial planning services also must be registered with the Securities and Exchange Commission, or with state regulatory authorities as well. Registration consists of:

- submission of Form ADV

- payment of the filing fees

- passage of the NASD Series 65 — Investment Advisor Examination

While all financial planners must be Registered Investment Advisors, please do not assign a greater importance to this than it deserves. The Series 65 examination merely tests knowledge of SEC rules, not expertise or competence, and there are no continuing education requirements.

Notice that I continually use the phrase "Registered Investment Advisor" instead of the acronym "RIA." That's because the SEC frowns on use of the initials. Why? Because the SEC recognizes that the mere filing of Form ADV (see Chapter 86) does not bestow any expertise upon the planner, and the agency does not want consumers to be misled into thinking a person is an expert just because they happen to be an "RIA." Thus, legitimate planners who are registered with the SEC refer to themselves as being Registered Investment Advisors, not RIAs.

Because the law requires all planners to register, do not work with any planner who has not done so.

Chapter 84 - The Four Ways Planners Get Paid

No matter who your planner is or what type of organization he works for, all planners are compensated in one of four ways: commission only, fee-only, fee-plus-commission, and fee offset. We'll look at each of these fee schedules one by one.

Compensation Method #1: Commission Only

Planners who are commission-only are different from traditional stockbrokers and insurance salespeople (who also are commission-only). Traditional stockbrokers make money by selling investments, such as stocks, bonds and mutual funds, while insurance agents sell life insurance, annuities, and sometimes mutual funds, too.

Like traditional brokers, commission-only planners almost always work for a bank, brokerage firm, or insurance company, and as far as their employers are concerned, they are salespeople — nothing more, nothing less. But what sets commission-only planners apart from traditional stockbrokers and insurance agents is their methodology.

If you were to ask a traditional stockbroker, "How should I invest $10,000?" he'll answer you, because brokers traditionally have been trained to focus on investments, not on non-investment-related matters such as taxes, mortgages or wills. This is not a criticism of traditional brokers: They know whether you should buy Ford stock vs. General Motors, but they are not trained to review broader financial issues, such as the tax implications of selling a stock.

That's the difference between a traditional stockbroker and a financial planner, who happens to hold a broker's license and work in a brokerage firm. If you ask a planner what to do with ten grand, he or she will not tell you. Instead, he or she will ask you lots of questions about your income and expenses, need for liquidity, how you feel about risk, and about your goals and objectives. They'll also want to discuss seemingly unrelated issues, such as family, job status, debt and budget issues, taxes, and estate matters. Only after analysis of

> *"With an evening coat and a white tie, anybody, even a stockbroker, can gain a reputation for being civilized."*
> —Oscar Wilde

all this information would a planner feel comfortable giving you investment recommendations.

So, go ahead and take investment and insurance advice from traditional stockbrokers and insurance agents, but don't let them pretend to be financial planners.

How do you tell them apart? The quickest way is this: Brokers and insurance agents tend to talk about their *products*, while planners tend to talk about *you*.

Financial planners who are compensated by commission only argue that anybody who pays a fee for financial planning is out of their mind. After all, they argue, the number-crunching and analysis that goes into your situation is all well and good, but if you never act on the recommendations, then the planning itself is of no value. Until you implement the plan, they argue — until you buy the investments or insurance that the planner says you need — the plan itself does you no good at all.

> It kills me when a person approaches me after a seminar and asks, "I have some money to invest. What looks good?"
>
> That's like phoning a physician and asking, "Hey, doc, what drugs are hot this week? I thought I'd try some."
>
> Stockbrokers believe that some investments are good and others are bad. Planners don't. Planners believe there's no such thing as a "good" or "bad" investment. Rather, planners seek "appropriate" investments and strategies designed to help each client achieve his or her goals.
>
> So while a planner might recommend the same investment as a broker, the planner's thought process and methodology that is used to arrive at that conclusion are very different from the broker's.

And since *all* investments and insurance products feature some form of transaction fees, expenses, sales charges, or commissions, you'll end up paying twice: once to be told what to do and again when you do it. So the commission-only planner argues that she is working in the consumer's best interests: If you don't like their recommendations, you are free to walk away, having spent no money on advice you're not using.

Thus, commission-only planners say their form of compensation demands that they emphasize the *implementation* phase of a financial plan. The result, they say, is that they produce better recommendations than other types of planners. They have to, they say, or you won't buy, and if you don't buy, they won't make any money.

The Problem with Commission-Only

Critics say commission-only planners can suffer from a serious conflict-of-interest. Since the planner makes money only when you buy, like stockbrokers and insurance agents, they only recommend products that have fat commissions. In other words, are they telling you to buy something because it's good for you or good for them?

Compensation Method #2: Fee-Only

To avoid this conflict, some people turn to *fee-only* planners, who do not earn commissions. Instead, they charge fees. This fee can be an hourly rate (usually ranging from $100 to $250 per hour) or a flat fee (usually $1,500 to $5,000 per year).

Whatever their rates, fee-only planners will conduct their analysis and give you recommendations, but you'll have to go elsewhere to buy the investment, insurance, or mortgage products they say you need. Because fee-only planners do not earn commissions, they argue that they do not have any conflict of interest.

Three Problems with Fee-Only Planners

Commission-only planners, in their own defense, offer three criticisms of fee-only planners.

BROOM HILDA   RUSSELL MYERS

Problem #1: Why They Do Not Earn Commissions

In order to sell investments and insurance products, you must hold a federal securities license and a state insurance license. Stockbrokers and insurance agents go through extensive training and testing, with subsequent auditing and review by federal and state regulators, including the SEC, the NASD, and state insurance commissions. There also are periodic continuing education requirements that must be fulfilled. With the exception of medicine, law, and accounting, the securities licensing exam is considered the most difficult. (The six-hour test has only a 30% pass rate.) It's similar with state insurance examinations. Maintaining a license requires passing state-mandated classes and tests, as well as ongoing continuing education requirements.

These licenses are the only government-recognized demonstrations of expertise and knowledge in the field of investments and insurance, and they constitute legal authorization for a person to make specific recommendations to you. So, commission-only planners argue that fee-only planners don't earn commissions simply because they aren't allowed to. And they're not allowed to because they do not have the required licensing, training, or experience.

For more on licensing, see the following chapter.

Problem #2: No Conflict, But No Interest, Either

While commission-only planners agree that their fee-only colleagues have no conflicts of interest, they say this lack of conflict creates a new problem.

Not too much of a turf war going on here, huh?

They say that because fee-only planners are compensated to analyze, not to implement, they are objective to the point of disinterest. It makes no difference to a fee-only planner whether your investments succeed or fail, since their fees are not based on performance. Say a fee-only planner tells you to put 30% of your money in stocks, so you go down the street to a stockbroker and buy them. When the stocks go down, you return to your planner who says, "I didn't mean those stocks!"

So commission-based planners say they are more accountable for their recommendations because they are implementation-oriented, not design-oriented like fee-only planners.

Problem #3: What They Earn vs. What You Pay

The final point commission-only planners make is this: Even though fee-only planners *earn* only fees, that doesn't mean you *pay* only fees. You've still got to implement, and that means you've still got to pay commissions or sales charges or transaction fees — *to somebody*. The fact that you're paying these expenses to someone else, rather than to your planner, might be small consolation.

Compensation Method #3: Fees-Plus-Commissions

The objections of the commission-only planners make sense. Still, it's nice to know that your planner is objective. So, which is the better choice? Before you choose, let's examine the third type of planner, the most common of all.

According to industry surveys, more than 70% of all financial planners charge their clients fees plus commissions. In other words, most planners do hold insurance and securities licenses. Therefore, they charge you fees for the analysis, then they sell you the investments you need and charge you commissions for doing so.

Many fee-plus-commission planners also charge asset management fees. These fees, anywhere from 1% to 3% of the value of the assets they are monitoring for you, are in addition to the fees and commissions you pay.

When Fees Are Really Commissions

Asset management fees, such as those charged by wrap accounts (see Chapter 26) are all the rage today. Although not yet used by a majority of planners, it is emerging as the compensation method of choice for both planners and consumers.

Consumers like asset management fees because they can avoid paying up-front commissions. Further, since the fee grows with the size of the assets, the planner's compensation is directly related to how well those assets perform. This puts the planner on the same team as the client: If the client's investments fall in value, so will the fee that the planner earns, while an increase in the client's account gives the planner increased compensation, too. This gives the planner a strong motivation to offer good recommendations.

And planners like asset management fees, too. Why? Because fees provide steady streams of income, enabling the planners to devote their energy to serving their existing clients. Commission-only and fee-only planners, on the other hand, must continually find new clients because their compensation comes from the commissions and fees that new clients pay. Asset-based planners do not have this concern — for the benefit of their clients.

Three Problems with Asset Management Fees

But while the benefits are strong, there can be some problems.

Problem #1: Asset-Based Fees Should be a Substitute, Not an Addition

The whole point to asset management fees is that they provide an alternative form of compensation for the advisor. Therefore, paying asset-based fees in addition to commissions defeats the purpose.

Problem #2: Asset-Based Fees Are Often Too Expensive

Many planners charge such exorbitantly high asset management fees that their clients would have been better off paying commissions or flat rates. Asset management fees never should be more than 2%, and the percentage should decrease as the size of the assets increase.

Problem #3: It's Not Really a Fee Anyway

Many financial planners who charge asset management fees claim — with the blessing of the regulators and the media — that they are "fee-only." It is argued that such planners are not earning commissions because the products they are recommending, such as no-load mutual funds, do not pay commissions, and that their only form of compensation is paid by the client.

This argument is nonsense. A *fee* is a fixed rate based on time or work. A *commission* is based on the size of the transaction. And since asset management fees are expressed as a percentage of the assets that a client gives the advisor for management, it is clear that asset management fees are commissions. They are simply another form of commissions.

Think about it. If you invest $10,000 in a mutual fund that has a 4% load, you are paying $400, of which your advisor will receive all or part as compensation. Thus, the more you invest, the more he is paid. If you don't invest at all, the advisor is not paid anything. *Sounds like a commission to me.*

But if your advisor charges you a 3% asset management fee, he or she will receive $300 on that $10,000 — but, again, only if you agree to invest the money. If you invest, the advisor is paid. And, again, the more you invest, the more she is paid. If you do not invest, nothing is paid. *Sounds like a commission to me.*

Don't misunderstand me: There's nothing wrong with asset management fees *per se.* What is wrong, though, is (a) charging a fee that's too high and (b) pretending that it's not a commission — even though it is a benign, even consumer-friendly commission.

> **It's easy to understand why advisors don't like to refer to asset management fees as "commissions." First, there is a negative connotation to the word — it reminds people of the conflict-of-interest issue. Second, unlike traditional commissions that are based on the size and frequency of transactions, this compensation method is not based on trading. Instead, it's based on results, which is how many feel it should be. Therefore, it is argued, asset management fees are fees, not commissions.**
>
> **It's more important that you understand what it is than what you call it.**

Compensation Method #4: Fee-Offset

Whereas fee-plus-commission planners are the most common, *fee-offset* planners are the most rare.

Planners who use this method charge fees to do the plan, just as fee-only planners do. The client is then free to go elsewhere to buy whatever investments or insurance products the planner recommends.

But here's where the fee-offset planner differs: If the client buys those products from the planner, or if the client agrees to pay asset management fees to the planner (either way providing the planner with additional compensation), the planner reduces his or her fee by whatever commissions or asset management fees the client incurred. Thus, a fee-offset planner will be paid one way or the other, but not both. Thus, it is the client's prerogative to choose the method they prefer.

Fee-offset planners say they have the most consumer-oriented method of all. Because they charge fees only, they have the same objectivity of fee-only planners. But because they are fully licensed, they are highly skilled in implementing their recommendations. All they are doing, they say, is reducing their compensation to be competitive in the marketplace.

Fee-offset planners wonder why consumers are willing to pay twice: once to be told what to do and once again to actually do it. Nobody would tolerate such practices in other industries, fee-offset planners contend, but consumers let financial planners get away with it all the time. Fee-offset planners avoid this redundancy for the benefit of their clients.

The Problems with Fee Offset

Fee-only planners don't go for those arguments, however. They accuse fee-offset planners of being commission-based in disguise, while fee-and-commission planners claim the fee-offset group cannot afford to maintain that aggressive fee schedule indefinitely. In other words, they say, fee-offset planners either must change to fee-plus-commission or they'll one day be out of business.

Chapter 85 - Ten Taboos Between You and Your Planner

Here are some things you should never do when working with a financial advisor:

1. **Never write a check made payable to your planner, other than for his fee.**

   Your checks should be made payable only to mutual funds, brokerage firms, or insurance companies. No legitimate planner would ever allow a client to write a check for investments or insurance payable to him personally or to his firm.

2. **Never allow your planner to list himself as a joint owner or beneficiary on your accounts.**

   Your money is yours, not your planner's. Keep it that way. The only place your advisor's name should appear on documents is as the advisor of record.

3. **Never lend money to your planner.**

   Period.

4. **Never give your planner discretionary authority.**

   This allows your advisor to execute transactions without your prior knowledge or consent. If your advisor earns commissions, this is a license to steal.

5. **Never let your planner sign your name to any document.**

   Forgery — however well-intentioned — is a felony.

6. **Never let your planner allow you to sign a blank form or contract.**

   It's a violation of NASD rules and a pretty dumb thing to do. Cross out sections that do not apply.

> *"He that won't be counseled can't be helped."*
> —Benjamin Franklin

7. **Never let your planner use his address on account statements instead of yours.**

You should receive routine, periodic statements directly from the mutual fund, brokerage firm, or insurance company. Never allow your planner to have such documents go to his office instead of to you.

8. **Never let your planner sell you an investment that isn't available from others.**

There can be only one reason why an advisor would want you to buy in-house, or proprietary, investment products: Because he makes additional compensation for doing so. If a product is not generally available, you could find it extremely difficult to sell in the future. Like a box of cereal, all investments and insurance policies your planner recommends should be available from any number of sources.

9. **Never let your planner share in your profits.**

Unless you invest a minimum of $500,000, or your net worth is at least $1 million (exclusive of homes, home furnishings and cars), it is an NASD violation for an advisor to share in the profits of a client's account. Besides, from a practical perspective, I'd never let an advisor share in my profits unless he was willing to reimburse me for my losses, too — and while you might find a planner offering the former, none would ever agree to the latter.

10. **Never let your planner assign any agreement with you to another advisor.**

One day, your planner may retire or sell his practice. If so, you immediately are relieved of any and all contractual obligations you may have had with your planner. Never let a planner — or his successor — let you think you are obligated to work with the successor. Assignment is an SEC violation.

Chapter 86 - How to Find a Planner

Now that you know the different ways financial planners are paid, you know one of the first questions to ask when interviewing them: How are they compensated? Make sure you understand how they earn a living and what your costs will be.

Interview two or three planners. Shop around as you would for a car or washing machine. To get the names of potential candidates, talk to your neighbors, friends, or co-workers. One note of caution, though: Before you ask someone for the name of their advisor, make sure the person you're asking is similar to you in age, income, net worth, and objectives.

Your neighbor might be very happy with his financial advisor, but if your neighbor is a real risk-taker and you're not, his planner might not be well suited to you. Likewise, if you make $20,000 a year, asking your rich uncle for the name of his advisor also might lead to a bad match.

Another good way to find an advisor is by watching some in action. Maybe you saw one on TV, at a seminar, or read a news article they wrote. If you were impressed, add them to your interview list.

Ten Points to Ponder About Prospective Planners

Once you identify a few planners to talk to, here are ten questions you should ask:

1. How many years have they been in business, and how did they get started?

If the planners you interview are former stockbrokers, their emphasis likely will be on investment management, whereas if they were insurance agents, they probably will emphasize insurance products.

2. What kind of people do they work with most often?

Do not tell the planner about yourself right away. Instead, ask them to describe their typical client. If they describe you, it could be a good match. If they describe someone totally different, you could be out of place.

As part of this question, ask how much money their typical clients invest. If you have $50,000 to invest, you don't want a planner who works primarily with millionaires, or you'll be ignored. Likewise, if you have $1 million and the planner works mostly with assets of fifty grand, the planner may not have the expertise you require. Ideally, you want a planner who works extensively with people like you.

3. What is the ratio of support staff to professional staff?

Too few and the advisor will never get any work done. Too many means his office is not operating well, and you're paying for the firm's big expenses.

Here's a good test: If the planner does not answer his own phone, he or his associates should return phone calls within one business day.

4. What is the planner's reputation in the field and in the local community?

Planners who have roots and who are well-known have reputations to protect and therefore tend to be more careful than the planner who just blew into town.

5. When setting your appointment, go to the planner's office instead of inviting him to your home.

It takes more effort on your part, but it will allow you to inspect his office. How often does the phone ring before it's answered? Is the office neat and organized? Is there a bustle of activity? Don't be taken in by offices that are too opulent, though. Remember: Clients pay the rent, not the owners! If there's a huge pile of papers, files, and documents all over the place, remember too that one day, your file will be somewhere in that mess!

6. Do you understand what they tell you?

Here's the easy way to know: If you understand what they're telling you, you should be able to repeat to others what they've said. If you can't, you might be getting bamboozled.

7. Does the planner have a clean record?

Don't be afraid to ask this question and, if you like, follow it up with a phone call to the regulatory authorities. If your planner has a securities license, see if there have been any complaints by calling the NASD.

If the planner has an insurance license, call your state insurance commission, too. Check with the SEC to see if your planner is a Registered Investment Advisor. All planners are required to provide clients with a copy of the planner's Form ADV Part II, which is the registration statement they filed with the SEC. It will disclose everything you need to know about their background, methodology, compensation, and other important data.

8. Ask about the planner's investment methods.

What types of investments does he normally work with? Are they high risk or low risk? Is your money accessible after it is invested or are there restrictions? Who makes decisions to buy or sell investments — you or the planner? Can the planner execute transactions without your prior approval?

Make sure you're comfortable with all the answers.

9. Get referrals.

This isn't a bad idea, but it's not that great, either. After all, no planner will give you a negative source. Still, you can use referrals to verify basic facts.

Do not ask the referrals how their investments are performing. (It's a bad basis from which to make a decision and it's rude, too.) Instead, ask what it's like to work with the planner. Do they return phone calls timely? Are mistakes often made or difficult to get corrected? How quickly and effectively are questions answered? How often do you hear from the planner? Why do they contact you — just to sell you something or with bona fide news? Questions about style can tell you a lot about substance.

10. Must you sign a contract?

What does it obligate you to do? Many financial planners do use contracts, but never sign one that doesn't let you cancel in 30 days or less. For planning work, never pay more than 50% in advance, with the balance payable upon completion of the work. When paying asset management fees, never pay for more than one year in advance.

And always pay only for what you are getting, and make sure you get what you pay for.

ric's money quiz

Here's a chance to see how well you learned the information contained in Part XIII – How to Choose a Financial Advisor. Don't worry if you get stumped — just re-read this part until it sinks in. Remember, your financial future depends on it.

The answers are at the end of the quiz. No peeking!

---

1. **A financial planner can help you with:**

   I. investments
   II. mortgages
   III. estate planning
   IV. insurance
   V. taxes

   ○ a. I
   ○ b. I, II
   ○ c. I, II, III
   ○ d. I, II, III, IV
   ○ e. I, II, III, IV, V

2. **Private money managers:**

   I. invest each client's money almost identically
   II. charge asset management fees up to 3% per year
   III. typically require a minimum investment of $100,000
   IV. often manage mutual funds

   ○ a. I and II
   ○ b. II and IV
   ○ c. I, II, and III
   ○ d. I, II, III, and IV

3. **It is illegal for your planner to:**

   ○ a. allow you to sign a blank form or contract
   ○ b. assign your agreement to another advisor without your permission
   ○ c. sign your name on a document if you're unavailable
   ○ d. all of the above

4. **In order to sell securities, planners must hold:**

   ○ a. at least two designations
   ○ b. a federal securities license
   ○ c. both a and b
   ○ d. neither a nor b

5. **Most planners are compensated through:**

   ○ a. fees
   ○ b. commissions
   ○ c. fees and commissions
   ○ d. salaries from their employer

6. **When working with a planner, it is okay to:**

   ○ a. write a check for the money you wish to invest payable to the planner
   ○ b. list your planner as joint owner or beneficiary on your accounts
   ○ c. give your planner discretionary authority
   ○ d. none of the above

7. **When choosing a planner to work with, you should consider:**

   ○ a. the planner's reputation
   ○ b. how long the planner has been in this business
   ○ c. the planner's investment methods
   ○ d. all of the above

8. **Asset management fees should never be more than _____ , and the percentage should _____ as the size of the assets increase.**

   ○ a. 2%, increase
   ○ b. 2%, decrease
   ○ c. 5%, increase
   ○ d. 5%, decrease

9. **A planner gives his client a brochure describing the planner's fee schedule. Which of the following fee schedules is prohibited by NASD rules?**

   ○ a. a fee schedule that charges a flat fee of more than $500 per year
   ○ b. a fee schedule that charges both fees and commissions
   ○ c. a fee schedule where the planner shares in the profits earned in the client's account
   ○ d. a fee schedule where the planner charges commissions only

10. **You should never work with a planner who is not a Registered Investment Advisor.**

   ○ a. True
   ○ b. False

Answers: 1-e (pg.594) 3-d (pg.609) 5-c (pg.605) 7-d (pg.611) 9-c (pg.613)
          2-d (pg.595) 4-b (pg.599) 6-d (pg.609) 8-b (pg.606) 10-a (pg.600)

Sources

Figure 1-1:   National Vital Statistics, March 21, 2002.

Figure 1-2:   National Vital Statistics, March 21, 2002.

Figure 1-3:   n/a

Figure 1-4:   Lino, Mark. 2002. Expenditures on Children by Families, 2001 Annual Report. U.S. Department of Agriculture, Center for Nutrition Policy and Promotion. Miscellaneous Publication No. 1528-2001.

Figure 1-5:   College websites

Figure 1-6:   Conde Nast Bridal Group

Figure 1-7:   Gallup

Figure 1-8:   n/a

Figure 1-9:   n/a

Figure 1-10: www.minneapolisfed.org (Federal Reserve Bank of Minneapolis).

Figure 1-11: Ibbotson Associates

Figure 1-12: National Automobile Dealers Association
Gaspricewatch.com
Boston Herald, January 5, 2003
www.nationalcarecorp.com
U.S. Department of Labor - Bureau of Labor Statistics
www.sgma.com (Sporting Goods Manufacturers Association)

Figure 1-13: www.taxfoundation.org (Tax Foundation).

Figure 1-14: www.taxadmin.org (Federation of Tax Administrators).

Figure 1-15: *The Value of a Dollar*

Figure 1-16: Federal Housing Finance Board.

Figure 1-17 to 1-20: n/a

Figure 2-1 to 2-4: n/a

Figure 2-5:   www.minneapolisfed.org (Federal Reserve Bank of Minneapolis)
www.forecasts.org (The Financial Forecast Center)

Figure 2-6:   www.federalreserve.gov, November 4, 2002 (Board of Governors of the Federal Reserve System)

Figure 2-7:   www.federalreserve.gov, November 4, 2002 (Board of Governors of the Federal Reserve System)

Figure 3-1 to 3-4: n/a

Figure 3-5:   Standard and Poor's, Moody's

Figure 3-6 to 3-8: n/a

Figure 3-9:   www.forecasts.org (The Financial Forecast Center)

Figure 3-10: n/a

Figure 3-11: Ibbotson Associates

Figure 4-1:   *Forbes,* January, 2003

Figure 4-2 to 4-4: Ibbotson Associates

Figure 4-5:   National Bureau of Economic Research.

Figure 4-6   *Fortune*, July 22, 2001

Figure 4-7:   *Fortune*, July 22, 2001

Figure 4-8:   Morgan Stanley Capital International

Figure 4-9:   *Fortune*, July 22, 2001

Figure 4-10: n/a

Figure 4-11: Hoover's Handbook of American Business, 2002

Figure 4-12, 4-13: n/a

Figure 4-14: Ibbotson Associates

Figure 4-15: Statistical Abstract of the U.S., 2002, Table 926

Figure 5-1:   n/a

Figure 5-2:   www.ici.org (Investment Company Institute)

Figure 5-3:   n/a

Figure 5-4 to 5-9: Ibbotson Associates

Figure 5-10 to 5-14: n/a

Figure 6-1 to 6-5: Ibbotson Associates

Figure 6-6: Callahan Associates

Figure 6-7, 6-8: Standard & Poor's

Figure 6-9:   n/a

Figure 6-10: *Money* Magazine

Figure 6-11: n/a

Figure 6-12: Ibbotson Associates; Morningstar and Thompson Financial

Figure 6-13: Standard and Poor's

Figure 6-14: Thompson Financial

Figure 6-15: n/a

Figure 6-16: n/a

Figure 6-17 to 6-23: n/a

Figure 6-24: Ibbotson Associates

Figure 6-25: Ibbotson Associates

Figure 7-1 to 7-4: n/a

Figure 7-5: *American Demographics* Magazine

Figure 7-6: www.yale.edu, www.harvard.edu, www.tufts.edu, www.princeton.edu, www.brown.edu

Figure 7-7: College Board

U.S. Department of Labor - Bureau of Labor Statistics

Figure 7-8: Peterson's Paying Less for College

Figure 8-1: Fannie Mae

Figure 8-2: Federal Home Loan Bank District

Figure 9-1: IRS Federal Estate Tax Table 2003

Figure 9-2 to 9-4: n/a

Figure 10-1 to 10-3: n/a

Figure 10-4: Institute of Management and Administration

Figure 10-5: U.S. Department of Health and Human Services

Figure 10-6: U.S. Department of Health and Human Services

Figure 10-7: *Atlantic Financial*: Don't Rely on Social Security Alone When Planning for Retirement

Figure 10-8: n/a

Figure 11-1: www.guardiandibrokerage.com (Guardian Disability Insurance Brokerage)

Figure 11-2: "Calvert-Henderson: Quality of Life Indicators 1960-1998" Trudy Karlson

Figure 11-3: n/a

Figure 11-4: U.S. Senate Special Committee on Aging

Figure 11-5: National Center for Health Statistics

Figure 11-6: John Hancock Life, $180/day, 6 yr. benefit, compound inflation; 90-day waiting period, 2003

Figure 11-7: Philadelphia Life Insurance Company

Figure 11-8: Philadelphia Life Insurance Company

Figure 11-9: n/a

Figure 11-10: A.M. Best; Standard and Poor's; Duff and Phelps

About the Author

Ric Edelman, CFS, RFC, CMFC, CRC, QFP is one of the nation's most acclaimed financial advisors. He and his firm have won more than 50 financial, business, community and philanthropic awards, and his commitment to teaching consumers about personal finance has established him as one of the most popular financial professionals in America.

ACCLAIMED FINANCIAL ADVISOR

In 2003, *Research Magazine* ranked Ric the #1 advisor in the nation for his focus on the individual client. He has earned three Awards of Excellence by Royal Alliance Associates[1], was named Ace Advisor of the Year by *Ticker Magazine*, named Financial Planner of the Year three times by World Invest Corporation and named one of the D.C. area's top financial professionals by *Washingtonian* magazine.

SUCCESSFUL ENTREPRENEUR

Ric's firm, Edelman Financial Services Inc., was named three times by *Inc.* magazine as the fastest-growing privately held financial planning firm in the country[2]. In 2003, *Bloomberg Wealth Manager* ranked EFS as the sixth-largest independent financial planning and investment management firm in the nation[3], with $1.7 billion in client assets under management. Other awards include Service Business of the Year by the Fairfax, Va. Chamber of Commerce, the Blue Chip Enterprise Award by the U.S. Chamber of Commerce, and the Washington, D.C. Entrepreneur of the Year Award by Ernst and Young.

BESTSELLING AUTHOR

Ric Edelman is a #1 *New York Times* bestselling author. His five books on personal finance include *Ordinary People, Extraordinary Wealth, The New Rules of Money, Discover the Wealth Within You* and *What You Need to Do Now,* and the personal finance classic, *The Truth About Money,* which was named Book of the Year by *Small Press* magazine. His books have collectively sold more than one million copies, been translated into several languages and have educated countless people worldwide.

---

1 1999 #1 Group Manager, 1998 Outstanding Achievement, 1997 New Colleague of the Year.
2 *Inc.* magazine's list of the fastest growing companies in America according to growth in net sales in the last 5 years.
3 *Bloomberg Wealth Manager* magazine, cover story July/August 2003. Based on a survey of 370 independent financial planning firms who offer comprehensive financial planning; more than 50 percent of client base are individuals; with client assets in excess of $25 million. Edelman Financial Services ranked #1 based on number of clients (6,500), #6 based on client assets ($1.7 billion) and #327 based on size of average client account ($230,000).

AWARD-WINNING TALK SHOW HOST

Winner of the A.I.R. Award for Best Talk Show Host, Ric hosts weekly radio and television shows in Washington, D.C., writes a syndicated advice column for *AARP Magazine* and newspapers around the country, publishes a monthly newsletter and has built one of the most comprehensive free educational resources on personal finance online at RicEdelman.com. He is also the author of a variety of video and audio educational systems that help people achieve their financial goals.

RENOWNED EDUCATOR

For nine years, Ric taught personal finance at Georgetown University. He is a state- and AICPA-approved instructor for continuing professional education. He is also a member of the NASD Board of Arbitrators.

Ric has been the subject of many feature stories in the media, has appeared on hundreds of radio stations and every major television network and has been quoted by dozens of newspapers and magazines. He also has testified before Congress and provided services to many agencies within the federal government, including as a delegate to the 1998 and 2002 National Summits on Retirement Savings. Ric is a sought-after speaker, widely acknowledged as one of the most entertaining and informative experts in his field.

Ric received an honorary doctorate from Rowan University in 1999. In 2002, the university named the school's new planetarium "The Ric and Jean Edelman Planetarium" in their honor.

CHARITY WORK

Ric is founder of the Edelman Center for Personal Finance Education, a nonprofit organization. He also serves as a member of the Board of the United Way of the National Capital Area and the Boys & Girls Clubs of Greater Washington, D.C. Ric also is a full partner of the American Savings Education Council and the Jump$tart Coalition for Personal Financial Literacy. He is a former board member of Junior Achievement of the National Capital Area and served for three years on the Grants Committee of the Foundation for Financial Planning, where he remains a major donor. Ric and his wife Jean also support the INOVA Hospital Foundation, Northern Virginia Family Service, Wolf Trap Foundation, Rowan University, the Leukemia and Lymphoma Society and many other charities.

12450 Fair Lakes Circle
Suite 200, Fairfax, VA 22033-3808
(703) 818-0800
FAX (703) 818-1910
redelman@ricedelman.com
ricedelman.com

Also Available from the Author

Ric's National Bestsellers *Ordinary People, Extraordinary Wealth,*
The New Rules of Money, The Truth About Money **and**
What You Need to Do Now

Also available on audio cassette by HarperAudio and in bookstores everywhere.

Subscribe to Ric's Award-Winning 12-page Monthly Newsletter

Inside Personal Finance with Ric Edelman will show you how to stretch your dollars farther and increase your wealth faster than you can ever imagine. And without the hype and hoopla you see elsewhere.

You'll get the latest on taxes; insurance; financial planning advice; estate planning; retirement and elder care; your IRA, 401(k) and 403(b) plans; saving and debt management; mortgage and home matters; and even issues affecting parents who wish to teach their kids the principles of sound money-management practices.

It's the most comprehensive source you'll ever find on the topic of personal finance. What's more, you'll find each topic explained in clear, concise, plain English … no gobbledygook.

Subscribe today! Call (888) 987-PLAN

Seminars on Video

How to Choose a Financial Advisor

Protecting Against the Cost of Long-Term Care

Why You Should Carry a Big, Long Mortgage and Never Pay It Off

How to Be a Successful Financial Planner

To Order Call Toll-Free 1-800-221-6597

Invite Ric to Speak at Your Next Conference

Ric is one of the most entertaining speakers in the field of personal finance. Call 703-818-0800 for more information.

Online with Ric!

Get the weekly email edition of the Edelman Advisor delivered right to you! The award-winning Ric Edelman brings you informative articles and helpful tips. Also get the first look at Ric's upcoming events! Sign up for Ric's free bi-weekly newsletter today!!

Ric on the Air

Radio MD, VA, DC & Internet

The Ric Edelman Show
Saturdays 10am-11:45 EST

Tune In for Ric's Report
Weekday Mornings

Live at www.wmal.com
Call in at 202-432-WMAL

TV MD, VA, & DC

The Truth About Money with Ric Edelman
Mondays
8:30-9:00pm EST
Call in at 703-912-1430

Index